BARRON'S
THE TRUSTED NAME IN TEST PREP

7 SAT
Practice
Tests
2023

Philip Geer, Ed.M.
and Stephen A. Reiss, M.B.A.

SAT® is a registered trademark of the College Board, which was not involved
in the production of, and does not endorse, this product.

Dedication

To my teaching colleagues in the United States, Singapore, Hong Kong, and Australia, particularly Dr. Peter Saunders and Dr. Robert Wilks, with whom I enjoyed many interesting discussions about the English language and other subjects over the years.

And, as always, to my wife Susan for all her help and support.

—Philip Geer

To Iris Lowe-Reiss, my in-home editor and wife-for-life. And thanks to my parents, Elinor and Oscar Reiss, who supported me in all of my endeavors.

To Jennifer Goodenough, my editor, cheerleader, and friend.

—Steve Reiss

Copyright © 2022, 2017 by Kaplan North America, LLC, dba Barron's Educational Series
Second edition © copyright 2016 by Kaplan, Inc., d/b/a Barron's Educational Series under the title *6 Practice Tests for the New SAT* and written by Philip Geer and Stephen A. Reiss.
First edition © copyright 2012 by Kaplan, Inc., d/b/a Barron's Educational Series under the title *6 SAT Practice Tests* and written by Philip Geer and Ira K. Wolf.

Published by Kaplan North America, LLC, dba Barron's Educational Series
1515 W Cypress Creek Road
Fort Lauderdale, FL 33309
www.barronseduc.com

ISBN: 978-1-5062-6459-2

10 9 8 7 6 5 4 3 2 1

Kaplan North America, LLC, dba Barron's Educational Series print books are available at special quantity discounts to use for sales promotions, employee premiums, or educational purposes. For more information or to purchase books, please call the Simon & Schuster special sales department at 866-506-1949.

About the Authors

Philip Geer has taught English language and literature for many years in the United States and abroad. He is the author of a number of textbooks and test preparation books, including the *GRE Verbal Workbook* and *Essential Words for the GRE*, and is the director of Mentaurs Educational Consultants.

Steve Reiss is the founder and owner of the Math Magician and the Reiss SAT Seminars, test preparation centers in San Diego. Jokingly referred to as "San Diego's most boring author," he has authored, co-authored, and edited more than seventy books for the test preparation industry. Reiss is also a member of Mensa, the high IQ society.

Table of Contents

PRACTICE TESTS

Introduction

The New Digital SAT

Beginning in the fall of 2023, the SAT will no longer be a paper test. International students will be the first to take this digital test followed by U.S. students in the spring of 2024. The new digital exam will continue to test mathematics, reading and grammar. However, the length of the test will be reduced from three hours to two and calculator use will be permitted on all math sections. The reading passages will also change, featuring shorter passages and fewer questions. In addition, the new computer-based exam will be adaptive, i.e., it will increase or decrease the level of difficulty based on the test taker's performance. As we learn more about the digital SAT, we will provide you with the very latest strategies and practice resources on the Barron's Online Learning Hub.

7 SAT Practice Tests

As you probably know, many colleges use the SAT as one of several ways to assess a student's readiness for college-level work. Other important measures used are high school grades and teacher recommendations. Unlike many countries, the United States does not have a common national exam that must be taken by all students to earn a high school diploma. In one sense, therefore, the SAT can be seen as a means to give colleges a common standard by which to assess students' proficiency.

The SAT tests skills in reading, mathematics, and writing, using predominantly multiple-choice questions. (Some of the mathematics questions require you to write answers in grids.) Because the test aims to assess readiness for college, the level of the material on it is about the level of work done in the first and second years of college. However, the SAT does not require you to have specialized knowledge of any subject.

The SAT is prepared by the College Board, an organization that promotes college education in the United States. Students can go to the College Board's website at *http://sat.collegeboard.org/home* for detailed information on when the test is given and how to register for it.

Students typically take the SAT in their junior or senior year of high school. They can also retake the test to improve their scores. The College Board has a policy called Score Choice that allows students to have only their best score report sent to colleges to which they have applied for admission. Some colleges accept Score Choice, and others do not. To find out if your selected colleges accept Score Choice and to find further information about how this process works, go to *http://sat.collegeboard.org/register/sat-score-choice*.

The SAT tests the skills that you have developed over the entire course of your education. Whenever you write an essay or solve a mathematics problem, you are developing these skills. However, this does not mean that you should not do additional preparation for this important test. Carefully focused preparation over several weeks (or, even better, a number of months) will almost certainly help you to do better—in many cases, much better. Experts with many years of experience preparing students for the SAT and students who have achieved high scores on the SAT agree that the best way to do well is to practice using well-designed materials that provide full explanations of the answers. This is where *7 SAT Practice Tests* will help you succeed!

The SAT Format

The SAT is a 3-hour test that contains three parts: a Reading Test, a Writing and Language Test, and a Math Test. The Math Test consists of one section where calculators may be used and one section where calculators may not be used.

Reading Test—65 minutes, 5 passages, 52 total questions

Passages (1 paired passage is included) are drawn from the following areas:

Science (2 passages, 1 with graphic)
Literature (1 passage)
Social Studies (2 passages, 1 with graphic)

Questions are broken down into the following categories:

10 Command of Evidence Questions
10 Words in Context Questions
32 Analysis Questions

Writing and Language Test—35 minutes, 4 passages, 44 total questions

Some passages will contain graphics, tables, or charts; they are drawn from the following areas:

Humanities (1 passage)
History/Social Studies (1 passage)
Science (1 passage)
Careers (1 passage)

Questions are broken down into the following categories:

24 Expression of Ideas Questions
20 Standard English Conventions Questions

Math Test, No Calculator—25 minutes, 20 total questions

15 Multiple-Choice and 5 Grid-In Questions as follows:

8 Heart of Algebra Questions
9 Passport to Advanced Math Questions
3 Additional Topics in Math Questions

Math Test, Calculator—55 minutes, 38 total questions

30 Multiple-Choice Questions and 8 Grid-In Questions as follows:

11 Heart of Algebra Questions
17 Problem Solving and Data Analysis Questions
7 Passport to Advanced Math Questions
3 Additional Topics in Math Questions

Your Test Scores

After you take the SAT, you will receive a number of scores that will help you to evaluate your performance and tell you where your strengths and weaknesses lie. These scores include the following.

Main section scores of 200–800 in each of the following:
English
Math

A composite score of 400–1600

This is the sum of your two main section scores.

Area scores of 10–40 in each of the following:

Reading

Writing and Language

Math

Cross-test scores of 10–40

These scores evaluate the level of your skills in analyzing texts and solving problems in Analysis in History/Social Studies and Analysis in Science questions.

Subscores of 1–15

These scores assess your skills in the following seven areas of Evidence-Based Reading and Writing and of Math:

- Expression of Ideas
- Standard English Conventions
- Words in Context
- Command of Evidence
- Heart of Algebra
- Problem Solving and Data Analysis
- Passport to Advanced Math

Percentile scores

You will receive a percentile ranking of 1 to 99 for your total composite score as well as for each of your section scores in Evidence-Based Reading and Writing and in Math. The percentiles tell you how well you performed compared with other students taking the test. For example, if you receive a composite percentile ranking of 92%, you have achieved a higher score than 92% of all students taking the test.

The Reading Test

The Reading Test contains 52 questions on 5 passages that test how well you understand what you read. There are three general question types:

- 10 *vocabulary questions* test how well you understand the meaning of words in the context in which they appear.
- 10 *command of evidence* questions assess your ability to find information in the passage to support your answer choice.
- 32 *analysis* questions that test a range of other skills. These can be categorized as questions on:
  1. the main idea or supporting details
  2. the point of view or attitude (e.g., of the author)
  3. the implications of what the author says
  4. inferences that can be made based on what is stated in the passage
  5. the argument made (e.g., logic and evidence)
  6. the author's use of language (e.g., tone)
  7. the graphic (if any)

Passages are selected from a wide variety of sources and deal with many different subjects. The College Board says, "The content of the passages is drawn from the humanities, literary fiction, social studies, and natural science."

Examples of Evidence-Based Reading Questions

The following passage is shorter than the ones that appear on the actual test. It is designed to familiarize you with the types of questions asked on the Reading Test section of the SAT.

> **DIRECTIONS:** Following each of the passages (or pairs of passages) below are questions about the passage (or passages). Read each passage carefully. Then, select the best answer for each question based on what is stated in the passage (or passages) and in any graphics that may accompany the passage.

The passage is from *The History of the Rise, Progress and Accomplishment of the Abolition of the African Slave Trade by the British Parliament* by Thomas Clarks (1808).

The disappointments, which I frequently experienced in these journeys, increased the poignancy of the suffering, which arose from a contemplation of the melancholy cases which I had thus traveled to bring forward to the public view. The reader at present can have no idea of these. I have been sixty miles to visit a person, of whom
(5) I had heard, not only as possessing important knowledge, but as espousing our opinions on this subject. I have at length seen him. He has applauded my pursuit at our first interview. He has told me, in the course of our conversation, that neither my own pen, nor that of any other man, could describe adequately the horrors of The Slave-trade, horrors which he himself had witnessed. He has exhorted me
(10) to perseverance in this noble cause. Could I have wished for a more favorable reception? —But mark the issue. He was the nearest relation of a rich person concerned in the traffic, and if he were to come forward with his evidence publicly, he should ruin all his expectations from that quarter.

In the same week I have visited another at a still greater distance. I have met
(15) with similar applause. I have heard him describe scenes of misery which he had witnessed, and on the relation of which he himself almost wept. But mark the issue again. —"I am a physician," says he: "through that window you see a spacious house. It is occupied by a West Indian. The medical attendance upon his family is of considerable importance to the temporal interests of mine. If I give you my evidence I lose his
(20) patronage. At the house above him lives an East Indian. The two families are connected: I fear, if I lost the support of one, I shall lose that of the other also: but I will give you privately all the intelligence in my power."

1. What are the "disappointments" that the author refers to in line 1?

   (A) realizing the horrors of the slave trade
   (B) having to travel very far to interview people
   (C) hearing the men he interviewed decline to make available to everyone their knowledge of the suffering caused by the slave trade
   (D) finding that the men interviewed were not sympathetic to his cause

This question is fact based, requiring you to identify specific information in the text. It also requires you to make an inference to identify the correct answer. You also need to follow the somewhat complicated language the author uses in his account to see that the "disappointments" are described toward the end of both the first paragraph and the second paragraph.

In the first paragraph, the author implies that he had high hopes that his visits would produce evidence about the suffering caused by the slave trade. At first, the author says the visits were positive because the man supported his cause against the slave trade. For example, lines 11–12 say, "Could I have wished for a more favorable reception?" We can infer that the author's disappointment arose from the fact that the man would not give evidence despite fully supporting the author's cause. The writer recounts a very similar experience in the second paragraph. He has his hopes raised by the positive reception he receives only to see them dashed when the man does not agree to make public his evidence about the slave trade. Thus, choice (C) is clearly the correct answer.

Choice (D) can be eliminated because the two men make it clear that they are sympathetic to the author's cause. Choice (A) makes some sense if you do not read carefully. It is reasonable to believe that the author would be disappointed by the horrors of the slave trade. However, the "disappointments" clearly refer to the author's learning that the two men would not make public their knowledge of the suffering caused by the slave trade, as explained in (C) above.

Choice (B) also makes some sense because it is reasonable to think that the author would be disappointed by having to travel so far. However, there is no evidence in the passage for this. Also, there is no evidence that he had hopes that visiting the two men would require only short journeys. Therefore, it is not likely that he would have been disappointed by the long length of the journey.

2. The author makes use of all the following *except*

   (A) direct quotation
   (B) indirect quotation
   (C) analogy
   (D) figurative language

This question requires you to identify the language strategies that the author uses.

Choice (A) *direct quotation* can be eliminated because the author uses a direct quotation in lines 17–22, "I am a . . . in my power." Choice (B) *indirect quotation* is incorrect because the author uses an indirect quotation in lines 7–10, "He has told . . . this noble cause." Choice (D) *figurative language* is incorrect because the author makes use of figurative language in lines 7–9, "He has told . . . himself had witnessed." The words "my own pen, nor that of any other man, could describe adequately" are figurative because a pen does not describe—a writer describes.

Choice (C) *analogy* is correct because no use is made of analogy, which is a comparison between two otherwise unlike things based on resemblance of a particular aspect.

3. The word "intelligence" as it is used in line 22 most nearly means

   (A) intellectual ability
   (B) ideas
   (C) support
   (D) information

This question tests your ability to figure out the meaning of a word in a particular context.

The context of line 22 is a doctor saying that he will give the author "intelligence." In the previous sentence, the doctor had referred to "evidence" (line 19) that he could give the author. Thus, we can infer that "intelligence" here refers to choice (D) *information*. This seems to be the correct answer, but we should examine the other choices to be sure it is the best choice.

Choice (A) *intellectual ability* is incorrect. This definition of intelligence, although one of the dictionary definitions of the word, does not make sense in this context. The doctor could not give the author intellectual ability. Choice (B) *ideas* makes some sense because ideas are part of intelligence. However, *ideas* does not fit well in this context because it is a very general term. Choice (D) *information* is more specific and thus a better choice. Choice (C) *support* makes some sense in context because the doctor is offering support. However, *support* is not a definition of intelligence. We can conclude, therefore, that Choice (D) *information* is the best answer.

4. The reason that the two men give only limited support to the cause of the author can best be described as

   (A) political
   (B) emotional
   (C) financial
   (D) religious

Like question 1, this is a fact-based question.

Choice (A) *political* can be eliminated because there is no evidence that politics played a part in the two men's decision to give only limited support to the author's cause. Choice (B) *emotional* makes some sense because it is reasonable that emotion would play a part in the men's decision. However, there is no clear evidence for this in the passage. Choice (D) *religious,* similar to choice (B) *emotional,* makes some sense because the men have strong moral convictions about the slave trade. However, there is no evidence that these convictions caused the men to give only limited support to the author's cause.

Choice (C) *financial* is the correct choice because both men say that, although they strongly support the author's cause (opposition to the slave trade), they are not willing to sacrifice their livelihood for it. The first man says in lines 11–13 that he is closely related to a rich person involved with the slave trade and he could not have "expectations" of money from the man if he came forward with his evidence. The second man, a doctor, says in lines 17–22 that he would lose the "patronage" of two rich families if he made his evidence public.

Developing Your Reading Skills

It is impossible to know what passages will appear on the test. So it is important to do extensive independent reading in a wide range of subjects, while thinking critically about what you read. Also, sharpen your skills by practicing regularly using *7 SAT Practice Tests*. The reading passages and their questions have been carefully designed to familiarize you with the sort of passages and questions that appear on the real test. If you do not understand a particular question or why an answer is either correct or incorrect, the explanation will tell you exactly what you need to know. The explanation will also tell you how you can identify clues that can help you find the correct answer. By taking the time to use this book, you will master the skills needed to answer all the types of questions that appear on the test.

Increasing Your Knowledge

As mentioned above, passages on the SAT are on a wide variety of subjects. Although the SAT is not primarily a test of knowledge, it is helpful to be familiar with the sorts of ideas, viewpoints, and ways of thinking that are likely to appear on the test. Once again, it must be stressed that it is vital you read regularly from a variety of sources and in a number of different subjects. Read a good novel or nonfiction book on a subject that interests you. As a student, your time is limited. So it is a good idea to concentrate on reading a quality current affairs magazine such as *Time*. Read critically, evaluating the information and how it is presented. Always keep a sharp eye out for words you do not know. If they are in *Time*, for example, there is a good chance they will be on the SAT.

Do not read about *just* those topics that interest you. Expand your horizons by sometimes reading about topics you do not know much about. After all, the SAT does not let you choose reading passages based on your interests.

Building Your Vocabulary

The SAT does not test advanced vocabulary as much as it did previously—the stress is now on understanding everyday words in somewhat unusual contests. However, you still need a good vocabulary to do well on the SAT because difficult words appear regularly in the reading passages questions. Difficult words will not be tested directly. The more of them you know, the easier you will find it to understand the passages and, in some cases, the questions on the passages.

Reading widely, as well as improving your skills and knowledge, will also boost your vocabulary. When you come across a word you do not know, look it up. As you work through *7 SAT Practice Tests*, use every opportunity to increase your vocabulary. When you go over a test you have completed, find out the meaning of all the words that are unfamiliar to you. It is a good idea to make a list of these newly acquired words and their meanings. Periodically review this list. After you have completed all 6 tests, you will have greatly expanded your vocabulary.

The Writing and Language Test

The Writing and Language Test consists of 4 passages and 44 questions. It evaluates your ability to identify and correct errors in grammar and usage and tests your ability to recognize writing that is correct, clear, logical, and concise. The test also requires you to correct several pieces of writing to improve their logical structure and other features. There are two general question types.

- 24 Expression of Ideas Questions

These questions require you to analyze the organization of a passage, improve word choice, and make structural changes in sentences and paragraphs to improve the clarity and impact of a passage.

- 20 Standard English Conventions Questions

These questions require you to recognize writing that adheres to the accepted rules of grammar and usage. You will need to recognize and correct errors in such areas as parallel construction, subject-verb agreement, verb tense, punctuation, and usage. You may also be required to make improvements in style, tone, and word choice.

Questions on informational graphics measure how accurately you interpret information presented in graphic form.

In the Writing and Language Test, you will encounter topics drawn from passages in the following areas: careers, humanities, science, history, and social studies.

Examples of Writing and Language Passages and Questions

The following is an example of the type of passages and questions that you will encounter on the Writing and Language section of the SAT.

DIRECTIONS: Questions follow each of the passages below. Some questions ask you how the passage might be changed to improve the expression of ideas. Other questions ask you how the passage might be altered to correct errors in grammar, usage, and punctuation. One or more graphics accompany some passages. You will be required to consider these graphics as you answer questions about editing the passage.

There are three types of questions. In the first type, a part of the passage is underlined. The second type is based on a certain part of the passage. The third type is based on the entire passage.

Read each passage. Then, choose the answer to each question that changes the passage so that it is consistent with the conventions of standard written English. One of the answer choices for many questions is "NO CHANGE." Choosing this answer means that you believe the best answer is to make no change in the passage.

The Romans had become masters of the **①** world; only to see the Mediterranean from one end to the other patrolled by organized rovers. For many years, as Roman commerce extended, the Mediterranean had become a profitable field of enterprise for this group of people. From every country **②** who they had overrun or occupied the conquests of the

(5) Roman Empire had let loose swarms of restless patriots who, if they could not save the liberties of their own countries, could prey upon their oppressor. Illyrians from the Adriatic, Greeks from the islands and the Asiatic ports, Syrians, Egyptians, Africans, Spaniards, Gauls, and disaffected Italians, many of them trained to the sea from their childhood, **③** took to the water in their light galleys with all the world before them. Under most circumstances

(10) society is protected against thieves by their inability to combine. However, the pirates of the Mediterranean had learned from the Romans the advantage of union, and had drifted into a vast **④** corporation.

1. (A) NO CHANGE
   (B) world. Only
   (C) world, only
   (D) world: only

This question concerns the correct use of grammar in structuring a sentence.

Choice (A) *world; only* is incorrect because the words after the semicolon are not an independent clause. That is, they cannot stand alone as a sentence. Similarly, choice (B) *world. Only* does not create a grammatically correct complete sentence beginning with the word "only." Choice (D) *world: only* is incorrect for the same reason—a complete sentence is not created here, in this case after the colon.

Choice (C) *world, only* is correct because it creates a dependent clause beginning with the adverb "only," which here means "with the final result." This clause adds additional information to the preceding independent clause: "The Romans had become masters of the world."

2. (A) NO CHANGE
   (B) that
   (C) whom
   (D) what

The second question requires you to choose the correct pronoun to begin a relative clause.

The clause beginning with the word "who" modifies the preceding noun "country," telling us *which* countries—that is, the countries overrun by the Romans. Because countries are things, not persons, either of two relative pronouns that refer to things—*which* or *that*—is needed. Choice (B) *that* is thus correct.

Choice (A) *who* is incorrect because, although it is relative pronoun, the word is used to refer to people, not things. Choice (C) *whom* is incorrect for the same reason as choice (A). Choice (D) *what* is not a relative pronoun and so can be eliminated.

3. (A) NO CHANGE
   (B) taking
   (C) taken
   (D) have taken

This question tests your ability to choose the correct tense of a verb to use in a particular context.

The writer is describing past events here. So choice (A) *took*, which is the past tense of "take," is correct.

Choice (B) *taking* is incorrect because it does not create a grammatically correct sentence and because "taking" is not the past tense of "take." Choice (C) *taken* is incorrect for the same reason as choice (B). Choice (D) *have taken* is the present perfect tense of the verb "take." The present perfect refers to action that began in the past and that continues to the present. This tense is incorrect here because the action described took place in the past and stopped sometime in the past.

4. (A) NO CHANGE
   (B) confederation
   (C) entourage
   (D) cabal

This question tests your ability to identify the correct word to use in a particular context. The context here is a description of how the pirates learned "the advantage of union" and as a result "drifted" into something. From the word "union" we know that the pirates must have formed some sort of cooperative arrangement. From the word "drifted" we know that this arrangement was not planned; rather, it happened gradually over time without an overall plan.

Choice (A) *corporation*—a large company or group of companies—is not a good choice because there is no indication that the pirates formed a company. Choice (C) *entourage*—a group of people surrounding an important person—is not correct because, although it refers to a group of people, there is no indication that the pirates came together around an important person. Choice (D) *cabal*—a secret political group—is not correct because, although it refers to a group of people, there is no indication that the pirates formed a secret political group.

Choice (B) *confederation*—an organization that consists of a number of parties in an alliance—is correct in this context because the pirates (having learned "the advantages of union") formed an alliance to further their common interests.

Preparing for the Writing and Language Test

7 SAT Practice Tests provides plenty of practice with and explanations about the full range of question types that appear in the Writing and Language Test. Terms from traditional grammar are frequently incorporated in questions to explain errors and how to correct them. This book does not provide detailed explanations of grammatical terms or review the fundamentals of grammar and usage. If you need more assistance in this area you should consult a suitable grammar book. A good one is *The McGraw-Hill Handbook of English Grammar and Usage*. For guidance on matters of style, the classic *The Elements of Style* by William Strunk, Jr. and E. B. White is highly recommended.

Points to Remember

As described on page 7, there are two basic types of questions on the Writing and Language Test. About half of the questions are Expression of Ideas Questions. These do not test grammar and usage. Rather, they test how clearly and effectively ideas are communicated. Many of these questions require you to improve the organization of a passage. Others require you to identify wording that makes the meaning clearer or the argument more persuasive. You are often asked to determine:

- The best sentence to introduce the focus of a paragraph
- The best sentence to conclude a paragraph
- Whether or not a particular sentence should be added or deleted
- The best place in the paragraph for a given sentence
- The best transitional word or phrase to begin a sentence
- Which answer best corrects wordiness or vagueness in the text
- Which answer best maintains a particular linguistic pattern
- Which answer best maintains the style or tone of the passage

The rest of the questions are Standard English Conventions Questions. Unlike the Expression of Ideas Questions, these test actual errors in grammar and usage. A wide variety of errors is tested, so it is impossible to describe all the types of errors that appear on the test. However, it is possible to identify the types of errors that regularly appear. Make sure you can correct errors in the following areas:

- *Sentence structure*: Your answer must create a grammatically correct complete sentence.
- *Punctuation*: This is often tested along with sentence structure. Frequently, a period or semi-colon must be used to correct a fragment and make a complete sentence. Remember that two independent clauses cannot be joined with a comma. The comma is tested in a number of other ways, one of which is the series comma. The series comma appears before the "and" in a list of three or more items and is correctly used in the following: baseball, football, and basketball.
- *Subject-verb agreement*: Remember that the main verb in the sentence must agree in number (singular or plural) with the main subject of the sentence. Often before the subject there will be nouns that are the subjects of prepositions—ignore these and find the main subject. Make sure it agrees with the verb in number.
- *Parallel structure*: Watch for unnecessary shifts in sentence structure, such as in the sentence "Ann loves swimming and to jog."
- *Verb tense*: Be on the lookout for incorrect tense changes. The change might be correct, but sometimes it is not.

The Math Test

There are 58 math questions on the SAT. The test is divided into two parts: no calculator allowed and calculator allowed.

The No Calculator Section

As the name implies, calculator use is not permitted on this portion of the Math Test. This part of the SAT will always be section 3 and will feature a calculator icon with a slash on each page. The test will have these additional features:

- The test taker must complete this section in 25 minutes.
- There will be 15 multiple-choice questions and 5 grid-in questions.
- Most, but not all, of the important formulas will appear in the reference guide on the first page.

The difficulty level of the questions will generally proceed from easy to medium to difficult. The test taker must complete the 20 questions in 25 minutes, which averages to 75 seconds per question. Many of the questions in the beginning of the multiple-choice section can be completed in 30 seconds or fewer, which provides more time for some of the time-consuming questions at the end.

The following question would likely show up somewhere in the middle of the test.

$$m = \frac{\left(\frac{3r}{1600}\right)\left(1 - \frac{3r}{1600}\right)^y}{\frac{3}{16}\left(1 + \frac{3r}{1600}\right)^{y-1}}P$$

The formula above shows the monthly payment m for a state loan provided to one of its county governments. The variables r and y represent the interest rate and months of the loan, respectively, and P is the dollar amount to be paid back. Which of the following choices expresses P in terms of m, r, and y?

(A) $P = \frac{(1 - 9r)^2}{1600}m$

(B) $P = \frac{1600}{(1 - 9r)^2}m$

(C) $P = \frac{\left(\frac{3r}{1600}\right)\left(1 - \frac{3r}{1600}\right)^y}{\frac{3}{16}\left(1 + \frac{3r}{1600}\right)^{y-1}}m$

(D) $P = \frac{\frac{3}{16}\left(1 + \frac{3r}{1600}\right)^{y-1}}{\left(\frac{3r}{1600}\right)\left(1 - \frac{3r}{1600}\right)^y}m$

This seemingly time-consuming question can be solved in 10 seconds—without lifting a pencil! The question shows a complex fraction, i.e., a fraction with fractions in the numerator and denominator. Let's model this question with an easier example.

Solve for P in the following equation:

$$m = \frac{2}{7}P$$

You could divide both sides of the equation by $\frac{2}{7}$, but that could be complicated. An alternative would be to multiply each side of the equation by $\frac{7}{2}$.

$$m = \frac{2}{7}P$$

$$\frac{7}{2}\left(m = \frac{2}{7}P\right)\frac{7}{2}$$

$$\frac{7}{2}m = P$$

By multiplying each side of the equation by the reciprocal, we are able to isolate P. In the sample question above, choice (D) multiplies each side of the equation by the reciprocal, which is

$$\frac{\frac{3}{16}\left(1 + \frac{3r}{1600}\right)^{y-1}}{\left(\frac{3r}{1600}\right)\left(1 - \frac{3r}{1600}\right)^{y}}.$$

The grid-in section of the no calculator Math Test also uses many of the strategies used in the multiple-choice section. Using estimation and logic will shave valuable seconds off the time needed to solve many of the questions. One strategy that is not available in the grid-in section is plug-and-check: there are no choices to plug in. The test taker must furnish the correct answer (or one of the correct answers) by writing it a grid. Look at the following grid-in example.

$$x^3 - 7x^2 + 3x - 21 = 0$$

What real value satisfies the equation above?

Solve this equation by grouping.

$$x^3 - 7x^2 + 3x - 21 = 0$$
$$x^2(x - 7) + 3(x - 7) = 0$$
$$(x^2 + 3)(x - 7) = 0$$
$$x^2 + 3 = 0 \quad x - 7 = 0$$
$$x^2 = -3 \quad x = 7$$
$$x = \pm i\sqrt{3}$$

The solution set contains two complex solutions and one real solution, 7. Grid in **7**.

Before we proceed to our discussion of the calculator section, let's conclude with some final tips about the grid-in section:

- There are no negative solutions to any of the questions.
- You do not need to simplify fraction answers. If the answer is $\frac{4}{8}$, you can grid it in as is without wasting time simplifying the solution. Just remember to grid in the fraction line too.
- Decimal or fraction answers are both acceptable, but mixed numbers must be grid in as improper fractions.

The Calculator Section

The calculator-allowed section of the Math Test will seem more like the questions that show up in your math classes in school. The calculator section will always be section 4 of the SAT and is recognizable by the calculator icon that appears at the top of each page.

Although calculator use is permitted, you should use the calculator solely for detailed calculations. The more calculations the test taker can do mentally, the more time she/he will save.

There are 38 questions in this section: 30 multiple-choice questions and 8 grid-in questions. The calculator section provides 55 minutes to complete the 38 questions, which works out to approximately 87 seconds per question. Similar to the no calculator section, the calculator portion begins with relatively easy questions, proceeds to medium-difficulty ones, and finally ends with the most challenging questions. Answer the easy questions quickly to gain additional time for the more difficult ones later. When the test taker arrives at the grid-in section, the difficulty level resets. It features easier questions at the beginning and more challenging ones at the end.

Many topics are covered in the calculator section. The following is a partial list of subjects that will appear among the 38 questions:

- Systems of equations
- Deriving and manipulating equations relating to lines, parabolas, and circles
- Real-life applications of linear and quadratic functions
- Special right triangles
- Parallel lines that are intersected by transversals

Many, but not all, of the formulas and math facts appear on the first page's reference section.

Let's investigate some sample questions from the calculator section.

The special theory of relativity shows that observers hypothetically moving at nearly the speed of light will perceive time moving more slowly than an observer at rest. The formula that models this phenomenon, called time dilation, is

$$d = \frac{t}{\sqrt{1 - v^2}}$$

In this formula, t represents some unit of time, v is the velocity of an object expressed as a fraction of light speed, and d is the dilation effect. Which of the following shows velocity expressed as a function of time and the dilation effect?

(A) $v = \pm\sqrt{1 - \frac{t^2}{d^2}}$

(B) $v = \pm\sqrt{1 + \frac{d^2}{t^2}}$

(C) $v = 1 - \frac{t^2}{d^2}$

(D) $v = 1 - \frac{d^2 t^2}{2}$

At first glance, this question can be daunting. After all, the typical test taker may know nothing about special relativity. However, closer inspection indicates the question is merely asking that $d = \frac{t}{\sqrt{1 - v^2}}$ be expressed in terms of v.

$$d = \frac{t}{\sqrt{1 - v^2}}$$

$$(\sqrt{1 - v^2})d = \frac{t}{\sqrt{1 - v^2}}(\sqrt{1 - v^2})$$

$$(\sqrt{1 - v^2})d = t$$

$$\frac{(\sqrt{1 - v^2})d}{d} = \frac{t}{d}$$

$$\sqrt{1 - v^2} = \frac{t}{d}$$

—(Continued)

$$\left(\sqrt{1-v^2}\right)^2 = \left(\frac{t}{d}\right)^2$$

$$1 - v^2 = \frac{t^2}{d^2}$$

$$-v^2 = \frac{t^2}{d^2} - 1$$

$$v^2 = 1 - \frac{t^2}{d^2}$$

$$\sqrt{v^2} = \sqrt{1 - \frac{t^2}{d^2}}$$

$$v = \pm\sqrt{1 - \frac{t^2}{d^2}}$$

Although this question assumes you have sophisticated knowledge of algebra, there is no need to possess outside knowledge of physics. The answer is choice (A).

Let's look at a typical grid-in question in the calculator-allowed Math Test.

$$(-5x^2 - 2x + 9) - (-3x^2 - 5x + 1)$$

If the expression above is written in the form of $ax^2 + bx + c$, what is the value of $a + b + c$?

Simplify the expression by combing like terms.

$$(-5x^2 - 2x + 9) - (-3x^2 - 5x + 1) = -2x^2 + 3x + 8$$
$$a = -2 \qquad b = 3 \qquad c = 8$$
$$a + b + c = 9$$

Grid in **9**.

Calculator Tips

- Make sure your calculator has fresh batteries the week of the test.
- Do not purchase a calculator for the test that is more sophisticated than the one you use in school. A graphing calculator may be useful, but most of the graphs can be sketched quickly by hand.
- Try to do as many of the calculations as you can mentally; use your calculator to make computations that would waste valuable time if done by hand.

Using This Book

The 6 tests in this book are modeled on actual SAT tests. They closely resemble the SAT you will take in format, content, and level of difficulty. If you work diligently on them, you will greatly improve the skills you need to do well when test day comes around.

Work through the book, starting with the first test. When you go over your answers, carefully read the answer explanation for every question you answered incorrectly so that you fully understand the question and how to answer it.

A good approach is to use Practice Test 1 as a diagnostic, doing it under timed test conditions. Then do the next 4 practice tests section by section. This will enable you to concentrate on developing the skills needed for each section of the test. Finally, take Practice Test 6 as a posttest to see how much you have improved and to give yourself a final practice before the actual SAT test.

Taking the Test

First: Familiarize yourself with the format and instructions of each section of the test *before* the test. Why waste precious minutes reading instructions *during* the test?

- Do not clutter your mind with tips and tricks. You need to concentrate on the *test*, not on how to "beat" the test. The SAT is carefully designed. So if someone has told you that you can "game" the test—for example, that (C) answers are correct less frequently than (A), (B), and (D) answers—they are wrong.

- There is no point in rushing through the test without understanding what you are doing. Work as quickly as you can. However, make sure you do not work so fast that you do not understand the material. Strike a balance between speed and accuracy. Generally, it is better to answer fewer questions with greater accuracy than to answer more questions with less accuracy.

- Answer every question. There is no penalty for incorrect answers. So even if you have no idea what the correct answer is, choose an answer. If you can eliminate one or more choices, so much the better because this means that your odds of guessing right will improve.

- If you make an informed guess on a question, do not change it unless you are pretty sure your new choice is correct. First hunches tend to be better than second thoughts.

Practice Tests

ANSWER SHEET
Practice Test 1

Section 1: Reading

1. Ⓐ Ⓑ Ⓒ Ⓓ
2. Ⓐ Ⓑ Ⓒ Ⓓ
3. Ⓐ Ⓑ Ⓒ Ⓓ
4. Ⓐ Ⓑ Ⓒ Ⓓ
5. Ⓐ Ⓑ Ⓒ Ⓓ
6. Ⓐ Ⓑ Ⓒ Ⓓ
7. Ⓐ Ⓑ Ⓒ Ⓓ
8. Ⓐ Ⓑ Ⓒ Ⓓ
9. Ⓐ Ⓑ Ⓒ Ⓓ
10. Ⓐ Ⓑ Ⓒ Ⓓ
11. Ⓐ Ⓑ Ⓒ Ⓓ
12. Ⓐ Ⓑ Ⓒ Ⓓ
13. Ⓐ Ⓑ Ⓒ Ⓓ

14. Ⓐ Ⓑ Ⓒ Ⓓ
15. Ⓐ Ⓑ Ⓒ Ⓓ
16. Ⓐ Ⓑ Ⓒ Ⓓ
17. Ⓐ Ⓑ Ⓒ Ⓓ
18. Ⓐ Ⓑ Ⓒ Ⓓ
19. Ⓐ Ⓑ Ⓒ Ⓓ
20. Ⓐ Ⓑ Ⓒ Ⓓ
21. Ⓐ Ⓑ Ⓒ Ⓓ
22. Ⓐ Ⓑ Ⓒ Ⓓ
23. Ⓐ Ⓑ Ⓒ Ⓓ
24. Ⓐ Ⓑ Ⓒ Ⓓ
25. Ⓐ Ⓑ Ⓒ Ⓓ
26. Ⓐ Ⓑ Ⓒ Ⓓ

27. Ⓐ Ⓑ Ⓒ Ⓓ
28. Ⓐ Ⓑ Ⓒ Ⓓ
29. Ⓐ Ⓑ Ⓒ Ⓓ
30. Ⓐ Ⓑ Ⓒ Ⓓ
31. Ⓐ Ⓑ Ⓒ Ⓓ
32. Ⓐ Ⓑ Ⓒ Ⓓ
33. Ⓐ Ⓑ Ⓒ Ⓓ
34. Ⓐ Ⓑ Ⓒ Ⓓ
35. Ⓐ Ⓑ Ⓒ Ⓓ
36. Ⓐ Ⓑ Ⓒ Ⓓ
37. Ⓐ Ⓑ Ⓒ Ⓓ
38. Ⓐ Ⓑ Ⓒ Ⓓ
39. Ⓐ Ⓑ Ⓒ Ⓓ

40. Ⓐ Ⓑ Ⓒ Ⓓ
41. Ⓐ Ⓑ Ⓒ Ⓓ
42. Ⓐ Ⓑ Ⓒ Ⓓ
43. Ⓐ Ⓑ Ⓒ Ⓓ
44. Ⓐ Ⓑ Ⓒ Ⓓ
45. Ⓐ Ⓑ Ⓒ Ⓓ
46. Ⓐ Ⓑ Ⓒ Ⓓ
47. Ⓐ Ⓑ Ⓒ Ⓓ
48. Ⓐ Ⓑ Ⓒ Ⓓ
49. Ⓐ Ⓑ Ⓒ Ⓓ
50. Ⓐ Ⓑ Ⓒ Ⓓ
51. Ⓐ Ⓑ Ⓒ Ⓓ
52. Ⓐ Ⓑ Ⓒ Ⓓ

Section 2: Writing and Language

1. Ⓐ Ⓑ Ⓒ Ⓓ
2. Ⓐ Ⓑ Ⓒ Ⓓ
3. Ⓐ Ⓑ Ⓒ Ⓓ
4. Ⓐ Ⓑ Ⓒ Ⓓ
5. Ⓐ Ⓑ Ⓒ Ⓓ
6. Ⓐ Ⓑ Ⓒ Ⓓ
7. Ⓐ Ⓑ Ⓒ Ⓓ
8. Ⓐ Ⓑ Ⓒ Ⓓ
9. Ⓐ Ⓑ Ⓒ Ⓓ
10. Ⓐ Ⓑ Ⓒ Ⓓ
11. Ⓐ Ⓑ Ⓒ Ⓓ

12. Ⓐ Ⓑ Ⓒ Ⓓ
13. Ⓐ Ⓑ Ⓒ Ⓓ
14. Ⓐ Ⓑ Ⓒ Ⓓ
15. Ⓐ Ⓑ Ⓒ Ⓓ
16. Ⓐ Ⓑ Ⓒ Ⓓ
17. Ⓐ Ⓑ Ⓒ Ⓓ
18. Ⓐ Ⓑ Ⓒ Ⓓ
19. Ⓐ Ⓑ Ⓒ Ⓓ
20. Ⓐ Ⓑ Ⓒ Ⓓ
21. Ⓐ Ⓑ Ⓒ Ⓓ
22. Ⓐ Ⓑ Ⓒ Ⓓ

23. Ⓐ Ⓑ Ⓒ Ⓓ
24. Ⓐ Ⓑ Ⓒ Ⓓ
25. Ⓐ Ⓑ Ⓒ Ⓓ
26. Ⓐ Ⓑ Ⓒ Ⓓ
27. Ⓐ Ⓑ Ⓒ Ⓓ
28. Ⓐ Ⓑ Ⓒ Ⓓ
29. Ⓐ Ⓑ Ⓒ Ⓓ
30. Ⓐ Ⓑ Ⓒ Ⓓ
31. Ⓐ Ⓑ Ⓒ Ⓓ
32. Ⓐ Ⓑ Ⓒ Ⓓ
33. Ⓐ Ⓑ Ⓒ Ⓓ

34. Ⓐ Ⓑ Ⓒ Ⓓ
35. Ⓐ Ⓑ Ⓒ Ⓓ
36. Ⓐ Ⓑ Ⓒ Ⓓ
37. Ⓐ Ⓑ Ⓒ Ⓓ
38. Ⓐ Ⓑ Ⓒ Ⓓ
39. Ⓐ Ⓑ Ⓒ Ⓓ
40. Ⓐ Ⓑ Ⓒ Ⓓ
41. Ⓐ Ⓑ Ⓒ Ⓓ
42. Ⓐ Ⓑ Ⓒ Ⓓ
43. Ⓐ Ⓑ Ⓒ Ⓓ
44. Ⓐ Ⓑ Ⓒ Ⓓ

ANSWER SHEET
Practice Test 1

Section 3: Math (No Calculator)

1. Ⓐ Ⓑ Ⓒ Ⓓ   5. Ⓐ Ⓑ Ⓒ Ⓓ   9. Ⓐ Ⓑ Ⓒ Ⓓ   13. Ⓐ Ⓑ Ⓒ Ⓓ

2. Ⓐ Ⓑ Ⓒ Ⓓ   6. Ⓐ Ⓑ Ⓒ Ⓓ   10. Ⓐ Ⓑ Ⓒ Ⓓ   14. Ⓐ Ⓑ Ⓒ Ⓓ

3. Ⓐ Ⓑ Ⓒ Ⓓ   7. Ⓐ Ⓑ Ⓒ Ⓓ   11. Ⓐ Ⓑ Ⓒ Ⓓ   15. Ⓐ Ⓑ Ⓒ Ⓓ

4. Ⓐ Ⓑ Ⓒ Ⓓ   8. Ⓐ Ⓑ Ⓒ Ⓓ   12. Ⓐ Ⓑ Ⓒ Ⓓ

16.

17.

18.

19.

20.

ANSWER SHEET
Practice Test 1

Section 4: Math (Calculator)

1. Ⓐ Ⓑ Ⓒ Ⓓ
2. Ⓐ Ⓑ Ⓒ Ⓓ
3. Ⓐ Ⓑ Ⓒ Ⓓ
4. Ⓐ Ⓑ Ⓒ Ⓓ
5. Ⓐ Ⓑ Ⓒ Ⓓ
6. Ⓐ Ⓑ Ⓒ Ⓓ
7. Ⓐ Ⓑ Ⓒ Ⓓ
8. Ⓐ Ⓑ Ⓒ Ⓓ

9. Ⓐ Ⓑ Ⓒ Ⓓ
10. Ⓐ Ⓑ Ⓒ Ⓓ
11. Ⓐ Ⓑ Ⓒ Ⓓ
12. Ⓐ Ⓑ Ⓒ Ⓓ
13. Ⓐ Ⓑ Ⓒ Ⓓ
14. Ⓐ Ⓑ Ⓒ Ⓓ
15. Ⓐ Ⓑ Ⓒ Ⓓ
16. Ⓐ Ⓑ Ⓒ Ⓓ

17. Ⓐ Ⓑ Ⓒ Ⓓ
18. Ⓐ Ⓑ Ⓒ Ⓓ
19. Ⓐ Ⓑ Ⓒ Ⓓ
20. Ⓐ Ⓑ Ⓒ Ⓓ
21. Ⓐ Ⓑ Ⓒ Ⓓ
22. Ⓐ Ⓑ Ⓒ Ⓓ
23. Ⓐ Ⓑ Ⓒ Ⓓ
24. Ⓐ Ⓑ Ⓒ Ⓓ

25. Ⓐ Ⓑ Ⓒ Ⓓ
26. Ⓐ Ⓑ Ⓒ Ⓓ
27. Ⓐ Ⓑ Ⓒ Ⓓ
28. Ⓐ Ⓑ Ⓒ Ⓓ
29. Ⓐ Ⓑ Ⓒ Ⓓ
30. Ⓐ Ⓑ Ⓒ Ⓓ

31.
32.
33.
34.
35.
36.
37.
38.

Practice Test 1

READING TEST

65 MINUTES, 52 QUESTIONS

Turn to Section 1 of your answer sheet to answer the questions in this section.

> **DIRECTIONS:** Following each of the passages (or pairs of passages) below are questions about the passage (or passages). Read each passage carefully. Then, select the best answer for each question based on what is stated in the passage (or passages) and in any graphics that may accompany the passage.

Questions 1–10 are based on the following passage.

This passage is from Peter Matthiessen, *Indian Country*, © 1984 by Peter Matthiessen.

The traditionals have always been wary of the white man's consumer mentality, and now they were worried about what could happen when the Black Mesa mine was dead, when a depen-
(5) dent and poverty stricken people, having been left with waste and desecration where a sacred mountain had once stood, found themselves forced to accept more leases and more desola-tion. This threat was increased by the prospect
(10) of legal "termination," or dissolution of a people as a cultural unit, with which Indians are threat-ened every other year. Termination legislation, which had already wiped out a number of small tribes, not only withdraws all federal aid, but
(15) turns the Indians over to the mercies of state jurisdiction and property taxation, forcing a people with no other recourse to put their last resource—land—upon the market. ("That is all we have. When the land is gone, we will walk
(20) away from our homes with our beds upon our backs.") By eliminating an Indian nation, ter-mination quiets Indian claims to tribal lands that were never ceded to the U.S. government by treaty, which happens to describe almost
(25) all the "federal" land in the Far West; instead, the people must accept whatever monetary settlement has been bestowed upon them by the Court of Claims, which was set up not to administer justice but to expedite adjudication
(30) of land titles and head off any future claims that Indians might make on lands already coveted by the white economy.

The Hopi chairman's brother, Wayne, a pros-perous Mormon, proprietor of a thriving Hopi
(35) craft shop, with holdings in the family ranch and a construction company, complains in his progressive newspaper, *Qua Toqti*, of the poor attitude of the traditionals toward "their fellow tribesmen in business," and criticizes white sup-
(40) porters of the traditionals for "wanting to keep us in our 'primitive' state." He has declared, "We will never go back to our cornfields and orchards unless we are forced to." In another column in the newspaper, Wayne Sekaquaptewa inquires,
(45) "When will someone come along to convince us that we are squabbling like untrained children

1   1   1

over everything in the name of our useless religion?" (Sekaquaptewa believes that the true story of the Hopi may be found in the Book of (50) Mormon.) Not surprisingly, Qua Toqti vociferously supports the eviction of the "enemy Navajo" from Hopi land.

The progressives feel that there is no place for old, slow Hopi ways in a world that is going (55) on without them; they look down on the traditionals, with their wood stoves and kerosene lamps and outhouses, their "useless religion." (I notice, however, that outhouses in Oraibi and Hotevilla are not locked to keep out witches, (60) as are the Christian outhouses of Walpi.) The traditionals know that those who follow the lead of the progressives will be assimilated— that is, swept away into a competitive economy for which they have no training. So long as the (65) Hopi hold their land, those still able to make corn grow in the slow, patient techniques of dry farming will survive even when all help has been taken away, proceeding as best as they can according to their sacred instructions until (70) the Day of Purification restores harmony and balance to all land and life, until the bad road taken by the white man comes to its inevitable end, as foretold in the stark etching on the Life Plan Rock.

1. According to the author, the Court of Claims referred to in line 28

    (A) adjudicates cases fairly
    (B) almost always favors Indian claims to land over white claims to land
    (C) has little real effect on Indian affairs
    (D) is biased toward white people in its judgments

2. The word *quiets* as it is used in line 22 most nearly means

    (A) reduces in volume
    (B) softens
    (C) lessens
    (D) eliminates

3. The author most likely put quotation marks around the word "federal" in line 25 to

    (A) show that he understands that the term is an informal, unofficial one
    (B) remind the reader the notion of a federal government is a controversial one
    (C) emphasize that most of the land in the Far West is owned not by the states but by the U.S. government
    (D) indicate that ownership of most of the land claimed by the U.S. government in the Far West is open to dispute

4. Which of the following words, as it is used in the passage, can most accurately be described as sarcastic?

    (A) "forced" (line 8)
    (B) "mercies" (line 15)
    (C) "vociferously" (lines 50–51)
    (D) "stark" (line 73)

5. What does the author aim to imply in lines 58–60: "I notice, however, that outhouses in Oraibi and Hotevilla are not locked to keep out witches, as are the Christian outhouses of Walpi"?

    (A) Traditional Hopi religion has not developed even to the point at which it believes in witches.
    (B) Followers of traditional Hopi religion are careless in the practice of their religion compared to the progressives, who scrupulously follow the teachings of Christianity.
    (C) Followers of traditional Hopi religion might be less superstitious than the Hopi followers of the white man's predominant religion, Christianity.
    (D) Progressive Indians are, sensibly, aware of the danger presented by witches.

6. The traditionals believe that

   (A) the only way in which the Hopi can survive as a distinct culture is to follow the lead of the progressives and adapt to the white man's ways

   (B) Hopi religion is based on a misplaced faith that balance will eventually be restored in the world

   (C) it is very possible that the truth about the origin and destiny of the Hopi is to be found in the Book of Mormon

   (D) the only chance that the Hopi have to survive as a cultural unit is to cling to their traditional ways

7. The author's main purpose in citing the views of Wayne Sekaquaptewa is to help

   (A) present the views of the progressives in the Hopi nation

   (B) show that progressive Hopis are more realistic than traditional Hopis

   (C) illustrate the influence of Mormonism on Hopi society

   (D) show that Indians, if given the opportunity, can be as successful in business as whites

8. Which of the following statements best describes the author's view of the "Day of Purification" referred to in line 70?

   (A) He believes it will come as long as enough Hopis abandon their traditional culture and adopt the ways of the white man.

   (B) He is certain that it will come one day, precisely as predicted in Hopi teaching.

   (C) He thinks that it is a myth believed by a primitive culture that contains no truth, even on a symbolic level.

   (D) He respects it as an important Hopi belief and sees it as symbolic of a future time that may very possibly come to pass.

9. Which word or phrase would traditional Hopi be most likely to use to describe the white man?

   (A) trustworthy

   (B) altruistic

   (C) materialistic

   (D) respectful of nature

10. Which choice provides the best evidence for the answer to the previous question?

   (A) "The . . . desolation." (lines 1–9)

   (B) "Termination . . . market." (lines 12–18)

   (C) "The . . . state.'" (lines 33–41)

   (D) "The . . . religion.'" (lines 53–57)

Questions 11–20 are based on the following passages.

Each of the following passages is from the beginning of short stories by F. Scott Fitzgerald in *Flappers and Philosophers*, originally published in 1920.

PASSAGE 1

This unlikely story begins on a sea that was a blue dream, as colorful as blue-silk stockings, and beneath a sky as blue as the irises of children's eyes. From the western half of
(5) the sky the sun was shying little golden disks at the sea—if you gazed intently enough you could see them skip from wave tip to wave tip until they joined a broad collar of golden coin that was collecting half a mile out and would
(10) eventually be a dazzling sunset. About half-way between the Florida shore and the golden collar a white steam-yacht, very young and graceful, was riding at anchor and under a blue-and-white awning aft a yellow-haired girl reclined in
(15) a wicker settee reading *The Revolt of the Angels,* by Anatole France. She was about nineteen, slender and supple, with a spoiled alluring mouth and quick gray eyes full of a radiant curiosity. Her feet, stockingless, and adorned rather
(20) than clad in blue-satin slippers which swung nonchalantly from her toes, were perched on the arm of a settee adjoining the one she occupied. And as she read she intermittently regaled herself by a faint application to her tongue of a
(25) half-lemon that she held in her hand. The other half, sucked dry, lay on the deck at her feet and rocked very gently to and fro at the almost imperceptible motion of the tide.

The second half-lemon was well-nigh pulp-
(30) less and the golden collar had grown astonishing in width, when suddenly the drowsy silence which enveloped the yacht was broken by the sound of heavy footsteps and an elderly man topped with orderly gray hair and clad in a
(35) white-flannel suit appeared at the head of the companionway. There he paused for a moment until his eyes became accustomed to the sun, and then seeing the girl under the awning he uttered a long even grunt of disapproval. If he
(40) had intended thereby to obtain a rise of any sort he was doomed to disappointment. The girl calmly turned over two pages, turned back one, raised the lemon mechanically to tasting distance, and then very faintly but quite unmis-
(45) takably yawned.

PASSAGE 2

The sunlight dripped over the house like golden paint over an art jar, and the freckling shadows here and there only intensified the rigor of the bath of light. The Butterworth and
(50) Larkin houses flanking were entrenched behind great stodgy trees; only the Happer house took the full sun, and all day long faced the dusty road-street with a tolerant kindly patience. This was the city of Tarleton in southernmost
(55) Georgia, September afternoon.

Up in her bedroom window Sally Carrol Happer rested her nineteen-year-old chin on a fifty-two-year-old sill and watched Clark Darrow's ancient Ford turn the corner. The car
(60) was hot—being partly metallic it retained all the heat it absorbed or evolved— and Clark Darrow sitting bolt upright at the wheel wore a pained, strained expression as though he considered himself a spare part, and rather likely to break.
(65) He laboriously crossed two dust ruts, the wheels squeaking indignantly at the encounter, and then with a terrifying expression he gave the steering-gear a final wrench and deposited self and car approximately in front of the Happer
(70) steps. There was a heaving sound, a death-rattle, followed by a short silence; and then the air was rent by a startling whistle. Sally Carrol gazed down sleepily. She started to yawn, but

1 1 1

finding this quite impossible unless she raised
(75) her chin from the window-sill, changed her
mind and continued silently to regard the car,
whose owner sat brilliantly if perfunctorily at
attention as he waited for an answer to his
signal. After a moment the whistle once more
(80) split the dusty air.

11. The phrase "quick gray eyes" (line 18) is most
    likely used to suggest that the girl portrayed in
    Passage 1 is

    (A) alert
    (B) nervous
    (C) shifty
    (D) distracted

12. The phrase "adorned rather than clad" (lines 19–20)
    suggests that the girl described in Passage 1

    (A) is indifferent to how her feet look
    (B) likes to make herself attractive
    (C) is wearing slippers because they are the most
        practical footwear for a passenger on a yacht
    (D) does not know much about fashion

13. The word closest in meaning to the word *rise* as it
    is used in line 40 in Passage 1 is

    (A) increase
    (B) greeting
    (C) reaction
    (D) wave

14. What can most reasonably be inferred about the
    man portrayed in Passage 1?

    (A) He is the girl's grandfather.
    (B) He does not enjoy being on a yacht.
    (C) He does not often come on deck because his
        illness confines him to bed below deck.
    (D) He does not approve of the girl spending so
        much of her time reading.

15. In Passage 2 the author uses the words and
    phrases "tolerant kindly patience" (line 53),
    "indignantly" (line 66), and "death-rattle"
    (lines 70–71) mainly to

    (A) satirize the way of life in Tarleton
    (B) help the reader imagine what is being
        described
    (C) exaggerate and distort reality to give the
        reader a fresh perspective
    (D) encourage the reader to sympathize with the
        people described in the scene

16. The whistle mentioned in line 72 of Passage 2 was
    most likely produced by

    (A) a passerby
    (B) Clark Darrow's car
    (C) Clark Darrow
    (D) a policeman

17. One can reasonably infer that the words "sat bril-
    liantly if perfunctorily at attention" in Passage 2
    (lines 77–79) suggest that Clark Darrow regards
    his visit to the Happer house largely as

    (A) a dramatic way to demonstrate his romantic
        interest in Sally Happer
    (B) a great honor
    (C) an uninteresting routine duty to be per-
        formed, albeit in a somewhat showy manner
    (D) an exciting change from his regular activities

18. The word *evolved* as it is used in line 61 means

    (A) gave off
    (B) developed gradually
    (C) devised
    (D) retained

19. Which of the following words best describes both of the girls as they are portrayed in Passage 1 and Passage 2?

   (A) pretty
   (B) relaxed
   (C) intelligent
   (D) indolent

20. In both Passage 1 and Passage 2 the arrival of a male character

   (A) primarily helps to create humor
   (B) is followed by a condemnation of self-indulgence
   (C) interrupts a tranquil mood
   (D) establishes a serious atmosphere

Questions 21–31 are based on the following passage.

This passage is from Paul Fussell, "Hiroshima: A Soldier's View," © 1981 by The New Republic.

In an exchange of views not long ago in *The New York Review of Books,* Joseph Alsop and David Joravky set forth the by now familiar argument on both sides of the debate about
(5) the "ethics" of the bomb. It's not hard to guess which side each chose once you know that Alsop experienced capture by the Japanese at Hong Kong early in 1942, while Joravky came into no deadly contact with the Japanese: a
(10) young, combat-innocent soldier, he was on his way to the Pacific when the war ended. The editors of *The New York Review* gave the debate the tendentious title "Was the Hiroshima Bomb Necessary?" surely an unanswerable question
(15) (unlike "Was It Effective?") and one precisely indicating the intellectual difficulties involved in imposing *ex post facto* a rational and even a genteel ethics on this event. In arguing the acceptability of the bomb, Alsop focuses on
(20) the power and fanaticism of War Minister Anami, who insisted that Japan fight to the bit- ter end, defending the main islands with the same techniques and tenacity employed at Iwo Jima and Okinawa. Alsop concludes: "Japanese
(25) surrender could never have been obtained, at any rate without the honor-satisfying blood- bath envisioned by . . . Anami, if the hideous destruction of Hiroshima and Nagasaki had not finally galvanized the peace advocates into tear-
(30) ing up the entire Japanese book of rules." The Japanese plan to deploy the undefeated bulk of their ground forces, over two million men, plus 10,000 kamikaze planes, plus the elderly and all the women and children with sharp-
(35) ened spears they could muster in a suicidal defense makes it absurd, says Alsop, to "hold the common view, by now hardly challenged

by anyone, that the decision to drop the two bombs on Japan was wicked in itself, and that (40) President Truman and all others who joined in making or who [like Robert Oppenheimer] assented to this decision shared in the wicked-ness." And in explanation of "the two bombs," Alsop adds: "The true, climactic, and success-(45) ful effort of the Japanese peace advocates . . . did not begin in deadly earnest until *after* the second bomb had destroyed Nagasaki. The Nagasaki bomb was thus the trigger to all the developments that led to peace." At this time the (50) army was so unready for surrender that most looked forward to the forthcoming invasion as an indispensable opportunity to show their mettle, enthusiastically agreeing with the army spokesman who reasoned early in 1945, "Since (55) the retreat from Guadalcanal, the Army has had little opportunity to engage the enemy in land battles. But when we meet in Japan proper, our Army will demonstrate its invincible superior-ity." This possibility foreclosed by the Emperor's (60) post-A-bomb surrender broadcast, the shocked, disappointed officers of one infantry battalion, anticipating a professionally impressive defense of the beaches, killed themselves in the follow-ing numbers: one major, three captains, ten first (65) lieutenants, and twelve second lieutenants.

David Joravsky, now a professor of history at Northwestern, argued on the other hand that those who decided to use the A-bombs on cit-ies betray defects of "reason and self-restraint." (70) It all needn't have happened, he says, "if the U.S. government had been willing to take a few more days and to be a bit more thoughtful in opening up the age of nuclear warfare." I've already noted what "a few more days" would (75) mean to the luckless troops and sailors on the spot, and as to being thoughtful when "opening up the age of nuclear warfare," of course no one was focusing on anything as portentous as that, which reflects a historian's tidy hind-sight. The

(80) U.S. government was engaged not in that sort of momentous thing but in ending the war con-clusively, as well as irrationally remembering Pearl Harbor with a vengeance. It didn't know then what everyone knows now about leuke-(85) mia and various kinds of carcinoma and birth defects. Truman was not being sly or coy when he insisted that the bomb was "only another weapon." History, as Eliot's "Gerontion" notes,

. . . has many cunning passages, contrived (90)   corridors
And issues, deceives with whispering
   ambitions,
Guides us by vanities . . .
         Think
(95) Neither fear not courage saves us.
Unnatural vices
Are fathered by our heroism. Virtues
Are forced upon us by our impudent
   crimes.

(100)   Understanding the past requires pretending that you don't know the present. It requires feel-ing its own pressure on your pulses without any *ex post facto* illumination. That's a harder thing to do than Joravsky seems to think.

(105) *Ex post facto* means "after the fact."

1   1   1

21. In the opening part of the passage, "In an exchange . . . the war ended" (lines 1–11), what assumption does the author appear to be making?

   (A) A soldier who is captured by the enemy will always feel hatred toward the enemy that will distort that person's judgment about the enemy.
   (B) A person's opinions are determined to a large extent by his or her experiences.
   (C) The views of a soldier who has not experienced combat about the enemy cannot be taken seriously.
   (D) It is not possible for anyone to reach an objective judgment about an emotional topic like the ethics of the dropping of A-bombs on Hiroshima.

22. Why does the author say that the question "Was the Hiroshima Bomb Necessary?" is unanswerable?

   (A) Americans are still so deeply divided about this event that no definitive answer can yet be given.
   (B) The word "necessary" in the question requires that the answer to the question be "no," because the Japanese could have been defeated without the use of the atomic bomb, albeit at the cost of great loss of life.
   (C) Ethical issues can never be conclusively decided.
   (D) Questions about the past are meaningless because the past remains the past no matter what is decided about it in retrospect.

23. What does the "Japanese book of rules" mentioned in line 30 refer to?

   (A) the guidelines Japanese peace advocates had been following before the destruction of Hiroshima and Nagasaki
   (B) the deeply held values governing Japanese conduct, especially in regard to national pride, individual honor, and conduct in war
   (C) the plan devised at the highest levels of Japanese government to defend the homeland against invasion at all costs
   (D) the code of conduct of Japanese soldiers

24. What information, if it came to light, would support Joseph Alsop's contention, cited by the author in lines 18–27, that the only way Japan could have been induced to surrender other than by the dropping of the atomic bomb would have been an "honor-satisfying bloodbath"?

   (A) sociological studies suggesting that Japanese people place less value on honor than is generally thought
   (B) evidence that the case being made by peace advocates in Japan was being received with increasing interest by the Japanese populace
   (C) surveys of public opinion in Japan near the end of the war suggesting that the vast majority of the population would fight to the death to defend Japan
   (D) documents showing that the civilian population was poorly organized and unmotivated to fight trained Allied soldiers to defend Japan

25. Which of the following statements would the author be most likely to agree with?

(A) There is little chance that Kamikaze planes would have been used by the Japanese military against a U.S.-led invasion.

(B) In considering the morality of the atomic bombing of Japan, Americans tend to ignore the fact that Japanese culture places great stress on honor, even if it requires great sacrifice.

(C) There is little reason to think that Japanese civilians would defend their country as ferociously as Japanese soldiers.

(D) The ferocity of the fighting at Iwo Jima and Okinawa has been greatly exaggerated by Hollywood movies.

26. What phrase best expresses what the author means by "a genteel ethics" in line 18?

(A) middle class values

(B) religious morals

(C) generally accepted social norms

(D) the morality of polite society

27. What information, if discovered, would support the argument made by Joseph Alsop, cited in lines 44–49 ("The true, climactic . . . led to peace") that the dropping of an atomic bomb on Nagasaki was morally justifiable?

(A) evidence that a secret offer of unconditional surrender by the Japanese emperor had been received one day after the atom bomb was dropped on Hiroshima

(B) studies by the U.S. military arguing persuasively that Japanese civilians would not make an effective fighting force

(C) information showing that the Japanese military had nearly run out of fuel at the time the A-bomb was dropped on Nagasaki

(D) documents showing that the Japanese leaders possessed secret information that led them to believe (incorrectly) after the atomic bomb was dropped on Hiroshima that the Americans did not possess another atomic bomb that was ready for use, and it would be several months before another one would be ready

28. Which of the following words or phrases is closest in meaning to the word *tidy* as it is used in line 79?

(A) clean

(B) orderly

(C) substantial

(D) satisfactory

29. The phrase, "as well as irrationally remembering Pearl Harbor with a vengeance" (lines 82–83), suggests that the author believes that

    (A) in deciding to drop atomic bombs on Hiroshima and Nagasaki, officials in the U.S. government were partly motivated by a desire for revenge against the Japanese

    (B) U.S. government officials were not acting at all rationally in deciding to drop atomic bombs on Japanese cities

    (C) in their desire to drop atomic bombs on Japanese cities, the U.S. government was motivated entirely by the memory of the surprise Japanese attack on Pearl Harbor

    (D) the U.S. government allowed itself to be distracted from the main business of decisively and expeditiously ending the war by a desire for vengeance for Japan's surprise attack on Pearl Harbor

30. The word *illumination* as it is used in line 103 most nearly means

    (A) exaggeration
    (B) intellectual enlightenment
    (C) pretension to knowledge
    (D) spiritual enlightenment

31. The lines from T. S. Eliot's poem "Gerontion" serve mainly to

    (A) remind historians that to understand an event in the past they must imagine that they are ignorant of what the consequences of the event were

    (B) make the point that a heroic action might result in evil, and a cowardly action might result in good

    (C) encourage the reader to investigate what great poets have written about both the heroism war inspires and the horrors it entails

    (D) reinforce the point that the consequences of an action (for good or ill) are not known by those who decide to take the action at the time of their decision

Questions 32–42 are based on the following passage.

This passage is from David Alpaugh, "The Professionalization of Poetry" in *Heavy Lifting*, © 2007 by Alehouse Press.

As colleges and universities increasingly make the education, publication, sustenance, and honoring of American poets their business, writing program professionals have assumed
(5) a number of nonpoetic responsibilities. It has become part of their business to attract students and sponsor an ever-growing body of work produced by graduates and colleagues. Such practical concerns have led professionals to tolerate
(10) aesthetic trends designed not so much to make poetry better as to make it easier to produce and publish.

Most obvious is the "prosification" of poetry—the publication of flat, pedestrian
(15) prose with the assurance, explicit or implied, that it is the real thing. The notion that lineation is a magic wand that can turn prose into poetry has been uncritically accepted by too many literary editors. So many poets publish lineated
(20) prose today that it would be unfair to single out one or two. In "On the Prosing of Poetry," poet Joan Houlihan makes a similar argument, providing poems by writers such as Donald Hall, John Balaban, John Brehm, and Robert Creeley
(25) as examples. She writes, "We have reached the point [where] we are being asked to believe that a text block, chopped randomly into flat, declarative lines, is a poem."

If the profusion of prose made to look like
(30) poetry is disconcerting, it is equally annoying when similar fare is dished up under the faddish moniker "prose poem," a form in which text is set like prose in ragged or justified type, line breaks thereby losing significance. The "poem"
(35) part of the equation promises greater density and compression than we normally expect from prose, achieved through poetic devices such as rhythm, imagery, metaphor, simile, and figures of speech.

(40)   William Blake and Christopher Smart wrote prose poems long before the term was invented. Poe and Baudelaire more consciously a century later. In our own time Russell Edson has written brilliantly in this genre, producing a body of *(45)* original work that can hold its own with the best poetry of our time.

The current popularity of the genre is attested to by Peter Johnson, editor of *The Best of the Prose Poem: An International Journal.* "I have *(50)* read so many prose poems," he complains, "that I feel as if a large gray eraser is squatting in the hollow of my head. I am not even sure what my criteria are, anymore." At least one prestigious graduate writing program understands the *(55)* genre well enough to offer students an entire course in "The Prose Poem."

The jury is still out on definitions. Some critics deny that the term has any meaning at all. Others concede that the term is muddied, *(60)* since it is difficult to define the genre without opening the door to the heightened prose of many a novelist and short story writer. Still, the term leads us to expect a combination of and tension between prose and poetic elements. *(65)* Unfortunately, these expectations aren't always met.

Examples abound. Here are two excerpts from "Doubt," by Fanny Howe, which appeared in *The Best American Poetry: 2001*, edited by *(70)* David Lehman and Robert Hass, both long associated with writing programs:

Virginia Woolf committed suicide in 1941 when the German bombing campaign against England was at its peak and when she was read- *(75)* ing Freud whom she had staved off until then.

Edith Stein, recently and controversially beatified by the Pope, who had successfully worked to transform an existential vocabulary into a theological one, was taken to Auschwitz *(80)* in August 1942.

These excerpts are part of a "prose poem" that goes on for four pages. Howe offers interesting insights in a style appropriate for a scholarly or critical journal. But it's hard to find *(85)* any definition from Aristotle to the present that would admit such writing as poetry, certainly not under the term free verse or open form; for it has been the concern of responsible poets in those movements to find non- *(90)* traditional, personalized strategies for making poetry musical. "Poetry atrophies, when it gets too far from music," Ezra Pound observes in his *ABC of Reading.* Howe's piece lacks the rhythmical, metaphorical texture needed to fulfill the *(95)* poetry part of the prose-poem equation. In her author's note Howe explains that she "can no longer make distinctions" between poetry and prose. It is unfortunate that the editors of an anthology entitled *The Best American Poetry* are *(100)* equally unable to make a distinction that readers who buy a book with that title have a right to expect.

The ever-increasing prosification of poetry assures prospective students that they needn't *(105)* employ meter or rhyme or cadence or figurative language, or any of the devices, for that matter, in a standard poet's dictionary; that the drabbest encyclopedia prose, even technical jargon, can be hailed as "poetry" of the highest order. *(110)* It's the profession's way of redefining the art downward to accommodate its talent pool.

32. The phrase "aesthetic trends" in line 10 most nearly means

(A) movements in the arts designed to challenge conventional notions of artistic beauty

(B) literary theories about what makes one text "better" than another

(C) fashions in what is regarded as worthwhile in the arts and literature

(D) the increasing tendency of poetry to be like prose

33. In line 14, *pedestrian* most nearly means

    (A) pedantic
    (B) undistinguished
    (C) popular
    (D) static

34. Based on what he says in the first paragraph of the passage the author would probably agree that

    (A) quite a few people involved in teaching the writing of poetry at American colleges and universities care more about furthering their careers than encouraging the writing and publication of good poetry
    (B) most of the people involved in teaching the writing of poetry in American colleges and universities care more about maintaining a high standard of poetry than they do about encouraging the production of poetry, regardless of its quality
    (C) many of those who teach the writing of poetry in American colleges and universities do so because they are unable to write good poetry themselves
    (D) most teachers of the writing of poetry in American colleges and universities are, as a rule, unable to distinguish good poetry from bad poetry

35. The "real thing" in line 16 refers to

    (A) prose poems
    (B) good prose
    (C) poetry
    (D) original writing of any type

36. It is most likely that the author used the phrase "dished up" rather than the word "published" in line 31 in order to

    (A) suggest that prose poetry is, in many ways, like fast food
    (B) colorfully emphasize his dislike for currently fashionable prose poetry
    (C) create the impression in the reader's mind that he is not above using colloquial language
    (D) demonstrate that he is capable of poetic expression as well as critical analysis

37. In line 35, "equation" most nearly means

    (A) the combination of poetic elements with elements from prose to create prose poetry
    (B) the use of poetic devices in prose to create poetic prose
    (C) the poetic elements in prose poetry that can be quantified
    (D) the widespread but incorrect belief that the production of good poetry (of any sort) is, like everything, governed by precise, definable laws

38. According to the author, William Blake and Christopher Smart

    (A) were not aware that some of their work was prose
    (B) worked primarily in the genre of prose poetry
    (C) did not consciously set out to write work that would later come to be called prose poetry
    (D) were largely responsible for the creation of the literary genre now known as prose poetry

39. The author's tone in lines 53–56 ("At least one . . . 'The Prose Poem.'") is most accurately described as

    (A) ironic
    (B) sarcastic
    (C) self-deprecating
    (D) ambivalent

40. The phrase "heightened prose" in line 61 refers to

(A) poetic prose
(B) the prose of poets
(C) pretentious writing
(D) profoundly meaningful prose

41. Which of the following statements would the author of this passage be likely to agree with?

(A) Prose poetry never succeeds as poetry.
(B) Writing free verse frees a poet from having to follow the conventions of poetry as a genre.
(C) Any distinction between poetic prose and prose poetry is meaningless.
(D) To be considered poetry a piece of writing must make significant use of rhythm and metaphor.

42. The author includes the two excerpts from "Doubt" (lines 72–80) primarily to

(A) provide examples to support his contention that many prose poems being written do not successfully combine prose elements and poetic elements
(B) provide support for the view that prose poetry is a legitimate genre
(C) demonstrate that prose poems can make effective use of traditional poetic devices
(D) show that prose poems are uniquely suited for literary criticism because they combine the analytic precision of prose with the intuitive insight of poetry

Questions 43–52 are based on the following passage.

This passage is from S. Jeffress Williams, Kurt Dodd, Kathleen Krafft Gohn, 1990, Coasts in Crisis, Coastal Change: U.S. Geological Survey Circular 1075.

Diverse and complex natural processes continually change coasts physically, chemically, and biologically, at scales that range from microscopic (grains of sand) to global (changes
(5) in sea level). Regional and local characteristics of coasts control the differing interactions and relative importance of these natural processes.

Coastal lands and sediments are constantly in motion. Breaking waves move sand along the
(10) coast, eroding sand in one area and depositing it on an adjacent beach. Tidal cycles bring sand onto the beach and carry it back into the surf. Rivers carry sediment to the coast and build deltas into the open water. Storms cause deep
(15) erosion in one area and leave thick overwash deposits in another. Plants retain sediment in wetlands and impede movement of coastal dunes. Natural processes that change the water level also affect coastal dynamics. Taken indi-
(20) vidually, each natural process of coastal transport is complex; taken collectively, they create an intricate system that attempts to achieve a dynamic balance.

Winds create waves that ripple across the
(25) surface of lakes and seas until they break on the shallowing bottom and crash into the shore. In many areas, prevailing winds produce waves that consistently approach the coast at oblique angles. Even the slightest angle between the
(30) land and the waves will create currents that transport sediment along the shore. These longshore currents are a primary agent of coastal movement; they are a major cause of sand migration along barrier and mainland beaches.
(35) Tides ebb and flood in response to the gravitational attraction of the moon and sun; exceptional high and low tides occur each month when the sun and moon are aligned. Tides help

determine where the waves break—low on the
(40) beach at low tide, high on the beach at high
tide—and, therefore, where sand is deposited
and removed. Rip tides, or undertow, occur
along most beaches and can move significant
amounts of sand offshore.

(45)   Storm systems along coasts contain high
winds, create large waves, and cause storm
surges that raise water levels as much as 7
meters above normal. Although storms are spo-
radic, they are the primary cause of beach
(50) erosion along many coasts. Storms carry sand
seaward, forming offshore bars; much of this
sand migrates landward during calm weather.
Some areas are more storm prone than others.
Storms often are concentrated in specific sea-
(55) sons; along the eastern seaboard, for example,
hurricanes occur in the late summer and early
fall, and storms are especially frequent during the winter months. These seasonal trends
result in a general difference between the win-
(60) ter "eroding" beach and the summer "building"
beach that is most common along parts of the
west coast.

In addition to the daily cycles of tides, many
other forces lead to significant changes in water
(65) level. Predominantly closed bodies of water
such as lakes experience dramatic water-level
changes in response to precipitation, spring
snowmelt, and evaporation.

Other local changes in water level occur
(70) when the land either rises or falls relative to
the water. Along tectonically active coasts, such
as the coast of earthquake-prone southern
California, land may rise as much as 4 centimeters per century. The Earth's crust in parts
(75) of Alaska and the Great Lakes area, which was
pressed down by the weight of the massive ice
sheets that blanketed the north during the last
great ice age, is now rising due to the retreat of
the glaciers.

(80)   Global changes in sea level result from tectonic processes, such as the down- or up-warp-
ing of the ocean basins, or from changes in the

total volume of water in the oceans. During the
last great ice age, which began 36,000 years ago,
(85) huge amounts of ocean water were transformed
into glaciers, resulting in a 100-meter drop in
the global sea level. We are still emerging from
that ice age, and sea level has been rising continuously over the last 20,000 years; during the
(90) past century, the rate of sea level rise has aver-
aged 10–15 centimeters per century worldwide.

The slope of a coast is critical to determining
how water-level changes will affect it. Steeply
sloping coasts experience small shifts in their
(95) coastlines as the water level changes; however,
because wave action along steep coasts is concentrated within a narrow zone, small water-
level increases can result in significant erosion
of bluffs or dunes. On a gently sloping coast, like
(100) the U.S. east coast or around the Gulf of Mexico,
small changes in water level cause the coastline
to shift dramatically; however, the gentle slope
absorbs and dissipates the waves' energy along
a broad front.

Longshore Current

Beach

Longshore current direction

incoming waves

43. The most appropriate title for the passage would be

(A) Ocean Coasts
(B) The Ocean and the Land
(C) Coastal Slope and Sea-level Change
(D) Coastal Change

44. The word *continually* as it is used in lines 1–2 most nearly means

(A) continuously
(B) regularly occurring
(C) gradually
(D) eternally

45. The word *shallowing* as it is used in line 26 most nearly means

(A) becoming more shallow
(B) shallow
(C) varying
(D) becoming less shallow

46. Which of the following, mentioned in the second paragraph, are not elaborated on in the rest of the passage?

(A) waves
(B) tides
(C) storms
(D) plants

47. If waves hit a shore so that there is no angle between the land and the waves

(A) an undertow will be created
(B) sediment will be deposited along the shore as a result
(C) sediment will not be moved along the shore as a result
(D) currents will be created along the shore

48. Which of the following provides evidence for the answer to the previous question?

(A) "Breaking . . . beach." (lines 9–11)
(B) "Winds . . . shore." (lines 24–26)
(C) "Even . . . shore." (lines 29–31)
(D) "These . . . beaches." (lines 31–34)

49. In the diagram the arrows in the section marked "Beach" probably represent

(A) waves coming onto the beach and then back into the ocean, carrying sand along the shore
(B) areas of the beach that are not affected by waves
(C) areas of the beach most affected by a long-shore current
(D) waves that have no effect on the shore

50. According to the passage, which of the following does not affect sea level?

(A) tides
(B) glaciers melting
(C) storms
(D) the slope of coasts

51. Large water-level changes in the ocean off the U.S. east coast would most likely

(A) cause a great deal of erosion on beaches there
(B) increase rainfall along the U.S. east coast
(C) shift the location of coastlines there significantly
(D) cause beaches to disappear in many places on the U.S. east coast

52. If the Earth's climate became warmer, ocean levels would be likely to

(A) fall
(B) rise
(C) remain the same
(D) rise briefly, then fall dramatically

STOP If there is still time remaining, you may review your answers.

2   2   2

WRITING AND LANGUAGE TEST

35 MINUTES, 44 QUESTIONS

Turn to Section 2 of your answer sheet to answer the questions in this section.

DIRECTIONS: Questions follow each of the passages below. Some questions ask you how the passage might be changed to improve the expression of ideas. Other questions ask you how the passage might be altered to correct errors in grammar, usage, and punctuation. One or more graphics accompany some passages. You will be required to consider these graphics as you answer questions about editing the passage.

There are three types of questions. In the first type, a part of the passage is underlined. The second type is based on a certain part of the passage. The third type is based on the entire passage.

Read each passage. Then, choose the answer to each question that changes the passage so that it is consistent with the conventions of standard written English. One of the answer choices for many questions is "NO CHANGE." Choosing this answer means that you believe the best answer is to make no change in the passage.

Questions 1–11 are based on the following passage and supplementary material.

Highlights of Women's Earnings

In 2011, women who were full-time wage and salary workers had median usual weekly earnings of $684, about 82 percent of median earnings for male full-time wage and salary workers ($832). In 1979, the first year for which ❶ comparing earnings data are available, women earned 62 percent of what men earned.

❷ Women working full time in management, business, and financial operations jobs had median weekly earnings of $977 in 2011, which is more than women earned in any

1. (A) NO CHANGE
   (B) comparison
   (C) comparable
   (D) comparability

2. (A) NO CHANGE
   (B) Women worked
   (C) Women have worked
   (D) Women, those working

other major occupational category. ❸ The second highest paying job group for women was professional and related occupations, in which their median weekly earnings were $919. Within professional and related occupations, women who were lawyers ($1,631), pharmacists ($1,898), and physicians ($1,527) had the highest earnings.

The occupational distributions of female and male full-time workers differ ❹ significantly compared with men. Relatively few women work in construction, production, or transportation occupations, and women are

3. At this point, the writer is considering adding the following sentence:

Within management, business, and financial operations occupations, women who were chief executives and computer and information systems managers had the highest median weekly earnings ($1,464 and $1,543, respectively).

Should the writer make this addition here?

(A) Yes, because the information in this sentence provides a contrast with the information in the previous sentence.

(B) Yes, because it provides more information about the earnings of women in a sub-category of workers mentioned in the previous sentence.

(C) No, because the information in this sentence is too specific for a report of this kind.

(D) No, because no supporting evidence is given for the information in this sentence.

4. (A) NO CHANGE
   (B) significantly. It is relative that few
   (C) significantly. Compared with men relatively few
   (D) significantly compared with men, relatively. Few

2   2   2

Distribution of full-time wage and salary employment, by sex and major occupation group, 2011 annual averages

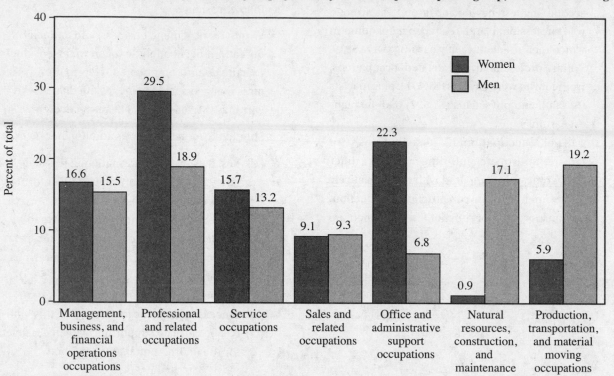

far more concentrated in ⑤ <u>natural resources occupations</u>.

Women are more likely than men to work in professional and related ⑥ <u>occupations. Being within this category, though,</u> the proportion of women employed in the higher paying job groups is much smaller than the proportion of men employed in them. In 2011, 8 percent of

5. Which choice most accurately and effectively represents the information in the graph?

(A) NO CHANGE
(B) sales and related occupations
(C) office and administrative support occupations
(D) management, business, and financial operations occupations

6. (A) NO CHANGE
(B) occupations. Within this occupational category, though,
(C) occupations. Looking at those which are within this category, though,
(D) occupations which are within this category. Though

2   2   2

female professionals were employed in ❼ the relative high-paying computer and engineering fields, compared with 44 percent of male professionals. Professional women were more likely to work in education and healthcare occupations, in which the pay is generally lower ❽ than computer and engineering jobs. ❾ Sixty-nine percent of female professionals worked in the education and healthcare fields in 2011, compared with 30 percent of male professionals.

Women are more likely than men to work part time—that is, less than 35 hours per week on a sole, or principal, job. Women who worked part time made up 26 percent of all female wage and salary workers in 2011. ❿ Similarly, 13 percent of men in wage and salary jobs worked part time. Unlike full-time workers, women and men who worked part time had similar median earnings. Median weekly earnings for female part-timers were $235 in 2011, ⓫ a little different than the $226 median for their male counterparts.

7. (A) NO CHANGE
   (B) relating to
   (C) relation to the high-paying
   (D) the relatively high-paying

8. (A) NO CHANGE
   (B) than that which would be earned in
   (C) than it is in
   (D) than what employees get paid in

9. The writer is considering deleting the underlined sentence. Should he keep it or delete it?

   (A) Keep it, because it provides a detail that supports the main topic of the paragraph.
   (B) Keep it, because it helps link the paragraph it is in to the following paragraph.
   (C) Delete it, because it contradicts information provided earlier in the passage.
   (D) Delete it, because the information it provides is not relevant to what is described in the paragraph it is in.

10. (A) NO CHANGE
    (B) In contrast,
    (C) Consequently,
    (D) Notwithstanding this,

11. (A) NO CHANGE
    (B) with little difference than
    (C) little different from
    (D) and this is a little different than

2   2   2

Questions 12–22 are based on the following passage.

Arctic Science

The Arctic is a gigantic "natural laboratory" of surprising ⓬ divergence that offers exciting research possibilities in almost every branch of science.

⓭ The field lines of the magnetic field surrounding the Earth converge in the polar regions. This means that charged particles from the sun enter the Earth's atmosphere in these regions, producing ⓮ ostentatious effects such as the aurora, magnetic storms, and ionospheric disturbances, which may black out radio communication.

Lower in the atmosphere, the high-velocity westerly jet stream is affected by processes of energy exchange at the Earth's surface in the Arctic—by sea ice distribution and ocean and land temperatures—and ⓯ in turn effects the weather and climate of the entire hemisphere or even the whole Earth.

Nowhere else is ice and snow in all its forms—sea ice, glaciers, permafrost, river and lake ice—as widespread and diverse as in the Arctic. Alaska is an ideal laboratory for studying these ice ⓰ forms. It is from individual ice crystals under a microscope to the millions of square kilometers of sea ice as seen by a satellite. The solution of practical problems associated with avalanches, building roads and houses on permafrost, extracting petroleum from ice-covered waters, and numerous others,

12. (A) NO CHANGE
    (B) diversity
    (C) discrepancy
    (D) incongruity

13. Which choice is the best transition from the previous paragraph to this one?

    (A) Scientists from several nations have worked for many years in this "laboratory."
    (B) Recent studies show that climate change in the Arctic predicts climate change elsewhere on Earth.
    (C) When one examines this large-scale natural laboratory, starting in outer space above the Arctic, a number of fascinating features become apparent.
    (D) This article will concentrate on the magnetic field in the polar regions.

14. (A) NO CHANGE
    (B) glaring
    (C) conspicuous
    (D) protrusive

15. (A) NO CHANGE
    (B) in turn affects
    (C) in turn effect
    (D) in turn affect

16. Which choice most effectively combines the sentences at the underlined portion?

    (A) forms from individuals, ice
    (B) forming from individual ice
    (C) which form from individual ice
    (D) forms, from individual ice

depends on fundamental research that can be conducted in the Alaska setting. **17**

[1] A major ocean covers a large area around the pole in the Northern Hemisphere. [2] This ocean is largely ice covered and exhibits a wide range of dynamic behavior of its ice and water masses. [3] Since from 5 to 7% of the world's potentially most devastating earthquakes occur in Alaska, this is an ideal location for the study of the Earth's structure and its often violent surface movements. [4] Alaska is also part of the Pacific "Rim of **18** Fire," this is where tectonic activity has created a unique and dangerous environment. [5] Within its boundary, Alaska encloses **19** a long island, the arc associated with a deep ocean trench, 40 active volcanoes, and heavy earthquake activity. **20**

These brief examples illustrate the uniqueness and diversity in structure, dynamics, and behavior of the arctic regions as an important part of the whole Earth. Other nations are expending great efforts in the study of the Arctic because they understand that the keys to many of our planet's present and future problems may lie in this **21** region if the United States is to participate in this process in any meaningful way. It must begin **22** involving in arctic research now.

17. Which choice most effectively establishes the main topic of the paragraph?

(A) The most important scientific research in Alaska is done using satellite images.
(B) Scientists first began studying Alaska in 1960.
(C) Alaska is an excellent setting for scientists to study snow and ice.
(D) Although fundamental research is conducted in Alaska, the most important research is about finding solutions to practical problems associated with snow and ice.

18. (A) NO CHANGE
(B) Fire," being
(C) Fire," where
(D) Fire." It is where

19. (A) NO CHANGE
(B) a long island of arc
(C) a long island arc
(D) a long island for an arc

20. For the sake of the logic and cohesion of this paragraph, sentence 3 should be placed

(A) where it is now
(B) after sentence 1
(C) after sentence 4
(D) after sentence 5

21. For the sake of clarity of expression and meaning, the underlined portion of the sentences should be written as follows:

(A) as it is now
(B) region if the United States is to participate in this process. In any meaningful way, it
(C) region. If the United States is to participate in this process in any meaningful way, it
(D) region, if the United States is to participate in this process, in any meaningful way. It

22. (A) NO CHANGE
(B) to involve itself
(C) to involve it
(D) to involve

2   **2**   **2**

Questions 23–33 are based on the following passage.

Dining Roman Style

㉓ The prodigality of the Romans in matters of eating is well-known, **㉔** extensive to all matters connected with the pleasures of the table. In their rooms, their couches, and all the furniture of their entertainments, **㉕** this was where magnificence and extravagance were carried to their highest point. The rich had several of these apartments, to be used at different

23. The writer is considering adding the following sentence to the beginning of this paragraph:

One of the most important apartments in the whole house was the triclinium, or dining room, named for the three beds that encompassed the table on three sides, leaving the fourth open to the attendants.

Should the writer make this addition here?

(A) Yes, because the focus of this paragraph is the triclinium. This sentence thus serves as an appropriate topic sentence.

(B) Yes, because this sentence introduces the topic of Roman sleeping arrangements, which is discussed further in the rest of the paragraph.

(C) No, because the focus of the paragraph is on Roman extravagance in dining.

(D) No, because the information given in the sentence is repeated elsewhere in the paragraph.

24. (A) NO CHANGE
(B) and it extended
(C) it extended
(D) extends

25. (A) NO CHANGE
(B) it was magnificence and extravagance that were carried
(C) this was where they carried magnificence and extravagance
(D) magnificence and extravagance were carried

2   2   2

seasons, or on various occasions. 26 Lucullus celebrated, for his wealth and profuse expenditure, had a certain standard of expenditure for each 27 triclinium. Telling his servants which hall he was to sup in, they knew exactly the style of entertainment to be prepared. There is a well-known story of the way in which he deceived Pompeii and Cicero, when they insisted on going home with him to see his family supper, by merely sending word home that he would sup in the Apollo, one of the most splendid of his halls, in which he never gave an entertainment for less than 50,000 denarii. Sometimes the 28 ceiling was contriving to open and let down a second course of meats, with showers of flowers and perfumed waters, while rope-dancers performed over the heads of the company.

The triclinium was 29 twice as long, for it was broad, and divided, as it were, into two parts—the upper occupied by the table and the couches, the lower left empty for the convenience of the attendants and spectators. Around the former the walls, up to a certain height, were

26. (A) NO CHANGE
(B) Lucullus, celebrated for his wealth and profuse expenditure,
(C) Lucullus was celebrating his wealth and profuse expenditure, they
(D) Lucullus celebrating his wealth and profuse expenditure, and he

27. Which choice most effectively combines the sentences at the underlined portion?

(A) triclinium, in telling his servants
(B) triclinium, when he told his servants
(C) triclinium, so that when his servants were told
(D) triclinium, being that he told his servants

28. (A) NO CHANGE
(B) ceiling was contrived
(C) ceiling contrived
(D) ceiling had contrived

29. (A) NO CHANGE
(B) in length twice what it was in breadth,
(C) twice as long if it was broad,
(D) twice as long as it was broad,

ornamented with valuable hangings. **30** The decorations of the rest of the room were noble, and yet **31** <u>owing to</u> the destination; garlands, entwined with ivy and vine-branches, divided the walls into compartments bordered with fanciful ornaments; in the center of each of which were painted with admirable elegance young Fauns, or half-naked Bacchantes, carrying vases and all the furniture of festive meetings. Above the columns was a large frieze, divided into twelve compartments; each of these was surmounted by one of the signs of the **32** <u>Zodiac, contained in it</u> paintings of the meats which were in highest season in each month; so that under Sagittary (December) **33** <u>there were</u> shrimps, shellfish, and birds of passage; under Capricorn (January), lobsters, sea fish, wild boar and game; under Aquarius (February), ducks, plovers, pigeons, and water rails.

30. At this point the writer is considering adding the following sentence:

There is another well-known story of how Lucullus entertained guests in the upper part of the triclinium.

Should the writer make this addition here?

(A) No, it should not be added because the paragraph is not mainly about the triclinium.

(B) No, it should not be added because it concerns something that is not the focus of the paragraph, which is a description of the triclinium.

(C) Yes, it should be added because it provides evidence that guests were entertained in the triclinium.

(D) Yes, it should be added because it helps the reader visualize how the triclinium was used.

31. (A) NO CHANGE
    (B) appropriate to
    (C) surprising for
    (D) foreign to

32. (A) NO CHANGE
    (B) Zodiac, wherein contained were
    (C) Zodiac, contained within were
    (D) Zodiac and contained

33. (A) NO CHANGE
    (B) there was
    (C) was
    (D) being

2   2   2

Questions 34–44 are based on the following passage.

Causes of Woman's Subjection
(originally published in 1887)

Writers on the question of the origin of woman's subjection to man differ as to the cause of the universal ㉞ corruption of woman in all periods and nations.

One of the greatest minds of the century ㉟ thrown a ray of light on this gloomy picture by tracing the origin of woman's slavery to the same principle of selfishness and love of power in man that has thus far dominated all weaker nations and classes. ㊱ The slavish instinct of an oppressed class has led it to

34. (A) NO CHANGE
    (B) criticism
    (C) knowledge
    (D) fear

35. (A) NO CHANGE
    (B) throwing
    (C) has thrown
    (D) being thrown

36. At this point, the writer is considering adding the following sentence:

    This brings hope of final emancipation, for as all nations and classes are gradually, one after another, asserting and maintaining their independence, the path is clear for woman to follow.

    Should the writer make this addition here?

    (A) Yes, because this sentence provides clear examples of the male domination of nations and classes described in the preceding sentence. These examples serve as a link to the description of female subservience described in the following sentence.
    (B) Yes, because this sentence explains what the "ray of light" mentioned in the preceding sentence is. This sentence says that women's freedom will come about as a result of women asserting their independence just as other oppressed groups did to attain independence.
    (C) No, because the issue of national and class emancipation is not related to the issue of women's emancipation.
    (D) No, because there is nothing stated in the preceding sentence that suggests that women will achieve "final emancipation." On the contrary, it suggests that male domination of nations, classes, and women will continue forever.

toil patiently through the ages, **37** given all and asking little, cheerfully sharing with man all perils and privations by land and sea, that husband and sons might attain **38** honor and success, while justice and freedom for herself is her latest and highest demand.

Another writer asserts that the tyranny of man over woman has its roots, after all, in his nobler **39** feelings; his love, his chivalry, and his desire to protect woman in the barbarous periods of pillage, lust, and war. **40** But anywhere that the roots are traced to, the results at this hour are equally disastrous to woman. Her best interests and happiness do not seem to have been consulted in the arrangements made for her **41** protection, as being bought and sold, caressed and crucified at the will and pleasure of her master. But if a chivalrous desire to protect woman has always been the mainspring of man's dominion over her, it should have prompted him to place in her hands the same weapons of defense he has found to be most effective against wrong and oppression.

It is often asserted that as woman has always been man's slave—subject—inferior—dependent, under all forms of government and religion, slavery must be her normal condition. This might have some weight **42** if not the vast majority of men also been enslaved for centuries to kings and popes, and orders of nobility, who, in the progress of civilization, have reached complete equality. And did we not also see the great changes in woman's condition,

37. (A) NO CHANGE
    (B) give
    (C) giving
    (D) gave

38. For the sake of clarity of meaning and effectiveness of expression, the underlined portion of the sentence should be written as follows:

    (A) as it is now
    (B) honor and success, justice and freedom for herself have been
    (C) honor and success, justice and freedom
    (D) honor and success. Justice and freedom

39. (A) NO CHANGE
    (B) feelings his love
    (C) feelings: his love
    (D) feelings and they are his love

40. For the sake of clarity of expression and meaning, the underlined portion of the sentence should be written as follows:

    (A) as it is now
    (B) wherever the roots may be traced,
    (C) the roots may be traced anywhere,
    (D) anywhere one traces the roots, it will be found that

41. Write the underlined portion of the sentence to form two distinct sentences that make sense.

    (A) protection. Being she was bought
    (B) protection. She, as bought
    (C) protection. She has been bought
    (D) protection. She, bought

42. (A) NO CHANGE
    (B) were it not
    (C) was it not
    (D) had not

2   2   2

the marvelous transformation in her character, from a toy in the Turkish harem, or a drudge in the German fields, **43** <u>or a leader</u> of thought in the literary circles of France, England, and America!

In an age when the wrongs of society are adjusted in the courts and at the ballot-box, material force yields to reason and majorities. Woman's steady march onward, and her growing desire for a broader outlook, prove that she has not reached her normal condition, and that society has not yet **44** <u>acquiesced</u> all that is necessary for its attainment.

43. (A) NO CHANGE
    (B) to a leader
    (C) but a leader
    (D) for a leader

44. (A) NO CHANGE
    (B) conceded
    (C) assented
    (D) complied

STOP If there is still time remaining, you may review your answers.

3   3

MATH TEST (NO CALCULATOR)

25 MINUTES, 20 QUESTIONS

Turn to Section 3 of your answer sheet to answer the questions in this section.

DIRECTIONS: For questions 1–15, solve each problem and choose the best answer from the given options. Fill in the corresponding circle on your answer document. For questions 16–20, solve the problem and fill in the answer on the answer sheet grid. Please use scrap paper to work out your answers.

Notes:
- You **CANNOT** use a calculator on this section.
- All variables and expressions represent real numbers unless indicated otherwise.
- All figures are drawn to scale unless indicated otherwise.
- All figures are in a plane unless indicated otherwise.
- Unless indicated otherwise, the domain of a given function is the set of all real numbers x for which the function has real values.

REFERENCE INFORMATION

The arc of a circle contains 360°.
The arc of a circle contains 2π radians.
The sum of the measures of the angles in a triangle is 180°.

3   3

1. Which of the following is an equation for the line graphed above?

(A) $y = -x + 2$

(B) $y = x + 2$

(C) $y = 2$

(D) $x - y = 2$

2. If $f(x) = x^2 + 2$ and $g(x) = 2x + 3$, what is the value of $g(3) - f(-2)$?

(A) 15

(B) 9

(C) 3

(D) 4

3.
$$2x - 3y = 24$$
$$x + 4.5y = -12$$

In the system of equations above, what is the value of the product of x and y?

(A) 12

(B) 18

(C) −24

(D) −36

4. A shoe manufacturer wants to come up with a general rule to correlate the number of holes with the length of their shoelaces. The following table shows the number of holes in a shoe and the length, in inches, of its shoelace.

Holes	Length
4	12
6	18
8	24

If the table above represents a linear function, a hiking boot that has 18 holes should have shoelaces that are how long?

(A) 45 inches

(B) 48 inches

(C) 54 inches

(D) 63 inches

5. If $m = 2x^3 + 3x - 11$ and $n = 4x^2 + 5x - 7$, what is $3n - m$ in terms of x?

(A) $-2x^3 - 4x^2 - 2x - 18$

(B) $-(2x^3 + 3x^2 - 5x - 6)$

(C) $2x^3 - 12x^2 - 12x + 10$

(D) $-2x^3 + 12x^2 + 12x - 10$

6. If $\frac{1}{3x - 1} = \frac{2}{x}$ then $x = $?

(A) $\frac{2}{5}$

(B) 2

(C) $\frac{5}{2}$

(D) 3

7. Jenna needs to take a taxicab ride in Chicago to go to an important job interview. The taxi service she has selected provides the following fee schedule:

First $\frac{1}{4}$ mile: $2.00

Each $\frac{1}{4}$ mile after: $1.25

Excluding a tip, Jenna's fare was $15.75. How many miles did she travel?

(A) 2
(B) 2.5
(C) 2.75
(D) 3

8.
$$\frac{2}{3}x - \frac{5}{9}y = -7$$
$$bx - \frac{10}{3}y = 17$$

In the system of equations above, b is a constant. If the system has no solution, what is the value of b?

(A) -3.75
(B) 3.75
(C) 4
(D) 4.4

9. $\sqrt{n - b} = n - 2$

If $b = -4$, what is the solution set to the equation above?

(A) $\{-5\}$
(B) $\{0\}$
(C) $\{5\}$
(D) $\{0, 5\}$

10. In a homecoming game, a girls' basketball team scored $\frac{1}{3}$ of its points during the first quarter, $\frac{1}{4}$ of its points during the second quarter, $\frac{1}{3}$ of its points in the third quarter, and 8 points in the fourth quarter. How many points did the team score in the game?

(A) 84
(B) 90
(C) 96
(D) 102

11. If $x^2 + y^2 = 12$ and $xy = -13$, what is the value of $2(x - y)^2$?

(A) -26
(B) 1
(C) 38
(D) 76

12. The number of bacteria in petri dish #1 is A. Petri dish #2 contains twice as many as dish #1 and is represented by the value B. Petri dish #3 has 17 more bacteria than the quantity in dish #2 and is represented by C. Which of the following expressions shows C in terms of A?

(A) $C = 3A - 17$
(B) $C = 2A + 17$
(C) $C = 2A$
(D) $C = A + 17$

3   3

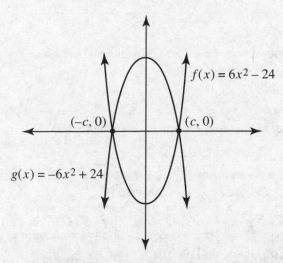

$f(x) = 6x^2 - 24$

$(-c, 0)$ $(c, 0)$

$g(x) = -6x^2 + 24$

Note: Figure not drawn to scale

13. The functions f and g, defined by $f(x) = 6x^2 - 24$ and $g(x) = -6x^2 + 24$, are graphed in the xy-plane above. The graphs above intersect at the points $(c, 0)$ and $(-c, 0)$. What is the value of c?

(A) -2

(B) 0

(C) 2

(D) 4

14. Which of the following is an equivalent form of $\dfrac{7}{2 - 3i}$ (Note: $i = \sqrt{-1}$)?

(A) $3.5 + 4i$

(B) $\dfrac{14 + 21i}{13}$

(C) $1 + 3i$

(D) $-\dfrac{14 + 21i}{5}$

15. What are the solutions to $6x^2 + 12x - 15 = 0$?

(A) $2 \pm \sqrt{14}$

(B) $\dfrac{2 \pm \sqrt{14}}{2}$

(C) $\dfrac{-2 \pm \sqrt{14}}{2}$

(D) $-2 \pm 4\sqrt{2}$

Grid-in Response Directions

In questions 16–20, first solve the problem, and then enter your answer on the grid provided on the answer sheet. The instructions for entering your answers follow.

- First, write your answer in the boxes at the top of the grid.
- Second, grid your answer in the columns below the boxes.
- Use the fraction bar in the first row or the decimal point in the second row to enter fractions and decimals.

- Grid only one space in each column.
- Entering the answer in the boxes is recommended as an aid in gridding but is not required.
- The machine scoring your exam can read only what you grid, so you **must grid-in your answers correctly to get credit.**
- If a question has more than one correct answer, grid-in only one of them.
- The grid does not have a minus sign; so no answer can be negative.
- A mixed number *must* be converted to an improper fraction or a decimal before it is gridded.

  Enter $1\frac{1}{4}$ as $\frac{5}{4}$ or 1.25; the machine will interpret 11/4 as $\frac{11}{4}$ and mark it wrong.

- **All decimals must be entered as accurately as possible.** Here are three acceptable ways of gridding

$$\frac{3}{11} = 0.272727\ldots$$

- Note that rounding to .273 is acceptable because you are using the full grid, but you would receive **no credit** for .3 or .27, because they are less accurate.

3

3

16. If $2x - 6 = 18$, what is the value of $x - 3$?

17. A farmer has 200 feet of fencing to surround a small plot of land. He wants to maximize the amount of space possible using a rectangular formation. The enclosed area will be against the side of a barn so he only needs one of the lengths of the rectangular area to be enclosed by fencing. What is the maximum area that can be enclosed by the fence (ignore the square unit label)?

18. $x^3 - 6x^2 + 2x - 12 = 0$

For what real value of x is the equation above true?

19. If $r = 3\sqrt{3}$ and $2r = \sqrt{3x}$, what is the value of x?

20. $(4{,}264 + 200m^2) + 6(12m^2 - 125)$

The expression shown above can be written in the form of $am^2 + b$, where a and b are constants. What is the value of $2a + b$?

MATH TEST (CALCULATOR)

55 MINUTES, 38 QUESTIONS

Turn to Section 4 of your answer sheet to answer the questions in this section.

DIRECTIONS: For questions 1–30, solve each problem and choose the best answer from the given options. Fill in the corresponding circle on your answer document. For questions 31–38, solve the problem and fill in the answer on the answer sheet grid. Please use scrap paper to work out your answers.

Notes:

- The **use of** a calculator on this section IS permitted.
- All variables and expressions represent real numbers unless indicated otherwise.
- All figures are drawn to scale unless indicated otherwise.
- All figures are in a plane unless indicated otherwise.
- Unless indicated otherwise, the domain of a given function is the set of all real numbers x for which the function has real values.

REFERENCE INFORMATION

The arc of a circle contains 360°.
The arc of a circle contains 2π radians.
The sum of the measures of the angles in a triangle is 180°.

1. If $\frac{m-4}{3} = \frac{x}{9}$, what is x in terms of m?

   (A) $x = 3m + 6$

   (B) $x = \frac{1}{3}m - \frac{4}{3}$

   (C) $x = 3(m - 4)$

   (D) $x = 3m - 4$

2. After researching the future cost of a four year college education, Sergio and Maria began saving for their daughter's tuition. After two years, they had accrued $2,870 for their college fund. After five years, the account balance was $7,150. If Sergio and Maria continue to save at the same rate as they have for the past five years, approximately what will the savings be after 78 months?

   (A) $7,846.33
   (B) $8,413.17
   (C) $9,290.02
   (D) $9,4107.63

3. The cube less the square of a number is twice the number. If x is a positive integer, what is its value?

   (A) 1
   (B) 2
   (C) 4
   (D) 8

Fish	6–12 inches	13–24 inches	Total
Bullhead	26	18	44
Trout	31	47	78
Mullet	53	44	97
Total	110	109	219

4. A popular fishing site recorded the number of fish caught on a particular day as shown in the table above. If a certain fish caught that day was 11 inches long, what is the probability that the fish was a mullet?

   (A) .242
   (B) .316
   (C) .482
   (D) .546

5. A light year, the distance that light travels in one year, is 5.87×10^{12} miles. The Andromeda Galaxy is 1.3×10^{19} miles distant from Earth. How many light years distant is the Earth from the Andromeda Galaxy?

   (A) 2.2×10^5
   (B) 2.2×10^6
   (C) 3.4×10^8
   (D) 3.4×10^9

6. Conner needs to plan a production budget for a computer firm. In order to maximize profit, he needs to buy m computer frames at $18.75 and r keyboards at $13.25 each. If the cost of this transaction must be less than $139.00, which of the following inequalities represents Conner's model for profit maximization?

   (A) $18.75m + 13.25r < 139$
   (B) $18.75m + 13.25r \leq 139$
   (C) $18.75r + 13.25m < 139$
   (D) $18.75r + 13.25m \leq 139$

Day	Thursday	Friday	Saturday
Chance of rain	65%	74%	31%

7. The coach of the Denver High School baseball team will have to cancel an upcoming tournament if the weather conditions forecast rain. The table presents the probability of rain for the next three days. If it doesn't rain on Friday or Saturday, the coach can plan on holding the tournament at his high school. What is the probability that it will rain on Thursday but not Friday or Saturday?

   (A) 18.7%
   (B) 16.3%
   (C) 14.9%
   (D) 11.7%

4   4

8. For what value of m does the system of equations have an infinite number of solutions?

$$7x - 4y = 13$$
$$mx - 10y = 32.5$$

(A) 14

(B) 17.5

(C) 21

(D) 32.5

9. Californians are very concerned about the continued drought conditions in their state. They are therefore curious about the price and quality of different water plans. A certain popular water plan charges a service fee of $31.50 per month. Each gallon of water used costs $.17 per gallon plus a local tax of 7.3% (the monthly service charge is tax exempt). Which of the following functions models the monthly cost of the plan?

(A) $f(x) = (.17x + .073)(31.5)$

(B) $f(x) = 31.5 + (.073x)(.17)$

(C) $f(x) = 31.5 + (1.073)(.17 + x)$

(D) $f(x) = 31.5 + (1.073)(.17x)$

Questions 10 and 11 refer to the table below.

The Environmental Protection Agency (EPA) has demonstrated that newer automobile emission standards have had a strong positive correlation with cleaner air in large metropolitan areas. Thus, it is the EPA's responsibility to get older cars off the road.

Cars in Operation in 1997

Age of Car	Millions of Cars
<3 years old	21.5
3–5 years old	29.9
6–8 years old	22.2
9–11 years old	16.7
≥12 years old	14.4

10. What percent of cars in operation in 1997 were between 6 and 11 years old?

(A) 37.2

(B) 41.3

(C) 48.1

(D) 53.2

11. 1.3% of all cars were 20 years old and older. What percent of the 12 years and older category does this number represent?

(A) 8.3

(B) 9.4

(C) 11.3

(D) 14.8

Questions 12 and 13 refer to the graph below.

TV/Device Viewing Hours Daily

The advent of television, iPhones, and tablets is vying for students' study time. Experts are concerned that the prolonged use of electronic devices adversely affects SAT scores. The graph demonstrates the correlation between hours spent viewing daily and their effect on SAT scores.

12. Which of the following can be inferred from the graph?

   (A) The impact of viewing 3 versus 4 hours resulted in the same SAT score.
   (B) All students who watched one hour or less of television/devices daily scored 1200 or higher on the SAT.
   (C) SAT scores varied inversely with daily television/device viewing.
   (D) SAT scores varied directly with daily television/device viewing.

13. Given the data in the graph, which equation could be the line of best fit?

   (A) $y = 2.3x - 4.8$
   (B) $y = .86x + .23$
   (C) $y = -6.2x - 5.9$
   (D) $y = -2.04x + 15.8$

Questions 14 and 15 refer to the information below.

Home values in America have increased since the 2008 slump in housing prices. Over the past six years, home prices have increased at an annual rate of 3.72%.

14. Which of the following functions models the increase in home values?

   A = accumulated value of the home over time
   P = the purchase price of the home
   t = time in years
   r = rate expressed as a decimal

   (A) $A = P(.0372)^t$
   (B) $A = P(.9628)^t$
   (C) $A = P(1.0372)^t$
   (D) $A = P(3.72)^t$

15. A home costing \$187,650 purchased in 2010 would be worth how much in 2013?

   (A) \$194,455
   (B) \$205,996
   (C) \$209,380
   (D) \$217,357

16. A retailer was unable to sell all of her sofas, so she reduced the price of a sofa by 40%. Once she saw the sofas were beginning to sell, she increased the price by 40%. After the 40% price increase, what percent is the new price of the original price?

   (A) 100%
   (B) 84%
   (C) 75%
   (D) 60%

17. If $5x + 3y = 16$ and $4x + 15y = 26$, what is the value of $3x + 6y$?

    (A) 15
    (B) 14
    (C) 11
    (D) 7.5

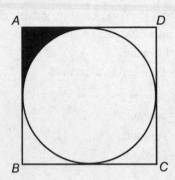

18. A coin toss board is shown above. If square $ABCD$ has perimeter 64, what is the probability of a coin landing on the shaded portion of the board?

    (A) .363
    (B) .182
    (C) .098
    (D) .053

19. Given the equation in the xy-plane, $-5x + 6y = -7$, which of the following equations is perpendicular to the graph of the equation above?

    (A) $-6x + 10y = 7$
    (B) $6x + 5y = 15$
    (C) $6x - 20y = 15$
    (D) $5x + 6y = -18$

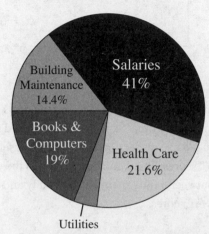

Operating Costs Deerfield HS

20. The above pie chart represents the operating costs for Deerfield High School in 2014.

    The cost for health care benefits in 2014 is $4,100,000. What is the cost for utilities?

    (A) $586,113
    (B) $637,431
    (C) $759,259
    (D) $817,437

21. The tables below provide the distributions of majors of students at College A and College B.

College A

Major	Frequency
Psychology	300
Pre-Med	1,400
Nursing	200
Business	100
Art History	100

College B

Major	Frequency
Psychology	600
Pre-Med	300
Nursing	200
Business	400
Art History	600

Which of the following is true about the data shown for these two colleges?

(A) The standard deviation of majors at College A is larger.

(B) The standard deviation of majors at College B is larger.

(C) The standard deviation of majors at College A is the same as the standard deviation of College B.

(D) The standard deviation of both data sets cannot be calculated.

Question 22 refers to the graph below.

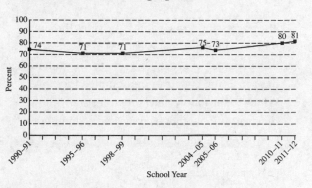

The graph above reflects the average percent of freshman high school students in America who graduate from high school within four years.

22. Which of the following can be inferred from the graph above?

(A) From 2006 to 2012 there was approximately an 11% increase in the percent of high school graduates.

(B) There was a steady increase in the number of high school graduates between 1991 and 2012.

(C) The number of high school graduates decreased from 2006 to 2012.

(D) The state of the national economy had a marked increase on the percent of high school graduates.

23.
$$2{,}500\left[1+\frac{r}{1{,}200}\right]^{12}$$

The expression shown above provides the sum of money, in dollars, that is earned in a year by an initial deposit of $2,500 in a savings institution that pays an annual rate r% compounded monthly. Which of the following expressions shows how much additional money is earned at an interest rate of 6% than at an interest rate of 3.2%?

(A) $2{,}500\left[1+\dfrac{6-3.2}{1{,}200}\right]^{12}$

(B) $2{,}500\left[1+\dfrac{\frac{6}{3.2}}{1{,}200}\right]^{12}$

(C) $\dfrac{2{,}500\left[1+\frac{6}{1{,}200}\right]^{12}}{2{,}500\left[1+\frac{3.2}{1{,}200}\right]^{12}}$

(D) $2{,}500\left[1+\dfrac{6}{1{,}200}\right]^{12}-2{,}500\left[1+\dfrac{3.2}{1{,}200}\right]^{12}$

24. The square root of x varies inversely with y.

When $x = 196$, $y = -\dfrac{1}{2}$.

Find the value of x when $y = -3$.

(A) 3

(B) $\dfrac{49}{9}$

(C) $\dfrac{49}{3}$

(D) 49

Questions 25–27 refer to the graph below.

A girls' softball coach was recruiting for Behrens High School's spring softball team. The coach wanted to see if age was a determining factor in gauging the distance each girl could throw a softball.

Softball Throws by Age and Distance

25. Which of the following statements can be concluded from the graph?

(A) There is a weak negative correlation between age and the distance thrown.

(B) There is a strong positive correlation between age and the distance thrown.

(C) There is no correlation between age and distance thrown.

(D) There is an inverse relationship between age and distance thrown.

26. Which of the following functions is a line of best fit for the graph?

(A) $y = 5.14x - 123.5$

(B) $y = -43.27x - 231.3$

(C) $y = 33.33x - 299.6$

(D) $y = 14.2 - 2.01x$

27. Given the data in the graph, what would be the predicted distance of a throw from a person who is 18 years old?

    (A) 247 feet
    (B) 277 feet
    (C) 300 feet
    (D) 319 feet

28. If $i = \sqrt{-1}$, what is the value of $3(2 - 4i)^2$?

    (A) $-12 - 4i$
    (B) $-12 - 16i$
    (C) $-36 - 48i$
    (D) -84

29. There are nine students in a statistics class. After a recent test, the average (arithmetic mean) score was 79%. What must a tenth student's score be to raise the class average to 81%?

    (A) 87
    (B) 89
    (C) 94
    (D) 99

30. The number of students in an elementary class, s, decided to spend D dollars for a present for their favorite teacher, Mrs. Konopka. Each student was to contribute an equal amount. Because 15 students refused to contribute, each of those remaining agreed to contribute an additional, equal amount. What was the additional amount each had to contribute, in dollars?

    (A) $(s - 15) \div D$
    (B) $(s^2 - 15) \div D$
    (C) $\dfrac{15D}{s^2 - 15s}$
    (D) $\dfrac{s^2 - 15s}{15D}$

Grid-in Response Directions

In questions 31–38, first solve the problem, and then enter your answer on the grid provided on the answer sheet. The instructions for entering your answers follow.

- First, write your answer in the boxes at the top of the grid.
- Second, grid your answer in the columns below the boxes.
- Use the fraction bar in the first row or the decimal point in the second row to enter fractions and decimals.

Either position is acceptable

- Grid only one space in each column.
- Entering the answer in the boxes is recommended as an aid in gridding but is not required.
- The machine scoring your exam can read only what you grid, so you **must grid-in your answers correctly to get credit.**
- If a question has more than one correct answer, grid-in only one of them.
- The grid does not have a minus sign; so no answer can be negative.
- A mixed number *must* be converted to an improper fraction or a decimal before it is gridded.

  Enter $1\frac{1}{4}$ as $\frac{5}{4}$ or 1.25; the machine will interpret 11/4 as $\frac{11}{4}$ and mark it wrong.

- **All decimals must be entered as accurately as possible.** Here are three acceptable ways of gridding

$$\frac{3}{11} = 0.272727\ldots$$

- Note that rounding to .273 is acceptable because you are using the full grid, but you would receive **no credit** for .3 or .27, because they are less accurate.

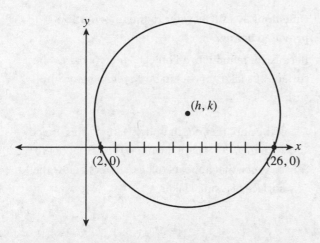

31. In the xy-plane, the circle shown above has center (h, k). If the radius of the circle is 13, what is the value of k?

32. A manufacturer of surgical equipment measures its profit by using the following function:

    $P(x) = 11,000x - 6750$, where x is the number of units the company sells in a three month period

    If the company's profit over a three month period was $9,321,250, how many units did it sell?

33. Kari wants to buy a new service plan for a data and internet bundle. One plan offers a monthly fee of $24.00 and $.007 for each minute of use. Another plan offers a flat monthly fee of $36.50. After how many minutes of use will the two plans charge the same monthly cost (round your answer to the nearest minute)?

34. A "standard candle" is a way for astronomers to calculate the distance to an object in space. The apparent brightness of an object varies indirectly with the square of the distance. For example, a galaxy that is 1,000,000 times farther than another would appear to be 1,000 times dimmer. Similarly, a nebula that is 900 times more distant than another would appear 30 times as dim. If a star appeared to be 16 times dimmer than another star, how many times farther away is the more distant star?

35. If $x^{\frac{y}{4}} = 81$ for positive integers x and y, what is one possible value of y?

36. A central angle in a circle has a measure of 34.4° and the measure of its sector is 139.6 square units. To the nearest tenth of a unit, what is the measure of the circle's radius (use π = 3.14)?

Questions 37 and 38 refer to the information provided below.

Because of refraction, an object 5 meters below the surface of a lake appears to be 4 meters below the surface.

37. If the apparent depth under water varies directly with the actual depth, what is the actual depth of a rock that appears to be 6 meters below the surface of a small lake?

38. A diver inadvertently left his keys in his shorts when he was swimming. The keys fell out of his shorts and went to the bottom of his swimming pool. The keys appeared to be 9 feet below the surface. What is the difference between the actual depth of the keys and the apparent depth?

STOP If there is still time remaining, you may review your answers.

ANSWER KEY
Practice Test 1

Section 1: Reading

1. **D**	14. **D**	27. **D**	40. **A**
2. **C**	15. **B**	28. **B**	41. **D**
3. **D**	16. **C**	29. **A**	42. **A**
4. **B**	17. **C**	30. **B**	43. **D**
5. **C**	18. **A**	31. **D**	44. **B**
6. **D**	19. **B**	32. **C**	45. **A**
7. **A**	20. **C**	33. **B**	46. **D**
8. **D**	21. **B**	34. **A**	47. **C**
9. **C**	22. **B**	35. **C**	48. **C**
10. **A**	23. **B**	36. **B**	49. **A**
11. **A**	24. **C**	37. **A**	50. **D**
12. **B**	25. **B**	38. **C**	51. **C**
13. **C**	26. **D**	39. **B**	52. **B**

Number Correct   _____

Number Incorrect   _____

Section 2: Writing and Language

1. **C**	12. **B**	23. **A**	34. **A**
2. **A**	13. **C**	24. **B**	35. **C**
3. **B**	14. **C**	25. **D**	36. **B**
4. **C**	15. **B**	26. **B**	37. **C**
5. **C**	16. **D**	27. **C**	38. **D**
6. **B**	17. **C**	28. **B**	39. **C**
7. **D**	18. **C**	29. **D**	40. **B**
8. **C**	19. **C**	30. **B**	41. **C**
9. **A**	20. **D**	31. **B**	42. **D**
10. **B**	21. **C**	32. **D**	43. **B**
11. **C**	22. **B**	33. **A**	44. **B**

Number Correct   _____

Number Incorrect   _____

PRACTICE TEST 1

ANSWER KEY
Practice Test 1

Section 3: Math (No Calculator)

1. **A**	5. **D**	9. **C**	13. **C**
2. **C**	6. **A**	10. **C**	14. **B**
3. **C**	7. **D**	11. **D**	15. **C**
4. **C**	8. **C**	12. **B**	

16. **9**   17. **5,000**   18. **6**   19. **36**

20. **4,058**

Number Correct   _____

Number Incorrect   _____

ANSWER KEY
Practice Test 1

Section 4: Math (Calculator)

1. **C**	9. **D**	17. **B**	25. **B**
2. **C**	10. **A**	18. **D**	26. **C**
3. **B**	11. **B**	19. **B**	27. **C**
4. **C**	12. **C**	20. **C**	28. **C**
5. **B**	13. **D**	21. **A**	29. **D**
6. **A**	14. **C**	22. **A**	30. **C**
7. **D**	15. **C**	23. **D**	
8. **B**	16. **B**	24. **B**	

31. **5**   32. **848**   33. **1,786**   34. **256**

35. **1, 2, 4, 8, or 16**   36. **21.6**   37. **7.5 or 15/2**   38. **2.25**

Number Correct _____

Number Incorrect _____

SCORE ANALYSIS

Reading and Writing Test

Section 1: Reading $\underline{\hspace{2cm}} = \underline{\hspace{2cm}}$ (A)

correct   raw score

Section 2: Writing $\underline{\hspace{2cm}} = \underline{\hspace{2cm}}$ (B)

correct   raw score

To find your Reading and Writing test scores, consult the chart below; find the ranges in which your raw scores lie and read across to find the ranges of your test scores.

$\underline{\hspace{3cm}} + \underline{\hspace{3cm}} = \underline{\hspace{3cm}}$ (C)

range of Reading   range of Writing   range of Reading + Writing
test scores   test scores   test scores

To find the range of your Reading and Writing Scaled Score, multiply (C) by 10.

Test Scores for the Reading and Writing Sections

Reading Raw Score	Writing Raw Score	Test Score
44–52	39–44	35–40
36–43	33–38	31–34
30–35	28–32	28–30
24–29	22–27	24–27
19–23	17–21	21–23
14–18	13–16	19–20
9–13	9–12	16–18
5–8	5–8	13–15
less than 5	less than 5	10–12

Math Test

Section 3: $\underline{\hspace{2cm}} = \underline{\hspace{2cm}}$ (D)

correct   raw score

Section 4: $\underline{\hspace{2cm}} = \underline{\hspace{2cm}}$ (E)

correct   raw score

Total Math raw score: (D) + (E) = $\underline{\hspace{2cm}}$

To find your Math Scaled Score, consult the chart below; find the range in which your raw score lies and read across to find the range for your scaled score.

Scaled Scores for the Math Test

Raw Score	Scaled Score	Raw Score	Scaled Score
50–58	700–800	20–25	450–490
44–49	650–690	15–19	400–440
38–43	600–640	11–14	350–390
32–37	550–590	7–10	300–340
26–31	500–540	less than 7	200–290

Answer Explanations

Section 1: Reading Test

1. **(D)** The author says, "the Court of Claims . . . was set up not to administer justice but to expedite adjudication of land titles and head off any future claims that Indians might make on lands already coveted by the white economy" (lines 28–32).

2. **(C)** In lines 12–18 ("Termination . . . market") the author explains the effect of termination legislation on Indian nations and their land. One of these effects is to *lessen* Indian claims on land because some Indian nations are eliminated by termination and so cannot claim land not previously ceded to the U.S. by treaty.

3. **(D)** Quotation marks are sometimes used, as in this case, to indicate that an assertion made by one party is open to dispute by another party. The U.S. government regards most of the land not ceded to it by treaty with Indian nations as its own, but others—notably many Indian nations—do not agree.

4. **(B)** The author used the word *mercies* in the course of his description of termination legislation that "had already wiped out a number of small tribes" (lines 13–14) and "turns the Indians over to the mercies of state jurisdiction and property taxation" (lines 15–16). It is clear from this context he is using it sarcastically because the Indians are very unlikely to be shown mercy—in fact, they will almost certainly be treated without mercy, in the author's view.

5. **(C)** In the sentence preceding the one cited in the question, the author describes the attitude of the progressives toward the traditionals and their "useless religion" (line 57) as one of scorn for outdated beliefs and practices. The observation that it is the progressives rather than the traditionals who feel it necessary to keep witches out of outhouses suggests that the author believes that it is the progressives rather than the traditionals who are superstitious.

6. **(D)** This is the only statement about the traditionals supported by the passage: "The traditionals know . . . been taken away" (lines 60–68).

7. **(A)** The first paragraph of the passage describes the bleak future the Hopi face, focusing on the views of the traditionals. The second paragraph describes what Wayne Sekaquaptewa, a leading progressive, thinks about the views of the traditionals.

8. **(D)** Although the author does not say that he agrees with the traditionals, he takes a sympathetic view of them and their beliefs throughout the passage. Also, he shows respect for Hopi beliefs in general. In lines 60–74 ("The traditionals know . . . Life Plan Rock") he describes the views of the traditionals very sympathetically, suggesting strongly that he agrees with them that their only chance of survival as a distinct culture is to cling to their traditional beliefs and practices. We can infer, however, that because he is not a Hopi he does not agree with the literal meaning of the Day of Purification, but rather that he sees it as symbolic of a future that may come to pass in which the Hopi survive amid the ruins of the white man's world.

9. **(C)** The author says, "The traditionals have always been wary of the white man's consumer mentality" (lines 1–2). There is no evidence to support other choices.

10. **(A)** This line provides the best evidence because it describes the white men as having, in the view of the Hopis, a "consumer mentality." Having such a mentality (outlook) entails being materialistic.

11. **(A)** The girl's eyes are also described as "full of a radiant curiosity" (lines 18–19), so it makes sense that the phrase "quick gray eyes" is used to suggest that the girl is alert.

12. **(B)** The word *clad* means "clothed," whereas the word *adorned* means "made attractive," suggesting the girl likes to make herself attractive.

13. **(C)** Immediately before the word *rise* is used, the old man is described as grunting: "There he paused . . . grunt of disapproval" (lines 36–39), suggesting that he intended to communicate something to the girl. Thus, in context, *rise* means "reaction."

14. **(D)** The elderly man is described as "utter[ing] a long even grunt of disapproval" (line 39) when he sees the girl sitting and reading a book. It cannot be conclusively inferred that he is disapproving of her reading a novel, but the fact that the grunt is described as one of "disapproval" means that he does not approve of something. There is some evidence for (A), (B), and (C), but none of it is as strong as the evidence for (D). Thus, (D) is the best choice.

15. **(B)** The author is mainly concerned with vividly describing the scene. He uses these words and phrases to *personify* (portray inanimate objects as having human emotions) the house and car in Passage 2 to help the reader imagine the scene.

16. **(C)** It is not stated who or what produced the whistle mentioned in line 72, but it is reasonable to infer that the "signal" referred to in line 79 was the whistle mentioned in line 72. Choices (A) and (D) are possible, but there is no evidence for them. Choice (B) makes some sense because sounds are described as coming from the car, but it is more reasonable to infer that the whistle was a signal.

17. **(C)** Choice (C) is the best answer because *perfunctorily* means "done routinely and with little interest." The fact that Clark Darrow is sitting in this way suggests that visiting the Happer house is probably part of his routine. "Sat brilliantly . . . at attention" suggests that he regards the visit as something to be done in a somewhat showy manner. (A) Although "sat brilliantly . . . at attention" suggests that Clark Darrow regards the visit as something to be done dramatically, the word *perfunctorily* suggests that he regards the visit as something done as a duty, and which he has little interest in. If Clark Darrow were visiting the Happer house to show his romantic interest in Sally he would probably not be sitting *perfunctorily*. (B) Although the words "sat brilliantly . . . at attention" suggest that he could regard his visit as an honor, one would not normally respond to a great honor by sitting *perfunctorily* (in a manner suggesting that one regards it as a duty). (D) The fact that Clark Darrow sits *perfunctorily* shows that he regards the visit as a routine duty, not as an exciting change from his regular activities.

18. **(A)** In this context, *evolved* means "gave off." The author says "The car was hot [and] retained all the heat it absorbed or evolved" (lines 59–61). We can infer that the car's engine produced heat that it gave off.

19. **(B)** Both of the girls are depicted as being *relaxed*. The girl in Passage 1 is sitting in a wicker settee, very relaxed, reading a book, and Sally Happer in Passage 2 is resting her chin on a window sill, gazing down sleepily at the car. (A) *Pretty* is not the correct choice because, although there is some suggestion that the girl in Passage 1 is pretty ("slender and supple . . . alluring mouth," lines 17–18), nothing is suggested about Sally Happer's appearance. (C) There is a suggestion that the girl in Passage 1 is *intelligent* ("quick gray eyes full of a radiant curiosity," lines 19–20), but there is nothing to suggest that Sally is intelligent. (D) Neither

girl can be described as *indolent* (habitually lazy) because not enough information is provided to show whether they are frequently lazy.

20. **(C)** In Passage 1 "the drowsy silence" (line 31) is broken by the "heavy footsteps" of the elderly man. In Passage 2 Sally Happer looks down "sleepily" (line 73) at Clark Darrow's noisy arrival in his old Ford. (A) In Passage 1 the arrival of the elderly man does not mainly create humor. In Passage 2 there is a stronger suggestion than there is in Passage 1 that the arrival of the male character is intended, at least in part, to be humorous. However, in neither passage does the male character's arrival mainly serve to create humor. (B) It is possible that the elderly man grunts because he condemns the girl's self-indulgence, but there is nothing to suggest a condemnation of self-indulgence in Passage 2. (D) In Passage 1 the elderly man interrupts the mood briefly, but this does not really change the atmosphere; the girl ignores him and continues reading and eating a lemon. In Passage 2 Clark Darrow's arrival does not create a serious atmosphere. On the contrary, it creates a somewhat comical atmosphere.

21. **(B)** The author says in the first few lines of the passage, "It's not hard to guess which side [of the debate about the ethics of using the atomic bomb] each chose once you know that Alsop experienced capture by the Japanese at Hong Kong early in 1942, while Joravsky came into no deadly contact with the Japanese" (lines 5–9). This statement makes the assumption that Alsop's and Joravsky's opinions about whether the use of the atomic bomb was ethical are determined by their experience in the war.

22. **(B)** The author's point is that the question does not fairly and objectively present the crucial issue for debate because it can only be answered "no." A person, such as the author, who on balance favored the use of the atomic bomb, is forced to answer "no" because, strictly speaking, dropping the atomic bomb was not really necessary because the war could have been ended by other means.

23. **(B)** From the context it can be inferred that the atomic bombing of Hiroshima and Nagasaki prompted peace advocates in Japan to call into serious question deeply held Japanese values about national pride and individual honor because the atomic bombing radically changed their significance. A short-hand term for these values is "the Japanese book of rules."

24. **(C)** Such opinion surveys would support Joseph Alsop's contention that a bloodbath would have been inevitable without the use of the atomic bomb because they show that most Japanese would have joined the fight against the invaders and fought fiercely.

25. **(B)** The author quotes Joseph Alsop: "It [is] absurd . . . to hold the common view . . . that the decision to drop the two bombs on Japan was wicked in itself" (lines 36–39). We can see from this that the author agrees with Mr. Alsop's view that most Americans mistakenly condemn the dropping of the atomic bombs on Japan. It is reasonable to infer that one of the reasons the author believes that they make this mistake is that they tend to ignore the great stress placed on honor in Japanese culture, leading them to believe that the Japanese would not have fought an invasion fiercely. The author quotes Joseph Alsop's conclusion: "Japanese surrender could never have been obtained, at any rate without the honor-satisfying bloodbath envisioned by . . . Anami" (lines 24–27) without the dropping of the atomic bombs on Japan.

26. **(D)** The word *genteel* means "belonging to polite society," so "genteel ethics" are the ethics, or moral values, of polite society. The term suggests that such morality is removed from the harsh realities of life, and is able to stand apart and make fine moral judgments free of involvement in the events that are judged.

27. **(D)** The discovery of documents showing that the Japanese leadership possessed information leading them to (incorrectly) believe that the Americans would not have a second atomic bomb ready for use for several months would suggest Joseph Alsop's argument that dropping an atomic bomb on Nagasaki was morally justifiable because it would strengthen the likelihood that the Japanese would have fought to the death to defend their country, even if it meant a "bloodbath" (lines 26–27).

28. **(B)** In context, the word *tidy* means "orderly." The author is saying that the historian can use hindsight to analyze events of the past in an orderly manner. An example of this is that they know the implications (such as "opening up the age of nuclear warfare") of events, whereas the people involved in them could not know such implications. Thus, the historian, using hindsight, can fit everything into an orderly view of what happened.

29. **(A)** The words "as well as" signal that in dropping atomic bombs on Japan, U.S. government officials were motivated not only by a desire to end the war but also by a desire for revenge against the Japanese for attacking Pearl Harbor and starting the war in the Pacific.

30. **(B)** In context, the word *illumination* means "intellectual enlightenment." The author is saying that to understand the past one must put aside one's knowledge of subsequent events and not consider any intellectual enlightenment that comes with considering these later events.

31. **(D)** The lines from the poem "Gerontion" suggest that when a person acts it is difficult for the person to know the consequences of those actions, and that neither acting from fear nor from courage ensures that history will judge the person's acts as being virtuous. In the context of the passage, these lines are appropriate because the author is arguing that the people who decided to drop atomic bombs on Japan could not know the full implications of their decision. Perhaps "unnatural vices" (the consequences of the atomic bombings) were "fathered by [their] heroism" (lines 96–97) in their deciding to drop the bombs, or perhaps their "impudent crimes" (dropping the bombs) resulted in their being considered virtuous.

32. **(C)** The word *aesthetic* in this context means "relating to aesthetics, theories of what is beautiful." Thus, "aesthetic trends" are fashions in what is considered beautiful and thus worthwhile in the arts and literature.

33. **(B)** In context, *pedestrian* means "undistinguished, ordinary." The author is contrasting ordinary prose made to appear somewhat like poetry with "the real thing" (line 16), which is poetry. It thus makes sense that he describes it rather negatively.

34. **(A)** The author says that writing professionals have made it their business to attract students to their poetry writing programs, and that in so doing having assessed the value of poetry more on the basis of "practical concerns" (lines 8–9) than on its aesthetic merit. It is reasonable to infer from this that quite a few of these writing program professionals care more about their careers than they do about encouraging the production of good poetry.

35. **(C)** In lines 13–16 ("Most obvious is . . . the real thing") the author discusses the phenomenon of poetry becoming more like prose. The "real thing" refers to writing that has not lost the essential character of poetry—that is, *poetry*.

36. **(B)** In lines 29–34 ("If the profusion . . . thereby losing significance") the author expresses his dislike for prose poetry. Using the informal expression "dished up" helps him to express this dislike colorfully.

37. **(A)** In lines 34–35 the author refers to the "'poem' part of the equation." From this we can infer that in order to create a prose poem it is necessary to add poetic elements to prose elements. (Prose elements + poetic elements = prose poem.)

38. **(C)** In lines 42–43 ("Poe and Baudelaire . . . a century later") the author says that Poe and Baudelaire wrote prose poems "more consciously" than Blake and Smart before them. This suggests that the author is saying that Blake and Smart did not consciously decide to write work that would come to be called prose poetry; rather, they wrote in this style because it was one of a number of forms they used in the course of composing their poems.

39. **(B)** The author makes the comment in lines 53–56 immediately after citing Peter Johnson, who says, "I am not even sure what my criteria [for deciding what a prose poem is] are, anymore" (lines 52–53). Thus, we can infer that the author is being sarcastic in saying that one graduate writing program understands the genre well enough to offer an entire course in it. Also, in the paragraph after this comment, the author says that the definition of the genre of prose poetry is still very controversial.

40. **(A)** In lines 59–62 ("Others concede that . . . short story writer") the author says that some critics believe that it is difficult to exclude "the heightened prose of many a novelist and short story writer" from the genre of prose poetry. Since the definition of prose poetry is being discussed, it can be inferred that "heightened prose" refers to prose that has characteristics of poetry.

41. **(D)** Throughout the passage the author describes distinctions between poetry and prose. In lines 34–39 ("The 'poem' part . . . figures of speech") he says that a prose poem is made poetic by the use of poetic devices such as rhythm and metaphor. In lines 88–91 ("for it has . . . making poetry musical") he mentions the importance of music in even free and open verse. In lines 93–95 ("Howe's piece lacks . . . prose-poem equation") he stresses that rhythm and metaphor are essential to poetry.

42. **(A)** In the paragraph immediately preceding the one in which he cites the two excerpts from "Doubt," the author says that the term *prose poem* leads one to expect a work designated as such to be comprised of "a combination of and tension between prose and poetic elements" (lines 63–64), but that "these expectations aren't always met" (lines 65–66). The sentence "Examples abound" (line 67) signals that the two excerpts from "Doubt" are examples in which prose poetry does not meet these expectations.

43. **(D)** The passage describes various processes that change coasts.

44. **(B)** In context, *continually* means "regularly occurring." The processes affecting coasts the passage describes are not continuous (uninterrupted) but rather occur quite often.

45. **(A)** Waves are described as traveling across the surface of lakes and seas and then breaking as they near the shore. From this we can infer that *shallowing* means "becoming more shallow."

46. **(D)** In lines 16–18 ("Plants . . . dunes") the author describes the effects plants have on wetlands and coastal dunes. He does not elaborate on this in the rest of the passage as he does on waves, tides, and storms.

47. **(C)** In lines 29–31 ("Even . . . shore") the author says even a slight angle between the land and waves "will create currents that transport sediment along the shore." From this we can infer that if there is no angle, sediment will not be moved along the shore.

48. **(C)** This provides the best evidence for the previous question because, as described in the explanation of that question, it allows us to infer the correct answer.

49. **(A)** This can be inferred from what the passage says about how currents in the ocean can transport sediment along the shore: "Even the slightest angle between the land and the waves will create currents that transport sediment along the shore." (lines 29–31).

50. **(D)** The passage does not say that the slope of coasts affects sea level. In the last paragraph he describes how "the slope of a coast is critical to determining how water-level changes will affect it" (lines 92–93). All of the others are described as affecting sea level.

51. **(C)** The author says, "On a gently sloping coast, like the U.S. east coast . . . small changes in water level cause the coastline to shift dramatically" (lines 99–102).

52. **(B)** In lines 80–91 ("Global . . . worldwide") the author describes how during the last great ice age "huge amounts of water were transformed into glaciers, resulting in a 100-meter drop in the global sea level." Because a colder climate caused sea levels to fall we can deduce that a warmer climate would cause glaciers to melt and thus sea levels to rise.

Section 2: Writing and Language Test

1. **(C)** The adjective *comparable* (admitting of comparison) is the best choice. Comparable data would be needed to allow an accurate comparison of women's earnings in different years.

2. **(A)** This is the best choice. The participial phrase beginning with the word "working" modifies the noun "women," which is the subject of the sentence.

3. **(B)** The previous sentence gave the earnings of women working full-time in management, business, and financial occupations. Choice (B) provides more detailed information about the earnings of chief executives and computer and information systems managers, which is a sub-category of the larger category mentioned in the previous sentence.

4. **(C)** Choice (A) makes no sense. This choice creates two new grammatical sentences that make good sense.

5. **(C)** Of the choices given, the chart shows that women are far more concentrated in this category than the others mentioned.

6. **(B)** Choice (A) makes no sense. This choice creates two new sentences that make good sense.

7. **(D)** The adjective "relative" makes little sense in context. The adverb "relatively" makes good sense because it is saying that these fields are high-paying in comparison to other fields.

8. **(C)** The given sentence has an error in parallelism because it compares "pay" and "jobs," which are not comparable. This choice corrects the error so that pay in two occupational categories is compared.

9. **(A)** This information provides important support for the main point of the paragraph.

10. **(B)** This is the best choice because it makes a *contrast* between the wages of men and women in working part-time.

11. **(C)** Although the given choice is grammatically correct, standard usage is "little different from." Choice (A) would be correct if it read "which is little different than."

12. **(B)** This choice makes good sense in context. A clue is "offers exciting research possibilities in almost every branch of science." A diverse "laboratory" would allow many types of research.

13. **(C)** This sentence provides an effective transition from the first paragraph, which introduces the idea of the Arctic as a "natural laboratory" offering "research possibilities in almost every branch of science," to the second paragraph, which discusses one of these areas of research.

14. **(C)** *Conspicuous* (attracting attention) makes good sense because the atmospheric effects described would attract attention.

15. **(B)** This choice makes good sense. The jet stream is "affected by" (influenced by) processes of heat exchange and then ("in turn") affects Earth's weather and climate. Note that the verb *affects* (influences) is correct in context. Choice (A) *in turn effects* is incorrect because the verb *effect* means "to bring about."

16. **(D)** This is the best choice. The adjective prepositional phrase beginning with the word "from" and ending with the word "satellite" describes the noun "forms," telling more about them.

17. **(C)** This is the correct choice because the focus of the paragraph is on the great value of the Arctic as a place to study "snow in all its forms."

18. **(C)** This is the only choice that makes sense and is grammatical and concise. Choice (D) is grammatically correct; however, it is not as good of a choice as choice (C) because it unnecessarily creates two short sentences.

19. **(C)** This is the only choice that is grammatical. The adjectives "long" and "island" modify the noun "arc," which is the direct object of the verb "encloses."

20. **(D)** Choice (A) is incorrect because sentence 3 does not belong in its present position in the paragraph. Sentence 4 and sentence 5 describe "Alaska's relation to" the "Rim of Fire," which has a lot of earthquakes. Sentence 3 draws a conclusion based on these two sentences.

21. **(C)** This is the only choice that is grammatical and makes sense. Choice (A) is grammatical but doesn't make sense. It creates a new sentence that follows logically from the preceding sentence.

22. **(B)** This choice is correct because the reflexive pronoun *itself* refers back to its antecedent, the pronoun *it*, which here is used in place of "the United States."

23. **(A)** The main topic of this paragraph is the triclinium. This sentence is an effective topic sentence for the paragraph because it describes the triclinium.

24. **(B)** *Extensive* is incorrect usage in context. The conjunction "and" effectively links the two independent clauses.

25. **(D)** The given sentence is incorrect. It is not grammatical because the prepositional phrase in the first part of the sentence beginning with "In" and ending with "entertainments" refers to "magnificence and extravagance," which should come immediately after the prepositional phrase. This choice corrects the error.

26. **(B)** The given sentence is not grammatical and makes little sense. This choice corrects the error by making "celebrated for his wealth and profuse expenditure" an appositive phrase referring to Lucullus.

27. **(C)** This choice effectively links the two main ideas expressed in the sentence: one, the fact that Lucullus had a certain standard of expenditure for each triclinium and, second, that *as a result* (expressed in choice (C) by the word "so") when he told his servants which hall he wanted to sup in they knew what type of entertainment to prepare.

28. **(B)** This choice corrects the given sentence, which is not grammatical.

29. **(D)** The given sentence makes little sense because it says "The triclinium was twice as long" but doesn't say what it was twice as long as. This choice corrects this error and makes good sense.

30. **(B)** This is the correct answer because the sentence introduces a subject that is not directly concerned with the focus of the paragraph. This sentence interrupts the description of the walls of the triclinium in the sentences preceding and following it. The sentence should not be added but not for the reason given in choice (A), which is false. The passage is mainly about the triclinium. Choice (C) is incorrect for two reasons. First, it does not provide evidence that guests were entertained in the triclinium. It merely states that there is a story relevant to this. Second, the sentence would interrupt the logical sequence of the paragraph because it is not concerned with the focus of the passage, which is a description of the triclinium. Choice (D) is incorrect because the sentence is not concerned with the main focus of the paragraph and interrupts the description of the walls of the triclinium.

31. **(B)** Choice (A) makes no sense in context. "Appropriate to" is the best choice. The decorations were "noble," so it would have been easy for them to be inappropriate to the destination, "yet" they were not.

32. **(D)** Choice (A) does not create a grammatical sentence. Choice (D) corrects this to make a grammatical sentence. Note that this choice creates an independent clause beginning with the subject "each."

33. **(A)** The independent clause beginning with the word *there* is existential—that is, it is pointing out the existence of something. The verb must agree with the plural subject, "shrimps, shellfish, and birds of passage." Note that the word "there" is not the subject of the clause.

34. **(A)** This is the best choice. In context, *corruption* means "change from original state."

35. **(C)** Choice (A) is not grammatical. Choice (C) casts the verb "throw" in the present perfect tense and makes good sense because the writer's actions ("throwing a ray of light," that is) began in the past and is still continuing at present.

36. **(B)** This sentence follows logically from the preceding sentence. It explains how women can follow the same path to liberation as other groups oppressed by men.

37. **(C)** Choice (A) is not grammatical. This choice is correct because one of the uses of the present progressive is to emphasize that action is continuing over a period of time. Clues to the answer are the verbs "asking" and "sharing."

38. **(D)** This is the only grammatically correct choice; all of the other choices create a run-on sentence. This choice creates two grammatically correct sentences.

39. **(C)** Choice (C) and choice (D) are both grammatically correct. However, choice (C) is better because it is less wordy and follows standard usage. The colon is often used, as it is here, to introduce several ideas. In this instance, "love," "chivalry," and "desire to protect women" all tell what man's "nobler feelings" are.

40. **(B)** This is the best choice because it is clear and concise. Choice (A) and choice (D) are grammatically correct but their meaning is not as clear as that of choice (B).

41. **(C)** This is the only choice that creates two grammatical sentences that make sense.

42. **(D)** This is the only choice that is grammatical and makes good sense. This choice creates an adverb clause of condition (beginning with "had" and ending with "equality") modifying the verb "might have."

43. **(B)** This is the only choice that makes a grammatical sentence. It is required by the structure of the sentence. The preposition *from* earlier in the sentence must be followed by the preposition *to* (*from* this *to* that).

44. **(B)** *Conceded* (granted) makes good sense because the author is saying that women have not yet attained equality ("her normal condition") because society has not granted them everything necessary for them to achieve it. Choice (A) would be correct if it was "acquiesced *to*."

Section 3: Math Test (No Calculator)

1. **(A)** The line crosses the y-axis at $(0, 2)$. So b, which is the y-intercept, is 2. Using $\frac{\text{rise}}{\text{run}}$ to identify the slope, we go down 1 unit and move to the right 1 unit. Thus, the slope, m, equals -1. With the slope equaling -1 and the y-intercept at 2, the equation of the line in the graph is $y = -x + 2$.

2. **(C)** Given that $g(x) = 2x + 3$, then $g(3) = 2(3) + 3 = 9$. Since $f(x) = x^2 + 2$, then

$$f(-2) = (-2)^2 + 2 = 6$$

Thus, $g(3) - f(-2) = 9 - 6 = 3$.

Choice (A) is incorrect because it is the sum of $g(x)$ and $f(x)$. Choice (B) is incorrect because it is the value of $g(3)$. Choice (D) is incorrect because it is the result of improper calculation.

3. **(C)** Multiply $x + 4.5y = -12$ by -2. Attain the same coefficient of x but with different signs. Solve by elimination.

$$2x - 3y = 24$$
$$-2(x + 4.5y = -12)$$

Solve by eliminating x.

$$\begin{array}{r} 2x - 3y = 24 \\ + -2x - 9y = 24 \\ \hline -12y = 48 \\ y = -4 \end{array}$$

Replace y with -4 in $2x - 3y = 24$.

$$2x - 3(-4) = 24$$
$$2x + 12 = 24$$
$$2x = 12$$
$$x = 6$$

The product of x and y is $(6)(-4) = -24$.

This problem could also have been solved by using the substitution method.

$$x + 4.5y = -12$$
$$x = -4.5y - 12$$

$(-4.5y - 12)$ would be substituted for x in $2x - 3y = 24$.

4. **(C)** You may have noticed that the length of the shoelace is three times the number of holes. For example, a 4-hole lace is 12 inches long and an 8-hole lace is 24 inches long. Therefore, the hiking boot will need shoelaces that are 54 inches long because $18 \times 3 = 54$.

5. **(D)** Substituting for m and n into $3n - m$ results in the following:

$$3(4x^2 + 5x - 7) - (2x^3 + 3x - 11) =$$
$$12x^2 + 15x - 21 - 2x^3 - 3x + 11 =$$

Combine like terms by adding and subtracting those terms with variables raised to the same power.

$$-2x^3 + 12x^2 + 12x - 10$$

6. **(A)** Cross-multiply the proportion and solve for x.

$$\frac{1}{3x - 1} = \frac{2}{x}$$
$$(2)(3x - 1) = (1)(x)$$
$$6x - 2 = x$$
$$-2 = -5x$$
$$\frac{2}{5} = x$$

7. **(D)** Subtract $2.00 from $15.75 to count the first quarter mile.

$$\$15.75 - \$2.00 = \$13.75$$

Divide $13.75 by $1.25 to calculate the remaining quarter miles.

$$\$13.75 \div \$1.25 = 11$$

The taxi traveled a total of 12 quarter miles. Divide 12 by 4 to find the equivalent number of miles.

$$12 \div 4 = 3$$

8. **(C)** If the system of equations has no solution, each equation has the same slope and a different y-intercept, thus making the lines parallel. In this system of equations, the x's and y's must be multiples of one another.

Find the multiple by dividing $-\frac{10}{3}y$ by $-\frac{5}{9}y$.

$$-\frac{10}{3}y \div -\frac{5}{9}y = 6$$

Multiply $\frac{2}{3}$ by 6 to find the value of b.

$$\frac{2}{3} \times 6 = 4$$

Make sure the constants are different to ensure the lines are parallel.

$-7(6)$ does not equal 17 because -42 does not equal 17.

9. **(C)** Square both sides of the equation to get rid of the radical.

$$\sqrt{n-(-4)} = n - 2$$
$$(\sqrt{n--4})^2 = (n-2)^2$$
$$n + 4 = n^2 - 4n + 4$$
$$0 = n^2 - 5n$$
$$0 = n(n-5)$$

$n = 0$ or $n - 5 = 0$
$n = 0$ or $n = 5$

Check each solution in the original equation to ascertain any extraneous solutions.

Check 5:

$$\sqrt{5-(-4)} = 5 - 2$$
$$\sqrt{9} = 3$$
$$3 = 3$$

Check 0:

$$\sqrt{0-(-4)} = 0 - 2$$
$$\sqrt{4} = -2$$
$$2 \neq -2$$

We accept 5 as the solution and reject 0.

10. **(C)** Let $x =$ the number of points scored in the game.

$$\tfrac{1}{3}x + \tfrac{1}{4}x + \tfrac{1}{3}x + 8 = x$$
$$\tfrac{11}{12}x + 8 = x$$
$$8 = \tfrac{1}{12}x$$
$$96 = x$$

11. **(D)** Expand $(x - y)^2$

$$(x - y)^2 = x^2 - 2xy + y^2$$

It was given that $x^2 + y^2 = 12$ and $xy = -13$. Therefore, $-2xy = 26$.

$$(x - y)^2 = 12 + 26 = 38$$

Multiply the equation by 2.

$$2(x - y)^2 = (2)(38) = 76$$

12. **(B)** Dish #2 has B bacteria, which is twice the number in dish #1. Therefore, $2A = B$. Dish #3 has C bacteria, which is 17 more than B. Given that $B = 2A$ and $C = B + 17$, then $C = 2A + 17$.

13. **(C)** The two functions f and g intersect when their x and y values are the same. Set each of the functions equal and solve for x.

$$6x^2 - 24 = -6x^2 + 24$$

Add $6x^2$ and 24 to both sides to isolate x^2.

$$6x^2 - 24 + 6x^2 + 24 = -6x^2 + 24 + 6x^2 + 24$$
$$12x^2 = 48$$
$$x^2 = 4$$

Find the square root of each side of the equation.

$$x^2 = 4$$
$$x = \pm 2$$

Since we are looking for c rather than $-c$, its value is 2.

14. **(B)** Rationalize the denominator by multiplying the numerator and the denominator by $2 + 3i$, the conjugate of $2 - 3i$.

$$\frac{7}{2 - 3i} \times \frac{2 + 3i}{2 + 3i} =$$
$$\frac{7(2 + 3i)}{4 - 9i^2} =$$
$$\frac{14 + 21i}{4 + 9} = \frac{14 + 21i}{13}$$

Note that if $i = \sqrt{-1}$, then $i^2 = -1$.

15. **(C)** Solve the equation by first dividing all of the terms by 3.

$$(6x^2 + 12x - 15) \div 3 = 0 \div 3$$
$$2x^2 + 4x - 5 = 0$$

The equation cannot be factored so use the quadratic equation to solve.

$$x = \frac{-b \pm \sqrt{b^2 - 4ac}}{2a}$$
$$a = 2 \quad b = 4 \quad c = -5$$
$$\frac{-4 \pm \sqrt{(4)^2 - 4(2)(-5)}}{2(2)}$$
$$\frac{-4 \pm \sqrt{16 + 40}}{4} =$$
$$\frac{-4 \pm \sqrt{56}}{4} = \frac{-2 \pm \sqrt{14}}{2}$$

16. **9** Solve for x.

$$2x - 6 = 18$$
$$2x = 24$$
$$x = 12$$
$$x - 3 = 9$$

There is a faster way to solve this problem. Divide $2x - 6 = 18$ by 2.

$$\frac{2x - 6 = 18}{2}$$
$$x - 3 = 9$$

17. **5,000**

House Wall

The area of a rectangle is found by using the formula Area = (length)(width). Using the diagram we get

$$f(x) = (200 - 2x)(x) = -2x^2 + 200x$$

The lead term is negative and the function is quadratic, resulting in a parabola that opens down. Its vertex is a maximum of the function, which provides the maximum enclosed area of the fence. Begin finding the vertex by using the formula $x = -\dfrac{b}{2a}$.

$$a = -2 \quad b = 200$$

$$-\frac{200}{2(-2)} = 50$$

Replace x with 50 in $f(x) = -2x^2 + 200x$

$$f(50) = -2(50)^2 + 200(50) = 5,000$$

This can be demonstrated with the diagram below.

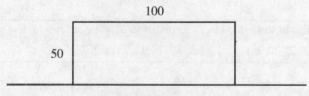

House Wall

The maximum area enclosed by the fencing is 5,000 square feet. Confirm the calculation by using the formula Area = (length)(width).

$$\text{Area} = 100 \times 50 = 5,000$$

18. **6** Begin factoring $x^3 - 6x^2 + 2x - 12 = 0$ by grouping.

$$(x^3 - 6x^2) + (2x - 12) = 0$$

Extract the largest common factor from each of the parentheses.

$$x^2(x - 6) + 2(x - 6) = 0$$

Place x^2 and 2 in its own parentheses.

$$(x^2 + 2)(x - 6) = 0$$

Set each of the parentheses equal to 0.

$$x^2 + 2 = 0 \text{ or } x - 6 = 0$$

$$x^2 = -2 \text{ or } x = 6$$

$x^2 = -2$ becomes $x = \pm i\sqrt{2}$, neither of which is a real number. Therefore, the real solution to $x^3 - 6x^2 + 2x - 12 = 0$ is $x = 6$.

19. **36** $r = 3\sqrt{3}$ and $2r = \sqrt{3x}$; therefore, $2r$ also equals $(2)(3\sqrt{3})$ or $6\sqrt{3}$. Set $6\sqrt{3}$ equal to $\sqrt{3x}$ and solve for x.

Remove the radicals by squaring both sides.

$$6\sqrt{3} = \sqrt{3x}$$
$$(6\sqrt{3})^2 = (\sqrt{3x})^2$$
$$108 = 3x$$
$$36 = x$$

20. **4,058** Simplify $6(12m^2 - 125)$ and combine like terms.

$$(4,264 + 200m^2) + 6(12m^2 - 125)$$
$$4,264 + 200m^2 + 72m^2 - 750$$
$$272m^2 + 3,514$$

This calculation shows that $a = 272$ and $b = 3,514$. Therefore, $2a + b$ equals $2(272) + 3,514 = 4,058$.

Section 4: Math Test (Calculator)

1. **(C)** Cross-multiply and solve for x.

$$\frac{m - 4}{3} = \frac{x}{9}$$
$$3x = 9(m - 4)$$
$$x = 3(m - 4)$$

2. **(C)** The phrase "... at the same rate ..." means use the linear model $y = mx + b$. Find the slope by using the ordered pairs (2, \$2,870) and (5, \$7,150).

$$m = \frac{y_2 - y_1}{x_2 - x_1} = \frac{7150 - 2870}{5 - 2} = \frac{4280}{3} = 1426.67$$

Replace m with 1426.67.

$$y = 1426.67x + b$$

Replace x and y with either point.

$$2870 = 2(1426.67) + b$$
$$16.67 = b$$
$$y = 1426.67x + 16.67$$

Replace x with 78 months, but remember to first convert it to years.

$$78 \text{ months} = 6.5 \text{ years}$$
$$y = 1426.67(6.5) + 16.66$$
$$y = 9,290.02$$
$$\$9,290.02$$

3. **(B)** Let x = the positive integer

$$x^3 - x^2 = 2x$$
$$x^3 - x^2 - 2x = 0$$
$$x(x^2 - x - 2) = 0$$
$$x(x - 2)(x + 1) = 0$$

$$x = 0 \quad x - 2 = 0 \quad x + 1 = 0$$
$$x = 0 \quad x = 2 \quad x = -1$$

Since x is a positive integer, $x = 2$.
If factoring is difficult, try a plug-and-check strategy.

$$(2)^3 - 2^2 = 2(2)$$
$$8 - 4 = 4$$
$$4 = 4$$

4. **(C)** According to the table, 110 fish were caught that were 6–12 inches long. Of that amount, 53 were mullets. Divide 53 by 110 to find the probability that a particular fish caught that measured 6–12 inches was a mullet.

$$\frac{53}{100} \approx .482$$

5. **(B)** Divide the miles to the Andromeda Galaxy by the miles in a light year to find the light years to the Andromeda Galaxy.

$$\frac{1.3 \times 10^{19}}{5.87 \times 10^{12}} \approx .22 \times 10^7 = 2.2 \times 10^6$$

In scientific notation, the first number is expressed such that $1 \leq x < 10$ and the second number is 10 expressed to a power.

6. **(A)** The cost for m computers at \$18.75 each is \$18.75m. The cost for r keyboards at \$13.25 each is \$13.25r. The cost must be less than \$139, so we arrive at

$$18.75m + 13.25r < 139$$

Choices (B) and (D) can automatically be eliminated because each features $\leq$ (less than or equal to). The problem stipulates the cost must be less than \$139.

7. **(D)** The probability of rain on Thursday is 65%. Since the probability of rain on Friday and Saturday is 74% and 31%, respectively, subtract each from 100% to find the probability of no rain on both days.
No rain on Friday: $100\% - 74\% = 26\%$
No rain on Saturday: $100\% - 31\% = 69\%$
Each day's forecast is independent of the others so multiply the three probabilities.

$$(.65)(.26)(.69) = .1166 \approx 11.7\%$$

8. **(B)** A system of equations has an infinite number of equations when the lines are the same. For example,

$$x + y = 6$$
$$2x + 2y = 12$$

has infinite solutions because $2(x + y) = (6)(2)$. Both equations are multiples of one another. Observe the following:

$$7x - 4y = 13$$
$$mx - 10y = 32.5$$
$$(32.5) \div 13 = 2.5$$
$$(-10) \div (-4) = 2.5$$

In order for the system of equations to have infinite solutions, m must be 2.5 times greater than 7.

$$7 \times 2.5 = m$$
$$17.5 = m$$

9. **(D)** The cost of x gallons of water at \$.17/gallon is $.17x$. The tax applied is found by $[.17x + (.073)(.17x)]$, which can be rewritten as $(1.073)(.17x)$. Add the monthly service charge to get

$$f(x) = 31.5 + (1.073)(.17x)$$

10. **(A)** Use the formula $\dfrac{\text{part}}{\text{whole}} = \dfrac{n}{100}$ to find the percent of those operating cars that were in the category 6 to 11 years old.

$$6\text{–}8: 22.2$$
$$9\text{–}11: 16.7$$

The number of cars (in millions) that are between 6 and 11 years old is 38.9 because $22.2 + 16.7 = 38.9$.
Total cars: 104.7

$$\frac{38.9}{104.7} = \frac{n}{100}$$

Cross-multiply and solve for n.

$$104.7n = 38,900$$
$$n = 37.2\%$$

11. **(B)** Find the number of cars that were 20 years old and older.

$$(.013)(104.7) = 1.36 \text{ million}$$

Use the formula $\dfrac{\text{part}}{\text{whole}} = \dfrac{n}{100}$ to find the percent of cars 12 years old and older that are 20 years old and older.

$$\frac{1.36}{14.4} = \frac{n}{100}$$

Cross-multiply and solve for n.

$$14.4n = 136$$
$$n = 9.4\%$$

12. **(C)** Inverse variation means one variable increases proportionally to the decrease in the other variable. SAT scores generally dropped as daily television/device watching increased.

13. **(D)** The data appear to descend to the right, indicating a negative slope. Therefore, choices (A) and (B) can be eliminated. Choose two points in the center of the data and derive the equation of the line that connects them.

$$(1, 14) \ (2, 12)$$
$$m = \frac{y_2 - y_1}{x_2 - x_1}$$
$$m = \frac{12 - 14}{2 - 1}$$
$$m = -2$$
$$y = -2x + b$$

Substitute either point for x and y.

$$14 = -2(1) + b$$
$$16 = b$$

The equation of a line of best fit could be $y = -2x + 16$. Choice (D) is the closest to this equation.

14. **(C)** A = accumulated value of the home over time; P = the purchase price of the home; t = time in years. The formula for the growth of the home over time is the exponential equation $A = P(1.0372)^t$. The addition of 1 and .0372 insures growth in the calculations.

15. **(C)** Input the information provided in the question into the formula $A = P(1.0372)^t$. We substitute 3 for t because three years have elapsed from 2010 to 2013.

$$A = 187,650(1.0372)^3 = \$209,380$$

16. **(B)** To facilitate making calculations, assume the original price was \$100. Find the price after the reduction.

$$100 - (.40)(100) = 60$$

Next, find the price after the increase.

$$60 + (.40)(60) = 84$$

The new price is $\frac{84}{100}$ of the original price, which is 84%.

17. **(B)** Although the system of equations can be solved using either the elimination or the substitution method (or even via graphing), a quicker way to calculate the value of $3x + 6y$ is to add the equations together.

$$\begin{array}{r} 5x + 3y = 16 \\ +4x + 15y = 26 \\ \hline 9x + 18y = 42 \end{array}$$

Next, multiply by $\frac{1}{3}$.

$$\frac{1}{3}(9x + 18y = 42)$$
$$3x + 6y = 14$$

18. **(D)** Subtract the area of the square from the area of the circle.

Area of a square: side $\times$ side (s^2)

Divide the perimeter by 4 and square that value:

$$\left(\tfrac{64}{4}\right)^2 = 16^2 = 256$$

The area of the square is 256 square units.

$$\text{Area of a circle} = \pi r^2$$

The diameter of the circle is equal to the length of one of the sides of the square. Each side is 16 so the radius is 8 because the radius of a circle is one-half of the diameter.

$$\pi(8)^2 \approx 201.1$$

Subtract the area of the circle from the area of the square.

$$256 - 201.1 = 54.9$$

Divide the remaining area by 4 to find the shaded area.

$$54.9 \div 4 = 13.73$$

Divide the measure of the shaded area by the area of the square to find the probability of a coin landing in the shaded area.

$$13.73 \div 256 = .053$$

The diagram is assumed to be drawn to scale so choice (A), .363, would appear to be much too large.

19. **(B)** The slopes of perpendicular lines are the opposite reciprocal of one another. Transform $-5x + 6y = -7$ to slope-intercept form to determine its slope.

$$-5x + 6y = -7$$
$$6y = 5x - 7$$
$$y = \tfrac{5}{6}x - \tfrac{7}{6}$$

The slope of the line $-5x + 6y = -7$ is $\tfrac{5}{6}$. The slope of a line perpendicular to $-5x + 6y = -7$ is $-\tfrac{6}{5}$. Only choice (B) has slope $-\tfrac{6}{5}$.

$$6x + 5y = 15$$
$$5y = -6x + 15$$
$$y = -\tfrac{6}{5}x + 3$$

Expressed in slope-intercept form, the slope of $6x + 5y = 15$ is $-\tfrac{6}{5}$.

Choices (A), (C), and (D) are incorrect because their slopes are $\tfrac{3}{5}$, $\tfrac{3}{10}$, and $-\tfrac{5}{6}$, respectively.

20. **(C)** Find the percentage that is utility expense in 2015.

$$100\% - (14.4 + 41 + 21.6 + 19) = 4\%$$

Set up a proportion comparing an item's percentage of the budget to its dollar expenditure.

$$\frac{21.6}{4,100,000} = \frac{4}{x}$$

Cross-multiply and solve for x.

$$(21.6)(x) = (4)(4,100,000)$$
$$21.6x = 16,400,000$$
$$x = \$759,259$$

21. **(A)** The standard deviation is a measure of how far the data set values are from the mean. In the data set for College B, the large majority of the data are in three of the five possible values, which are the three values closest to the mean. In the data set for College A, the data are more spread out, with many values at the minimum and maximum values. Therefore, by observation, the data for College A have a larger standard deviation.

22. **(A)** The percent of high school graduates in 2006 was 73% and in 2012 the percent had increased to 81%. Divide 81 by 73 to find the percent increase.

$$81 \div 73 = 1.109$$

The increase was 10.9%; the closest answer to this figure is 11%.

23. **(D)** The formula indicates the amount of money earned at a savings institution on a $2,500 deposit, compounded monthly at $r\%$. To find the additional dollars earned at 6% versus 3.2%, find the difference between the annual earnings at each rate.

$2,500\left[1 + \frac{6}{1,200}\right]^{12}$ represents the amount earned each year at 6%.

$2,500\left[1 + \frac{3.2}{1,200}\right]^{12}$ represents the amount earned at 3.2%.

Find their difference by subtracting the smaller expression from the larger.

$$2,500\left[1 + \frac{6}{1,200}\right]^{12} - 2,500\left[1 + \frac{3.2}{1,200}\right]^{12}$$

24. **(B)** Inverse variation uses the model $xy = k$ where k is a constant. Since the question stipulates that the square root of x varies inversely with y, use the model $\sqrt{x}y = k$.

$$\sqrt{196} \times -\frac{1}{2} = k$$
$$-7 = k$$

Now input $y = -3$ into the equation.

$$\sqrt{x} \times -3 = -7$$
$$\sqrt{x} = \frac{7}{3}$$
$$(\sqrt{x})^2 = \left(\frac{7}{3}\right)^2$$
$$x = \frac{49}{9}$$

25. **(B)** The graph shows an unmistakable upward rise to the right; as the age increases, so, too, does the distance thrown. Choice (A), which indicates a weak negative correlation in the graph, can be discarded; the graph clearly moves vertically as age increases.

26. **(C)** Find the line of best fit by selecting two points that lie within the data.

$$(12, 100) \quad (15, 200)$$

Find the slope of a line that connects the two points.

$$\frac{y_2 - y_1}{x_2 - x_1} = \frac{200 - 100}{15 - 12} \approx 33.33$$
$$y = 33.33x + b$$

Use either point to find b.

$$100 = 33.33(12) + b$$
$$-299.6 = b$$
$$y = 33.33x - 299.6$$

27. **(C)** Substitute 18 for x in the equation $y = 33.33x - 299.6$.

$$y = 33.33(18) - 299.6 \approx 300 \text{ feet}$$

28. **(C)** Expand $(2 - 4i)^2$:

$$(2 - 4i)^2 = 4 - 16i + 16i^2$$
$$= 4 - 16i - 16$$
$$= -12 - 16i$$

Multiply $-12 - 16i$ by 3:

$$3(-12 - 16i) = -36 - 48i$$

29. **(D)** If nine students earned an average score of 79%, the class amassed 711 points because $9 \times 79 = 711$. In order for ten students to have an average score of 81, the class must collect 810 points because $10 \times 81 = 810$. Subtracting we get: $810 - 711 = 99$. The tenth student must earn a score of 99% to raise the class average to 81%.

30. **(C)** If the entire class contributed equally, the cost per student, in terms of s and D, would be $\frac{D}{s}$. However, 15 of the students do not contribute this sum, so $15\frac{D}{s}$ needs to be split among the remaining $s - 15$ students.

$\frac{15\frac{D}{s}}{s - 15}$ can be rewritten as $\left(15\frac{D}{s}\right)\left(\frac{1}{(s - 15)}\right)$. Multiplying the numerators and denominators, we arrive at $\frac{15D}{s^2 - 15s}$.

31. **5** The length of the segment connecting $(2, 0)$ and $(26, 0)$ is 24 because $26 - 2 = 24$. Extend (h, k) to this segment to create an altitude. From $(h, 0)$ to $(2, 0)$ is 12 units because a segment drawn from the center and perpendicular to a segment bisects the segment. Given that the radius of the circle is 13, use the Pythagorean theorem to calculate the height, k, of the circle.

$$a^2 + 12^2 = 13^2$$
$$a^2 + 144 = 169$$
$$a^2 = 25$$
$$a = 5$$

The reader may realize that the triangle is the Pythagorean triple 5-12-13.

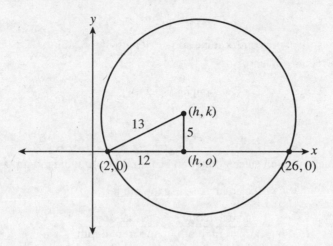

The value of k is 5.

32. **848** Replace $P(x)$ with \$9,321,250, the company's profit.

$$9{,}321{,}250 = 11{,}000x - 6{,}750$$
$$9{,}328{,}000 = 11{,}000x$$
$$848 = x$$

33. **1,786** Kari needs to set the plans equal to each other while leaving the number of minutes as a variable.

Let $x =$ the number of minutes at \$.007 per minute

Plan 1: $24 + .007x$

Plan 2: 36.50

$$24 + .007x = 36.50$$
$$.007x = 12.50$$
$$x = 1{,}786$$

At 1,786 minutes, the two data plans have equal monthly costs.

34. **256** The way to calculate the distance of a star is to square the apparent dimness to find the distance. For example, the galaxy that is 1000 times dimmer is 1,000,000 times farther away $(1000^2 = 1{,}000{,}000)$. The nebula that is 30 times as dim is 900 times further away $(30^2 = 900)$. Therefore, a star that is 16 times dimmer than another would be 256 times distant than the brighter star because $16^2 = 256$.

35. **1, 2, 4, 8, or 16** The equation $x^{\frac{y}{4}} = 81$, where x and y are positive integers, can be written as follows:

$$3^4 = 81$$
$$9^2 = 81$$
$$81^1 = 81$$
$$(81^2)^{\frac{1}{2}} = 81$$
$$(81^4)^{\frac{1}{4}} = 81$$

If $x^{\frac{y}{4}} = 81$, and x and y are positive integers, then $\frac{y}{4}$ can equal 4, 2, 1, $\frac{1}{2}$, or $\frac{1}{4}$. Therefore, the value of y can be 16, 8, 4, 2, or 1.

36. **21.6** The area of a sector is found by using the formula

$$A = \frac{m}{360}\pi r^2$$

where m = measure of the central angle and r = length of the radius.
Input the known data and solve for r.

$$139.6 = \frac{34.4}{360}\pi r^2$$
$$465.33 \approx r^2$$
$$21.6 \approx r$$

37. **7.5 or $\frac{15}{2}$** Direct variation calculations can be found by using the model $\frac{y_1}{x_1} = \frac{y_2}{x_2}$.

In the situation with the refracted images, use the model

$$\frac{\text{actual depth}}{\text{apparent depth}} = \frac{\text{actual depth}}{\text{apparent depth}}$$
$$\frac{5}{4} = \frac{n}{6}$$
$$30 = 4n$$
$$7.5 = n$$

38. **2.25** Use the model $\dfrac{\text{actual depth}}{\text{apparent depth}} = \dfrac{\text{actual depth}}{\text{apparent depth}}$ to find the actual depth of the keys.

$$\frac{n}{9} = \frac{5}{4}$$
$$45 = 4n$$
$$11.25 = n$$

The question asks for the difference between the actual depth and the apparent depth, so subtract 9 from 11.25.

$$11.25 - 9 = 2.25$$

ANSWER SHEET
Practice Test 2

Section 1: Reading

1. Ⓐ Ⓑ Ⓒ Ⓓ	14. Ⓐ Ⓑ Ⓒ Ⓓ	27. Ⓐ Ⓑ Ⓒ Ⓓ	40. Ⓐ Ⓑ Ⓒ Ⓓ
2. Ⓐ Ⓑ Ⓒ Ⓓ	15. Ⓐ Ⓑ Ⓒ Ⓓ	28. Ⓐ Ⓑ Ⓒ Ⓓ	41. Ⓐ Ⓑ Ⓒ Ⓓ
3. Ⓐ Ⓑ Ⓒ Ⓓ	16. Ⓐ Ⓑ Ⓒ Ⓓ	29. Ⓐ Ⓑ Ⓒ Ⓓ	42. Ⓐ Ⓑ Ⓒ Ⓓ
4. Ⓐ Ⓑ Ⓒ Ⓓ	17. Ⓐ Ⓑ Ⓒ Ⓓ	30. Ⓐ Ⓑ Ⓒ Ⓓ	43. Ⓐ Ⓑ Ⓒ Ⓓ
5. Ⓐ Ⓑ Ⓒ Ⓓ	18. Ⓐ Ⓑ Ⓒ Ⓓ	31. Ⓐ Ⓑ Ⓒ Ⓓ	44. Ⓐ Ⓑ Ⓒ Ⓓ
6. Ⓐ Ⓑ Ⓒ Ⓓ	19. Ⓐ Ⓑ Ⓒ Ⓓ	32. Ⓐ Ⓑ Ⓒ Ⓓ	45. Ⓐ Ⓑ Ⓒ Ⓓ
7. Ⓐ Ⓑ Ⓒ Ⓓ	20. Ⓐ Ⓑ Ⓒ Ⓓ	33. Ⓐ Ⓑ Ⓒ Ⓓ	46. Ⓐ Ⓑ Ⓒ Ⓓ
8. Ⓐ Ⓑ Ⓒ Ⓓ	21. Ⓐ Ⓑ Ⓒ Ⓓ	34. Ⓐ Ⓑ Ⓒ Ⓓ	47. Ⓐ Ⓑ Ⓒ Ⓓ
9. Ⓐ Ⓑ Ⓒ Ⓓ	22. Ⓐ Ⓑ Ⓒ Ⓓ	35. Ⓐ Ⓑ Ⓒ Ⓓ	48. Ⓐ Ⓑ Ⓒ Ⓓ
10. Ⓐ Ⓑ Ⓒ Ⓓ	23. Ⓐ Ⓑ Ⓒ Ⓓ	36. Ⓐ Ⓑ Ⓒ Ⓓ	49. Ⓐ Ⓑ Ⓒ Ⓓ
11. Ⓐ Ⓑ Ⓒ Ⓓ	24. Ⓐ Ⓑ Ⓒ Ⓓ	37. Ⓐ Ⓑ Ⓒ Ⓓ	50. Ⓐ Ⓑ Ⓒ Ⓓ
12. Ⓐ Ⓑ Ⓒ Ⓓ	25. Ⓐ Ⓑ Ⓒ Ⓓ	38. Ⓐ Ⓑ Ⓒ Ⓓ	51. Ⓐ Ⓑ Ⓒ Ⓓ
13. Ⓐ Ⓑ Ⓒ Ⓓ	26. Ⓐ Ⓑ Ⓒ Ⓓ	39. Ⓐ Ⓑ Ⓒ Ⓓ	52. Ⓐ Ⓑ Ⓒ Ⓓ

Section 2: Writing and Language

1. Ⓐ Ⓑ Ⓒ Ⓓ	12. Ⓐ Ⓑ Ⓒ Ⓓ	23. Ⓐ Ⓑ Ⓒ Ⓓ	34. Ⓐ Ⓑ Ⓒ Ⓓ
2. Ⓐ Ⓑ Ⓒ Ⓓ	13. Ⓐ Ⓑ Ⓒ Ⓓ	24. Ⓐ Ⓑ Ⓒ Ⓓ	35. Ⓐ Ⓑ Ⓒ Ⓓ
3. Ⓐ Ⓑ Ⓒ Ⓓ	14. Ⓐ Ⓑ Ⓒ Ⓓ	25. Ⓐ Ⓑ Ⓒ Ⓓ	36. Ⓐ Ⓑ Ⓒ Ⓓ
4. Ⓐ Ⓑ Ⓒ Ⓓ	15. Ⓐ Ⓑ Ⓒ Ⓓ	26. Ⓐ Ⓑ Ⓒ Ⓓ	37. Ⓐ Ⓑ Ⓒ Ⓓ
5. Ⓐ Ⓑ Ⓒ Ⓓ	16. Ⓐ Ⓑ Ⓒ Ⓓ	27. Ⓐ Ⓑ Ⓒ Ⓓ	38. Ⓐ Ⓑ Ⓒ Ⓓ
6. Ⓐ Ⓑ Ⓒ Ⓓ	17. Ⓐ Ⓑ Ⓒ Ⓓ	28. Ⓐ Ⓑ Ⓒ Ⓓ	39. Ⓐ Ⓑ Ⓒ Ⓓ
7. Ⓐ Ⓑ Ⓒ Ⓓ	18. Ⓐ Ⓑ Ⓒ Ⓓ	29. Ⓐ Ⓑ Ⓒ Ⓓ	40. Ⓐ Ⓑ Ⓒ Ⓓ
8. Ⓐ Ⓑ Ⓒ Ⓓ	19. Ⓐ Ⓑ Ⓒ Ⓓ	30. Ⓐ Ⓑ Ⓒ Ⓓ	41. Ⓐ Ⓑ Ⓒ Ⓓ
9. Ⓐ Ⓑ Ⓒ Ⓓ	20. Ⓐ Ⓑ Ⓒ Ⓓ	31. Ⓐ Ⓑ Ⓒ Ⓓ	42. Ⓐ Ⓑ Ⓒ Ⓓ
10. Ⓐ Ⓑ Ⓒ Ⓓ	21. Ⓐ Ⓑ Ⓒ Ⓓ	32. Ⓐ Ⓑ Ⓒ Ⓓ	43. Ⓐ Ⓑ Ⓒ Ⓓ
11. Ⓐ Ⓑ Ⓒ Ⓓ	22. Ⓐ Ⓑ Ⓒ Ⓓ	33. Ⓐ Ⓑ Ⓒ Ⓓ	44. Ⓐ Ⓑ Ⓒ Ⓓ

Section 3: Math (No Calculator)

1. Ⓐ Ⓑ Ⓒ Ⓓ
2. Ⓐ Ⓑ Ⓒ Ⓓ
3. Ⓐ Ⓑ Ⓒ Ⓓ
4. Ⓐ Ⓑ Ⓒ Ⓓ

5. Ⓐ Ⓑ Ⓒ Ⓓ
6. Ⓐ Ⓑ Ⓒ Ⓓ
7. Ⓐ Ⓑ Ⓒ Ⓓ
8. Ⓐ Ⓑ Ⓒ Ⓓ

9. Ⓐ Ⓑ Ⓒ Ⓓ
10. Ⓐ Ⓑ Ⓒ Ⓓ
11. Ⓐ Ⓑ Ⓒ Ⓓ
12. Ⓐ Ⓑ Ⓒ Ⓓ

13. Ⓐ Ⓑ Ⓒ Ⓓ
14. Ⓐ Ⓑ Ⓒ Ⓓ
15. Ⓐ Ⓑ Ⓒ Ⓓ

16.

17.

18.

19.

20.

ANSWER SHEET
Practice Test 2

Section 4: Math (Calculator)

1. Ⓐ Ⓑ Ⓒ Ⓓ   9. Ⓐ Ⓑ Ⓒ Ⓓ   17. Ⓐ Ⓑ Ⓒ Ⓓ   25. Ⓐ Ⓑ Ⓒ Ⓓ

2. Ⓐ Ⓑ Ⓒ Ⓓ   10. Ⓐ Ⓑ Ⓒ Ⓓ   18. Ⓐ Ⓑ Ⓒ Ⓓ   26. Ⓐ Ⓑ Ⓒ Ⓓ

3. Ⓐ Ⓑ Ⓒ Ⓓ   11. Ⓐ Ⓑ Ⓒ Ⓓ   19. Ⓐ Ⓑ Ⓒ Ⓓ   27. Ⓐ Ⓑ Ⓒ Ⓓ

4. Ⓐ Ⓑ Ⓒ Ⓓ   12. Ⓐ Ⓑ Ⓒ Ⓓ   20. Ⓐ Ⓑ Ⓒ Ⓓ   28. Ⓐ Ⓑ Ⓒ Ⓓ

5. Ⓐ Ⓑ Ⓒ Ⓓ   13. Ⓐ Ⓑ Ⓒ Ⓓ   21. Ⓐ Ⓑ Ⓒ Ⓓ   29. Ⓐ Ⓑ Ⓒ Ⓓ

6. Ⓐ Ⓑ Ⓒ Ⓓ   14. Ⓐ Ⓑ Ⓒ Ⓓ   22. Ⓐ Ⓑ Ⓒ Ⓓ   30. Ⓐ Ⓑ Ⓒ Ⓓ

7. Ⓐ Ⓑ Ⓒ Ⓓ   15. Ⓐ Ⓑ Ⓒ Ⓓ   23. Ⓐ Ⓑ Ⓒ Ⓓ

8. Ⓐ Ⓑ Ⓒ Ⓓ   16. Ⓐ Ⓑ Ⓒ Ⓓ   24. Ⓐ Ⓑ Ⓒ Ⓓ

31. 32. 33. 34.

35. 36. 37. 38.

1   1   1

Practice Test 2

READING TEST

65 MINUTES, 52 QUESTIONS

Turn to Section 1 of your answer sheet to answer the questions in this section.

DIRECTIONS: Following each of the passages (or pairs of passages) below are questions about the passage (or passages). Read each passage carefully. Then, select the best answer for each question based on what is stated in the passage (or passages) and in any graphics that may accompany the passage.

Questions 1–10 are based on the following passage.

This passage is from Dai Sijie, *Balzac and the Little Chinese Seamstress,* © 2001 by Alfred A. Knopf. (English translation Copyright © by Ina Rilke 2001.)

The events portrayed take place during the Cultural Revolution in China. Two boys, the narrator and his friend Luo, have recently been sent by the government to a remote village to work as laborers as part of their "re-education." The stated goal of the Cultural Revolution was to preserve "true" Communist ideology in the country by purging remnants of capitalist and traditional elements from Chinese society, and to re-impose Maoist thought as the dominant ideology within the Party.

The village headman sat cross-legged in the centre of the room, close to the coals burning in a hearth that was hollowed out of the floor; he was inspecting my violin. Among the pos-
(5) sessions brought to this mountain village by the two "city youths"—which was how they saw Luo and me—it was the sole item that exuded an air of foreignness, of civilization, and therefore aroused suspicion.

(10)   One of the peasants came forward with an oil lamp to facilitate identification of the strange object. The headman held the violin upright and peered into the black interior of the body, like an officious customs officer searching for
(15) drugs. Raising the violin to eye level, he shook it, as though convinced something would drop out of the sound holes. His investigation was so enthusiastic I was afraid the strings would break.

Just about everyone in the village had come
(20) to the house on stilts way up on the mountain to witness the arrival of the city youths. Men, women and children swarmed inside the cramped room, clung to the windows, jostled each other by the door. When nothing fell out of
(25) my violin, the headman held his nose over the sound holes and sniffed long and hard.

Still no clues.

He ran his calloused fingertips over one string, then another . . . . The strange resonance
(30) froze the crowd, as if the sound had won some sort of respect.

"It's a toy," said the headman solemnly.

This verdict left us speechless. Luo and I exchanged furtive, anxious glances. Things were
(35) not looking good.

One peasant took the "toy" from the head-man's hands, drummed with his fists on its back, then passed it to the next man. For a while my violin circulated through the crowd and

(40) we—two frail, skinny, exhausted and risible city youths—were ignored. We had been tramping across the mountains all day, and our clothes, faces and hair were streaked with mud. We looked like pathetic little reactionary soldiers

(45) from a propaganda film after their capture by a horde of Communist farm workers.

"A stupid toy," a woman commented hoarsely.

"No," the village headman corrected her, "a bourgeois toy."

(50) I felt chilled to the bone despite the fire blazing in the centre of the room.

"A toy from the city," the headman continued, "go on, burn it!"

His command galvanized the crowd.

(55) Everyone started talking at once, shouting and reaching out to grab the toy for the privilege of throwing it on the coals.

"Comrade, it's a musical instrument," Luo said as casually as he could, "and my friend

(60) here's a fine musician. Truly."

The headman called for the violin and looked it over once more.

Then he held it out to me.

"Forgive me, comrade," I said, embarrassed,

(65) "but I'm not that good."

I saw Luo giving me a surreptitious wink. Puzzled, I took my violin and set about tuning it.

"What you are about to hear, comrade, is a Mozart sonata," Luo announced, as coolly as

(70) before.

I was dumbfounded. Had he gone mad? All music by Mozart or indeed by any other Western composer had been banned years ago. In my sodden shoes my feet turned to ice. I shiv-

(75) ered as the cold tightened its grip on me.

"What's a sonata?" the headman asked warily.

"I don't know," I faltered. "It's Western."

"Is it a song?"

(80) "More or less," I replied evasively.

At that instant the glint of the vigilant Communist reappeared in the headman's eyes, and his voice turned hostile.

"What's the name of this song of yours?"

(85) "Well, it's like a song, but actually it's a sonata."

"I'm asking you what it's called!" he snapped, fixing me with his gaze.

"*Mozart . . .*" I muttered.

(90) "*Mozart* what?"

"*Mozart is Thinking of Chairman Mao,*" Luo broke in.

The audacity! But it worked: as if he had heard something miraculous, the headman's

(95) menacing look softened. He crinkled up his eyes in a wide, beatific smile.

"Mozart thinks of Mao all the time," he said.

"Indeed, all the time," agreed Luo.

As soon as I had tightened my bow there

(100) was a burst of applause, but I was still nervous. However, as I ran my swollen fingers over the strings, Mozart's phrases came flooding back to me like so many faithful friends. The peasants' faces, so grim a moment before, softened

(105) under the influence of Mozart's limpid music like parched earth under a shower, and then, in the dancing light of the oil lamp, they blurred into one.

I played for some time, Luo lit a cigarette and

(110) smoked quietly, like a man.

This was our first taste of re-education. Luo was eighteen years old. I was seventeen.

1. Until the narrator plays the violin the villagers regard it chiefly as

   (A) a dangerous weapon
   (B) a wondrous, almost magical device
   (C) something alien
   (D) a traditional Chinese musical instrument

2. What word most accurately describes how the narrator views the villagers?

   (A) bourgeois
   (B) materialistic
   (C) reactionary
   (D) uncivilized

3. The narrator says, "Things were not looking good" (lines 34–35) because

   (A) the headman doesn't understand how delicate the violin is, and so the narrator and Luo are afraid that he might accidentally break it
   (B) the headman has discovered the truth about the violin—that it's a toy—and Luo and the narrator are afraid that he will keep it for himself
   (C) the headman has just concluded that the violin is a toy, and therefore something regarded as bourgeois
   (D) Luo and the narrator believe that the headman's verdict about the violin suggests that he has total control of the village

4. The word *coolly* as it is used in line 69 most nearly means

   (A) stylishly
   (B) calmly
   (C) arrogantly
   (D) resignedly

5. What is the most likely reason that the villagers in the crowd regard burning the violin as a "privilege" (line 56)?

   (A) They believe that the person who destroys the violin will be richly rewarded by the headman.
   (B) They see it as an honor to be the person who destroys a symbol of bourgeois decadence.
   (C) They believe that the person who destroys the violin will be likely to become the next headman.
   (D) They believe that the person who destroys the violin will be rewarded in the afterlife.

6. What is the most likely reason that Luo gives the narrator "a surreptitious wink" (line 66)?

   (A) to reassure the narrator that it is all right if his violin playing is not very good
   (B) to indicate to the narrator that he has a plan, and that the narrator should go along with it
   (C) to remind the narrator that they should be loyal Communists
   (D) to warn the narrator that they are in a very difficult situation

7. The fact that the narrator "took [his] violin and set about tuning it" (line 67) after Luo had winked at him suggests that the narrator

   (A) has no idea at all what Luo was trying to communicate to him by winking at him
   (B) wants to distract the attention of the villagers
   (C) trusts his friend even though he does not understand his plan
   (D) is annoyed with Luo for trying to involve him in a duplicitous plan

1   1   1

8. The most likely reason that the narrator exclaims "The audacity!" (line 93) is that

   (A) he believes it is audacious of Luo to interrupt when the headman is waiting for a reply from the narrator
   (B) he thinks that making up a song title called *Mozart is Thinking of Chairman Mao* shows disrespect for one of the great Western classical composers
   (C) he thinks that making up a song title shows disrespect to the headman
   (D) he thinks it is very bold of Luo to make up a song title called *Mozart is Thinking of Chairman Mao* because the headman could have reacted angrily and said that the narrator and Luo were trying to trick him

9. The author makes use of all of the following *except*

   (A) parody
   (B) description of details
   (C) a building up of tension in the narrative
   (D) simile

10. It can be inferred from the fact that Luo "smoked quietly, like a man" (line 110) that

   (A) he is worried about what will happen when the narrator stops playing the Mozart sonata
   (B) he is planning another way to fool the gullible headman
   (C) he is justifiably satisfied with himself for orchestrating a daring and successful plan to gain the favor of the villagers
   (D) he realizes that he has been accepted as a full-fledged adult member of the village

Questions 11–20 are based on the following passage.

This passage is from Irving Kristol, *Reflections of a Neoconservative*, © 1983 by Irving Kristol.

Throughout history, artists and writers have been candidly contemptuous of commercial activity between consenting adults, regarding it as an activity that tends to coarsen and trivialize
(5) the human spirit. And since bourgeois society was above all else a commercial society—the first in all of recorded history in which the commercial ethos was sovereign over all others—their exasperation was bound to be all the more
(10) acute. Later on, the term "philistinism" would emerge to encapsulate this sentiment.

Though a commercial society may offer artists and writers all sorts of desirable things—freedom of expression especially, popularity
(15) and affluence occasionally—it did (and does) deprive them of the status that they naturally feel themselves entitled to. Artists and writers and thinkers always have taken themselves to be Very Important People, and they are out-
(20) raged by a society that merely tolerates them, no matter how generously.

A commercial society, a society whose civilization is shaped by market transactions, is always likely to reflect the appetites and prefer-
(25) ences of common men and women. Each may not have much money, but there are so many of them that their tastes are decisive. Artists and intellectuals see this as an inversion of the natural order of things, since it gives "vulgarity,"
(30) the power to dominate where and when it can. By their very nature "elitists" (as one now says), they believe that a civilization should be shaped by an aristocracy to which they will be organically attached, no matter how perilously.

(35) In sum, intellectuals and artists will be (as they have been) restive in a bourgeois-capitalist society. The popularity of romanticism in the century after 1750 testifies to this fact, as the artists led an "inner emigration" of

(40) the spirit—which, however, left the actual world unchanged. But not all such restiveness found refuge in escapism. Rebellion was an alternative route, as the emergence of various socialist philosophies and movements early in the nine-
(45) teenth century demonstrated.

Socialism (of whatever kind) is a romantic passion that operates within a rationalist framework. It aims to construct a human community in which everyone places the common good—
(50) as defined, necessarily, by an intellectual and moral elite—before his own individual interests and appetites. The intention was not new—there isn't a religion in the world that has failed to preach and expound it. What was new was
(55) the belief that such self-denial could be realized, not through a voluntary circumscription of individual appetites, but even while the aggregate of human appetites was being increasingly satisfied by ever-growing material prosperity.
(60) "Scientific" socialism promised to remove the conflict between actual and potentially ideal human nature by creating an economy of such abundance that appetite as a social force would, as it were, wither away.

(65) Behind this promise, of course, was the profound belief that modern science—including the social sciences, and especially including scientific economics—would gradually but ineluctably provide humanity with modes of
(70) control over nature (and human nature, too) that would permit the modern world radically to transcend all those limitations of the human condition previously taken to be "natural." The trouble with implementing this belief, however,
(75) was that the majority of men and women were no more capable of comprehending a "science of society" than they were of practicing austere self-denial. A socialist elite, therefore, was indispensable to mobilize the masses for their own
(80) ultimate self-transformation.

The appeal of any such movement to intellectuals is clear enough. As intellectuals, they are qualified candidates for membership in the elite that leads such movements, and they
(85) can thus give free expression to their natural impulse for authority and power. They can do so, moreover, within an ideological context, which reassures them that they are disinterestedly serving the "true" interests of the people.

11. The assertion made in lines 1–5 that "Throughout history, artists and writers have been candidly contemptuous of commercial activity between consenting adults, regarding it as an activity that tends to coarsen and trivialize the human spirit" could be best strengthened by

(A) evidence supporting the assertion
(B) an explanation of the word "candidly" (line 2)
(C) a fuller definition of "artists and writers" (line 1)
(D) an explanation of the term "commercial activity" (lines 2–3)

12. The phrase "between consenting adults" (line 3) is used to

(A) exclude commercial activity that is forced upon a person or is necessary for the person's survival from the sort of commercial activity that artists and writers have contempt for
(B) remind the reader that all meaningful activity of any sort is between free adults
(C) suggest that nearly all adults, if given the freedom to do so, resist the urge to engage in commercial activity
(D) suggest that bourgeois society, more than any other, depends on the freely given consent of adults

13. According to the author, the term "philistinism" (line 10) arose because

   (A) artists and writers became aware that they would increasingly have to participate in commercial activities
   (B) artists and writers became increasingly frustrated and annoyed as society became more commercial and bourgeois
   (C) a new word had to be found to refer to the new commercial ethos that was emerging in the eighteenth century
   (D) artists and writers needed a word to conveniently describe their changing role in bourgeois society

14. In line 27 *decisive* most nearly means

   (A) beyond doubt
   (B) vital
   (C) having the power to decide
   (D) characterized by decision and firmness

15. According to the author, as society became more commercial

   (A) artists and writers became increasingly constrained in their range of subjects
   (B) artists and writers generally tended to follow this trend and increasingly worked only for financial reward
   (C) artists and writers became relatively poorer as compared to people who weren't artists or writers
   (D) the status of artists and writers became lower

16. Which of the following best describes the author's attitude about the tastes of common men and women becoming predominant in commercial society?

   (A) unhappiness that higher art and literature as well as other intellectual pursuits have been devalued in commercial society
   (B) resignation to an unfortunate turn of events in history
   (C) celebration that at last the voices of common men and women are being heard
   (D) a non-committal attitude as to whether this is a favorable or unfavorable development

17. According to the author, romanticism

   (A) led to the creation of socialist philosophies and movements
   (B) culminated in rebellions in the early nineteenth century
   (C) had no effect on the real world
   (D) was most popular among common men and women after 1750

18. Which choice provides the best evidence for the answer to the previous question?

   (A) lines 1–5 ("Throughout . . . spirit.")
   (B) lines 37–41 ("The . . . unchanged.")
   (C) lines 46–48 ("Socialism . . . framework.")
   (D) lines 65–73 ("Behind . . . natural.'")

1   1   1

19. "Appetite as a social force would, as it were, wither away" (lines 63–64) means

(A) the desire of individuals to have and do what they like would gradually cease to have an effect on the nature of society

(B) common men and women would no longer regard the consumption of goods and services as legitimate

(C) individual taste would gradually be determined by individuals rather than by society

(D) society would gradually come to realize that individual appetites cannot be controlled by intellectual and moral elites

20. In lines 88–89 *disinterestedly* most nearly means

(A) without genuine interest

(B) genuinely

(C) impartially, and not motivated by self-interest

(D) with no emotion

Questions 21–31 are based on the following passages.

Passage 1 is from Samuel P. Huntington, "The Clash of Civilizations?" © 1993 by the Council on Foreign Relations, Inc. Passage 2 is from Albert L. Weeks, "Do Civilizations Hold?" © 1993 by Albert L. Weeks.

PASSAGE 1

Civilization identity will be increasingly important in the future, and the world will be shaped in large measure by the interactions among seven or eight major civilizations. These
(5) include Western, Confucian, Japanese, Islamic, Hindu, Slavic-Orthodox, Latin American, and possibly African civilization. The most important conflicts of the future will occur along the cultural fault lines separating these civilizations
(10) from one another. Why will this be the case?

First, differences among civilizations are not only real; they are basic. Civilizations are differentiated from each other by history, language, culture, tradition and, most important, religion.
(15) The people of different civilizations have different views on the relations between God and man, the individual and the group, the citizen and the state, parents and children, husband and wife, as well as differing views of the rela-
(20) tive importance of rights and responsibilities, liberty and authority, equality and hierarchy. These differences are the product of centuries. They will not soon disappear. They are far more fundamental than differences among political
(25) ideologies and political regimes. Differences do not necessarily mean conflict, and conflict does not necessarily mean violence. Over the centuries, however, differences among civilizations have generated the most prolonged and
(30) the most violent conflicts.

Second, the world is becoming a smaller place. The interactions between peoples of different civilizations are increasing; these increasing interactions intensify civilization

PRACTICE TEST 2

(35) consciousness and awareness of differences between civilizations and commonalities within civilizations. Enhanced civilization-consciousness of people, in turn, invigorates differences and animosities stretching or thought to stretch (40) back deep into history.

Third, the processes of economic modernization and social change throughout the world are separating people from longstanding local identities. They also weaken the nation state (45) as a source of identity. In much of the world religion has moved in to fill this gap, often in the form of movements that are labeled "fundamentalist." Such movements are found in Western Christianity, Judaism, Buddhism, and (50) Hinduism, as well as in Islam. In most countries and most religions the people active in fundamentalist movements are young, college-educated, middle-class technicians, professionals, and business persons. The "unsecularization (55) of the world," George Weigel has remarked, "is one of the dominant social facts of life in the late twentieth century." The revival of religion . . . provides a basis for identity and commitment that transcends national boundaries and unites (60) civilizations.

Fourth, the growth of civilization-consciousness is enhanced by the dual role of the West. On the one hand, the West is at a peak of power. At the same time, however, (65) and perhaps as a result, a return to the roots phenomenon is occurring among non-Western civilizations. Increasingly one hears references to trends toward a turning inward and "Asianization" in Japan, the end of the Nehru leg- (70) acy and the "Hinduization" of India, the failure of Western ideas of socialism and nationalism and hence "re-Islamization" of the Middle East. A West at the peak of its power confronts non-Wests that increasingly have the desire, the will (75) and the resources to shape the world in non-Western ways.

PASSAGE 2

Huntington's classification identifies determinants on a grand scale by "civilizations." His endeavor, however, has its fault lines. The (80) lines are the borders encompassing each distinct nation state and mercilessly chopping the alleged civilizations into pieces. With the cultural and religious glue of these "civilizations" thin and cracked, with the nation (85) state's political regime providing the principal bonds, crisscross fracturing and cancellation of Huntington's macro-scale, somewhat anachronistic fault lines are inevitable.

The world remains fractured along political (90) and possibly geopolitical lines; cultural and historical determinants are a great deal less vital and virulent. Politics, regimes, and ideologies are culturally, historically, and "civilizationally" determined to an extent. But it is willful, day- (95) to-day, crisis-to-crisis, war-to-war political decision-making by nation-state units that remains the single most identifiable determinant of events in the international arena. How else can we explain repeated nation-state (100) "defections" from their collective "civilizations"? As Huntington himself points out, in the Persian Gulf War "one Arab state invaded another and then fought a coalition of Arab, Western, and other states."

(105) Raymond Aron described at length the primacy of a nation state's political integrity and independence, its inviolable territoriality and sovereign impermeability. He observed that "men have believed that the fate of cultures was (110) at stake on the battlefields at the same time as the fate of provinces." But, he added, the fact remains that sovereign states "are engaged in a competition for power [and] conquests . . . . In our times the major phenomenon [on the (115) international scene] is the heterogeneity of state units [not] supranational aggregations."

21. The term "cultural fault lines" (line 9) suggests that

    (A) like geological continental plates, civilizations are distinct from each other, and sometimes collide
    (B) like geological continental plates, civilizations are relatively stable, with little meaningful interaction between them
    (C) future civilizational conflict will occur in areas difficult to predict
    (D) civilizations are subject to the same laws as all natural processes, such as those governing the movement of the Earth's tectonic plates

22. The word *basic* as it is used in line 12 most nearly means

    (A) important
    (B) distinct
    (C) fundamental
    (D) elementary

23. The author of Passage 1 would be most likely to agree with the statement that

    (A) differences between cultures nearly always lead to conflict between these cultures
    (B) most people in the world identify more strongly with the religion they belong to than the political party they belong to
    (C) the differing values of people of different civilizations are more superficial than is generally believed
    (D) it is not possible to make meaningful generalizations about the moral and other values of the world's seven or eight major civilizations

24. What would the author of Passage 1 most likely consider to be the most important implication of the statement, "Over the centuries, however, differences among civilizations have generated the most prolonged and the most violent conflicts" (lines 27–30)?

    (A) Differences among civilizations rather than differing political ideologies are likely to cause serious future conflict in the world.
    (B) All future conflicts among civilizations will be violent and long-lasting.
    (C) Differences among civilizations cause wars of great destruction, but these wars serve, paradoxically, to purify and thus strengthen civilizations.
    (D) There will ultimately be a major conflict between all the major civilizations of the world resulting in the destruction of all but one of them.

25. The author of Passage 1 would most likely agree that

    (A) the growth of trans-national companies is likely to sharply reduce the likelihood of conflict between civilizations
    (B) the wide availability of the World Wide Web has lessened, though not eliminated, the likelihood of major civilizational conflict
    (C) the increased frequency of large movements of people between nations belonging to different civilizations has raised the likelihood of conflict between civilizations
    (D) the availability and affordability of modern air transport has, most importantly, fostered understanding between people of different civilizations

26. According to the author of Passage 1, many young, well-educated technicians, professionals, and business persons around the world are turning to religion because

   (A) social change in many countries has brought more people into contact with the major world religions
   (B) economic and technological modernization in poorer countries has given people greater leisure, and thus young people have more opportunity to pursue different spiritual paths
   (C) young people in rapidly developing countries believe that identifying with a major world religion will make them more attractive as employees to multi-national companies
   (D) they identify less strongly with their local traditions and nation, and so seek identity in religion, especially in fundamentalist religious movements

27. The author of Passage 2

   (A) believes that Raymond Aron is correct in his statement that "men have believed that the fate of cultures was at stake on the battlefields at the same time as the fate of provinces"
   (B) believes that the term "civilization" is virtually synonymous with the term "nation-state"
   (C) asserts that ideologies develop independently of civilizations
   (D) suggests that nation-states almost never act to undermine the "civilization" to which they belong

28. The author of Passage 2 says "Politics, regimes, and ideologies are culturally, historically, and 'civilizationally' determined to an extent" (lines 92–94). In the context of the author's main argument, this sentence is most accurately described as

   (A) a central thesis
   (B) a reasonable inference
   (C) a proviso
   (D) a partial concession

29. The meaning of the word *vital* as it is used in line 91 most nearly means

   (A) essential
   (B) fatal
   (C) full of energy
   (D) influential

30. The author of Passage 1 would be most likely to respond to the example of the Persian Gulf War cited in Passage 2 (lines 101–104) by saying that

   (A) there will continue to be cases in which nation-states act against the interest of the civilization to which they belong, but the more significant trend is for civilizational loyalty to take precedence over loyalty to the nation-state
   (B) most of the Arab states involved in the Persian Gulf War owe their allegiance primarily to the West, not to Islamic civilization
   (C) the Arab states that allied themselves with the West in the Persian Gulf War were forced to do so for larger geo-political and economic reasons that transcend civilizational concerns
   (D) civilizational loyalty cannot be assessed by the amount of intra-civilizational aggression that occurs

31. The author of Passage 2 most likely put quotation marks around the word *civilizations* in line 82 to

   (A) suggest that it is very possible that what Huntington defines as civilizations are not in actuality civilizations
   (B) make it clear that his definition of civilization is not the same as Huntington's
   (C) suggest the term "civilization" has no meaning at all
   (D) express his scorn for scholars who use important terms carelessly

Questions 32–41 are based on the following passage.

This passage is from Milton Friend, *Why bother about wildlife disease?*: U.S. Geological Survey Circular 1401, 2014.

What are zoonoses? The common dictionary definition in scientific journals and media
coverage of zoonotic disease conveys the limited concept of infectious disease transmis-
(5) sible from animals to humans. However, that
perspective is inadequate. Zoonotic disease is
multidimensional and ecologically complex,
as are many of the pathogens involved. Like
those pathogens, the definition of zoonosis has
(10) followed an evolutionary path. Here, it is sufficient to recognize that zoonoses are infectious
diseases transmissible between vertebrate animals and humans and vice versa. In addition,
the animal component has an essential role in
(15) maintaining the pathogen in nature for diseases
transmitted to humans; for example, foxes and
rabies. Humans serve that same role for diseases being transmitted to lower vertebrates;
for example, measles and great apes. These
(20) revelations have direct ramifications for wildlife
conservation.

The general importance of zoonoses for
humanity has waxed and waned over time in
concert with changing conditions including
(25) changes in the number of human cases and
(or) exposures associated with enzootic areas,
such as chronic disease presence and activity
levels, for specific zoonoses. The occurrence
of major epizootics or epidemics involving the
(30) expansion of established geographic range for
specific diseases and (or) the appearance of
"new" zoonoses within a geographic area is also
of great concern. Rabies is a well-established
zoonosis and, except for anthrax, perhaps the
(35) next earliest zoonosis to confront humans. The
first recorded description of canine rabies dates
back to about 500 B.C. Rabies is an important
zoonosis in much of the world, because death is

the outcome once clinical signs appear. Human
(40) deaths from rabies are rare in the United States,
but the disease is diagnosed annually in wildlife
and other animals where it continues to cause
periodic epizootics. A recent major rabies epizootic that occurred among raccoons in the
(45) mid-Atlantic and northeastern United States
illustrates that even a zoonosis of antiquity can
reassert its prominence in the modern era as a
challenge for humans and wildlife alike.

Throughout history, zoonoses also have
(50) been the cause of humanity at local, regional, and global levels. Globally, an estimated
200–500 million people were sickened during
the 1917–19 H1N1 influenza virus "Spanish
flu" pandemic, more than 20 million of whom
(55) died. The specter of that pandemic contributed
greatly to the unprecedented global response
following the 1997 diagnoses of highly pathogenic H5N1 avian influenza virus in Asia and
the subsequent spread of that virus throughout
(60) much of Asia and Europe.

The emergence of highly pathogenic H5N1
is just one of a number of recent Emerging
Infectious Diseases (EIDs) that have wildlife
roots, including numerous diseases that have
(65) caused epizootics of great concern for society.
The World Health Organization reported that in
2006, 39.5 million people were currently infected with HIV/AIDS worldwide and that for the
next year alone (2007), 18 billion dollars would
(70) be needed to prevent future HIV transmission
and provide care for those already infected. A
myriad of other emerging zoonoses followed
HIV/AIDS to the headlines of major newspa-
pers as well as serving as subject matter for
(75) major media venues of all types. These diseases
have also become a major focus for scientific
investigations and the development of specialized programs and facilities to address them.

Some emerging zoonoses cause major eco-
(80) nomic impacts for agriculture because of their
presence in food production species such as

poultry (H5N1) and swine (Nipah virus). For example, the highly pathogenic H5N1 avian influenza virus that appeared in Asia during (85) 1997 and reached 51 countries by early 2010 caused billions of dollars in losses for the poultry industries of those countries. West Nile virus (WNV) also stands out because of its geographic spread across the United States and within (90) North America following the 1999 New York City index cases involving human fatalities, fatal cases in horses, and the thousands and thousands of wild birds killed.

Threats from EIDs are unlikely to decrease, (95) because the ever-changing relations between humans and the environment are a major factor driving disease emergence. The separation between the relevance of zoonoses to wildlife management and conservation and to public (100) health issues has rigidly existed in the past but has been greatly eroded by the current wave of EIDs, many of which are zoonoses. Further, the great costs of zoonoses for society demand that these diseases be aggressively dealt with. (105) For example, of the 868 zoonoses identified at the start of the 21st century, a review of 56 of them revealed approximately 2.5 billion cases of human illness and 2.7 million human deaths worldwide per year.

The "Rebirth" of Zoonoses

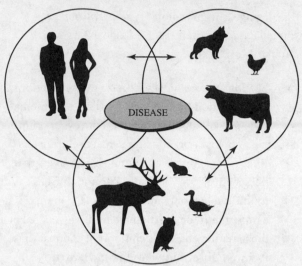

"...emerging zoonotic diseases are among the most important public health threats facing society."

(Mahy and Brown, 2000)

32. According to the author

(A) the effects of zoonoses on human beings have remained relatively consistent through human history

(B) zoonoses have had little effect on human activities

(C) zoonoses have often been the decisive factor in the extinction of civilizations

(D) the effects of zoonoses on human beings have varied considerably through human history

33. Which choice provides evidence for the answer to the previous question?

    (A) "Zoonotic . . . involved." (lines 6–8)
    (B) "The . . . zoonoses." (lines 22–28)
    (C) "Human . . . epiczootics." (lines 39–43)
    (D) "A myriad . . . types." (lines 71–75)

34. The author probably puts the word *new* in quotation marks (line 32) to show that

    (A) every appearance of a zoonosis involves an entirely new pathogen
    (B) experts have not been able to determine if any given recent zoonosis is different from previous ones
    (C) while a given zoonosis might be new to a particular geographic area, it is probably not new to Earth
    (D) zoonotic diseases are a relatively recent phenomenon in human history

35. The term *epizootics* as it is used in line 29 most nearly means

    (A) diseases harbored in humans that can be transmitted to animals
    (B) all diseases affecting animals
    (C) diseases in animals that occur at a greater than expected rate
    (D) epidemics that are caused by pathogens harbored in animals and transmitted to humans

36. According to the information provided in the passage, rabies

    (A) is maintained in nature by animals
    (B) affects only domesticated animals
    (C) is no longer a threat to human life
    (D) cannot be transmitted from an animal to a human

37. Which of the following is a reasonable inference that can be made from the information given in the passage?

    (A) Most new zoonoses are the result of the evolution of an entirely new pathogen.
    (B) Pathogens involved in a zoonosis never move outside their geographic area of origin.
    (C) The emergence of an entirely new pathogen that causes diseases in animals that can be transmitted to humans is relatively rare.
    (D) Scientists have been unable to identify the pathogens involved in most zoonoses.

38. The word *specter* as it is used in line 55 most nearly means

    (A) apparition
    (B) haunting image
    (C) effect
    (D) repetition

39. Which of the following could we reasonably infer to be one of the "ramifications for wildlife conservation" (lines 20–21)?

    (A) authorities acting to prohibit all but the most essential interactions between animals and humans
    (B) wildlife conservations coming to realize that eventually all vertebrates except humans will become extinct
    (C) authorities acting to outlaw the use of domestic animals to produce food for human consumption
    (D) biologists and other specialists more closely monitoring interactions between humans and animals

1   1   1

40. In the figure on page 108 the arrows indicate that

(A) all zoonoses move first from humans to domestic animals, then from domestic animals to wildlife, and finally from wildlife back to humans

(B) it cannot be determined whether pathogens in humans move to wildlife and domestic animals or vice versa

(C) zoonoses can move from any of the three categories of life shown to any other category

(D) zoonoses move in one direction (e.g., from humans to wildlife) while at the same time pathogens that cause them move in the other direction (e.g., from wildlife to humans)

41. Specialists interested in learning how zoonotic diseases are spread would probably be least interested in observing activities at

(A) zoos
(B) pet shops
(C) farms
(D) supermarkets

Questions 42–52 are based on the following passage.

The following passage is from Alexis de Tocqueville, *Democracy in America,* translated from French into English by Henry Reeve and originally published in 1835. Alexis de Tocqueville was a French writer and visitor to the United States.

I hold it to be a detestable maxim that, politically speaking, the people have a right to do anything; and yet I have asserted that all authority originates in the will of the majority. Am I,
(5) then, in contradiction with myself?

A general law, which bears the name of justice, has been made and sanctioned, not only by a majority of this or that people, but by a majority of mankind. The rights of every
(10) people are therefore confined within the limits of what is just. A nation may be considered as a jury which is empowered to represent society at large and to apply justice, which is its law. Ought such a jury, which represents society, to
(15) have more power than the society itself whose laws it executes?

When I refuse to obey an unjust law, I do not contest the right of the majority to command, but I simply appeal from the sovereignty of the
(20) people to the sovereignty of mankind. Some have not feared to assert that a people can never out step the boundaries of justice and reason in those affairs which are peculiarly its own; and that consequently full power may be given to
(25) the majority by which it is represented. But this is the language of a slave.

A majority taken collectively is only an individual, whose opinions, and frequently whose interests, are opposed to those of another indi-
(30) vidual, who is styled a minority. If it be admitted that a man possessing absolute power may misuse that power by wronging his adversaries, why should not a majority be liable to the same reproach? Men do not change their characters
(35) by uniting with one another; nor does their patience in the presence of obstacles increase

1   1   1

with their strength. I cannot believe it; the power to do everything, which I should refuse to one of my equals, I will never grant to any (40) number of them.

I do not think that, for the sake of preserving liberty, it is possible to combine several principles in the same government so as really to oppose them to one another. The form (45) of government that is usually termed mixed has always appeared to me a mere chimera. Accurately speaking, there is no such thing as a mixed government in the sense usually given to that word, because in all communities (50) some one principle of action may be discovered which preponderates over the others. England in the eighteenth century, which has been especially cited as an example of this sort of government, was essentially an aristocratic state, (55) although it comprised some great elements of democracy; for the laws and customs of the country were such that the aristocracy could not but preponderate in the long run and direct public affairs according to its own will.

(60) I am therefore of the opinion that social power superior to all others must always be placed somewhere; but I think that liberty is endangered when this power finds no obstacle which can retard its course and give it time to (65) moderate its own vehemence.

Unlimited power is in itself a bad and dangerous thing. Human beings are not competent to exercise it with discretion. There is no power on earth so worthy of honor in itself or (70) clothed with rights so sacred that I would admit its uncontrolled and all-predominant authority. When I see that the right and the means of absolute command are conferred on any power whatever, be it called a people or a king, an (75) aristocracy or a democracy, a monarchy or a republic, I say there is the germ of tyranny, and I seek to live elsewhere, under other laws.

The main evil of the present democratic institutions of the United States does not arise, (80) as is often asserted in Europe, from their weak-

ness, but from their irresistible strength. I am not so much alarmed at the excessive liberty which reigns in that country as at the inadequate securities which one finds there against (85) tyranny; if an individual or a party is wronged in the United States, to whom can he apply for redress? If to public opinion, public opinion constitutes the majority; if to the legislature, it represents the majority and implicitly obeys (90) it; if to the executive power, it is appointed by the majority and serves as a passive tool in its hands. The public force consists of the majority under arms; the jury is the majority invested with the right of hearing judicial cases; and in (95) certain states even the judges are elected by the majority. However iniquitous or absurd the measure of which you complain, you must submit to it as well as you can.

42. The word *sanctioned* as it is used in line 7 most nearly means

(A) disseminated
(B) tolerated
(C) penalized
(D) officially approved

43. The word *people* in line 8 refers to

(A) the members of a particular society
(B) all human beings
(C) the members of the ruling majority in a country
(D) various types of human beings

44. The author says, " The rights of . . . what is just" (lines 9–11). If this is true, then

(A) a person can do something unjust if a majority of people in his or her society approve of it
(B) human rights vary from society to society
(C) people do not have the right to do something unjust
(D) people who act unjustly have no human rights

45. According to the author

(A) it is possible for a majority to establish an unjust law
(B) what is decided by a majority in a society is always just
(C) what is just cannot be decided by human beings
(D) what is just can only be decided by the members of that society for that society

46. The word *principles* as it is used in line 43 most nearly means

(A) standards of proper behavior
(B) basic truths
(C) elements determining intrinsic nature and characteristic behavior
(D) fundamental assumptions

47. The author believes that "social power superior to all others must always be placed somewhere [in society]" (lines 60–62) because he thinks that

(A) every society is dominated by its aristocracy
(B) the majority in each society will decide where the dominant interest of the society lies
(C) every society is dominated by a single powerful interest group
(D) every society is unified around one dominant principle

48. Which choice provides the best evidence for the answer to the previous question?

(A) lines 20–23 ("Some . . . own.")
(B) lines 30–34 ("If . . . reproach?")
(C) lines 41–44 ("I . . . another.")
(D) lines 81–87 ("I . . . redress?")

49. The author believes that

(A) once superior power is placed in the hands of a single group, nothing will be able to limit its power
(B) to preserve freedom it is necessary for there to be some opposition to the dominant power group in a society
(C) individual liberty is not possible when a society is dominated by a single principle
(D) individual liberty is only possible when society is dominated by a powerful minority

50. The author makes use of all of the following *except*

(A) rhetorical questions
(B) analogies
(C) examples from history to support his argument
(D) citations of scholarly studies to support his argument

51. Based on what is stated in the passage, which of the following would the author be most likely to favor for the United States?

(A) election of the President by a majority of the popular vote
(B) election of all judges by popular vote
(C) abolition of the national army
(D) appointment of judges to life terms by a non-government body of respected lawyers, judges, and law professors

52. What would be the most appropriate title for this passage?

(A) The Decline of Freedom
(B) Tyranny by the Majority
(C) The Injustices of Democracy
(D) Democracy in Action

STOP   If there is still time remaining, you may review your answers.

2   2   2

WRITING AND LANGUAGE TEST

35 MINUTES, 44 QUESTIONS

TURN TO SECTION 2 OF YOUR ANSWER SHEET TO ANSWER THE QUESTIONS IN THIS SECTION.

> **DIRECTIONS:** Questions follow each of the passages below. Some questions ask you how the passage might be changed to improve the expression of ideas. Other questions ask you how the passage might be altered to correct errors in grammar, usage, and punctuation. One or more graphics accompany some passages. You will be required to consider these graphics as you answer questions about editing the passage.
>
> There are three types of questions. In the first type, a part of the passage is underlined. The second type is based on a certain part of the passage. The third type is based on the entire passage.
>
> Read each passage. Then, choose the answer to each question that changes the passage so that it is consistent with the conventions of standard written English. One of the answer choices for many questions is "NO CHANGE." Choosing this answer means that you believe the best answer is to make no change in the passage.

Questions 1–11 are based on the following passage and supplementary material.

Mercury Threatens Fish in National Parks

[1] The national park network in the United States ❶ is comprising some of the most pristine and sensitive wilderness in North America. [2] Additionally, variation (up to 20-fold) in site-specific fish THg concentrations within individual parks ❷ suggest that more intensive sampling in some parks will be required to effectively characterize Hg contamination in western national parks. [3] There is concern that via global distribution, Mercury (Hg) contamination could threaten the ecological ❸ virtue of aquatic communities in the parks and the wildlife that depends on it. [4] In this study, we examined Hg concentrations in non-migratory freshwater fish in 86 sites across 21 national parks in the Western United States. [5] Across all parks, sites, and

1. (A) NO CHANGE
   (B) is comprised of
   (C) is being comprised of
   (D) comprised of

2. (A) NO CHANGE
   (B) suggests
   (C) suggesting
   (D) having suggested

3. (A) NO CHANGE
   (B) morality
   (C) ethics
   (D) integrity

2   2   2

species, fish total Hg (THg) concentrations ranged from 9.9 to 1,109 nanograms per gram wet weight (ng/g ww) ❹ and this means 77.7 ng/g ww. [6] We found substantial variation in fish THg concentrations among and within parks, suggesting that patterns of Hg risk are driven by processes occurring at a combination of scales. ❺

Across all fish sampled, only 5 percent had THg concentrations exceeding a benchmark (200 ng/g ww) associated with ❻ malicious responses within the fish themselves. However, Hg concentrations in 35 percent of fish sampled were above a benchmark for risk to highly sensitive avian consumers (90 ng/g ww), and THg concentrations in 68 percent of fish sampled were above exposure levels recommended by the Great Lakes Advisory Group (50 ng/g ww) for unlimited consumption by ❼ humans: of the fish assessed for risk to human consumers (that is, species that are large enough to be consumed by recreational or subsistence anglers), only one individual fish from Yosemite National Park had a muscle Hg concentration exceeding the benchmark (950 ng/g ww) ❽ at which no human consumption is advised. Zion, Capital Reef, Wrangell-St. Elias, and Lake Clark National Parks all contained sites in which most fish exceeded benchmarks for the protection ❾ of human and wildlife health.

4. (A) NO CHANGE
   (B) by means of
   (C) with a mean of
   (D) in means of

5. For the sake of the cohesion of this paragraph, sentence 2 should be placed
   (A) where it is now
   (B) after sentence 3
   (C) after sentence 4
   (D) after sentence 6

6. (A) NO CHANGE
   (B) murderous
   (C) toxic
   (D) venomous

7. (A) NO CHANGE
   (B) humans; of
   (C) humans, of
   (D) humans. Of

8. (A) NO CHANGE
   (B) where it is advised no humans consume
   (C) which is advised for no human consumption
   (D) which advises no human consumption

9. (A) NO CHANGE
   (B) of human, and, wildlife health.
   (C) of: human and wildlife health.
   (D) of human and wildlife, health.

There were no consistent patterns in inter-annual variability across the 10 sites sampled over separate years. Significant differences in mean Hg concentrations were observed at 5 of 10 sites. Fish THg concentrations increased significantly from the first sampling to the second at two sites: **10** Sunup Lake and Center Basin Lake. Conversely, fish THg concentrations decreased significantly from the first sampling event to the second in three sites— **11** Lake Clark, Mirror Lake, and Ypsilon Lake.

10. Which choice most accurately represents the information in the graph?

(A) NO CHANGE

(B) Gladys Lake and Upper Lena Lake

(C) Sunup Lake and Nanita Lake

(D) Ypsilon Lake and Sunup Lake

11. Which choice most accurately represents the information in the graph?

(A) NO CHANGE

(B) Lake Clark, Poudre Lake, and Ypsilon Lake

(C) Upper Lena Lake, Poudre Lake, and Ypsilon Lake

(D) Upper Lena Lake, Mirror Lake, and Lake Clark

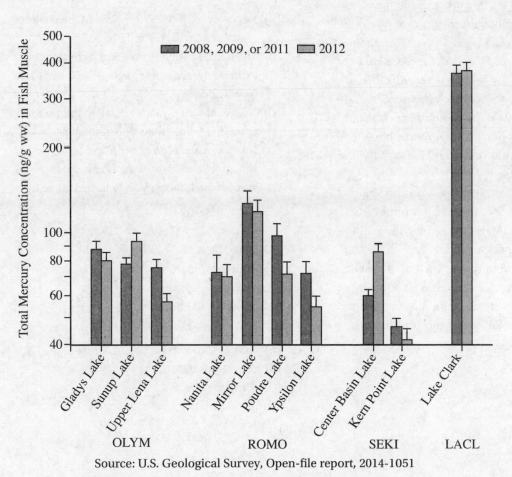

Source: U.S. Geological Survey, Open-file report, 2014-1051

Questions 12–22 are based on the following passage.

You're a What? Ornithologist

Ornithologists study birds in their natural habitats or in ⓵⓶ the underline{laboratory and it may also be that they} write research reports and proposals for grants, teach classes, present research to the ⓵⓷ underline{public while they have} administrative duties related to these activities.

⓵⓸ underline{Many questions about ornithology are best answered by observing birds in the wild during fieldwork.} Ornithologists and their students have done fieldwork in locations as remote as the Andes Mountains in South America and as nearby as the forests of southern Ohio and the ⓵⓹ underline{Midwest: fieldwork} usually involves surveying, or counting, birds and monitoring their nests. Fieldwork is where many ornithologists learn how to collect data for research. For example, they will watch and record different species foraging to discover where and what they eat. During fieldwork, ornithologists might also attach metal or plastic bands to a bird's leg to help identify individual birds and aid with survival estimates.

[1] Much of the research that ornithologists do is in the lab. [2] But not all ornithologists work outdoors. [3] For example, ⓵⓺ underline{feather collecting} during fieldwork are analyzed in the lab for a variety of purposes, including genetic mapping. [4] And some studies of migratory behavior or mate choice might involve observing birds in special cages. [5] Ornithologists

12. Select from the following the choice that forms two distinct sentences that make sense.

   (A) laboratory. Besides these things, they may write
   (B) laboratory. Besides, they may also write
   (C) laboratory. And, besides this, they may write
   (D) laboratory. They also may write

13. (A) NO CHANGE
   (B) public, and have
   (C) public, doing all this while having
   (D) public, when having

14. The writer is considering deleting the underlined sentence. Should the writer do this?

   (A) Yes, because it does not relate to the content of the paragraph it would be in.
   (B) Yes, because the information it contains is expressed later in the passage, so it would be redundant.
   (C) No, because it provides detailed information about fieldwork done by ornithologists.
   (D) No, because it is an appropriate topic sentence to introduce the second paragraph, which focuses on fieldwork done by ornithologists.

15. (A) NO CHANGE
   (B) Midwest, fieldwork
   (C) Midwest. Fieldwork
   (D) Midwest; fieldwork

16. (A) NO CHANGE
   (B) collections of feathers
   (C) feathers collected
   (D) feathers, having been collected

often write reports about their research or publish articles in scientific journals focused on biology, ecology, conservation, or **⑰** <u>managing wildlife</u>. [6] And ornithologists who do research also write grant proposals to seek funding for specific research. **⑱**

⑲ <u>Although they educate people</u> through writing about birds, ornithologists share their knowledge by teaching college courses. But education is not limited to teaching college students. Outreach activities **⑳** <u>did include</u> giving talks and making presentations to natural resources managers of government and other nonprofit organizations as well as to people in public interest groups, bird watching clubs, and schools.

Ornithologists need an advanced degree for most jobs. For most professional jobs, ornithologists need a master's degree that includes a research thesis. Those who want to develop their own research projects, work in high-level management positions, or teach at a university usually need a Ph.D. in **㉑** <u>a regimen</u> related to their work.

It is estimated that there are about 6,000 ornithologists employed in the United States. **㉒** <u>For statistics' purposes</u>, they are included among zoologists and wildlife biologists. Their median annual wage is $57,710.

17. (A) NO CHANGE
    (B) wildlife management
    (C) wildlife being managed
    (D) managed wildlife

18. For the sake of the cohesion of this paragraph, sentence 2 should be placed

    (A) where it is now
    (B) before sentence 1
    (C) before sentence 4
    (D) before sentence 6

19. (A) NO CHANGE
    (B) Whether they educate people
    (C) In addition to educating people
    (D) And if people are educated

20. (A) NO CHANGE
    (B) might include
    (C) including
    (D) included

21. (A) NO CHANGE
    (B) an instruction
    (C) a discipline
    (D) a preparation

22. (A) NO CHANGE
    (B) For statistical purposes,
    (C) For statistic purpose,
    (D) For purpose of a statistic

PRACTICE TEST 2

Questions 23–33 are based on the following passage.

Understanding Jainism

[1] The oldest continuous monastic tradition in India is Jainism, the path of the Jinas, or victors. [2] This tradition is traced to Vardhamana Mahavira (The Great Hero; ca. 599–527 B.C.), the twenty-fourth and last of the Tirthankaras (Sanskrit for fordmakers). [3] According to legend, Mahavira was born to a **㉓** family ruling in the town of Vaishali, located in the modern state of Bihar. [4] At the age of thirty, he **㉔** abdicated his wealthy life and devoted himself to fasting and self-mortification in order to purify his consciousness and discover the meaning of existence. [5] Following the example of the teacher Parshvanatha (ninth century B.C.), he attained enlightenment and spent the rest of his life meditating and teaching a dedicated group of disciples who formed a monastic order following rules **㉕** he lay down. [6] His life's work complete, he entered a final fast and deliberately died of starvation. [7] He never again dwelt in a house, owned property, **㉖** nor did he ever wear clothing of any sort. **㉗**

The ancient belief system of the Jains rests on a concrete understanding of the working of karma, **㉘** its effects on the living soul (jiva), and the conditions for extinguishing action and the soul's release. According to the Jain view, the soul is a living substance that combines with various kinds of nonliving matter and through action **㉙** accumulate particles of matter that adhere to it and determine its fate. Most of the matter perceptible to human senses, including all animals and plants, is attached in various degrees to living souls and is in this sense alive. Any action has conse-

23. (A) NO CHANGE
    (B) ruling family
    (C) a ruler family
    (D) a ruled family

24. (A) NO CHANGE
    (B) renounced
    (C) seceded from
    (D) defected from

25. (A) NO CHANGE
    (B) he had lain
    (C) he has lain
    (D) he laid

26. (A) NO CHANGE
    (B) nor did he wear
    (C) or wore
    (D) nor wore

27. For the sake of the cohesion of this paragraph, sentence 7 should be placed

    (A) where it is now
    (B) after sentence 2
    (C) after sentence 3
    (D) after sentence 4

28. (A) NO CHANGE
    (B) its affects on the
    (C) it effects the
    (D) its affecting the

29. (A) NO CHANGE
    (B) accumulates
    (C) accumulated
    (D) accumulating

2   2   2

quences that necessarily follow the embodied soul, but the worst accumulations of matter come from violence against other living beings. The ultimate Jain **30** discipline, therefore, rests on complete inactivity and absolute nonviolence (ahimsa) against any living beings. Some Jain monks and nuns wear face masks to avoid accidentally inhaling small organisms, and all practicing believers try to remain **31** vegetarians by extreme renunciation, including the refusal of all food, lies at the heart of a discipline that purges the mind and body of all desires and actions and, in the process, burns off the consequences of actions performed in the past. In this sense, Jain renunciants may recognize or **32** bolster deities, but they do not view the *Vedas as sacred texts and instead concentrate on the atheistic, individual quest for purification and removal of karma. The final goal is the extinguishing of self, a "blowing out" (nirvana) of the individual self. **33**

*The *Vedas* are the oldest scriptures of Hinduism.

30. The word *discipline* most nearly means

(A) a systematic method to obtain obedience
(B) punishment to correct undesirable behavior
(C) training that produces moral improvement
(D) a branch of learning

31. How should the underlined portions be rewritten?

(A) NO CHANGE
(B) vegetarians. Extreme renunciation, including
(C) vegetarians, extreme renunciation includes
(D) vegetarians. Extreme renunciation, and this includes

32. (A) NO CHANGE
(B) awe
(C) revere
(D) marvel

33. Which choice most effectively establishes the main topic of the paragraph?

(A) the religious beliefs and practices of Jainism
(B) the importance of vegetarianism in Jainism
(C) how the beliefs of Jainism changed throughout history
(D) the relationship between human beings and other living things

2   2   2

Questions 34–44 are based on the following passage.

What Is Civilization?

[1] To know what civilization is by study and observation is better than to rely upon a formal definition. [2] For instance, it may be used in a narrow sense to indicate the character and quality of the civil relations. [3] Those tribes or nations having a well-developed social order, with government, laws, and other fixed social **34** customs said to be civilized, while those peoples without these characters are assumed to be uncivilized. [4] It may also be considered in a somewhat different sense, when the arts, industries, sciences, and habits of life are stimulated—civilization **35** was determined by the degree in which these are developed. [5] Whichever view is accepted, it involves a contrast of present ideals with past ideals, of an undeveloped with a developed state of human progress. [6] For, indeed, the word is used in so many different ways that it admits of a loose interpretation. **36**

37 But whatever notion we have of civilization, it is difficult to draw a fixed line between civilized and uncivilized peoples. Lewis H. Morgan, in his *Ancient Society*, asserts that civilization began with the phonetic **38** alphabet. He says that all human activity prior to this could be classified as savagery or barbarism. But there is a broader conception of civilization which recognizes all phases of human achievement, from the making of a stone axe to the construction of the airplane; from the rude hut to the magnificent palace; from crude moral and religious conditions to the more

34. (A) NO CHANGE
(B) customs, and they are said to be civilized,
(C) customs, said civilized,
(D) customs are said to be civilized,

35. (A) NO CHANGE
(B) being
(C) is being
(D) has been

36. For the sake of the logic and cohesion of this paragraph, sentence 6 should be placed
(A) where it is now
(B) before sentence 4
(C) after sentence 4
(D) before sentence 2

37. The writer is considering deleting the underlined sentence. Should the writer do this?
(A) Yes, because it is unrelated to the ideas discussed in the second paragraph.
(B) Yes, because it contradicts what is said in the first paragraph.
(C) No, because it provides an appropriate link between the first and second paragraphs.
(D) No, because it provides one more definition of the word "civilization."

38. Which choice most effectively combines the sentences at the underlined portion?
(A) alphabet that is
(B) alphabet, and it is his opinion that
(C) alphabet and that
(D) alphabet, that is

2   2   2

refined conditions of ❸❾ humans in association. If we consider that civilization involves the whole process of human achievement, it must admit of a great variety of qualities and degrees of development; ❹⓿ hence it appears to be a relative term applied to the variation of human life. So we might say of the Chinese, the East Indians, and the American Indians, that they each have well-established customs, habits of thought, and standards of life, differing from other nations, ❹❶ which is expressing different types of civilization.

When a member of a primitive tribe invented the bow-and-arrow, ❹❷ or it began to chip a flint nodule in order to make a stone axe, civilization began. As soon as people began to cooperate with one another in obtaining food, building houses, or for protection against wild animals and wild ❹❸ men, that is when they began to treat each other civilly, they were becoming civilized. We may say then in reality that civilization has been a continuous process ❹❹ as the first beginning of man's conquest of himself and nature to the modern complexities of social life with its multitude of products of industry and cultural arts.

39. (A) NO CHANGE
    (B) humans associating
    (C) human association
    (D) association among humans

40. (A) NO CHANGE
    (B) furthermore
    (C) likewise
    (D) finally

41. (A) NO CHANGE
    (B) and that is expressing
    (C) expressed as
    (D) expressing

42. (A) NO CHANGE
    (B) or they began
    (C) or began
    (D) or were beginning

43. For the sake of clarity of meaning and effectiveness of expression, the underlined portion of the sentence should be rewritten as follows:

    (A) NO CHANGE
    (B) men, that is, when they began to treat each other civilly, they
    (C) men—that is, when they began to treat each other civilly—they
    (D) men that is when they began to treat each other civilly, they

44. (A) NO CHANGE
    (B) from the first beginning of man's conquest of himself and nature to
    (C) from the first beginning of man's conquest of himself within
    (D) during the first beginning of man's conquest of himself and nature beyond

STOP If there is still time remaining, you may review your answers.

PRACTICE TEST 2

MATH TEST (NO CALCULATOR)

25 MINUTES, 20 QUESTIONS

Turn to Section 3 of your answer sheet to answer the questions in this section.

DIRECTIONS: For questions 1–15, solve each problem and choose the best answer from the given options. Fill in the corresponding circle on your answer document. For questions 16–20, solve the problem and fill in the answer on the answer sheet grid. Please use scrap paper to work out your answers.

Notes:
- You **CANNOT** use a calculator on this section.
- All variables and expressions represent real numbers unless indicated otherwise.
- All figures are drawn to scale unless indicated otherwise.
- All figures are in a plane unless indicated otherwise.
- Unless indicated otherwise, the domain of a given function is the set of all real numbers x for which the function has real values.

REFERENCE INFORMATION

Area Facts	Volume Facts	Triangle Facts

$A = \ell w$

$A = \frac{1}{2} bh$

$A = \pi r^2$
$C = 2\pi r$

$V = \ell w h$

$V = \frac{4}{3}\pi r^3$

$V = \frac{1}{3}\pi r^2 h$

$V = \pi r^2 h$

$V = \frac{1}{3}\ell w h$

$a^2 + b^2 = c^2$

The arc of a circle contains 360°.
The arc of a circle contains 2π radians.
The sum of the measures of the angles in a triangle is 180°.

---

1. If $\dfrac{r-2}{6} = n$ and $n = 5$, what is the value of r?

   (A) 28
   (B) 30
   (C) 32
   (D) 42

2. If $i = \sqrt{-1}$, what is the value of $(5 + 3i)$ $+ (-4 + 7i)$?

   (A) $1 + 10i$
   (B) $9 + 10i$
   (C) $-41 + 2i$
   (D) $-1 - 5i$

3

3

3. Ted needs to purchase shirts and belts for the costumes in his school's play. He can buy s shirts and b belts but the quantity may not exceed 100 items. Which of the following inequalities represents the conditions of Ted's purchases?

(A) $s + b > 100$
(B) $s + b < 100$
(C) $s + b \leq 100$
(D) $sb \leq 100$

4. The total area of a right circular cone can be expressed as $TA = \pi rs + \pi r^2$ where TA is the total area, r is the radius of the base, and s is the slant height. Which of the following expresses s in terms of TA and r?

(A) $s = \frac{TA}{\pi r} - r$
(B) $s = TA(\pi r - r)$
(C) $s = (TA - r)\pi$
(D) $s = \frac{TA}{\pi r - r}$

5. What is the result when $3x^2 - 4x + 5$ is subtracted from $3x^3 - 13x + 4$?

(A) $3x^3 - 3x^2 - 9x - 1$
(B) $x^3 - 6x - 1$
(C) $x^5 - 4x^2 - 11$
(D) $3x^3 - 2x^2 - 6x - 9$

6. For what value(s) of x is the following expression undefined?
$$\frac{-5x^2y - 4xy}{6x^2 - 13x - 5}$$

(A) $-1, 5$
(B) 5
(C) $-\frac{1}{3}, \frac{5}{2}$
(D) $\frac{1}{3}, \frac{3}{2}$

7. Which of the following equations has the same x- and y-coordinates of the vertex as $y = 3(x - 4)(x + 6)$?

(A) $y = x^2 - 8x + 15$
(B) $y = 3(x^2 + 4x - 6)$
(C) $y = 3(x + 1)^2 - 75$
(D) $y = 3x^2 + 6x - 10$

8. An aquarium is in the shape of a right rectangular prism. The glass container has the following dimensions:

length: 3 feet
width: 2 feet

The water in the tank rises to a height of 1 foot. The water is poured into another aquarium that has the following dimensions:

length: 4 feet
width: 1 foot

If the water rises to a height of x feet in the second aquarium, what is the value of x?

(A) 1 foot
(B) 1.5 feet
(C) 2 feet
(D) 2.5 feet

9. Which of the following equations represents a line that is parallel to the line with equation
$$y = \frac{3}{2}x - \frac{7}{4}?$$

(A) $6x + 4y = 8$
(B) $-6x + 4y = 11$
(C) $x - 2y = -4$
(D) $3x + 2y = 7$

10. $n = 3.65 + .35x$

$m = 4.25 + .15x$

In the equations above, m and n represent the heights of bamboo plants, in feet, x weeks after September 15. What was the height of the two plants when their heights were equal?

(A) 1.5

(B) 3.0

(C) 4.7

(D) 4.8

11. $\dfrac{3i}{2 - i}$

If the expression above is written in the form $a + bi$, where a and b are real numbers, what is the value of a? (Note $i = \sqrt{-1}$)

(A) -6

(B) $\dfrac{6}{5}$

(C) $-\dfrac{3}{5}$

(D) $\dfrac{5}{3}$

12. The function g is defined by $g(x) = 2x^2 + 15x - 8$. The x-coordinate of the vertex of the graph is contained within which of the following intervals?

(A) $-\dfrac{1}{2} < x < 8$

(B) $-2 < x < 2$

(C) $-3.65 < x < -2$

(D) $-4 < x < 6$

13. $h(x) = bx^2 + 30$

For the function h defined above, b is a constant and $h(6) = 138$. What is the value of $h(-4)$?

(A) 24

(B) 64

(C) 78

(D) 86

14. $\sqrt{2x} = x - 4$

What value(s) of x satisfy the equation above?

I. 8

II. 2

III. Both 8 and 2

(A) I only

(B) II only

(C) I and II

(D) Neither value satisfies the equation.

15. $P = -1.6x^2 + 2.6xy - 11.4$

The equation above represents a profit function used by an event coordinator at a city museum. In the equation, P represents profit earned, x represents paid admissions ($x > 0$), and y is any rental discount that is offered. Which of the following represents y in terms of x and P?

(A) $y = \dfrac{1.6xP + 11.4}{2.6x}$

(B) $y = \dfrac{P + 1.6x^2 + 11.4}{2.6x}$

(C) $y = \dfrac{1.6x^2 - 11.4}{2.6x}$

(D) $y = \dfrac{P \pm \sqrt{2.6x}}{11.4}$

Grid-in Response Directions

In questions 16–20, first solve the problem, and then enter your answer on the grid provided on the answer sheet. The instructions for entering your answers follow.

- First, write your answer in the boxes at the top of the grid.
- Second, grid your answer in the columns below the boxes.
- Use the fraction bar in the first row or the decimal point in the second row to enter fractions and decimals.

- Grid only one space in each column.
- Entering the answer in the boxes is recommended as an aid in gridding but is not required.
- The machine scoring your exam can read only what you grid, so you **must grid-in your answers correctly to get credit**.
- If a question has more than one correct answer, grid-in only one of them.
- The grid does not have a minus sign; so no answer can be negative.
- A mixed number *must* be converted to an improper fraction or a decimal before it is gridded.

  Enter $1\frac{1}{4}$ as $\frac{5}{4}$ or 1.25; the machine will interpret 11/4 as $\frac{11}{4}$ and mark it wrong.

- **All decimals must be entered as accurately as possible**. Here are three acceptable ways of gridding

$$\frac{3}{11} = 0.272727\ldots$$

- Note that rounding to .273 is acceptable because you are using the full grid, but you would receive **no credit** for .3 or .27, because they are less accurate.

3

3

16. A line passes through the points $(x, 6)$ and $(9, 0)$. If the slope of the line connecting the two points is $\frac{2}{3}$, what is the value of x?

17. Jerry has joined a gymnasium for which he pays dues of $75 each month, plus a daily rate of $10 for each day that he uses the facilities. The function shown below can be used to determine the cost in dollars per month for being a member of this club.

$f(d) = 75 + 10d$, where d is the number of days

Jerry spent $155 in January, $195 in February, and $225 in March. If he spent a total of $850 for the months of January, February, March, and April, what was the total number of days that he spent at the club for those four months?

18. Two sides of a triangle are 7 and 11 inches. If a third side of the triangle is also an integer, what is the product of the smallest and largest values that the side could be?

19. In triangle ABC, the measure of angle B is $90°$, $BC = 80$, and $AC = 100$. Triangle DEF is similar to triangle ABC where vertices D, E, and F correspond with vertices A, B, and C. The scale factor of triangle DEF to triangle ABC is $\frac{1}{10}$. What is the value of $\cos D$?

20. A customer at the produce section of a food store bought cucumbers and heads of lettuce. The quantity she purchased of the heads of lettuce was 6 fewer than 5 times the number of cucumbers. If cucumbers cost $.30 each and a head of lettuce costs $.70 and her cost was $7.20, how many cucumbers did she buy?

STOP   If there is still time remaining, you may review your answers.

4   4

MATH TEST (CALCULATOR)

55 MINUTES, 38 QUESTIONS

Turn to Section 4 of your answer sheet to answer the questions in this section.

DIRECTIONS: For questions 1–30, solve each problem and choose the best answer from the given options. Fill in the corresponding circle on your answer document. For questions 31–38, solve the problem and fill in the answer on the answer sheet grid. Please use scrap paper to work out your answers.

Notes:
- The **use of** a calculator on this section IS permitted.
- All variables and expressions represent real numbers unless indicated otherwise.
- All figures are drawn to scale unless indicated otherwise.
- All figures are in a plane unless indicated otherwise.
- Unless indicated otherwise, the domain of a given function is the set of all real numbers x for which the function has real values.

REFERENCE INFORMATION

Area Facts

$A = \ell w$

$A = \frac{1}{2} bh$

$A = \pi r^2$

$C = 2\pi r$

Volume Facts

$V = \ell w h$

$V = \pi r^2 h$

$V = \frac{4}{3} \pi r^3$

$V = \frac{1}{3} \pi r^2 h$

$V = \frac{1}{3} \ell w h$

Triangle Facts

$a^2 + b^2 = c^2$

The arc of a circle contains 360°.
The arc of a circle contains 2π radians.
The sum of the measures of the angles in a triangle is 180°.

Questions 1 and 2 refer to the following information.

A graphic novelist earns income directly proportional to the number of books she sells. Her income at a recent book signing was $1,320 when 800 books were sold.

1. What would be the income for the novelist at a show in which she sold 12,000 books?

(A) $1,140
(B) $1,980
(C) $19,800
(D) $21,080

4   4

2. The graphic novelist has to pay certain expenses, called overhead, on all of her sales. The amount of the overhead costs is 32% of the income she earns from book sales. After she pays her overhead costs, what would be her income on sales of 5,000 books?

(A) $2,640
(B) $5,610
(C) $7,610
(D) $7,620

3. In a linear function $f(4) = 6$ and $f(-2) = 14$. What is the value of $f(9)$?

(A) $\frac{20}{3}$
(B) $\frac{2}{3}$
(C) $-\frac{2}{3}$
(D) -3

4. The average (arithmetic mean) of $2x - 4$, $x + 4$, and $3x - 6$ is $x + 4$. What is the value of $-2x + 3$?

(A) -9
(B) -6
(C) 6
(D) 12

5. Shelley is a salesperson for a local furniture store. She receives a $24.00 commission for every recliner she sells and $63.00 for every dinette set. If Shelley sells r dinette sets and d recliners during a work shift, which expression represents her pay for that day?

(A) $63r + 24d$
(B) $24r + 63d$
(C) $24r - 63d$
(D) $63r - 24d$

6. Ephraim has two summer jobs. The first, as a delivery person, pays $11.50 per hour. Ephraim's second job, as a math tutor, pays $15.00 per hour. He wants to work no more than 20 hours per week, and he wants to earn at least $270.00 weekly. If x and y represent the hours he works as a delivery person and as a tutor, respectively, which system of inequalities correctly models the situation?

(A) $x + y < 20$
$11.50x + 15y > 270$

(B) $x + y \leq 20$
$11.50x + 15y \geq 270$

(C) $x + y > 20$
$11.50x + 15y \leq 270$

(D) $x + y \geq 270$
$11.50x + 15y \leq 20$

7. If $n > 0$ then n^2 is

(A) greater than n
(B) equal to n
(C) less than n
(D) there is not enough information to solve this problem.

8. $y = x^2 + 2x - 24$

The equation above represents a parabola in the xy-plane. Which of the following equations below shows the x-intercepts of the parabola as constants or coefficients?

(A) $y - 24 = x(x + 2)$
(B) $y = (x + 1)^2 - 25$
(C) $y = (x + 6)(x - 4)$
(D) $y = x(x + 2) - 24$

PRACTICE TEST 2

4

 4

9. A fabric warehouse manager has found that for every 500 square yards of fabric in stock, 13 square yards cannot be sold due to defects. If a recent shipment contained 273 square yards of defective fabric, how many square yards were in the entire shipment?

(A) 10,000
(B) 10,500
(C) 11,000
(D) 23,500

Questions 10 and 11 refer to the graph below.

A botanist was exploring the impact a local red ant population had on local nurseries. An experiment was devised to investigate any correlation between red ant populations and the annual yield of white roses. A scatter plot of the data is shown below.

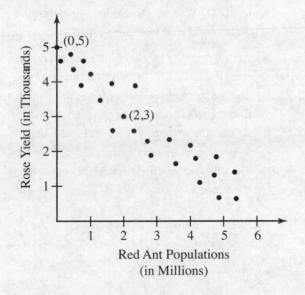

10. A line of best fit is constructed within the data. Which of the following functions best models the data?

(A) $f(x) = -4.88x + 4.66$
(B) $f(x) = 1.15x + 7.88$
(C) $f(x) = 1.27x + 4.88$
(D) $f(x) = -1.14x + 4.88$

11. A grower uses a pesticide that will reduce the ant population by 60%. If the grower currently has five million ants, which of the following is the closest to his rose yield after using the pesticide?

(A) 1,000
(B) 1,800
(C) 3,000
(D) 4,200

Questions 12 and 13 refer to the table below.

Table of the Seven Lightest Chemical Elements (by atomic mass)

Atomic Mass	Name of Chemical Element	Symbol	Atomic Number
1.0079	Hydrogen	H	1
4.0026	Helium	He	2
6.941	Lithium	Li	3
9.0122	Beryllium	Be	4
10.811	Boron	B	5
12.0107	Carbon	C	6
14.0067	Nitrogen	N	7

12. Which element is approximately equal to the sum of the weights of Helium and Lithium?

(A) Nitrogen
(B) Boron
(C) Beryllium
(D) Lithium

13. Which element is about 30% more massive than Lithium?

(A) Nitrogen
(B) Boron
(C) Beryllium
(D) Hydrogen

14. The equation of a circle is shown below.

$x^2 + y^2 - 6y + 4x = 36$

What is the circumference of this circle?

(A) 49π

(B) 36π

(C) 14π

(D) 12π

15. Sammie has done a survey of one hundred 16-year-old Florida students and found that 84% favored including an internship in their schools' curricula. She finds, however, that the margin of error in her survey is 6.9%. What can she do to reduce the margin of error?

(A) check similar surveys in other states

(B) reduce the survey size

(C) increase the survey size

(D) survey other age groups as well

16. The function g is defined by $g(x) = 2x^3 - 8x^2 - bx + 140$. In the xy plane, the graph of g intersects the x-axis at (2, 0), (−5, 0), and (m, 0). What is the value of b?

(A) −44

(B) 4

(C) 31

(D) 62

17. The standard form of an ellipse with major axis $2a$ in the xy-plane is $\dfrac{x^2}{a^2} + \dfrac{y^2}{b^2} = 1$. Which of the following expresses x in terms of y, a, and b?

(A) $x = \dfrac{(ab)^2}{y - x}$

(B) $x = \pm\sqrt{a^2 + b^2 - y^2}$

(C) $x = a^2 + b^2 - y^2$

(D) $x = \pm\dfrac{\sqrt{a^2b^2 - a^2y^2}}{b}$

18. Even though she is only twenty-seven years old, Cheryl is interested in beginning a retirement plan. The graph above shows the value of a market fund investment compared to a Certificate of Deposit (CD). Which of the following **cannot** be concluded by Cheryl from the graph?

(A) At one year, the market fund is worth more than the CD.

(B) The market fund shows exponential growth and the CD shows linear growth.

(C) At a point between years 1 and 2, the two funds have the same value.

(D) The initial investment in each account was the same.

19. Which of the following is a step in solving the equation $\sqrt{x - 7} = x - 7$?

(A) $x - 7 = x - 7$

(B) $2x = 14$

(C) $(x - 8)(x - 7) = 0$

(D) $(x + 7)(x - 6) = 0$

20. A game spinner has four colors equally spaced: red, green, blue, and yellow. What is the probability that a single, six-sided die will land on a prime number followed by a spin of yellow or blue?

(A) $\frac{1}{4}$

(B) $\frac{1}{9}$

(C) $\frac{1}{12}$

(D) $\frac{1}{36}$

21. Gold has always been coveted for its aesthetic qualities. However, due to its malleability, it also has many industrial and electronic applications. Gold can be stretched so thinly that a single ounce can cover 100 square yards of surface. How many square feet can be covered with 2.5 ounces of gold?

(A) 2,250 square feet

(B) 1,125 square feet

(C) 750 square feet

(D) 150 square feet

22.

Number of Cans per Student	Frequency
8	14
9	16
10	7
11	7
12	8
13	5
14	2

At Santa Fe Elementary School, the 59 students in 4th grade participated in a canned food drive. The table above shows the number of cans contributed by each student. Which number of cans contains the median of this data set?

(A) 11

(B) 10

(C) 9

(D) 8

23. A learning therapist has shown that students can increase reading levels by increasing required summer reading. She models the increase using the formula $y = 1.09x + .17$, where x represents the current grade reading level and y represents the improvement after the program. Which of the following represents the meaning of 1.09 in the equation?

(A) the difference between the students who use the program and those who do not

(B) the increase in the number of students using the reading program

(C) the increase in the reading level plus a constant of .17

(D) a 17% increase in reading level

Questions 24 and 25 refer to the information provided in the table below.

Rank	Country	GDP–per capita (US$)
1	Liechtenstein	141,100
2	Qatar	104,300
3	Luxembourg	81,100
4	Bermuda	69,900
5	Monaco	63,400
6	Singapore	60,500
7	Jersey	57,000
8	Falkland Islands (Islas Malvinas)	55,400
9	Norway	54,200
10	Brunei	50,000

The Gross Domestic Product (GDP) is a measure of a country's wealth. The per-capita income for a country is found by dividing the sum of all of the goods and services that a country produces by the country's population.

4

4

24. Which country exceeded the per capita income of Singapore by approximately 4.8%?

(A) Qatar

(B) Monaco

(C) Bermuda

(D) Norway

25. In 2014, the GDP of Singapore was $298,000,000,000. Which of the following is the best approximation of the size of Singapore's population?

(A) 493,000

(B) 874,000

(C) 4,900,000

(D) 6,100,000

	10th	11th
Female	17	18
Male	18	20

26. One lucky student at Bristol High School will be selected to attend a College for Kids camp at Johns Hopkins University. The table above represents the number of students in the 10th and 11th grades at the school. If a student is selected at random, what is the probability that the student will be in 10th grade or a male?

(A) .753

(B) .521

(C) .479

(D) .472

27. A great circle of a sphere contains the sphere's center. If the volume of a sphere is 374 cubic inches, what is the circumference of a great circle on that sphere? (Use $\pi = 3.14$)

(A) 4.47

(B) 28.07

(C) 56.14

(D) 62.74

Question 28 refers to the information below.

The half-life of an element is the amount of time that elapses until a certain mass of an element or compound decays to one-half its initial amount.

$$A = R_0\left(\frac{1}{2}\right)^x$$

28. A certain compound's half-life can be approximated using the equation above where

R_0 = the initial amount of the compound

A = the amount remaining after x years

x = the time elapsed in years

If 125 grams of the compound is left to decay over 2.3 years, how many grams will remain?

(A) 16.7

(B) 25.4

(C) 29.6

(D) 41.1

29. Twenty-one students entered into a foul shooting contest in basketball. Each student was given five foul shots to attempt. The table below lists the number of foul shots made and the number of students who made that many foul shots.

Successful Foul Shots	Frequency
0	2
1	4
2	4
3	7
4	3
5	1

If a student who successfully shot at least two foul shots was chosen at random, what is the probability that he/she successfully shot exactly 4 foul shots?

(A) $\frac{1}{7}$

(B) $\frac{1}{5}$

(C) $\frac{2}{5}$

(D) $\frac{3}{5}$

Question 30 refers to the system of equations below.

30. $4a + n = 2a - 3$
    $4b + m = 2b - 3$

If n is m plus 1, which of the following is true?

(A) a is b minus $\frac{1}{2}$

(B) a is b plus $\frac{1}{2}$

(C) a is b plus 1

(D) a is b minus 2

Grid-in Response Directions

In questions 31–38, first solve the problem, and then enter your answer on the grid provided on the answer sheet. The instructions for entering your answers follow.

- First, write your answer in the boxes at the top of the grid.
- Second, grid your answer in the columns below the boxes.
- Use the fraction bar in the first row or the decimal point in the second row to enter fractions and decimals.

- Grid only one space in each column.
- Entering the answer in the boxes is recommended as an aid in gridding but is not required.
- The machine scoring your exam can read only what you grid, so you **must grid-in your answers correctly to get credit**.
- If a question has more than one correct answer, grid-in only one of them.
- The grid does not have a minus sign; so no answer can be negative.
- A mixed number *must* be converted to an improper fraction or a decimal before it is gridded.

    Enter $1\frac{1}{4}$ as $\frac{5}{4}$ or 1.25; the machine will interpret 11/4 as $\frac{11}{4}$ and mark it wrong.

- **All decimals must be entered as accurately as possible**. Here are three acceptable ways of gridding

$$\frac{3}{11} = 0.272727\ldots$$

- Note that rounding to .273 is acceptable because you are using the full grid, but you would receive **no credit** for .3 or .27, because they are less accurate.

31. It's the end of the school year and a tenth grade civics class is planning a barbecue to celebrate. The class has drinks and desserts but needs to plan the number of hamburgers it needs to buy. Hamburger patties are sold in packages of six hamburgers. Hamburger rolls come in packages of eight rolls. What is the smallest number of hamburgers that should be purchased to have no rolls left over from a package?

32. A World History class recently took its mid-term exam. The following table represents the array of scores.

		X	X	
		X	X	
X		X	X	
X	X	X	X	X
20%	**40%**	**60%**	**80%**	**100%**

If a thirteenth student took the exam the next day, what must that score be to arrive at a class mean score of 60%?

33. $2(2x^2 - 7.5x + 3) - (-4x^2 + 2x - 7)$

If the expression above is written in the form of $ax^2 + bx + c$, what is the value of $a + b + c$?

34. In a circle with center P, central angle MPN has a measure of $\frac{3\pi}{4}$ radians. The area of the sector formed by the central angle MPN is what fraction of the circle?

35. Cindy owns a candy store and sells individual candies as well as mixes. Her most popular mixture is the chocolate and mint collection. The ratio of chocolates to mints in this candy mix is 3 to 5. If she is mixing 7 pounds of the mix, how many pounds are chocolates?

36. $\frac{1}{3}c = 6$

$b - \frac{2}{3}c = -6$

The system of equations has solution (b, c). What is the value of b?

Questions 37 and 38 refer to the information provided below.

The sum of the measures of the interior angles of a polygon can be found by using the formula $(n - 2)(180)$ where n is the number of angles.

37. If the sum of the measures of a regular polygon is $1,260°$, what is the degree measure of one interior angle? (Note: Ignore the degrees symbol.)

38. A regular polygon has a side that measures 11 inches. If an **exterior** angle of the figure measures $45°$, what is the measure in inches of the perimeter of the polygon?

ANSWER KEY
Practice Test 2

Section 1: Reading

1. C	14. C	27. A	40. C
2. D	15. D	28. D	41. D
3. C	16. D	29. C	42. D
4. B	17. C	30. A	43. A
5. B	18. B	31. A	44. C
6. B	19. A	32. D	45. A
7. C	20. C	33. B	46. C
8. D	21. A	34. C	47. C
9. A	22. C	35. D	48. C
10. C	23. B	36. A	49. B
11. A	24. A	37. C	50. D
12. A	25. C	38. B	51. D
13. B	26. D	39. D	52. B

Number Correct   _____

Number Incorrect   _____

Section 2: Writing and Language

1. B	12. D	23. B	34. D
2. B	13. B	24. B	35. B
3. D	14. D	25. D	36. D
4. C	15. C	26. C	37. C
5. D	16. C	27. D	38. C
6. C	17. B	28. A	39. C
7. D	18. B	29. B	40. A
8. A	19. C	30. C	41. D
9. A	20. B	31. B	42. C
10. A	21. C	32. C	43. C
11. C	22. B	33. A	44. B

Number Correct   _____

Number Incorrect   _____

ANSWER KEY
Practice Test 2

Section 3: Math (No Calculator)

1. **C**	5. **A**	9. **B**	13. **C**
2. **A**	6. **C**	10. **C**	14. **A**
3. **C**	7. **C**	11. **C**	15. **B**
4. **A**	8. **B**	12. **D**	

16. **18**   17. **55**   18. **85**

19. **3/5 or .6**   20. **3**

    or

Number Correct _____

Number Incorrect _____

ANSWER KEY
Practice Test 2

Section 4: Math (With Calculator)

1. **C**	7. **D**	13. **C**	19. **C**	25. **C**
2. **B**	8. **C**	14. **C**	20. **A**	26. **A**
3. **C**	9. **B**	15. **C**	21. **A**	27. **B**
4. **A**	10. **D**	16. **D**	22. **C**	28. **B**
5. **A**	11. **C**	17. **D**	23. **C**	29. **B**
6. **B**	12. **B**	18. **A**	24. **B**	30. **A**

31. **24** 32. **40** 33. **4**

34. **3/8 or .375**

or

ANSWER KEY
Practice Test 2

35. **21/8 or 2.62 or 2.63**

or

or

36. **6**

37. **140**

38. **88**

Number Correct _____

Number Incorrect _____

SCORE ANALYSIS

Reading and Writing Test

Section 1: Reading   _____ = _____ (A)
                            # correct   raw score

Section 2: Writing   _____ = _____ (B)
                            # correct   raw score

To find your Reading and Writing test scores, consult the chart below; find the ranges in which your raw scores lie and read across to find the ranges of your test scores.

_____ + _____ = _____ (C)
   range of Reading   range of Writing   range of Reading + Writing
     test scores   test scores   test scores

To find the range of your Reading and Writing Scaled Score, multiply (C) by 10.

Test Scores for the Reading and Writing Sections

Reading Raw Score	Writing Raw Score	Test Score
44–52	39–44	35–40
36–43	33–38	31–34
30–35	28–32	28–30
24–29	22–27	24–27
19–23	17–21	21–23
14–18	13–16	19–20
9–13	9–12	16–18
5–8	5–8	13–15
less than 5	less than 5	10–12

Math Test

Section 3:   _____ = _____ (D)
                   # correct   raw score

Section 4:   _____ = _____ (E)
                   # correct   raw score

Total Math raw score: (D) + (E) = _____

To find your Math Scaled Score, consult the chart below; find the range in which your raw score lies and read across to find the range for your scaled score.

Scaled Scores for the Math Test

Raw Score	Scaled Score	Raw Score	Scaled Score
50–58	700–800	20–25	450–490
44–49	650–690	15–19	400–440
38–43	600–640	11–14	350–390
32–37	550–590	7–10	300–340
26–31	500–540	less than 7	200–290

Answer Explanations

Section 1: Reading Test

1. **(C)** In lines 7–9 the narrator says, "It [the violin] was the sole item that exuded an air of foreignness. . . ." In lines 11–12, it is described as a "strange object" in the eyes of the villagers. The headman "[holds] his nose over the sound holes and sniffed long and hard" (lines 25–26), but the villagers have no idea what it is until the headman strums a few strings and the violin produces a sound. The only term the villagers have for the violin is "toy." Choice (B) is too positive to describe the villagers' attitude to the violin; they are suspicious of it.

2. **(D)** The narrator says that the violin was the only item Luo and he had that "exuded an air of . . . civilization, and therefore aroused suspicion" (lines 7–9). We can infer from this that the narrator regards the villagers as uncivilized.

3. **(C)** After examining the violin thoroughly, the headman concludes that it's a toy. The narrator says, "This verdict left us speechless" (line 33). The narrator says, "Things were not looking good" (lines 34–35) because he knows that the villagers, as loyal Communists, would regard them as bourgeois.

4. **(B)** In context, *coolly* means "calmly." Earlier the narrator said that Luo spoke to the headman "as casually as he could" (line 59).

5. **(B)** We can infer from their comments and behavior that the villagers see themselves as loyal Communists, which means they follow Communist ideology and condemn bourgeois (middle class) values and pastimes, such as playing Western music, as decadent. Thus, the villagers would see it as an honor to be the person who destroys a symbol of bourgeois decadence. The sentence "We looked like . . . Communist farm workers" (lines 43–46) strongly suggests that the villagers are Communists and that the narrator and Luo are "reactionary" (the latter suggests they are bourgeois). Further clues are that the headman condemns the violin as "a bourgeois toy" (lines 48–49) and that the narrator describes the headman as "the vigilant Communist" (lines 81–82).

6. **(B)** In light of what happens after Luo winks at the narrator, we can infer that Luo winked at the narrator to indicate that he had a plan and that the narrator should follow it. Evidently, Luo's plan was to announce that the narrator would play "a Mozart sonata" (lines 68–69) and then say that the sonata was called *Mozart is Thinking of Chairman Mao*.

7. **(C)** The narrator says he was "puzzled" (line 67) by Luo's wink, but he nevertheless takes his violin and tunes it. This suggests he trusts his friend to act intelligently and responsibly even though the narrator does not know what his friend is planning to do.

8. **(D)** We can infer this because we know that the narrator realizes that he and Luo are in a tense, dangerous situation in which they are dependent on the headman.

9. **(A)** Parody is not used in the passage. (B) There is a lot of description of details—for example, "his calloused fingertips" (line 31). (C) Tension is built up until the climax at the end of the passage. (D) There are several similes—for example, "Mozart's phrases came flooding back to me like so many faithful friends" (lines 102–103).

10. **(C)** The narrator says that Luo was only eighteen years old when the events recounted in the passage occurred. It can be inferred that when Luo lights a cigarette and smokes it while the narrator plays the violin for the villagers he is feeling satisfied with the successful outcome of his daring plan. The fact that the narrator describes Luo as smoking "quietly, like a man"

suggests that he has just undergone an experience that made him more mature and that he is aware that he has become more mature.

11. **(A)** The assertion is about a matter of fact, and thus historical evidence would strengthen the assertion. Examples of this attitude on the part of artists and writers could be given.

12. **(A)** We can infer that the writer does not think that artists and writers would have contempt for commercial activity that is forced upon a person or that is necessary for their survival.

13. **(B)** The phrase "this sentiment" (line 11) refers to the "exasperation" (line 10) of artists and writers with highly commercial society. *Philistinism* (line 10)—*an attitude of smug ignorance and conventionalism toward artistic and cultural values*—neatly describes the attitude that artists and writers found exasperating.

14. **(C)** In context, *decisive* (line 27) means "having the power to decide." The author is explaining that in commercial society the tastes of common people are the most influential ones in determining the prevailing tastes of a society.

15. **(D)** In lines 5–8 ("And since . . . over all others . . .") we are told that bourgeois society was the first in which the "commercial ethos" was dominant, so we can infer that the author is discussing a time at which the society was becoming more commercial. In lines 15–17 we are told that "[commercial society] did (and does) deprive [artists and writers] of the status that they naturally feel themselves entitled to."

16. **(D)** The author is concerned mainly with describing the attitudes of artists and writers and their place in bourgeois society. In lines 22–25 he says, "A commercial society, a society whose civilization is shaped by market transactions, is always likely to reflect the appetites and preferences of common men and women." He does not express a view on whether this was a favorable or unfavorable development. His main concern is to describe its effect on artists and writers.

17. **(C)** The author says, "The popularity of romanticism in the century after 1750 testifies to this fact, as the artists led an 'inner emigration' of the spirit—which, however, left the actual world unchanged" (lines 37–41).

18. **(B)** Lines 37–41 ("The . . . unchanged") provide the best evidence. The author says that the activities of artists embracing romanticism did not affect the "actual world."

19. **(A)** The phrase "social force" refers to anything that affects the nature of society. According to the author, socialists believed that the creation of great material abundance would mean that the demand for goods and services, ("appetite," line 63) would no longer affect the nature of society.

20. **(C)** In context, *disinterestedly* means "impartially, not motivated by self-interest." The author is saying that one of the reasons that "scientific socialism" (line 60) is an appealing ideology to intellectuals is that it supports their belief that they are not exercising control over others because they enjoy power or prestige but because they want to help "mobilize the masses for their own ultimate self-transformation" (lines 79–80).

21. **(A)** "Fault lines" is a term in geology that refers to the place where two tectonic plates meet. The use of the term to refer to civilizations compares civilizations to continental plates, suggesting that, like continental plates, civilizations are distinct entities that sometimes collide, causing conflict between them.

22. **(C)** We can infer that the author uses the word *basic* to mean "fundamental" because immediately after the sentence in which he uses the word, he describes differences among civilizations that, in his view, determine the essential nature of civilizations: "Civilizations are differentiated . . . equality and hierarchy" (lines 12–21). Also, in line 24 he refers to the differences as "fundamental."

23. **(B)** The author says, "Civilizations are differentiated from each other by history, language, culture, tradition and, *most important, religion*" (lines 12–14) and "[These differences] are far more fundamental than differences among political ideologies . . ." (lines 23–25). We can infer from this that the author believes that most people identify more strongly with their religion than with their political party.

24. **(A)** The author is arguing that what he considers the most fundamental differences among civilizations (as described in lines 12–21; "Civilizations are differentiated . . . equality and hierarchy") have "over the centuries . . . generated the most prolonged and the most violent conflicts" (lines 27–30). Since the passage is mainly concerned with the cause of future conflict, it is reasonable to suppose that the author would consider the most important implication of the statement to be that differences among civilizations rather than differing political ideologies will cause serious future conflict in the world.

25. **(C)** The author says, "The interactions between peoples of different civilizations are increasing; these interactions intensify civilization consciousness and awareness of differences between civilizations and commonalities within civilizations" (lines 32–37). In lines 37–40 the author says, "Enhanced civilization-consciousness of people, in turn, invigorates differences and animosities stretching or thought to stretch back deep into history." From this information we can infer that the author would be very likely to agree that the increased large movements of large numbers of people belonging to different civilizations from one civilization to another has increased the likelihood of conflict between civilizations.

26. **(D)** The author says, "The processes of economic modernization and social change throughout the world are separating people from longstanding local identities. . . . In much of the world religion has moved in to fill this gap . . . . In most countries and most religions the people active in fundamentalist movements are young, college-educated, middle-class technicians, professionals, and business persons" (lines 41–54).

27. **(A)** The author of Passage 2 believes Raymond Aron's statement is correct because he agrees with Aron that although culture and civilization are important to people and play a part in determining events in the international arena, nation-states play the decisive role in determining such events.

28. **(D)** The author's main argument is that "It is willful, day-to-day, crisis-to-crisis, war-to-war political decision-making by nation-state units that remains the single most identifiable determinant of events in the international arena" (lines 94–98). In this context, the statement in lines 92–94 is most accurately described as a "partial concession" to Huntington's argument that politics, regimes, and ideologies are determined by culture, history, and civilization. The author says Huntington's argument is true "*to an extent*" (line 94), a statement that can be described as a partial concession to Huntington's argument.

29. **(C)** In context, *vital* means "full of energy." The author is explaining his view that political rather than cultural and historical factors have the most important role in determining events in "the world area." Thus, it makes sense that he describes the cultural and historical factors as less full of energy.

30. **(A)** The author of Passage 1 does not argue that *all* conflict is at present caused by conflicts between civilizations or that this will be true in the future. He argues that "the world will be shaped *in large measure* by the interactions among seven or eight major civilizations" (lines 2–4) and that "the most important conflicts of the future will occur along the cultural fault lines separating these civilizations from one another" (lines 7–10). Thus, he would be likely to say that the Persian Gulf War is an example of nation-states putting their interests ahead of the interests of the civilization to which they belong, but that this one example does not invalidate his argument that civilizational loyalty is becoming more important than loyalty to the nation-state in causing conflict in the world.

31. **(A)** After describing Huntington's classification as "[identifying] determinants [of international events] on a grand scale by 'civilizations'" (lines 77–78), the author of Passage 2 describes what he sees as the difficulties with Huntington's classification: "His endeavor, however, has its own fault lines. The lines are the borders encompassing each distinct nation and mercilessly chopping the alleged civilizations into pieces" (lines 79–82). From this we can infer that the author of Passage 2 has serious doubts about whether the term "civilization" can be applied to the entities described as such by Huntington.

32. **(D)** In lines 22–24 the author says, "The general importance of zoonoses for humanity has waxed and waned over time in concert with changing conditions . . . ."

33. **(B)** These lines provide the best evidence, as stated above.

34. **(C)** In his discussion of zoonoses the author makes clear that zoonoses are "maintain[ed] . . . in nature" (line 15) in certain animals and humans, so it can be inferred that all (or at least nearly all) zoonoses are not actually new in the sense that they didn't exist previously. In lines 22–33 the author discusses how zoonoses vary in range and says that a zoonosis can appear in an area that had not previously existed; in this sense it is "new."

35. **(D)** If we know what an epidemic is we can infer that an epizootic is an epidemic caused by zoonotic pathogens.

36. **(A)** The author says, "Rabies is a well-established zoonosis and, except for anthrax, perhaps the earliest zoonosis to confront humans" (lines 33–35).

37. **(C)** As discussed in the explanation to question 3, all (or nearly all) zoonoses exist in nature (that is, in humans or animals). The author does not discuss how often new zoonoses occur, but his discussion strongly suggests that it does not occur frequently.

38. **(B)** From the context we can infer that *specter* must mean "haunting image" because it is used to refer to the Spanish flu that killed and sickened so many people.

39. **(D)** The "revelations" (line 20) the author refers to are the knowledge humanity has gained about zoonoses. Later in the passage he describes a number of zoonoses that have had a serious effect on human and animal health. In lines 94–97 he says, "Threats . . . emergence." Thus, it can be inferred that one of the ramifications (implications or effects) for wildlife managers will be that it will play an increasing role in monitoring human-animal interaction that can lead to zoonotic disease.

40. **(C)** The three arrows all point in two directions, indicating that zoonoses can move from humans to domestic animals and vice versa, from wildlife to domestic animals and vice versa, and from wildlife to humans and vice versa.

41. **(D)** We can infer this because at zoos, pet shops, and farms there is a great deal of interaction between animals and humans, which can lead to the transmission of zoonotic disease from humans to animals or vice versa.

42. **(D)** In context *sanctioned* means "officially approved." The author says that a "majority of mankind" has approved a law (justice).

43. **(A)** The author says a law has been approved "not only by a majority of this or that people, but by a majority of mankind" (lines 7–9).

44. **(C)** This statement means that "people's" rights cannot include any that are not just. Thus, people do not have a right to do something that is not just.

45. **(A)** The author asks, "If it be admitted that a man possessing absolute power may misuse that power by wronging his adversaries, why should not a majority be liable to the same reproach?" (lines 30–34). This rhetorical question makes the point that the majority can take actions, such as passing laws, that "wrong" people. Such laws would be unjust.

46. **(C)** The sentence in which the word *principles* is used begins a discussion of the composition of government. Thus, we can infer that the word means the elements that make up a government.

47. **(C)** In the previous paragraph (lines 41–59; "I . . . will") the author argues that it is not possible to create a government in such a way that one "principle of action" (line 50) dominates. It follows from this that some group will dominate the society.

48. **(C)** These lines provide the best evidence for the answer to the previous question.

49. **(B)** The author says, "I think that liberty is endangered when this power [the dominant social power] finds no obstacle which can retard its course and give it time to moderate its own vehemence" (lines 62–65).

50. **(D)** Scholarly studies are not cited. All the others are used.

51. **(D)** The author believes that in order to preserve justice and liberty in a democracy, it is necessary for there to be institutions that can check the power of the majority. In the final paragraph of the passage he argues that this is particularly true of the United States where "democratic institutions" are very strong. He says that the majority controls all of the institutions of society, such as the legislature and juries. He says that in some states "even" judges are elected by the majority. Thus, we can conclude that he would probably support the appointment of judges to create an institution to protect the rights of the minority.

52. **(B)** As mentioned in the explanation to the previous question, the author believes that in America the majority controls all of the institutions of society. We can infer that he believes that unless there are institutions capable of checking the power of these majority-dominated institutions there would be a tyranny of the majority, in which the rights of minorities are infringed. Thus, "Tyranny by the Majority" would be an appropriate title for this passage.

Section 2: Writing and Language Test

1. **(B)** This is the only grammatically correct choice.

2. **(B)** *Suggests* is correct because this verb must agree in number with the simple subject, "variation." Note that the words "concentrations" and "parks" are the objects of prepositional phrases and so can be ignored when choosing the correct verb form for this question.

3. **(D)** This choice makes good sense in context; in context *integrity* means "being unimpaired."

4. **(C)** This makes good sense in context, in which a range of mercury contamination is being described. In this context, *mean* means "arithmetic mean" (average).

5. **(D)** This is the best choice because sentence 2 adds information directly relevant to that given in sentence 6 and makes a suggestion based on findings mentioned in both sentences. The word "additionally" in sentence 2 provides a clue to the answer to this question.

6. **(C)** In context, *toxic* means "caused by poison." This is the best choice because the topic of the passage is mercury contamination.

7. **(D)** This is the best choice because it creates two sentences, each giving information about a related but separate topic.

8. **(A)** The phrase "at which" refers to "the benchmark 950 ng/g ww." A benchmark is "a standard of reference against which things can be compared."

9. **(A)** This is the correct choice because it is correctly punctuated. "Of human and wildlife health" is a prepositional phrase in which the noun *health* is the object. The adjectives *human* and *wildlife* modify the noun *health*.

10. **(A)** This can be seen by comparing the increase or decrease of mercury concentrations at each location. This is shown in the bar graph.

11. **(C)** As in the previous question, the answer can be seen by comparing the increase or decrease in mercury concentration at each location.

12. **(D)** All of the choices are grammatical. However, the best answer is choice (D), which creates two clear and concise sentences.

13. **(B)** Choice (A) is grammatical but creates a sentence that is awkward and has an unclear meaning. Choice (D) is not grammatical. Choice (C) is grammatical but wordy. Choice (B) is clear and concise.

14. **(D)** This sentence is an effective topic sentence to introduce the paragraph it is in. It also helps link the first paragraph to the second paragraph.

15. **(C)** This is the best choice. It creates two clear and grammatical sentences. Choice (A) is incorrect because the information given after the colon does not relate directly to the information given before the colon. Choice (B) creates a run-on sentence. Choice (D) is acceptable but is not as good a choice as choice (C) because a semicolon is normally used to create a sentence containing two independent clauses containing closely related information. In this case two quite separate points are made, so a period is a better choice.

16. **(C)** This is the best choice in context. Choice (A) and choice (B) do not make sense. Choice (D) is acceptable but is wordy and awkward.

17. **(B)** The underlined phrase *managing wildlife* is one of four in a series of topics, so to maintain parallelism standard usage requires that all of the nouns be in the same form.

18. **(B)** This is the best choice because sentence 2 provides a good transition between the second paragraph, which is about fieldwork (outdoor work), and the third paragraph, which is about lab work (indoor work).

19. **(C)** This is the only choice that is grammatical and makes good sense. The author is stating another way ornithologists educate people. Choice (A) is grammatical but does not make sense because "although" signals a contrast, but there is no contrast made in the sentence.

20. **(B)** This is the best choice because the author is stating some of the things that outreach activities *might* be. Choice (A) is grammatical, but the past tense verb *did* makes no sense in context because the author is describing ongoing activities or activities that have been done in the past, are being done in the present, and almost certainly will be done in the future rather than something done only in the past.

21. **(C)** This is the correct choice in context, which requires a word meaning a "field of knowledge." A Ph.D. in a relevant discipline is required for certain occupations related to ornithology.

22. **(B)** This choice is correct because the phrase "For statistical purposes" is an adverbial prepositional phrase that modifies the verb *included* and it is standard usage. Note that a comma is not required after such introductory phrases but is correct to use in such cases and often useful in making the meaning clear.

23. **(B)** This is the correct expression. Choice (A) and choice (C) are not standard idiomatic usage.

24. **(B)** This is the best choice because it means "formally renounced." None of the other choices is correct usage in context.

25. **(D)** This choice is correct because "laid" is the simple past tense, which is correct in this context. Note that "lain" is the past participle of a different verb, "lie."

26. **(C)** Choice (A) is grammatical but wordy because the phrase "nor did he ever" is unnecessary as the words "never again" earlier in the sentence apply to all three verbs—"dwelt," "owned," and "wore."

27. **(D)** This is the best choice because sentence 4 describes what Mahavira did to "purify his consciousness and discover the meaning of existence." To do this he "renounced" his wealthy life and fasted. It follows that he would never live in a house again, and so forth.

28. **(A)** This is the only grammatically correct choice. Note that the simple subjects of the prepositional phrase beginning with "of" and ending with "release" are "working," "effects," and "conditions," which means they are (correctly) parallel.

29. **(B)** Choice (B) is the only grammatically correct choice. The subject of the two verbs "combines" and "accumulates" in the clause beginning with "that combines" and ending with "matter" is the pronoun "that." The verbs must agree with the subject in number.

30. **(C)** This choice makes the best sense. The sentence immediately before the one in which the word "discipline" appears describes how action, especially violence, has consequences for the soul. It therefore makes sense that the next sentence would describe training based on inactivity and nonviolence to make a moral improvement.

31. **(B)** The given sentence is not grammatical. Choice (B) creates two grammatical sentences. Choice (D) is grammatically correct, but it is awkward and not standard usage.

32. **(C)** This is the correct choice in the context, which requires a verb meaning "regard with reverence and profound honor."

33. **(A)** This is the correct answer because the focus of the paragraph is on "the ancient belief system of the Jains" and on the "discipline" (training) followed by Jains.

34. **(D)** This is the only choice that is grammatical.

35. **(B)** This is the only choice that is grammatical. It changes the verb "was" to the present participle of be, "being," creating a participial phrase modifying the noun "civilization."

36. **(D)** This is the correct answer because sentence 6 follows logically from sentence 1 and because sentence 2 gives an example of something mentioned in sentence 2.

37. **(C)** This sentence helps to relate what is discussed in the first paragraph to what is discussed in the second paragraph. The words "but whatever notion we have of civilization" refer back to what has been discussed in the first paragraph, and the rest of the sentence introduces the subject of the second paragraph.

38. **(C)** This is the best choice because it makes a compound sentence with two independent clauses linked by the coordinating conjunction "and." Note that a comma must be put before the word *and* because this choice creates a compound sentence. Choice (B) is acceptable but unnecessarily wordy in that there is no need to say "it is his opinion" because this is evident from the context.

39. **(C)** This is the standard phrase in this context. Choice (A) and choice (D) are non-standard and a bit wordy.

40. **(A)** This is the correct choice because what comes after the word *hence* is a consequence of what comes before the word *hence*.

41. **(D)** This is the only grammatically correct choice. The subjects of the verb *expressing* are "customs," "habits," and "standards."

42. **(C)** This is the only grammatically correct choice. In the phrase "or began" it is understood that the action is performed by "a member." "It" is incorrect because "it" cannot be used to refer to a person.

43. **(C)** This is the only choice that makes good sense and is grammatical. The adverb clause "when they began to treat each other civilly," together with the phrase "that is," is set off by dashes. The material set off by dashes amplifies what has just been said. Note that this use of dashes is often effective, but dashes should be used sparingly in formal writing.

44. **(B)** The construction *from* [something] *to* [something else] is required: *from* "the beginning of man's conquest . . ." *to* "the modern complexities . . . ."

Section 3: Math Test (No Calculator)

1. **(C)** Substitute 5 for n as provided in the original equation.

$$\frac{r-2}{6} = 5$$

Next, multiply both sides of the equation by 6 to isolate $r - 2$.

$$(6)\frac{r-2}{6} = 5(6)$$

$$r - 2 = 30$$

Add 2 to both sides of the equation.

$$r - 2 + 2 = 30 + 2$$
$$r = 32$$

2. **(A)** Simplify $(5 + 3i) + (-4 + 7i)$ by combining the real components of the expression first.

$$5 + -4 = 1$$

Next, combine the imaginary components.

$$3i + 7i = 10i$$

Add the two components with the real number followed by the imaginary.

$$1 + 10i$$

3. **(C)** The number of shirts (s) and belts (b) cannot exceed 100 items, but they can be equal to that sum. We therefore add the two quantities and ensure that they could not exceed 100 items.

$$s + b \leq 100$$

Choices (A) and (B) can be eliminated at once. The question suggests that the number of items cannot exceed 100 items. That implies the number of items could be equal to 100 but not more. Therefore, the symbol "$\leq$" is needed, but using "$<$" would be incorrect.

4. **(A)** Begin isolating s by first factoring the greatest common factor.

$$TA = \pi rs + \pi r^2$$
$$TA = \pi r(s + r)$$

Divide both sides of the equation by πr.

$$\frac{TA}{\pi r} = \frac{\pi r(s + r)}{\pi r}$$
$$\frac{TA}{\pi r} = s + r$$

Subtract r from each side of the equation.

$$\frac{TA}{\pi r} - r = s + r - r$$
$$\frac{TA}{\pi r} - r = s$$

5. **(A)** When adding or subtracting algebraic expressions, combine only like terms. Like terms are those that have the same variables raised to the same power.

$$(3x^3 - 13x + 4) - (3x^2 - 4x + 5) =$$
$$3x^3 - 3x^2 + (-13x + 4x) + (4 - 5) =$$
$$3x^3 - 3x^2 - 9x - 1$$

When adding and subtracting polynomials, we only combine like terms; we do not add exponents unless we are multiplying. Thus, choice (C) with an exponent of 5 should be immediately eliminated.

6. **(C)** Division by 0 is undefined. Set $6x^2 - 13x - 5$ equal to 0 and solve.

$$6x^2 - 13x - 5 = 0$$

Solve by factoring.

$$(3x + 1)(2x - 5) = 0$$

Set each of the parentheses equal to 0 and solve for the variable.

$$3x + 1 = 0 \text{ or } 2x - 5 = 0$$
$$3x = -1 \text{ or } 2x = 5$$
$$x = -\frac{1}{3} \quad x = \frac{5}{2}$$

$\dfrac{-5x^2\,y - 4xy}{6x^2 - 13x - 5}$ is undefined when $x = -\dfrac{1}{3} \quad x = \dfrac{5}{2}$

7. **(C)** Find the coordinates of the vertex of $3(x - 4)(x + 6)$ by multiplying.

$$y = 3(x - 4)(x + 6)$$
$$y = 3(x^2 + 2x - 24)$$

Begin to transform the equation from standard form to graphing form. First, move -24 to the right of the parentheses, remembering to first multiply it by 3.

$$y = 3(x^2 + 2x) - (24)(3)$$
$$y = 3(x^2 + 2x) - 72$$

Complete the square by squaring $\dfrac{b}{2}$. Remember to multiply that value by 3.

$$y = 3(x^2 + 2x + 1) - 72 - (3 \times -1)$$
$$y = 3(x^2 + 2x + 1) - 72 - 3$$
$$y = 3(x + 1)^2 - 75$$

The equation is now in graphing form. The vertex is $(-1, -75)$.

8. **(B)** The volume of the water is 6 cubic feet because the volume, length × width × height, is $3 \times 2 \times 1 = 6$. The same volume of water is then poured into another aquarium that has the dimensions 4 feet by 1 foot and that rises to a height of x feet. Calculate the height.

$$(4)(1)(x) = 6$$
$$4x = 6$$
$$x = 1.5$$

9. **(B)** Parallel lines have the same slope but distinct y-intercepts. The equation $y = \dfrac{3}{2}x - \dfrac{7}{4}$ has slope $\dfrac{3}{2}$ and y-intercept $-\dfrac{7}{4}$. Transform each of the equations to slope-intercept form, $y = mx + b$, to compare slopes and y-intercepts. Choice (B) offers the following:

$$-6x + 4y = 11$$

Transform to slope-intercept form by isolating y:

$$-6x + 6x + 4y = 6x + 11$$
$$4y = 6x + 11$$

Divide both sides of the equation by 4.

$$\frac{4}{4}y = \frac{6}{4}x + \frac{11}{4}$$

$$y = \frac{3}{2}x + \frac{11}{4}$$

$$m = \frac{3}{2} \quad b = \frac{11}{4}$$

$y = \frac{3}{2}x + \frac{11}{4}$ and $y = \frac{3}{2}x - \frac{7}{4}$ have the same slope but different y-intercepts so the two lines are parallel.

10. **(C)**

$$n = 3.65 + .35x$$

$$m = 4.25 + .15x$$

Setting $m = n$ will provide the number of weeks that passed when the two plants were the same height.

$$3.65 + .35x = 4.25 + .15x$$

Solve for x.

$$3.65 + .35x = 4.25 + .15x$$

$$.2x = .6$$

$$x = 3$$

After 3 weeks passed, the two plants were identical heights. Replace x with 3 in either equation to find the height when they were the same.

$$3.65 + .35(3) = 4.7$$

The two plants were both 4.7 feet three weeks after September 15.

11. **(C)** Rationalize the denominator by multiplying the numerator and the denominator by $2 + i$.

$$\frac{3i}{2 - i} \times \frac{2 + i}{2 + i} =$$

$$\frac{6i + 3i^2}{4 - i^2}$$

Substitute -1 for i^2 into the expression.

$$\frac{6i + 3(-1)}{4 - (-1)} = \frac{6i - 3}{5}$$

$\frac{6i - 3}{5}$ can be rewritten in the form of $a + bi$ as $-\frac{3}{5} + \frac{6i}{5}$. Therefore, $a = -\frac{3}{5}$.

12. **(D)** The x-coordinate of the vertex can be found using the formula $x = -\frac{b}{2a}$. Find the values of a and b.

$$g(x) = 2x^2 + 15x - 8$$

$$a = 2 \quad b = 15$$

$$x = -\frac{b}{2a} = -\frac{15}{4} = -3.75$$

Answer choice (D), $-4 < x < 6$, is the only interval among the answer choices that contains $x = -3.75$.

13. **(C)** Replace $h(x)$ with 138 and x with 6 in order to find b.

$$138 = b(6)^2 + 30$$
$$138 = 36b + 30$$
$$108 = 36b$$
$$3 = b$$

Replace b with 3 to find $h(-4)$.

$$h(-4) = 3(-4)^2 + 30$$
$$h(-4) = 78$$

14. **(A)** Square both sides of the equation to eliminate the radical.

$$(\sqrt{2x})^2 = (x - 4)^2$$
$$2x = x^2 - 8x + 16$$

Set the equation equal to 0 and factor.

$$2x = x^2 - 8x + 16$$
$$x^2 - 10x + 16 = 0$$
$$(x - 8)(x - 2) = 0$$

Solve for x.

$$x - 8 = 0 \qquad x - 2 = 0$$
$$x = 8 \qquad x = 2$$

Check both values to eliminate extraneous answers.

$$\sqrt{2 \times 8} = 8 - 4$$
$$4 = 4$$
$$\sqrt{2 \times 2} = 2 - 4$$
$$2 \neq -2$$

Only 8 is a solution because 2 is an extraneous solution.

15. **(B)** Use the basic steps of algebra to isolate y.

STEP 1 Add $1.6x^2$ and 11.4 to both sides of the equation.

$$P = -1.6x^2 + 2.6xy - 11.4$$
$$P + 1.6x^2 + 11.4 = -1.6x^2 + 2.6xy - 11.4 + 1.6x^2 + 11.4$$
$$P + 1.6x^2 + 11.4 = 2.6xy$$

STEP 2 Divide both sides of the equation by $2.6x$

$$\frac{P + 1.6x^2 + 11.4}{2.6x} = \frac{2.6xy}{2.6x}$$

$$\frac{P + 1.6x^2 + 11.4}{2.6x} = y$$

16. **18** The slope of a line can be found by using the formula $\frac{rise}{run}$ or $\frac{y_2 - y_1}{x_2 - x_1}$. Substitute $(9, 0)$ for x_2 and y_2 and $(x, 6)$ for x_1 and y_1. Set the value of that fraction to $\frac{2}{3}$, the slope of the line connecting these two points.

$$\frac{0 - 6}{9 - x} = \frac{2}{3}$$
$$\frac{-6}{9 - x} = \frac{2}{3}$$

Cross-multiply and solve for x.

$$2(9 - x) = (-3)(6)$$
$$18 - 2x = -18$$
$$-2x = -36$$
$$x = 18$$

17. **55** The dollar amount in April was $\$850 - \$155 - \$195 - \$225 = \$275$. The number of days for January can be found by solving the equation $155 = 75 + 10d$. Subtract 75 from each side to get $80 = 10d$. Then $d = 8$. In a similar manner, the number of days for each of February, March, and April can be determined by solving the equations $195 = 75 + 10d$, $225 = 75 + 10d$, and $275 = 75 + 10d$, respectively. We find that Jerry spent 12 days in February, 15 days in March, and 20 days in April. Thus, the total number of days spent at the club was $8 + 12 + 15 + 20 = 55$.

18. **85** The sum of two sides of a triangle is always larger than the length of the third side. Suppose that 11 is the measure of the longest side. Then $7 + x > 11$ and $x > 4$. The smallest integer that satisfies this inequality is 5.

Suppose the largest side is unknown, then $7 + 11 > x$ and $18 > x$. The largest value that satisfies this inequality is 17. Therefore, the product of the smallest value, 5, and the largest value, 17, is $5 \times 17 = 85$.

19. **$\frac{3}{5}$ or .6** The scale factor of triangle DEF to triangle ABC is $\frac{1}{10}$, so multiply the sides of triangle ABC by $\frac{1}{10}$.

$$(100)\left(\frac{1}{10}\right) = 10 = DF$$
$$(80)\left(\frac{1}{10}\right) = 8 = EF$$

Use the Pythagorean theorem to calculate the length of DE.

$$a^2 + 8^2 = 10^2$$
$$a^2 = 36$$
$$a = 6$$

The cosine function is found by using the ratio $\cos x = \dfrac{\text{adjacent side}}{\text{hypotenuse}}$. The side adjacent to angle D is 6 and the hypotenuse is 10 so $\dfrac{\text{adjacent side}}{\text{hypotenuse}} = \dfrac{3}{5} = .6$.

20. **3** This question can be answered by using a system of equations. "The quantity she purchased of the heads of lettuce was 6 fewer than 5 times the number of cucumbers" can be translated as $h + 6 = 5c$. Each head of lettuce costs \$.70 and each cucumber costs \$.30, so the cost for the vegetables, in terms of c and h, is $.3c + .7h$. Given that the cost of the purchase was \$7.20, we get the second equation in the system of equations.

$$.3c + .7h = 7.2$$

Transform $h + 6 = 5c$ to $h = 5c - 6$, and replace that value for h in $.3c + .7h = 7.2$.

$$.3c + .7(5c - 6) = 7.2$$
$$.3c + 3.5c - 4.2 = 7.2$$
$$3.8c = 11.4$$
$$c = 3$$

Section 4: Math Test (Calculator)

1. **(C)** Use the ratio of books sold to income earned to create a proportion.

$$\frac{800}{1320} = \frac{12,000}{x}$$

Cross-multiply and solve for x.

$$(800)(x) = (1,320)(12,000)$$
$$800x = 15,840,000$$
$$x = \$19,800$$

The graphic novelist would earn \$19,800 on sales of 12,000 books.
Choices (A) and (B) can be eliminated immediately. Each is much too close to the initial \$1,320 earned when 800 books were sold. Clearly, selling 12,000 books should yield a significantly higher figure as offered in choices (C) and (D).

2. **(B)** Use the ratio of books sold: income earned once again.

$$\frac{800}{1320} = \frac{5000}{x}$$

Cross-multiply and solve for x.

$$(1320)(5000) = (800)(x)$$
$$6,600,000 = 800x$$
$$8250 = x$$

The income earned before overhead costs are subtracted is \$8,250. Subtract 32% of that amount to find the novelist's net income.
\$8,250 − (8,250)(.32) = \$5,610. Note that choice (A) is incorrect because it represents the expenses, not the net income.

3. **(C)** A linear function that contains $f(4) = 6$ and $f(-2) = 14$ indicates that the points $(4, 6)$ and $(-2, 14)$ satisfy the function. Use these points to find the slope of the function.

$$m = \frac{y_2 - y_1}{x_2 - x_1} = \frac{14 - 6}{-2 - 4} = -\frac{4}{3}$$

Use the point-slope form of a line to create the linear function.

$$y - y_1 = m(x - x_1)$$

Substitute either point for x and y.

$$y - 6 = -\frac{4}{3}(x - 4)$$

Substitute 9 for x to find $f(9)$.

$$y - 6 = -\frac{4}{3}(9 - 4)$$

$$y - 6 = -\frac{20}{3}$$

$$y = -\frac{2}{3}$$

Therefore, $f(9) = -\frac{2}{3}$

4. **(A)** Add the three terms and divide the sum by 3. Set this value equal to $x + 4$, the average.

$$\frac{2x - 4 + x + 4 + 3x - 6}{3} = x + 4$$

$$\frac{6x - 6}{3} = x + 4$$

$$6x - 6 = 3x + 12$$

$$3x = 18$$

$$x = 6$$

Replace x with 6 in $-2x + 3$.

$$-2(6) + 3 = -9$$

5. **(A)** If Shelley sold 10 recliners and 10 dinette sets, her commission would be $10(24) + 10(63)$ $= 870$. In other words, multiply each commission by the number of units sold of a particular item. If she sold r dinette sets and d recliners, her commission would be $63r + 24d$.

6. **(B)** Ephraim will work as many as 20 hours per week but not more. Thus, $x + y \leq 20$ models the number of hours he wants to work for both jobs. His pay must be at least $270.00. He'll work x hours at $11.50 per hour as a delivery person and y hours at $15.00 per hour as a math tutor. Therefore, $11.50x + 15y \geq 270$ models his weekly earnings. Choice (B) is the only answer that features both of these conditions.

7. **(D)** Consider the three conditions that each satisfy $n > 0$:

(a) Let $n = 2$, then $n^2 = 4$

$$n^2 > n$$

(b) Let $n = 1$, then $n^2 = 1$

$$n^2 = n$$

(c) Let $n = \frac{1}{2}$, then $n^2 = \frac{1}{4}$

$$n^2 < n$$

Without more information about n, we cannot make a conclusion about n^2.

8. **(C)** The factored form of $y = x^2 + 2x - 24$ is $y = (x + 6)(x - 4)$. To find the x-intercepts, let $y = 0$.

$$0 = (x + 6)(x - 4)$$
$$x + 6 = 0 \qquad x - 4 = 0$$
$$x = -6 \quad x = 4$$

The factored form of $y = x^2 + 2x - 24$ shows the x-intercepts of the parabola as constants.

9. **(B)** Form a proportion using the ratio $\dfrac{\text{defects}}{\text{total shipment}}$

$$\frac{13}{500} = \frac{273}{n}$$

Cross-multiply and solve for n.

$$13n = (273)(500)$$
$$13n = 136{,}500$$
$$n = 10{,}500$$

A shipment of 10,500 square yards of fabric would produce 273 square yards of defective fabric.

10. **(D)** The data roughly correspond to a line with a negative slope, so only choices (A) and (D) should be considered. Using the points $(0, 5)$ and $(2, 3)$ we can get a sense of the slope:

$$\frac{\text{rise}}{\text{run}} = \frac{5 - 3}{0 - 2} = -1$$

Choice (D) is more closely aligned with slope -1. Choices (B) and (C) can be eliminated at once. The data appear to descend to the right as the number of ants increases, thus indicating a negative slope. Choices (B) and (C) incorrectly show positive slopes.

11. **(C)** After the grower uses the pesticide, his ant population will be reduced by 60%. Find 60% of 5,000,000 and subtract that amount from 5,000,000.

$$5{,}000{,}000 - (.60)(5{,}000{,}000) = 2{,}000{,}000$$

The graph indicates the point $(2, 3)$ is on the line of best fit. Thus, when the grower has 2,000,000 ants, he can expect a yield of 3,000 roses.

12. **(B)** The combined weights of Helium and Lithium are $4.0026 + 6.941 = 10.9436$. The weight of Boron is 10.811. That value is the closest to the combined weights of Helium and Lithium among the answer choices.

13. **(C)** The atomic weight of Lithium is 6.941. Multiply that number by .30 and add it to the weight of Lithium.

$$6.941 + (.30)(6.941) = 9.023$$

Of the elements listed in the table, Beryllium, with a weight of 9.0122, is approximately 30% heavier than Lithium.

14. **(C)** Change the equation of the circle to graphing form by completing the square for x and y. The general form of a circle in graphing form is $(x - h)^2 + (y - k)^2 = r^2$, where (h, k) is the circle's center, and r is its radius.

$$x^2 + y^2 - 6y + 4x = 36$$
$$(x^2 + 4x + 4) + (y^2 - 6y + 9) = 49$$
$$(x + 2)^2 + (y - 3)^2 = 49$$

The radius squared, r^2, is 49, so r is 7. Replace the measure of the radius, r, in the circumference formula.

$$C = 2\pi r$$
$$C = (2)(\pi)(7) = 14\pi$$

Choice (A) can be eliminated as it represents the area, not the circumference, of the circle.

15. **(C)** If Sammie interviewed every 16-year-old in Florida, she would have no margin of error: she would have all of the data! Thus, the larger the sample size, the smaller the margin of error. Sammie ought to interview additional students to reduce the margin of error in the sample.

16. **(D)** Use any of the given zeroes to solve for b. In the zero $(2, 0)$, $x = 2$ and $y = 0$. Substitute both in $g(x) = 2x^3 - 8x^2 - bx + 140$.

$$0 = 2(2)^3 - 8(2)^2 - b(2) + 140$$
$$0 = 124 - 2b$$
$$2b = 124$$
$$b = 62$$

17. **(D)** Begin isolating x by multiplying the equation by a^2b^2.

$$a^2b^2\left(\frac{x^2}{a^2} + \frac{y^2}{b^2} = 1\right)$$

$$b^2x^2 + a^2y^2 = a^2b^2$$

$$b^2x^2 = a^2b^2 - a^2y^2$$

$$\frac{b^2x^2}{b^2} = \frac{a^2b^2 - a^2y^2}{b^2}$$

$$x^2 = \frac{a^2b^2 - a^2y^2}{b^2}$$

$$\sqrt{x^2} = \pm\sqrt{\frac{a^2b^2 - a^2y^2}{b^2}}$$

$$x = \pm\frac{\sqrt{a^2b^2 - a^2y^2}}{b}$$

18. **(A)** At one year, the market fund was worth $600 and the CD was valued at $1,600. Thus, choice (A) cannot be concluded because it states incorrectly that the market fund is worth more than the CD.

19. **(C)** Square both sides of the equation to remove the radical.

$$(\sqrt{x-7})^2 = (x-7)^2$$
$$x - 7 = x^2 - 14x + 49$$
$$x = x^2 - 14x + 56$$
$$x^2 - 15x + 56 = 0$$
$$(x - 7)(x - 8) = 0$$

This last step reflects answer choice (C).

20. **(A)** Find the probability that a single, six-sided die will land on a prime number:

$$p \text{ (prime number)} = \frac{2,3,5}{1,2,3,4,5,6} = \frac{1}{2}$$

Remember, 1 is not a prime number.

Find the probability that the spinner will land on yellow or blue.

$$\frac{\text{yellow,blue}}{\text{red,green,blue,yellow}} = \frac{1}{2}$$

The two events, landing on a prime number and spinning yellow or blue, are independent so multiply the probabilities.

$$\frac{1}{2} \times \frac{1}{2} = \frac{1}{4}$$

21. **(A)** An ounce of gold covers 100 square yards of surface, but the question requires the answer to be in square feet.

1 yard = 3 feet

100 square yards is equivalent to 900 square feet, so one ounce of gold covers 900 square feet. Multiply 900 by 2.5 to find the area covered by 2.5 ounces of gold.

$$2.5 \times 900 = 2,250 \text{ square feet}$$

22. **(C)** You are told that 59 students participated in the canned food drive. The table arranges the number of cans per student in ascending order. Thus, the median student contribution is the number of cans contributed by the 30th student. Add the frequency of contributions until you arrive at the 30th student.

Number of Cans per Student	Frequency
8	14
9	16

Adding 14 and 16 yields a total of 30. The 30th student lies in the category of students who contributed 9 cans each.

23. **(C)** The learning therapist has demonstrated that her program increases students' reading levels. 1.09 in the equation ensures growth. For example, if a student is in the second grade and uses the program, we get the following:

$$x = 2$$
$$y = 1.09(2) + .17$$
$$y = 2.35$$

This means a student in second grade would read at a level more than 3 months in advance (assuming a 10-month school year) of students who are not in the reading program.

24. **(B)** The per-capita income of Singapore is $60,500. Multiply that value by .048 and add it to $60,500.

$$\$60,500 + (.048)(\$60,500) = \$63,404$$

At $63,400, Monaco's per capita income is closest to this value.

25. **(C)** The GDP is found by multiplying the total value of goods and services that a country produces. Use the formula GDP = (per capita income)(population).

Let x = the population size

$$298,000,000,000 = 60,500(x)$$
$$x = 4,925,619$$

Choice (C), 4,900,000, is the closest to this value.

26. **(A)** Use the probability formula:

$$P(x) = \frac{\text{desired outcomes}}{\text{all outcomes}}$$

There are 35 tenth graders and 38 boys. However, some of the tenth graders are boys and should not be counted twice. Thus:

P(10th grader or boy) = [(number of 10th graders) + (number of boys) − (number of 10th grade boys)] ÷ (total number of students)

$$P(\text{10th grader or boy}) = (35 + 38 - 18) \div (73)$$

$$P(\text{10th grader or boy}) = 55 \div 73 = .753$$

27. **(B)** Find the radius of the sphere by using the formula $V = \frac{4}{3}\pi r^3$.

$$374 = \frac{4}{3}(3.14)r^3$$
$$374 = 4.19r^3$$
$$89.26 = r^3$$
$$4.47 = r$$

The circumference of a circle is found by using the formula $C = 2\pi r$.

$$C = (2)(4.47)(3.14) = 28.07$$

Once you have calculated the length of the radius of the sphere, choice (A) can be eliminated. 4.47 is the radius of the circle, not its circumference.

28. **(B)**

$$A = R_0\left(\frac{1}{2}\right)^x$$

Input 2.3 for the number of years, x, and 125 for R_0, the initial amount of the compound.

$$A = 125\left(\frac{1}{2}\right)^{2.3}$$

$$A = 25.4$$

After 2.3 years, 125 grams of the compound will be reduced to 25.4 grams.

29. **(B)** Find the probability of selecting a student who successfully shot four foul shots by using the formula $\frac{\text{favored outcomes}}{\text{all outcomes}}$.

There are a total of 15 students who successfully shot two or more foul shots. Of those 15 students, 3 made exactly 4 baskets. Therefore, $\frac{3}{15}$, or $\frac{1}{5}$, of the students in the sample made exactly 4 baskets.

30. **(A)** Subtract the two equations and combine like terms.

$$4a + n = 2a - 3$$
$$\underline{- 4b + m = 2b - 3}$$
$$4a - 4b + n - m = 2a - 2b$$
$$2a - 2b + n - m = 0$$

Substitute $m + 1$ for n.

$$2a - 2b + m + 1 - m = 0$$
$$2a - 2b + 1 = 0$$
$$2a - 2b = -1$$
$$a - b = -\frac{1}{2}$$
$$a = b - \frac{1}{2}$$

31. **24** The least number of hamburgers and rolls to buy is the least common multiple (LCM) of 6 and 8. Multiply 6 and 8 by 1, 2, 3, and so on to find the least common multiple.

$$6: 6, 12, 18, \mathbf{24}, 30$$

$$8: 8, 16, \mathbf{24}, 32$$

$$24 \text{ is the LCM of 6 and 8}$$

In order to buy hamburger patties and rolls without any left over, 24 of each should be purchased.

32. **40** Add the scores of all twelve of the students.

$$(2 \times 20) + (1 \times 40) + (4 \times 60) + (4 \times 80) + (1 \times 100) = 740$$

In order for 13 students to average 60%, the class must amass 780 points because $13 \times 60 = 780$.

Since the first 12 students accumulated 740 points, then the thirteenth student must score a 40% on his/her test because $780 - 740 = 40$.

33. **4** First multiply $2(2x^2 - 7.5x + 3)$. Next multiply each term in the second polynomial by -1. Then combine like terms.

$$2(2x^2 - 7.5x + 3) - (-4x^2 + 2x - 7)$$
$$4x^2 - 15x + 6 + 4x^2 - 2x + 7$$
$$8x^2 - 17x + 13$$

The expression $8x^2 - 17x + 13$ yields $a = 8$, $b = -17$, and $c = 13$.

$$a + b + c = 8 - 17 + 13 = 4$$

34. $\dfrac{3}{8}$ **or .375** The area of a circle is surrounded by an angle of measure 2π radians. Find the ratio of the central angle, $\dfrac{3\pi}{4}$, to the entire circle.

$$\frac{\frac{3\pi}{4}}{\frac{2\pi}{1}} = \frac{3\pi}{4} \times \frac{1}{2\pi} = \frac{3}{8} \text{ or } .375$$

35. $\dfrac{21}{8}$ **or 2.62 or 2.63** Since the ratio of chocolates to mints is 3 to 5, the ratio of chocolates to the mix is $\dfrac{3}{3+5} = \dfrac{3}{8}$. Remember, there are 8 parts to the mix: 3 parts chocolate and 5 parts mints. Multiply 7 pounds by $\dfrac{3}{8}$ to find the number of pounds of chocolates in a 7-pound mix.

$$\frac{3}{8} \times 7 = \frac{21}{8} \text{ or } 2.62 \text{ or } 2.63$$

36. **6**

$$\frac{1}{3}c = 6$$
$$b - \frac{2}{3}c = -6$$

Solve for c in the first equation.

$$\frac{1}{3}c = 6$$
$$(3)\left(\frac{1}{3}c = 6\right)(3)$$
$$c = 18$$

Substitute 18 for c in the second equation and solve for b.

$$b - \frac{2}{3}c = -6$$
$$b - \left(\frac{2}{3}\right)(18) = -6$$
$$b - 12 = -6$$
$$b = 6$$

37. **140** Use the formula $(n - 2)(180)$ to find the number of angles included in the polygon.

$$(n - 2)(180) = 1{,}260$$
$$n - 2 = 7$$
$$n = 9$$

The regular polygon has 9 congruent interior angles. Divide 1,260 by 9 to find the measure of one of the angles.

$$1{,}260 \div 9 = 140$$

38. **88** An exterior angle and an interior angle of a polygon form a linear pair; the sum of their measures is 180°. Thus, one interior angle of the polygon measures 135° because $180° - 45° = 135°$.

The formula $(n - 2)(180)$ is used to calculate the sum of the measures of all of the interior angles of a polygon. Since n represents the number of congruent angles *and* congruent sides in a regular polygon, we can use $\frac{(n - 2)(180)}{n}$ to find the measure of a single angle.

$$\frac{(n - 2)(180)}{n} = 135$$

Solve for n.

$$\frac{(n - 2)(180)}{n} = 135$$

$$(n - 2)(180) = 135n$$

$$180n - 360 = 135n$$

$$-360 = -45n$$

$$n = 8$$

The polygon has 8 congruent sides and angles (an octagon). Since each side measures 11 inches, the perimeter is $8 \times 11 = 88$ inches.

ANSWER SHEET
Practice Test 3

Section 1: Reading

1. Ⓐ Ⓑ Ⓒ Ⓓ
2. Ⓐ Ⓑ Ⓒ Ⓓ
3. Ⓐ Ⓑ Ⓒ Ⓓ
4. Ⓐ Ⓑ Ⓒ Ⓓ
5. Ⓐ Ⓑ Ⓒ Ⓓ
6. Ⓐ Ⓑ Ⓒ Ⓓ
7. Ⓐ Ⓑ Ⓒ Ⓓ
8. Ⓐ Ⓑ Ⓒ Ⓓ
9. Ⓐ Ⓑ Ⓒ Ⓓ
10. Ⓐ Ⓑ Ⓒ Ⓓ
11. Ⓐ Ⓑ Ⓒ Ⓓ
12. Ⓐ Ⓑ Ⓒ Ⓓ
13. Ⓐ Ⓑ Ⓒ Ⓓ

14. Ⓐ Ⓑ Ⓒ Ⓓ
15. Ⓐ Ⓑ Ⓒ Ⓓ
16. Ⓐ Ⓑ Ⓒ Ⓓ
17. Ⓐ Ⓑ Ⓒ Ⓓ
18. Ⓐ Ⓑ Ⓒ Ⓓ
19. Ⓐ Ⓑ Ⓒ Ⓓ
20. Ⓐ Ⓑ Ⓒ Ⓓ
21. Ⓐ Ⓑ Ⓒ Ⓓ
22. Ⓐ Ⓑ Ⓒ Ⓓ
23. Ⓐ Ⓑ Ⓒ Ⓓ
24. Ⓐ Ⓑ Ⓒ Ⓓ
25. Ⓐ Ⓑ Ⓒ Ⓓ
26. Ⓐ Ⓑ Ⓒ Ⓓ

27. Ⓐ Ⓑ Ⓒ Ⓓ
28. Ⓐ Ⓑ Ⓒ Ⓓ
29. Ⓐ Ⓑ Ⓒ Ⓓ
30. Ⓐ Ⓑ Ⓒ Ⓓ
31. Ⓐ Ⓑ Ⓒ Ⓓ
32. Ⓐ Ⓑ Ⓒ Ⓓ
33. Ⓐ Ⓑ Ⓒ Ⓓ
34. Ⓐ Ⓑ Ⓒ Ⓓ
35. Ⓐ Ⓑ Ⓒ Ⓓ
36. Ⓐ Ⓑ Ⓒ Ⓓ
37. Ⓐ Ⓑ Ⓒ Ⓓ
38. Ⓐ Ⓑ Ⓒ Ⓓ
39. Ⓐ Ⓑ Ⓒ Ⓓ

40. Ⓐ Ⓑ Ⓒ Ⓓ
41. Ⓐ Ⓑ Ⓒ Ⓓ
42. Ⓐ Ⓑ Ⓒ Ⓓ
43. Ⓐ Ⓑ Ⓒ Ⓓ
44. Ⓐ Ⓑ Ⓒ Ⓓ
45. Ⓐ Ⓑ Ⓒ Ⓓ
46. Ⓐ Ⓑ Ⓒ Ⓓ
47. Ⓐ Ⓑ Ⓒ Ⓓ
48. Ⓐ Ⓑ Ⓒ Ⓓ
49. Ⓐ Ⓑ Ⓒ Ⓓ
50. Ⓐ Ⓑ Ⓒ Ⓓ
51. Ⓐ Ⓑ Ⓒ Ⓓ
52. Ⓐ Ⓑ Ⓒ Ⓓ

Section 2: Writing and Language

1. Ⓐ Ⓑ Ⓒ Ⓓ
2. Ⓐ Ⓑ Ⓒ Ⓓ
3. Ⓐ Ⓑ Ⓒ Ⓓ
4. Ⓐ Ⓑ Ⓒ Ⓓ
5. Ⓐ Ⓑ Ⓒ Ⓓ
6. Ⓐ Ⓑ Ⓒ Ⓓ
7. Ⓐ Ⓑ Ⓒ Ⓓ
8. Ⓐ Ⓑ Ⓒ Ⓓ
9. Ⓐ Ⓑ Ⓒ Ⓓ
10. Ⓐ Ⓑ Ⓒ Ⓓ
11. Ⓐ Ⓑ Ⓒ Ⓓ

12. Ⓐ Ⓑ Ⓒ Ⓓ
13. Ⓐ Ⓑ Ⓒ Ⓓ
14. Ⓐ Ⓑ Ⓒ Ⓓ
15. Ⓐ Ⓑ Ⓒ Ⓓ
16. Ⓐ Ⓑ Ⓒ Ⓓ
17. Ⓐ Ⓑ Ⓒ Ⓓ
18. Ⓐ Ⓑ Ⓒ Ⓓ
19. Ⓐ Ⓑ Ⓒ Ⓓ
20. Ⓐ Ⓑ Ⓒ Ⓓ
21. Ⓐ Ⓑ Ⓒ Ⓓ
22. Ⓐ Ⓑ Ⓒ Ⓓ

23. Ⓐ Ⓑ Ⓒ Ⓓ
24. Ⓐ Ⓑ Ⓒ Ⓓ
25. Ⓐ Ⓑ Ⓒ Ⓓ
26. Ⓐ Ⓑ Ⓒ Ⓓ
27. Ⓐ Ⓑ Ⓒ Ⓓ
28. Ⓐ Ⓑ Ⓒ Ⓓ
29. Ⓐ Ⓑ Ⓒ Ⓓ
30. Ⓐ Ⓑ Ⓒ Ⓓ
31. Ⓐ Ⓑ Ⓒ Ⓓ
32. Ⓐ Ⓑ Ⓒ Ⓓ
33. Ⓐ Ⓑ Ⓒ Ⓓ

34. Ⓐ Ⓑ Ⓒ Ⓓ
35. Ⓐ Ⓑ Ⓒ Ⓓ
36. Ⓐ Ⓑ Ⓒ Ⓓ
37. Ⓐ Ⓑ Ⓒ Ⓓ
38. Ⓐ Ⓑ Ⓒ Ⓓ
39. Ⓐ Ⓑ Ⓒ Ⓓ
40. Ⓐ Ⓑ Ⓒ Ⓓ
41. Ⓐ Ⓑ Ⓒ Ⓓ
42. Ⓐ Ⓑ Ⓒ Ⓓ
43. Ⓐ Ⓑ Ⓒ Ⓓ
44. Ⓐ Ⓑ Ⓒ Ⓓ

ANSWER SHEET
Practice Test 3

Section 3: Math (No Calculator)

1. Ⓐ Ⓑ Ⓒ Ⓓ   5. Ⓐ Ⓑ Ⓒ Ⓓ   9. Ⓐ Ⓑ Ⓒ Ⓓ   13. Ⓐ Ⓑ Ⓒ Ⓓ

2. Ⓐ Ⓑ Ⓒ Ⓓ   6. Ⓐ Ⓑ Ⓒ Ⓓ   10. Ⓐ Ⓑ Ⓒ Ⓓ   14. Ⓐ Ⓑ Ⓒ Ⓓ

3. Ⓐ Ⓑ Ⓒ Ⓓ   7. Ⓐ Ⓑ Ⓒ Ⓓ   11. Ⓐ Ⓑ Ⓒ Ⓓ   15. Ⓐ Ⓑ Ⓒ Ⓓ

4. Ⓐ Ⓑ Ⓒ Ⓓ   8. Ⓐ Ⓑ Ⓒ Ⓓ   12. Ⓐ Ⓑ Ⓒ Ⓓ

16.   17.   18.

19.   20.

ANSWER SHEET
Practice Test 3

Section 4: Math (Calculator)

1. Ⓐ Ⓑ Ⓒ Ⓓ
2. Ⓐ Ⓑ Ⓒ Ⓓ
3. Ⓐ Ⓑ Ⓒ Ⓓ
4. Ⓐ Ⓑ Ⓒ Ⓓ
5. Ⓐ Ⓑ Ⓒ Ⓓ
6. Ⓐ Ⓑ Ⓒ Ⓓ
7. Ⓐ Ⓑ Ⓒ Ⓓ
8. Ⓐ Ⓑ Ⓒ Ⓓ

9. Ⓐ Ⓑ Ⓒ Ⓓ
10. Ⓐ Ⓑ Ⓒ Ⓓ
11. Ⓐ Ⓑ Ⓒ Ⓓ
12. Ⓐ Ⓑ Ⓒ Ⓓ
13. Ⓐ Ⓑ Ⓒ Ⓓ
14. Ⓐ Ⓑ Ⓒ Ⓓ
15. Ⓐ Ⓑ Ⓒ Ⓓ
16. Ⓐ Ⓑ Ⓒ Ⓓ

17. Ⓐ Ⓑ Ⓒ Ⓓ
18. Ⓐ Ⓑ Ⓒ Ⓓ
19. Ⓐ Ⓑ Ⓒ Ⓓ
20. Ⓐ Ⓑ Ⓒ Ⓓ
21. Ⓐ Ⓑ Ⓒ Ⓓ
22. Ⓐ Ⓑ Ⓒ Ⓓ
23. Ⓐ Ⓑ Ⓒ Ⓓ
24. Ⓐ Ⓑ Ⓒ Ⓓ

25. Ⓐ Ⓑ Ⓒ Ⓓ
26. Ⓐ Ⓑ Ⓒ Ⓓ
27. Ⓐ Ⓑ Ⓒ Ⓓ
28. Ⓐ Ⓑ Ⓒ Ⓓ
29. Ⓐ Ⓑ Ⓒ Ⓓ
30. Ⓐ Ⓑ Ⓒ Ⓓ

31. (grid-in)
32. (grid-in)
33. (grid-in)
34. (grid-in)
35. (grid-in)
36. (grid-in)
37. (grid-in)
38. (grid-in)

1   1   1

Practice Test 3

READING TEST

65 MINUTES, 52 QUESTIONS

Turn to Section 1 of your answer sheet to answer the questions in this section.

DIRECTIONS: Following each of the passages (or pairs of passages) below are questions about the passage (or passages). Read each passage carefully. Then, select the best answer for each question based on what is stated in the passage (or passages) and in any graphics that may accompany the passage.

Questions 1–10 are based on the following passage.

This passage is from Sir Arthur Conan Doyle, *The Great Boer War*, published in 1900.

Take a community of Dutchmen of the type of those who defended themselves for fifty years against all the power of Spain at a time when Spain was the greatest power in the world.
(5) Intermix with them a strain of those inflexible French Huguenots who gave up home and fortune and left their country for ever at the time of the revocation of the Edict of Nantes. The product must obviously be one of the most rug-
(10) ged, virile, unconquerable races ever seen upon earth. Take this formidable people and train them for seven generations in constant warfare against savage men and ferocious beasts, in circumstances under which no weakling could
(15) survive, place them so that they acquire exceptional skill with weapons and in horsemanship, give them a country which is eminently suited to the tactics of the huntsman, the marksman, and the rider. Then, finally, put a finer temper
(20) upon their military qualities by a dour fatalistic Old Testament religion and an ardent and con-

suming patriotism. Combine all these qualities and all these impulses in one individual, and you have the modern Boer—the most formi-
(25) dable antagonist who ever crossed the path of Imperial Britain. Our military history has largely consisted in our conflicts with France, but Napoleon and all his veterans have never treated us so roughly as these hard-bitten farm-
(30) ers with their ancient theology and their inconveniently modern rifles.

Look at the map of South Africa, and there, in the very center of the British possessions, like the stone in a peach, lies the great stretch of the
(35) two republics, a mighty domain for so small a people. How came they there? Who are these Teutonic folk who have burrowed so deeply into Africa? No one can know or appreciate the Boer who does not know his past, for he is what his
(40) past has made him.

It was in 1652 that the Dutch made their first lodgment at the Cape of Good Hope. The Portuguese had been there before them, but, repelled by the evil weather, and lured for-
(45) wards by rumors of gold, they had passed the true seat of empire and had voyaged further

to settle along the eastern coast. Some gold there was, but not much, and the Portuguese settlements have never been sources of wealth
(50) to the mother country. The coast upon which they settled reeked with malaria. A hundred miles of poisonous marsh separated it from the healthy inland plateau. For centuries these pioneers of South African colonization strove to
(55) obtain some further footing, but save along the courses of the rivers they made little progress. Fierce natives and an enervating climate barred their way.

But it was different with the Dutch. That very
(60) rudeness of climate which had so impressed the Portuguese adventurer was the source of their success. Cold and poverty and storm are the nurses of the qualities which make for empire. It is the men from the bleak and barren lands
(65) who master the children of the light and the heat. And so the Dutchmen at the Cape prospered and grew stronger in that robust climate. They did not penetrate far inland, for they were few in number and all they wanted was to be
(70) found close at hand. But they built themselves houses, and they supplied the Dutch East India Company with food and water and pushed their settlements up the long slopes which lead to the great central plateau.
(75) For a hundred more years the history of the colony was a record of the gradual spreading of the Afrikaners over the huge expanse of veld which lay to the north of them. Cattle raising became an industry, but in a country where six
(80) acres can hardly support a sheep, large farms are necessary for even small herds. The diseases which follow the white man had in Africa, been fatal to the natives, and an epidemic of smallpox cleared the country for the newcomers. Further
(85) and further north they pushed. Already the settlers were showing that independence of control and that detachment from Europe which has been their most prominent characteristic. Even the sway of the Dutch Company had

(90) caused them to revolt. The local rising, however, was hardly noticed in the universal cataclysm which followed the French Revolution. After twenty years, during which the world was shaken by the titanic struggle between England
(95) and France the Cape Colony was added in 1814 to the British Empire.

1. Which of the following, according to the author, did *not* go into the making of "the modern Boer" (line 24)?

(A) Dutch ancestry
(B) seven generations of constant warfare
(C) a country well-suited to the tactics the Boer were good at
(D) a religion that valued pleasure above all else

2. What does the author mean by "treated us so roughly" (line 29)?

(A) was such a difficult foe to defeat on the battlefield
(B) denied us vital exports of farm products
(C) insulted our national honor
(D) slaughtered so many of our helpless women and children

3. What does the writer mean when he describes the Boers' rifles as "inconveniently modern" (lines 30–31)?

(A) The Boers' rifles were up-to-date but poorly designed.
(B) The Boers' rifles were very effective.
(C) The Boers' rifles were effective but inconveniently stored so that there was difficulty in getting them to the troops before battle.
(D) The Boers' rifles were old-fashioned.

1   1   1

4. The word *nurses* as it is used in line 63 most nearly means

(A) things that foster certain characteristics in people
(B) persons trained to look after the sick and injured
(C) persons who are skilled in conserving precious resources
(D) foods that are nutritious in a cold, inhospitable climate

5. What, according to the author, was the main reason that the Dutch, rather than the Portuguese, succeeded in establishing a successful colony in Africa?

(A) The Dutch had more financial support from their mother country.
(B) The Dutch were more ruthless than the Portuguese.
(C) The Dutch were stronger than the Portuguese because they were from a harsher climate.
(D) The religion of the Dutch placed more emphasis on colonization of other lands than did that of the Portuguese.

6. Which of the following words best describes the attitude of the writer toward the Boers?

(A) skeptical
(B) admiring
(C) hostile
(D) neutral

7. The word *temper* as it is used in line 19 most nearly means

(A) irritability
(B) hardness
(C) resilience
(D) disposition

8. The word *consuming* as it is used in lines 21–22 most nearly means

(A) reckless
(B) self-destructive
(C) deeply felt
(D) wasteful

9. Which of the following would the author be *least* likely to say is a characteristic of the modern Boer?

(A) readiness to compromise
(B) independent spirit
(C) determination
(D) patriotism

10. The author does which of the following?

(A) questions the premises of some of his central assertions
(B) recounts historical events
(C) cites authorities to support some of his assertions
(D) contrasts his view of the Boer with that of other writers

1   1   1

Questions 11–20 are based on the following passage.

This passage is from Simon Singh, *Fermat's Enigma*, © 1997 by Simon Singh.

The periodical cicadas, most notably *Magicicada septendecim*, have the longest life cycle of any insect. Their unique life cycle begins underground, where the nymphs patiently suck
(5) the juice from the roots of trees. Then, after 17 years of waiting, the adult cicadas emerge from the ground, swarm in vast numbers, and temporarily swamp the landscape. Within a few weeks they mate, lay their eggs, and die.

(10) The question that puzzled biologists was, *Why is the cicada's life cycle so long*? And is there any significance to the life cycle being a prime number of years? Another species, *Magicicada tredecim*, swarms every 13 years, implying that
(15) life cycles lasting a prime number of years offer some evolutionary advantage.

One theory suggests that the cicada has a parasite that also goes through a lengthy life cycle and that the cicada is trying to avoid. If the
(20) parasite has a life cycle of, say, 2 years then the cicada wants to avoid a life cycle that is divisible by 2, otherwise the parasite and the cicada will regularly coincide. Similarly, if the parasite has a life cycle of 3 years then the cicada wants
(25) to avoid a life cycle that is divisible by 3, otherwise the parasite and the cicada will once again regularly coincide. Ultimately, to avoid meeting its parasite the cicadas' best strategy is to have a long life cycle lasting a prime number of years.
(30) Because nothing will divide into 17, *Magicicada septendecim* will rarely meet its parasite. If the parasite has a 2-year life cycle they will meet only every 34 years, and if it has a longer life cycle, say 16 years, then they will meet only
(35) every 272 (16×17) years.

In order to fight back, the parasite has only two life cycles that will increase the frequency of coincidences—the annual cycle and the same 17-year cycle as the cicada. However, the para-
(40) site is unlikely to survive reappearing 17 years in a row, because for the first 16 appearances there will be no cicadas for it to parasitize. On the other hand, in order to reach the 17-year life cycle, the generations of parasites would first
(45) have to evolve through the 16-year life cycle. This would mean at some stage of evolution the parasite and cicada would not coincide for 272 years! In either case the cicada's long prime life cycle protects it.

(50) This might explain why the alleged parasite has never been found! In the race to keep up with the cicada, the parasite probably kept extending its life cycle until it hit the 16-year hurdle. Then it failed to coincide for 272 years,
(55) by which time the lack of coinciding with cicadas had driven it to extinction. The result is a cicada with a 17-year life cycle, which it no longer needs because its parasite no longer exists.

11. As it is used in line 3 *unique* most nearly means

(A) one of a kind
(B) strange
(C) interesting
(D) solitary

12. Which word best describes the author's use of the word *patiently* in line 4?

(A) humorous
(B) ironic
(C) anthropomorphic
(D) exaggerated

13. Which of the following is the main likely intended audience of this passage?

(A) biologists
(B) laypersons interested in biology
(C) children
(D) journalists

14. Scientists theorize that cicadas have a 17-year life cycle because

   (A) 17 years is the optimum length of time for cicadas to most efficiently use available food and other resources in order to reproduce

   (B) no parasite species can survive 17 years without reproducing

   (C) it evolved as the most advantageous way for cicadas to co-exist with a parasite that has now become extinct

   (D) it evolved as a successful defense against a parasite that no longer exists

15. The reason *Magicicada tredecim* has a 13-year life cycle rather than a 17-year one is probably because

   (A) it is a less advanced species than *Magicicada septendecim*

   (B) two species of cicada having the same life cycle would create unnecessary competition for both species, so one evolved a different long prime number life cycle

   (C) its parasite became extinct so it had no need to evolve a life cycle lasting a longer prime number of years

   (D) it has a parasite with a 16-year life cycle, which means that it will meet its parasite only once every 208 (16 × 13) years

16. According to the theory described in the passage, which of the following statements is *not* true?

   (A) The cicada wants to decrease the frequency with which its life cycle coincides with its parasite.

   (B) The cicada's parasite wants to increase the frequency with which its life cycle coincides with that of the cicadas.

   (C) For the cicada's parasite, the longer the life cycle of the cicadas the better.

   (D) To avoid meeting its parasite it is advantageous for cicadas to have a life cycle lasting a prime number of years.

17. Which of the following lines provides the best evidence for the answer to the previous question?

   (A) lines 1–3 ("The . . . insect.")
   (B) lines 17–19 ("One . . . avoid.")
   (C) lines 27–29 ("Ultimately . . . years.")
   (D) lines 39–42 ("However . . . parasitize.")

18. Which of the following most accurately describes the explanation given in the passage for the fact that *Magicicada septendecim* has a 17-year life cycle?

   (A) It is based on a scientific theory that has reasonably good empirical and theoretical support.

   (B) It is based entirely on conjecture.

   (C) It is based on a scientific theory that has good theoretical support but no empirical support.

   (D) It is based on a theory with excellent empirical support but almost no theoretical support.

19. If an organism is discovered that parasitizes *Magicicada septendecim* it would

   (A) totally invalidate the theory that *Magicicada septendecim* evolved a long life cycle lasting a prime number of years to protect itself from a parasite

   (B) demonstrate conclusively that *Magicicada septendecim* evolved a long life cycle lasting a prime number of years in order to protect itself from a parasite

   (C) suggest that the theory that *Magicicada septendecim* evolved a long life cycle lasting a prime number of years to protect itself from a parasite might not be true

   (D) show conclusively that certain parasites can survive 272 years without a host to parasitize

1   1   1

20. The passage does all of the following *except*

   (A) pose questions about an observed phenomenon
   (B) formulate hypotheses
   (C) cite specific scientific papers dealing with the phenomena discussed
   (D) make use of deductive reasoning

Questions 21–31 are based on the following passages.

Passage 1 is from "Sustainability and Renewable Resources" by Steven Hayward, Ph.D., Elizabeth Fowler, and Laura Steadman. Copyright © 2000 by the Mackinac Center for Public Policy, Midland, Michigan.

Passage 2 is from OECD/Nuclear Energy Agency (2000), "Nuclear Energy in a Sustainable Development Perspective," *www.oecd-nea.org/sd*.

PASSAGE 1

Sustainability of renewable resources can be defined in different ways. Maintaining the economic output of an ecosystem (e.g., in a commercially exploited forest) is one option
(5) and maintaining the integrity of the whole ecosystem (e.g., in an old-growth forest) is another possibility. In addition to the immediate value associated with its economic outputs, the ecosystem that supports the resource flows may
(10) have option values for possible future uses, and existence values simply because people value its continued existence. Ecosystems have information value as working models of complex interacting life-sustaining systems, about
(15) which we still have much to learn. Option and existence values are less tangible and more difficult to measure than the immediate economic output, but may be of comparable importance, especially in a long-term perspective.
(20)   Renewable resources are subject to a variety of stresses, often more powerful than those acting on non-renewables. They are inexhaustible in the sense that they can be continually recycled, but this does not mean they are
(25) infinite in amount and does not prevent their degradation. Renewable resources, including air, water, and land, are subject to pressures for different uses, which may be incompatible. Air and water are particularly susceptible to pollut-
(30) ants because of the ease with which they can be used as open-access resources for receiving

1   1   1

and disseminating waste. Habitat for plant and
animal species may be very sensitive to environmental impacts, and easily destroyed. Thus
(35) renewable resources should be seen as finite
and vulnerable to pressures.

For example, a river system can be dedicated
to a variety of purposes: power generation,
drinking water, irrigation, industrial use, sport
(40) and commercial fishing, recreation in various
forms such as rafting and canoeing, swimming,
sailing or motor-boating on lakes and reser-
voirs, scenery for hikers and campers, sites for
resorts or cottages, or pure wilderness. Once
(45) dedicated, it cannot be used again without disturbing the constituencies that use its features
and whose property values depend on them.
Some of these uses may degrade the quality
of the water, or spoil it for other uses. In some
(50) cases, so much water is withdrawn for various
uses that not much reaches the sea or ocean—
the Nile and the Colorado are in this condition at times. This in turn can have an impact
on coastal currents and water quality, salin-
(55) ity of water in the delta, etc. Policy for renewable resources, including pricing policy, should
reflect their scarcity value, multiple uses, and
susceptibility to degradation or irreversible loss.

PASSAGE 2

Many instances of unsustainable resource
(60) use can be attributed not only to a lack of
a well-functioning market, but to perverse
institutional or legal incentives, such as a lack
of property rights to resources, or (especially
in underdeveloped nations) a lack of ready
(65) resource alternatives. Groundwater resources
in the U.S., for instance, are often overused
because of subsidies, a lack of tradable rights
to water ("use it or lose it"), and a lack of clear
property rights to water tables. Overfishing in
(70) the oceans provides a better example. It is easy
to imagine that cattle might be scarce, just as

buffalo became scarce, if they were owned in
common and were taken from one vast domain,
rather than being privately owned on separate
(75) ranches. While the exact analogue to barbed
wire for fishing grounds in the ocean may be
hard to conceive, assigning ownership rights
to the ocean should not be much more difficult
than assigning ownership rights to the radio
(80) frequency spectrum, as is currently being done
throughout the world.

The United States should encourage developing nations to follow this general strategy.
Much of the destruction of forest resources that
(85) is of present concern is due to unsound government policies that private owners would not
likely have undertaken to the same extent, if at
all. Al Gore notes in *Earth in the Balance:* "the
most serious examples of environmental deg-
(90) radation in the world today are tragedies that
were created or actively encouraged by governments—usually in pursuit of some notion that
a dramatic reordering of the material world
would enhance the greater good."

(95) There is much enthusiasm for "getting the
incentives right." This produces nods of agreement on the general level, and furious disagree-
ment about its specific application. "Getting the
incentives right" should mean chiefly assigning
(100) property rights to environmental goods, rather
than using government power to set the "correct price" for the use of a commonly held environmental good. Any so-called "market-based
incentive" policy that involves government set-
(105) ting the "correct price" to establish a "level playing field" is inherently flawed, because it mis-
understands the nature of markets and prices.
The government will always lack the necessary
knowledge to set the "right" price, and such
(110) policies will usually introduce new distortions
into the marketplace that will likely be counter-
productive and wasteful of resources.

21. The term "option values" as it is used in line 10 refers to

   (A) optional financial transactions
   (B) uses other than the present ones to which an ecosystem could be put
   (C) commercial worth
   (D) values that can be converted to cash under certain circumstances

22. According to the author of Passage 1, a renewable resource such as land is "inexhaustible" (lines 22–23) but not "infinite in amount" (line 25). This means that a particular resource, such as a 10-acre tract of land,

   (A) can be used for activities without worrying about the effects of these activities on it for the foreseeable future
   (B) can be put to an infinite number of uses but eventually it will have no value for anything
   (C) can be used for first one purpose, then another, and another, and so on indefinitely, but the total amount of land cannot be increased
   (D) is inexhaustible in that the supply of land is infinite, but there are so many types of uses to which it can be put that it ultimately will not be worthwhile maintaining

23. According to the author of Passage 1, once a river system is reserved for certain uses

   (A) it can never be used for any other purpose
   (B) it can be used for other purposes, but this will affect those already using it
   (C) it is always harmful to the river's ecosystem to change those uses
   (D) it is inevitable that water quality in the system will be degraded

24. Which of the following provides evidence for the answer to the previous question?

   (A) "Renewable . . . non-renewables." (lines 20–22)
   (B) "Air . . . waste." (lines 28–32)
   (C) "Once . . . them." (lines 44–47)
   (D) "This . . . etc." (lines 53–55)

25. As it is used in line 61 *perverse* most nearly means

   (A) convoluted
   (B) corrupt
   (C) caused by selfishness
   (D) arising from obstinate persistence in an error

26. According to the author of Passage 2, a lack of tradable rights to water encourages people with rights to water to

   (A) speculate on price rises for water
   (B) use other unsustainable resources in place of water
   (C) conserve the water they have
   (D) use the water they have rights to

27. We can infer that the author of Passage 2 believes that cattle might become scarce if they "were owned in common and were taken from one vast domain" (lines 72–73) because

   (A) people would have little incentive to conserve cattle
   (B) cattle would be much easier to kill
   (C) fatal diseases would spread easily through the cattle population
   (D) private ownership is always better than common or public ownership

1   1   1

28. According to the information provided in the passage, we can infer that the author of Passage 2 believes that

(A) one of the most important roles of government in the conservation of unsustainable resources is to assign property rights to environmental goods

(B) if property rights are assigned to environmental goods there will be no more instances of unsustainable resource use

(C) the private market has no role in the conservation of unsustainable resources

(D) only government has the expertise, access to information, and manpower to set the price of a commonly held economic good

29. Passage 1 and Passage 2 differ in that

(A) Passage 1 provides four definitions of sustainability of renewable resources; Passage 2 discusses several examples of unsustainable resource use

(B) Passage 1 describes the difficulties involved in promoting the sustainable use of resources; Passage 2 discusses some important concepts related to the sustainable use of resources and argues for more government involvement in the conservation of resources

(C) Passage 1 outlines a policy for encouraging the sustainable use of resources; Passage 2 discusses the role of government in preserving the environment through promoting the sustainable use of resources

(D) Passage 1 discusses various issues related to the sustainability of renewable resources and makes some general recommendations about the issue; Passage 2 analyzes certain examples of unsustainable resource use and makes firm recommendations about how some such problems in this area can be corrected

30. What comment would the author of Passage 1 be most likely to make about the suggestion in Passage 2 that ownership rights should be assigned to the ocean?

(A) It might have some merit but the results would have to be closely monitored because habitats could be destroyed and what is done by one owner could have a great effect on the areas of the ocean owned by others.

(B) It has some merit, but ownership rights to the ocean should be given only for fishing.

(C) It would be an excellent idea both for fostering economic activity and for environmental conservation.

(D) It is a good idea as long as owners are prohibited from oil exploration and promise to provide scientists with information on the effects of their commercial activities on the ecosystem.

31. Based on the information provided in Passage 1 and Passage 2, which of the following would most accurately reflect the probable views of the author of Passage 1 about the main argument made in Passage 2?

(A) He would say that a market-based approach should be encouraged in some instances, but that there are many problems related to the sustainability of renewable resources that cannot be solved by this approach alone.

(B) He would agree with it with certain relatively minor reservations.

(C) He would say that it is entirely misguided because the free market has no place in the conservation of resources.

(D) He would say that it is unrealistic because most governments will not grant property rights to resources.

PRACTICE TEST 3

Questions 32–42 are based on the following passage.

This passage is from David Alpaugh, "What Poets Can Learn from Songwriters," © 2011 by David Alpaugh, © 2011 *Scene4 Magazine*.

    In *Finishing The Hat*, Stephen Sondheim zeroes in on the essential difference between the art of the lyricist and that of the poet: "Poetry doesn't need music," he writes, "lyrics
(5) do." Poetry is the art of "concision," written to stand on its own; lyrics, the art of "expansion," written to accommodate music.

    And yet, the line between song and poem is not as firm as Sondheim suggests. William
(10) Blake called his greatest books of poetry *Songs of Innocence* and *Songs of Experience*. Walt Whitman called the opening poem of *Leaves of Grass* "Song of Myself." In both cases, their work straddles the line between the genres. Blake's

(15)   Piping down the valleys wild,
    Piping songs of pleasant glee,
    On a cloud I saw a child,
    And he laughing said to me

    practically begs to be set to music, and has been
(20) by more than one composer. Whitman's great elegy, beginning

    In the dooryard fronting an old farm-house
    near the white-wash'd palings,
    Stands the lilac-bush tall-growing . . .

(25) is one of the loveliest "songs" in the Kurt Weill/ Langston Hughes musical, *Street Scene*.

    Perhaps the most significant divergence between these sister arts today is the way in which poets and songwriters imagine their
(30) audiences.

    Whereas poetry is aimed almost exclusively at a limited number of fellow poets, hundreds of millions of men and women listen to songs on iPods and smart phones and millions more sing
(35) them in showers, kitchens, and karaoke bars.

    Poets who want to achieve wider readership might consider the qualities that attract millions of intelligent men and women to their sister art. First in importance, the primary mission
(40) of the poem should be the same as the primary mission of the song: *to make the listener want to hear the song again and again*!

    If I'm satisfied with listening to a song once the song is a failure! Yet, how many times have
(45) I heard poets introduce their poems with words like these:

    "I think I may have read this poem here before. If so, I hope you'll bear with me. Hopefully there are others here who haven't
(50) heard it."

    Imagine Paul Simon saying, "If there's anyone here who has already heard 'Bridge Over Troubled Water' I apologize for boring you with it again." If Frost came back from the grave
(55) would audiences shout, "We only want to hear new work, Robert. Don't you dare read 'Birches' or 'The Road Not Taken'!" Frost acknowledged poetry's ambition to be heard again and again when he explained that his goal was "to lodge a
(60) few poems where they will be hard to get rid of."

    Too many poets programmatically eschew the memory cues songwriters unabashedly use to accomplish this mission. After talking to writing students, conditioned by their professors
(65) to tolerate no rhyme or meter in poetry, James Fenton suggests (in *American Scholar*) that they would "be happier if they accepted that the person who was studying creative writing, with the aim of producing poetry, was the same person
(70) who had a car full of country and western tapes, or whatever the music was that delighted them."

    The aversion to rhyme and meter, Fenton implies, is an artificially-acquired, counter-intuitive, schizophrenic taste. The popularity
(75) of rap, rock, and country music, as well as the

1   1   1

power of advertising, remind us that our desire for repetition is based on pulse and heartbeat and the nature of the human brain. It's suicidal for poets to reject their own biology!

(80)   Still, I hear critics admonishing me for ignoring the singing elephant in the room. It's not the lyric, they protest, but the music that makes us want to hear a song again and again. And music is something poets do not have in their arsenal.

(85)   Or do they? To be sure, poets cannot rely on actual musical tones; still the poems I love (formal or open) have a quasi-melodic structure that has an effect not unlike melody proper.

Melody seizes us, picks us up, and holds us (90) with the progression of its tones, never putting us back on the ground until the final notes stops vibrating. Great poems use purely verbal elements—syllables, words, accent—to build a rhetorical arc that provides a similar experience.

(95)   At a time when too many poets have so purged their "poetry" of repetition and melody that it reads and sounds like outright prose, songwriters continue to satisfy a human craving that cannot and should not be denied. Whether (100) or not poets can again become relevant to non-practitioners of their art may depend on how well they listen to their big sister.

32. Which of the following statements about Stephen Sondheim's description of the difference between the art of the lyricist and that of the poet would the author of this passage be most likely to agree with?

(A) It is simplistic, but contains an element of truth.
(B) It expresses a truth about only one relatively minor aspect of the difference between the two arts.
(C) It is fundamentally true, yet at times the difference between them is not so clear.
(D) It is impossible to meaningfully generalize either about lyrics or poetry.

33. The author quotes lines from Blake's *Songs of Innocence* in order to

(A) illustrate how very different a poem is from a lyric
(B) provide an example of a poem that is very much like a lyric
(C) show that only a simple poem can successfully be set to music
(D) show that there is no difference between melody in music and repetition in poetry

34. According to the author, one of the main reasons that poems are not as popular as songs is that

(A) poets tend to write for a limited audience, whereas songwriters tend to write for a mass audience
(B) poets are not sufficiently trained in music theory and composition
(C) poems have become too complex for most people to understand
(D) poems have become too much like songs, thus losing the distinctiveness that gives them their appeal

35. Which of the following provides evidence for the answer to the previous question?

(A) "Whereas . . . bars." (lines 31–35)
(B) "After . . . them.'" (lines 63–71)
(C) "The . . . biology!" (lines 74–79)
(D) "At . . . denied." (lines 95–99)

36. The meaning of the phrase "programmatically eschew" as it is used in line 61 is most nearly

(A) automatically embrace as part of a program
(B) slavishly copy
(C) avoid something because one thinks it is conformist
(D) avoid something because it isn't part of one's customary system

37. The quotation by James Fenton "[They would] be happier if they accepted that the person who was studying creative writing, with the aim of producing poetry, was the same person who had a car full of country and western tapes, or whatever the music was that delighted them" (lines 67–71) suggests that

    (A) more music lovers should enroll in writing courses aimed at producing poets
    (B) writing students should listen to more music
    (C) writing students wanting to become poets tend not to draw on their knowledge and appreciation of music in their attempts to produce poetry
    (D) writing students are not happy because their professors do not allow them to draw on their knowledge and appreciation of music in their writing of poetry

38. As it is used in line 74 *schizophrenic* most nearly means

    (A) characterized by delusional thought patterns
    (B) characterized by the coexistence of antagonistic qualities
    (C) outside the bounds of what is normally accepted
    (D) mentally unstable

39. The phrase "singing elephant in the room" as it is used in line 81 can be described accurately by all of the following words *except*

    (A) metaphorical
    (B) jocular
    (C) colorful
    (D) elegiac

40. As it is used in line 88 "melody proper" most nearly means

    (A) musical melody
    (B) properly used melody
    (C) poetic "melody"
    (D) melody like that in old-time songs

41. In the last line of the passage the author says, "Whether or not poets can again become relevant to non-practitioners of their art may depend on how well they listen to their big sister" (lines 99–102).

    The author is most likely suggesting that

    (A) to significantly increase their popularity of their work among people who are not poets themselves, poets should strongly consider learning some of the techniques that songwriters use and employing them when they write poetry
    (B) to become popular outside poetry circles poets should write poems just like song lyrics
    (C) how popular a poet becomes depends on how sophisticated his or her musical tastes are
    (D) young poets must heed the advice of senior poets, including listening to popular music to develop their sense of rhythm and melody

42. Based on the information in the passage, the author would be most likely to agree with the statement that

    (A) a poem can be both excellent and popular
    (B) popular poetry is almost by definition bad poetry
    (C) the more like a song a poem becomes the better it is
    (D) a poem without a lot of "musical" qualities cannot be a good poem

1   1   1

Questions 43–52 are based on the following passage.

This passage is from Preston Dyches, "Cassini Catches Titan Naked in the Solar Wind," NASA News and Features, January 28, 2015.

Researchers studying data from NASA's Cassini mission have observed that Saturn's largest moon, Titan, behaves much like Venus, Mars, or a comet when exposed to the raw
(5) power of the solar wind. The observations suggest that unmagnetized bodies like Titan might interact with the solar wind in the same basic ways, regardless of their nature or distance from the sun.

(10) Titan is large enough that it could be considered a planet if it orbited the sun on its own, and a flyby of the giant moon in Dec. 2013 simulated that scenario, from Cassini's vantage point. The encounter was unique within Cassini's mis-
(15) sion, as it was the only time the spacecraft has observed Titan in a pristine state, outside the region of space dominated by Saturn's magnetic field, called its magnetosphere.

"We observed that Titan interacts with the
(20) solar wind very much like Mars, if you moved it to the distance of Saturn," said Cesar Bertucci of the Institute of Astronomy and Space Physics in Buenos Aires, who led the research with colleagues from the Cassini mission. "We thought
(25) Titan in this state would look different. We certainly were surprised," he said.

The solar wind is a fast-flowing gale of charged particles that continually streams outward from the sun, flowing around the planets
(30) like islands in a river. Studying the effects of the solar wind at other planets helps scientists understand how the sun's activity affects their atmospheres. These effects can include modification of an atmosphere's chemistry as well as
(35) its gradual loss to space.

Titan spends about 95 percent of the time within Saturn's magnetosphere. But during a

Cassini flyby on Dec. 1, 2013, the giant moon happened to be on the sunward side of Saturn
(40) when a powerful outburst of solar activity reached the planet. The strong surge in the solar wind so compressed the sun-facing side of Saturn's magnetosphere that the bubble's outer edge was pushed inside the orbit of Titan. This
(45) left the moon exposed to, and unprotected from, the raging stream of energetic solar particles.

Using its magnetometer instrument, which is akin to an exquisitely sensitive compass, Cassini has observed Titan many times dur-
(50) ing the mission's decade in the Saturn system, but always within Saturn's magnetosphere. The spacecraft has not been able to detect a magnetic field coming from Titan itself. In its usual state, Titan is cloaked in Saturn's magnetic field.

(55) This time the influence of Saturn was not present, allowing Cassini's magnetometer to observe Titan as it interacted directly with the solar wind. The special circumstance allowed Bertucci and colleagues to study the shock-
(60) wave that formed around Titan where the full-force solar wind rammed into the moon's atmosphere.

At Earth, our planet's powerful magnetic field acts as a shield against the solar wind,
(65) helping to protect our atmosphere from being stripped away. In the case of Venus, Mars, and comets—none of which is protected by a global magnetic field—the solar wind drapes around the objects themselves, interacting directly with
(70) their atmospheres (or in the comet's case, its coma). Cassini saw the same thing at Titan. Researchers thought they would have to treat Titan's response to the solar wind with a unique approach because the chemistry of the hazy
(75) moon's dense atmosphere is highly complex. But Cassini's observations of a naked Titan hinted at a more elegant solution. "This could mean we can use the same tools to study how vastly different worlds, in different parts of the

(80) solar system, interact with the wind from the sun," Bertucci said.

Bertucci noted that the list of similarly unmagnetized bodies might include the dwarf planet Pluto, to be visited this year for the first (85) time by NASA's New Horizons spacecraft.

"After nearly a decade in orbit, the Cassini mission has revealed once again that the Saturn system is full of surprises," said Michele Dougherty, principal investigator of the Cassini (90) magnetometer at Imperial College, London. "After more than a hundred flybys, we have finally encountered Titan out in the solar wind, which will allow us to better understand how such moons maintain or lose their (95) atmospheres."

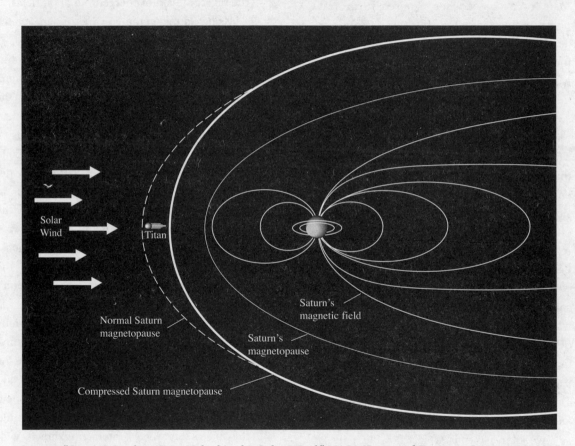

Source: "Cassini Catches Titan Naked in the Solar Wind," NASA News and Features, January 28, 2015.

43. According to the author

(A) all planets have a magnetosphere
(B) only Earth has a magnetosphere
(C) Earth and Saturn have a magnetosphere
(D) only comets have a magnetosphere

44. Which of the following provide evidence for the answer to the previous question?

(A) "The . . . sun." (lines 5–9) and
"Bertucci . . . spacecraft." (lines 82–85)
(B) "dominated . . . magnetosphere" (lines 17–18)
and "At . . . away." (lines 63–66)
(C) "The . . . river." (lines 27–30) and
"The . . . itself." (lines 51–53)
(D) "The . . . Titan." (lines 41–44) and
"In . . . coma." (lines 66–71)

45. From the information provided we can infer that

    (A) the strength of the solar wind varies
    (B) the solar wind does not affect the atmosphere of planets in orbit around the sun
    (C) the solar wind is stronger at Saturn than at Earth
    (D) no known force can affect the solar wind

46. Which of the following provides evidence for the answer to the previous question?

    (A) "The . . . sun." (lines 5–9)
    (B) "The . . . river." (lines 27–30)
    (C) "The . . . Titan." (lines 41–44)
    (D) "Researchers . . . complex." (lines 72–75)

47. Which of the following provides the best summary of the passage?

    (A) "Researchers . . . sun." (lines 1–9)
    (B) "We . . . said." (lines 19–26)
    (C) "Using . . . field." (lines 47–54)
    (D) "Researchers . . . said." (lines 72–81)

48. The word *elegant* as it is used in line 77 most nearly means

    (A) complex
    (B) tasteful and distinguished
    (C) ingenious and simple
    (D) stylish

49. In the drawing Titan is pictured

    (A) inside Saturn's magnetic field
    (B) outside Saturn's compressed magnetosphere
    (C) outside Saturn's normal magnetosphere
    (D) halfway between the sun and Saturn

50. The author most likely used the word *naked* in line 76 to

    (A) shock the reader
    (B) relate scientific findings to famous mythological figures
    (C) help the reader picture Titan as a god
    (D) dramatize the event described

51. The author makes use of all of the following *except*

    (A) quotations from experts
    (B) figurative language
    (C) description of natural phenomena
    (D) rhetorical questions

52. The author says, "The spacecraft has not been able to detect a magnetic field coming from Titan itself. In its usual state, Titan is cloaked in Saturn's magnetic field" (lines 51–54). From this we can infer that

    (A) Titan may have a magnetic field that is difficult to detect because of Saturn's powerful magnetic field
    (B) Titan definitely does not have its own magnetic field
    (C) Titan definitely has its own magnetic field
    (D) scientists will never be able to determine if Titan has its own magnetic field

STOP If there is still time remaining, you may review your answers.

WRITING AND LANGUAGE TEST

35 MINUTES, 44 QUESTIONS

Turn to Section 2 of your answer sheet to answer the questions in this section.

DIRECTIONS: Questions follow each of the passages below. Some questions ask you how the passage might be changed to improve the expression of ideas. Other questions ask you how the passage might be altered to correct errors in grammar, usage, and punctuation. One or more graphics accompany some passages. You will be required to consider these graphics as you answer questions about editing the passage.

There are three types of questions. In the first type, a part of the passage is underlined. The second type is based on a certain part of the passage. The third type is based on the entire passage.

Read each passage. Then, choose the answer to each question that changes the passage so that it is consistent with the conventions of standard written English. One of the answer choices for many questions is "NO CHANGE." Choosing this answer means that you believe the best answer is to make no change in the passage.

Questions 1–11 are based on the following passage.

Drawing in Ancient Egypt

Of the system upon which drawing was taught by the Egyptian masters, we know nothing. **❶** It was learning experience to determine the general proportions of the body, and the invariable relations of the various parts one with another; but they never troubled themselves to tabulate those proportions, or **❷** reducing them to a system. Nothing in what remains to us of their **❸** works that justify the belief that they ever possessed a canon based upon the length of the human finger or foot. Theirs was a teaching of routine,

1. For the sake of clarity of expression and meaning, the underlined portion of the sentence should be written as follows:

   (A) as it is now
   (B) Learning experience determining
   (C) Learning experience, determining
   (D) They had learned from experience to determine

2. (A) NO CHANGE
   (B) to reduce
   (C) having reduced
   (D) have to reduce

3. (A) NO CHANGE
   (B) works justifies
   (C) working justifies
   (D) workings justify

2   2   2

and not of theory. Models executed by the master ④ <u>copied</u> over and over again by his pupils,
until they could reproduce them with absolute
exactness. That they also studied from life is
shown by the facility with which they seized
a likeness, or ⑤ <u>converted</u> the characteristics
and movements of different kinds of animals.
They made their first attempts upon slabs of
limestone, on drawing boards covered with a
coat of red or white stucco, or on the backs
of old manuscripts of no value. New papyrus
was too dear to be spoiled by the scrawls of
tyros. ⑥ <u>They had neither pencil nor stylus.</u>
<u>They were making use of the reed, the end of</u>
<u>which, when steeped in water, opened out into</u>
<u>small fibers, and made a more or less fine brush</u>
<u>according to the size of the stem.</u> The palette
was of thin wood, in shape a rectangular
oblong, with a groove ⑦ <u>where</u> to lay the
brush at the lower end. At the upper end were

4. (A) NO CHANGE
   (B) copy
   (C) to copy
   (D) were copied

5. (A) NO CHANGE
   (B) yielded
   (C) rendered
   (D) furnished

6. Which choice most effectively combines the
   underlined sentences?

   (A) They had neither pencil nor stylus, they
       made use of the reed, the end of which,
       when steeped in water, opened out into
       small fibers, and made a more or less fine
       brush according to the size of the stem.
   (B) Having neither pencil nor stylus, made use
       of the reed, the end of which, when steeped
       in water, opened out into small fibers, mak-
       ing a more or less fine brush according to
       the size of the stem.
   (C) Having neither pencil nor stylus, they made
       use of the reed, the end of which, when
       steeped in water, opened out into small
       fibers, and made a more or less fine brush
       according to the size of the stem.
   (D) They had neither pencil nor stylus, they
       were making use of the reed, the end of
       which, when steeped in water, it opened out
       into small fibers, this made a more or less
       fine brush according to the size of the stem.

7. (A) NO CHANGE
   (B) which
   (C) in which
   (D) when

2   2   2

two or more cup-like hollows, each fitted with a cake of **8** <u>ink; black and red</u> being the colors most in use. A tiny pestle and mortar for color-grinding, and a cup of water in which to clip and wash the brush, completed the apparatus of the student. **9** Palette in hand, **10** <u>squatted</u> cross-legged before his copy, and, without any kind of support for his wrist, endeavored to reproduce the outline in black. The master looked **11** <u>across</u> his work when done, and corrected the errors in red ink.

8. (A) NO CHANGE
   (B) ink black and red
   (C) ink—black and red
   (D) ink (black and red)

9. At this point, the writer is considering adding the following sentence:

   The statues and bas-reliefs, which decorated the temples and tombs of ancient Egypt, were for the most part painted.

   Should the writer make this addition here?

   (A) Yes, because it helps the reader understand why students learned to draw.
   (B) Yes, because it introduces the main topic of the passage.
   (C) No, because this sentence provides extraneous details about how students learned to draw.
   (D) No, because this sentence does not follow logically from the sentence preceding it, which describes how students learned to draw.

10. (A) NO CHANGE
    (B) squatting
    (C) he squatted
    (D) a squat

11. (A) NO CHANGE
    (B) past
    (C) around
    (D) over

Questions 12–22 are based on the following passage.

You're a What? Acupuncturist

Got a headache? It could be your liver. And as part of your treatment, Jon Simon might stick a needle in your toe. Jon is an acupuncturist. He uses needles, herbs, and other devices to treat ailments such as headaches, back problems, and foot pain. Through his work, Jon **12** alleges Oriental medicine's centuries-old precept that the body is interconnected—head to toe and everything in between. It's a complex approach to well-being, he says, not a quick fix: "Acupuncture is more than just sticking needles in somebody's **13** body, its a whole system of healing."

Patients begin visits to Jon's New York City office by completing a form to describe their **14** condition, Jon reviews the form and then in an interview with the patient focuses on specific symptoms. "It may seem like I'm asking a bunch of unrelated questions," he says, "but I'm trying to find the nature of the complaint." Based on information gathered from the form and the interview, Jon **15** has recommended treatment.

The most common acupuncture treatment is **16** needling strategically inserting and manipulating thin, solid needles at specific points along the skin. Other treatment methods, often used in conjunction with needling, **17** including the prescriptions of herbs or herb mixtures; acupressure, which involves massaging instead of needling acupuncture points; and recommendations for lifestyle changes, such as dietary modifications and exercise. Jon usually gives a brief description of Oriental medicine **18** in case patients

12. (A) NO CHANGE
    (B) pleads
    (C) advocates
    (D) bears

13. (A) NO CHANGE
    (B) body. Its
    (C) body its
    (D) body. It's

14. For the sake of clarity of meaning and expression, the underlined portion of the sentence should be written as follows:

    (A) as it is now
    (B) condition. Jon reviews the form and then, in an interview with the patient, focuses
    (C) condition, Jon reviewing the form and then in an interview with the patient focusing
    (D) condition. Jon, reviewing the form, and then in an interview with the patient, focuses

15. (A) NO CHANGE
    (B) is recommending
    (C) had recommended
    (D) recommends

16. (A) NO CHANGE
    (B) needling: strategically
    (C) needling; strategically
    (D) needling. Strategically

17. (A) NO CHANGE
    (B) including the prescribing of
    (C) include prescriptions of
    (D) include to prescribe

18. (A) NO CHANGE
    (B) so that
    (C) whether
    (D) which

understand his suggested treatment. **19** Pain or illness results when the flow of energy is disrupted; by stimulating meridians via specific points on the skin, acupuncture eliminates disruption and restores balance.

[1] A study in the November 1998 *Journal of the American Medical Association* reports that between 1990 and 1997, patient visits to practitioners of alternative medicine increased about 47 percent. [2] And in a survey published in the January 2001 *American Demographics,* 70 percent of respondents had tried at least 1 of 8 selected forms of alternative medicine, including acupuncture. [3] **20** Surprisingly, the number of acupuncturists also has risen. [4] According to the Acupuncture and Oriental Medicine Alliance, the number of **21** licensed acupuncturists nearly tripled in less than a decade: from 525 in 1992 to 14,228 in 2000. [5] Data show that acupuncture and other forms of traditional Oriental medicine are gaining popularity as a treatment choice. **22**

19. At this point the writer is considering adding the following sentence.

Oriental medicine is based on the principle that human energy circulates along interconnected pathways known as meridians.

Should the writer make this addition here?

(A) Yes, because this sentence effectively links the preceding sentence to the following sentence. This sentence describes the principle of oriental medicine. The following sentence describes how illness results when processes this principle describes are disrupted.

(B) Yes, because this sentence describes more precisely than the preceding sentence how patients can better understand the principle of Oriental medicine.

(C) No, because this sentence is not directly relevant to the main topic of the passage, which is acupuncture.

(D) No, because this principle is disputed by Western medicine.

20. (A) NO CHANGE
    (B) Likely
    (C) Inexplicably
    (D) Not surprisingly

21. (A) NO CHANGE
    (B) licensing acupuncturists
    (C) license acupuncturists
    (D) acupuncturists with license

22. For the sake of the cohesion of this paragraph, sentence 5 should be placed

    (A) where it is now
    (B) before sentence 1
    (C) after sentence 1
    (D) after sentence 3

2   2   2

Questions 23–33 are based on the following passage.

Stained Glass

[1]

Stained glass is not one of the arts in which the method of production reveals itself at the first glance. Indeed, so few people when looking at a stained-glass window, whether a gorgeous and solemn one of the thirteenth or fourteenth century, or a crude and vulgar one of the nineteenth, realize the long and laborious process by which the result, good or bad, has been obtained. **㉓**

[2]

㉔ One hears it so often spoken of as <u>"painted glass" that it is not surprising that there should be a good deal of misconception on the point.</u> It must be clearly understood then that the color effects **㉕** <u>which are the glorious art</u> are not directly produced by painting at all, but by the **㉖** <u>window building up</u> of a multitude of small pieces of white and colored glass—glass, that is, colored in the making, and of which the artist must choose the exact shades he needs, cut them out to shape, and **㉗** <u>fitting them together</u> to form his design, using a separate piece for every color or shade of color.

Think about the passage as a whole as you answer question 23.

23. To make the passage most logical, paragraph 1 should be placed

   (A) where it is now
   (B) after paragraph 2
   (C) after paragraph 3
   (D) after paragraph 4

24. The writer is considering deleting the underlined sentence. Should the writer do this?

   (A) Yes, because the passage is mainly about the history of stained glass, not about how it is made.
   (B) Yes, because no evidence is provided to support the assertion that stained glass is "so often spoken of as 'painted glass.' "
   (C) No, because the following sentence would not make good sense if this sentence were deleted. The following sentence explains the "misconception" mentioned in this sentence.
   (D) No, because the focus of the passage is on common misconceptions about stained glass and this sentence introduces this topic.

25. (A) NO CHANGE
   (B) which are the glory of the art
   (C) which, glorifying the art,
   (D) which are glorious of the art

26. (A) NO CHANGE
   (B) window, it has been built up
   (C) window's being built up
   (D) window when building up

27. (A) NO CHANGE
   (B) having been fit together
   (C) he fits them together
   (D) fit them together

PRACTICE TEST 3

2   2   2

[3]

In twelfth and thirteenth century windows many of these pieces are only half an inch wide and from one to two inches long, and few are bigger than the palm of one's hand; so the reader can **28** humor himself, if he wishes, in trying to calculate the number of pieces in one of the huge windows of this date in the Cathedral of Canterbury, York, or Chartres, **29** and the labor that has involved this, the initial stage of the process.

[4]

When the window is finished these pieces are put together like a puzzle and joined by grooved strips of lead soldered at the joints, just as any "lattice" window is put together; but before this **30** is done the details of the design—features, folds of drapery, patterns, and so on—are painted on the glass in an opaque brownish enamel made of oxide of iron and other metals ground up with a "soft" glass (glass with a low melting-point). This is mixed with oil or gum and water in order to apply it, and then the glass is placed in a kiln and "fired" till the enamel is fused on and, if well fired, becomes part of the glass **31** itself, the only "painting" involved in the production of a stained-glass window. **32** Its' effect, in the hand of an artist, is to decorate and enrich what would **33** otherwise be somewhat crude and papery in effect.

28. (A) NO CHANGE
    (B) content
    (C) amuse
    (D) accommodate

29. (A) NO CHANGE
    (B) and the labor involved in this,
    (C) and the labor in which this is involved,
    (D) and the involving labor of this,

30. (A) NO CHANGE
    (B) has
    (C) is being
    (D) had been

31. Rewrite the underlined portion of the sentence to make two distinct sentences that make sense.

    (A) itself. Only the "painting" is
    (B) itself. The only "painting" is
    (C) itself. This is the only "painting"
    (D) itself. The "painting" is only

32. (A) NO CHANGE
    (B) It's
    (C) Its
    (D) It is

33. (A) NO CHANGE
    (B) nevertheless
    (C) subsequently
    (D) accordingly

2   2   2

Questions 34–44 are based on the following passage and supplementary material.

Global Trends in Literacy

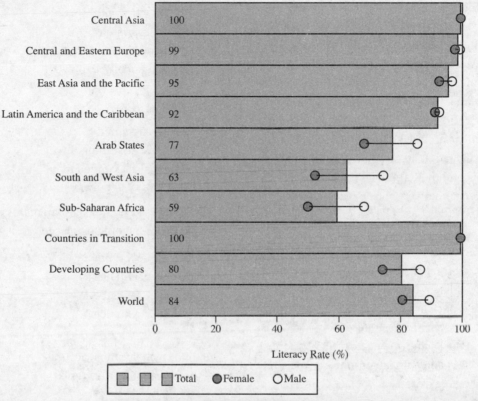

Adult Literacy Rate by Region and Sex, 2011

Region	Total
Central Asia	100
Central and Eastern Europe	99
East Asia and the Pacific	95
Latin America and the Caribbean	92
Arab States	77
South and West Asia	63
Sub-Saharan Africa	59
Countries in Transition	100
Developing Countries	80
World	84

Literacy Rate (%)

☐ ☐ ☐ Total   ●Female   ○Male

Note: 2011 data refer to the period 2005–2011.
Source: UNESCO Institute for Statistics, May 2013.

In 2011, the global adult literacy rate for the population aged 15 years and older was ❸❹ 74%. Regional averages of the adult literacy rate in 2011 were calculated for 151 countries and territories from eight regions, except ❸❺ North America and Western Europe due to the limited number of countries in the region that report literacy rates.

34. Which choice most accurately represents the information in the graph?

(A) NO CHANGE
(B) 64%
(C) 84%
(D) 94%

35. Which choice most accurately represents the information in the graph?

(A) NO CHANGE
(B) East Asia and the Pacific
(C) sub-Saharan Africa
(D) South and West Asia

2   2   2

[1] Adult literacy rates were below the global average in South and West Asia (63%) and sub-Saharan Africa (59%), where more than one-third of adults could not read and write. [2] However, the average for Latin America and the Caribbean **36** evades lower literacy rates in the Caribbean, where the adult literacy rate was only 69% in 2011. [3] Two regions, Central and Eastern Europe and Central Asia, were at or near universal literacy, with adult literacy rates of 99% and 100%, **37** consequently. [4] North America and Western Europe **38** also assumes near universal adult literacy. [5] In East Asia and the Pacific (adult literacy rate of 95%) and Latin America and the Caribbean (92%) at least nine out of ten adults were able to read and write. **39**

An examination of gender-disaggregated data reveals that in all regions with data, except Central Asia, female literacy rates were **40** higher than male literacy rates. The gap was especially large in the Arab States (male rate of 85% vs. female rate of 68%), **41** East Asia and the Pacific (male rate of 92% vs. female rate of 90%) and sub-Saharan Africa (male rate of 68% vs. female rate of 51%). Globally, 89% of men and 80% of women were able to read and write in 2011.

36. (A) NO CHANGE
    (B) harbors
    (C) conceals
    (D) curbs

37. (A) NO CHANGE
    (B) appropriately
    (C) respectively
    (D) sequentially

38. (A) NO CHANGE
    (B) also assumed
    (C) is also assuming
    (D) are also assumed to be

39. For the sake of the cohesion of this paragraph, sentence 2 should be placed

    (A) where it is now
    (B) after sentence 3
    (C) after sentence 4
    (D) after sentence 5

40. Which choice most accurately represents the information in the graph?

    (A) NO CHANGE
    (B) lower than
    (C) similar to
    (D) related to

41. Which choice most accurately represents the information in the graph?

    (A) NO CHANGE
    (B) South and West Asia (male rate of 74% vs. female rate of 52%)
    (C) Latin America and the Caribbean (male rate of 93% vs. female rate of 92%)
    (D) Central and Eastern Europe (male rate of 99% vs. female rate of 98%)

2   2   2

Adult literacy rates are projected to increase in almost all regions between 2011 and 2015. The exception is Central and Eastern Europe, where projections **42** implicate a small drop in adult literacy by one-half of a percentage point. The global adult literacy rate is projected to reach 86% in 2015, meaning that the target global literacy rate of 91%, a goal adopted by the World Education Forum in 2000, would be missed by 5%. Sub-Saharan Africa is projected to be **43** furthest from the 2015 target, and South and West Asia is projected to also come below the target for 2015. Central and Eastern Europe, Central Asia, and East Asia and the Pacific are projected to **44** reach, or come within one percentage point of the 2015 target.

42. (A) NO CHANGE
    (B) insinuate
    (C) connote
    (D) indicate

43. (A) NO CHANGE
    (B) above
    (C) right on
    (D) within

44. (A) NO CHANGE
    (B) reach or come within
    (C) reach or come, within
    (D) reach; or come within

STOP   If there is still time remaining, you may review your answers.

MATH TEST (NO CALCULATOR)

25 MINUTES, 20 QUESTIONS

Turn to Section 3 of your answer sheet to answer the questions in this section.

DIRECTIONS: For questions 1–15, solve each problem and choose the best answer from the given options. Fill in the corresponding circle on your answer document. For questions 16–20, solve the problem and fill in the answer on the answer sheet grid. Please use scrap paper to work out your answers.

Notes:
- You **CANNOT** use a calculator on this section.
- All variables and expressions represent real numbers unless indicated otherwise.
- All figures are drawn to scale unless indicated otherwise.
- All figures are in a plane unless indicated otherwise.
- Unless indicated otherwise, the domain of a given function is the set of all real numbers x for which the function has real values.

REFERENCE INFORMATION

Area Facts	**Volume Facts**	**Triangle Facts**

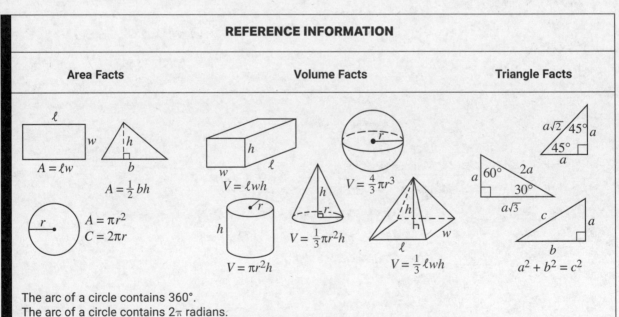

The arc of a circle contains 360°.
The arc of a circle contains 2π radians.
The sum of the measures of the angles in a triangle is 180°.

3

3

1. If $\dfrac{x+1}{4} = y$ and $y = 4$, what is the value of x?

   (A) 15
   (B) 13
   (C) 11
   (D) 8

2. Simplify $-2\left(\dfrac{x^2 - 8x - 180}{x + 10}\right)$ if $x \neq -10$

   (A) $x - 18$
   (B) $-2x + 36$
   (C) $-2x^2 + x$
   (D) $x + 10$

3. If $(x + n)^2 = x^2 + 19x + n^2$, what is the value of n^2?

   (A) 361
   (B) $\dfrac{361}{2}$
   (C) $\dfrac{361}{4}$
   (D) 38

4. Which of the following equations has only one x-intercept in the xy-plane?

   (A) $x^2 + 2x - 48 = y$
   (B) $x^2 + 11x + 30 = y$
   (C) $x^2 - 6x + 8 = y$
   (D) $x^2 + 6x + 9 = y$

5. If M represents the number of prime numbers less than 25 and r is their range, what is $2M - r$?

   (A) -3
   (B) 3
   (C) 8.9
   (D) 27

6. $y = -\dfrac{5}{8}x + 3$

   Which of the following is an equation of a line that is parallel to the equation above?

   (A) $5x + 8y = 48$
   (B) $5x - 8y = 24$
   (C) $6x + 3y = 22$
   (D) $3x - 5y = 17$

7. If $f(2) = 4$, $f(4) = 2$, and $g(2) = 6$, what is the value of $g(f(4))$?

   (A) 2
   (B) 4
   (C) 6
   (D) 8

8. If $2x + 3y = 17$ and $5x - 7y = 31$, what is the value of $\dfrac{7x - 4y}{8}$?

   (A) 6
   (B) 7
   (C) 8
   (D) 12

9. If the area of a rectangle is shown by the expression $16x^2 - 9y^2$ and the width is $4x - 3y$, what is the perimeter of the rectangle?

   (A) $4(x + y)$
   (B) $16x$
   (C) $64x^2 - 36y^2$
   (D) $2(x + y)$

10. In the xy-plane, the parabola with equation $y = (x - 6)^2$ intersects the line with equation $y = 36$ at two points, A and B. What is the length of AB?

    (A) 12
    (B) 16
    (C) 24
    (D) 48

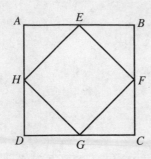

11. Square *EHGF* lies within square *ABCD* with *E*, *F*, *G*, and *H* all being midpoints. If the area of square *EHGF* is 64 units squared, what is the area of square *ABCD* (in square units)?

(A) 36

(B) 64

(C) $96\sqrt{2}$

(D) 128

12. In a 10-question true/false test, what is the probability of guessing correctly on exactly two of the questions from 6 through 8?

(A) $\frac{1}{3}$

(B) $\frac{3}{8}$

(C) $\frac{2}{3}$

(D) $\frac{7}{8}$

13. $2x^2 + y^2 = 360$

$y = 4x$

What is the value of x^2?

(A) 12

(B) 15

(C) 18

(D) 20

14. What are the solutions to $2x^2 + 8x - 12 = 0$?

(A) $x = -4 \pm 3\sqrt{10}$

(B) $x = -3 + \frac{\sqrt{10}}{10}$

(C) $x = -2 \pm \sqrt{10}$

(D) $x = 2 \pm \sqrt{10}$

15. $(ax - 7)(bx + 5) = 6x^2 + cx - 35$. If $ab = 6$ and $a - b = -1$, what are two possible values of c?

(A) $c = 2$ or $c = -4$

(B) $c = -11$ or $c = -1$

(C) $c = -2$ or $c = 4$

(D) $c = 12$ or $c = -5$

Grid-in Response Directions

In questions 16–20, first solve the problem, and then enter your answer on the grid provided on the answer sheet. The instructions for entering your answers follow.

- First, write your answer in the boxes at the top of the grid.
- Second, grid your answer in the columns below the boxes.
- Use the fraction bar in the first row or the decimal point in the second row to enter fractions and decimals.

Either position is acceptable

- Grid only one space in each column.
- Entering the answer in the boxes is recommended as an aid in gridding but is not required.
- The machine scoring your exam can read only what you grid, so you **must grid-in your answers correctly to get credit.**
- If a question has more than one correct answer, grid-in only one of them.
- The grid does not have a minus sign; so no answer can be negative.
- A mixed number *must* be converted to an improper fraction or a decimal before it is gridded.

  Enter $1\frac{1}{4}$ as $\frac{5}{4}$ or 1.25; the machine will interpret 11/4 as $\frac{11}{4}$ and mark it wrong.

- **All decimals must be entered as accurately as possible.** Here are three acceptable ways of gridding

$$\frac{3}{11} = 0.272727\ldots$$

- Note that rounding to .273 is acceptable because you are using the full grid, but you would receive **no credit** for .3 or .27, because they are less accurate.

3   3

16. Jamie is considering two different companies to rent him a mobile home trailer for one day. One service charges \$30 per day and \$0.25 per mile. The other service charges \$40 per day and \$0.20 per mile. At what number of miles is the cost for the two services equal?

19. $6x + 4y = 1,200$
    $4x + 6y = 1,700$

In the system of equations above, what is the value of $3x + 3y$?

20. $ax + by = 8$
    $4x + 6y = 48$

The system of equations above has infinite solutions. If a and b are constants, what is the value of $\frac{b}{a}$?

17. The graph of $f(x) = -2|x - m| + n$ is shown. What is the value of $-mn^{-1}$?

18. In a right triangle one of the acute angles measures $x°$, where $\sin x° = \frac{5}{8}$. What is the value of $\cos(90° - x°)$?

STOP   If there is still time remaining, you may review your answers.

MATH TEST (CALCULATOR)

55 MINUTES, 38 QUESTIONS

Turn to Section 4 of your answer sheet to answer the questions in this section.

DIRECTIONS: For questions 1–30, solve each problem and choose the best answer from the given options. Fill in the corresponding circle on your answer document. For questions 31–38, solve the problem and fill in the answer on the answer sheet grid. Please use scrap paper to work out your answers.

Notes:
- The **use of** a calculator on this section IS permitted.
- All variables and expressions represent real numbers unless indicated otherwise.
- All figures are drawn to scale unless indicated otherwise.
- All figures are in a plane unless indicated otherwise.
- Unless indicated otherwise, the domain of a given function is the set of all real numbers x for which the function has real values.

REFERENCE INFORMATION

Area Facts	Volume Facts	Triangle Facts

The arc of a circle contains 360°.
The arc of a circle contains 2π radians.
The sum of the measures of the angles in a triangle is 180°.

4

4

1. Warren has a streaming video account with an online movie channel. His cost for each movie he rents is $2.25 and his monthly membership fee is $4.00. If his invoice for the past month was $24.25, how many movies did Warren rent?

(A) 6
(B) 7
(C) 8
(D) 9

2. The legend on a map shows that 1 inch = 80 miles. The distance on a map shows that Hartford, Connecticut and Roanoke, Virginia are 5.05 inches apart. What is the actual distance between the two cities?

(A) 80 miles
(B) 205 miles
(C) 395 miles
(D) 404 miles

3. The density of an object is found by dividing the mass of the object by its volume. What is the volume, in milliliters, of an object with a mass of 48 grams and density of 4 grams per milliliter?

(A) 12
(B) 14
(C) 16
(D) 24

4. A customer service call center for a credit card company asks 1 in 8 of the callers to take a survey at the conclusion of the call. Approximately 20% of those solicited consent to the survey. If 400 callers were serviced between 2:00 and 3:00 one afternoon and 20% of the callers consented to the survey, how many callers did **not** consent to the survey?

(A) 20
(B) 30
(C) 35
(D) 40

5. The formula for the area of a trapezoid is

$$A = \tfrac{1}{2}(h)(b_1 + b_2)$$

Which of the following expresses b_1 in terms of h, A, and b_2?

(A) $\dfrac{2A}{h} - b_2$

(B) $\dfrac{h}{2A} - b_2$

(C) $b_2 + 2Ah$

(D) $\left(\dfrac{A}{2h}\right) - b_2$

6. A student is taking a series of classes at the recreational center in his neighborhood. Each class has a monthly fee of $5.75 and there is a single monthly membership cost of $11.50. If the total cost for March was $51.75, how many classes were taken?

(A) 5
(B) 6
(C) 7
(D) 8

7. If $2p - 4 \geq 6$, what is the least possible value of $2p + 4$?

   (A) 7
   (B) 14
   (C) 21
   (D) 28

8. Circle P has center $(4, -2)$. The point A $(7, 3)$ lies on the circle. What is the area of circle P?

   (A) 24π
   (B) 34π
   (C) 54π
   (D) 64π

Questions 9 and 10 refer to the graph below.

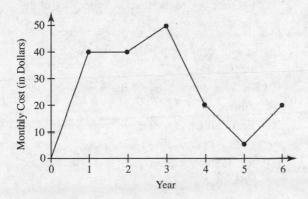

The monthly costs of certain internet plans have varied greatly over the six year period as illustrated in the graph.

9. What was the largest percent drop in price from one year to another?

   (A) 25
   (B) 50
   (C) 75
   (D) 85

10. What was the greatest decrease in internet plan price in the graph?

    (A) $40
    (B) $30
    (C) $25
    (D) $10

11. Given that $4a - 3b = 12$ and $6a + 8b = 17$, what is the value of $2a + b$?

    (A) $\dfrac{29}{5}$
    (B) $\dfrac{16}{5}$
    (C) $-\dfrac{18}{5}$
    (D) -9

12. Friendly Car Service charges a flat rate of $1.50 and $.55 per mile. Mustafa has only $11 to spend on his ride. Write an inequality that represents the maximum distance that Mustafa can travel.

    (A) $.55m - 1.50 \leq 11$
    (B) $.55m + 1.50 \leq 11$
    (C) $1.50m + .55 \geq 11$
    (D) $.55m + 1.50 \geq 11$

13. Pham is interested in starting a 4H Club at her high school. She randomly sampled a group of 200 students and found that 31.5% of the students in her sample thought that starting a club was a good idea. If her high school has 1,145 students enrolled, approximately how many will consider that starting the 4H club was a good idea?

    (A) 360
    (B) 340
    (C) 280
    (D) 225

4   4

Questions 14 and 15 refer to the graph below.

Cost of Citation (in Dollars)

14. The graph shows the number of drivers who have been caught texting while driving and the fines that were levied against them. Which of the following can be concluded from the graph?

(A) There is a strong negative correlation between higher fines and the number of drivers cited for texting while driving.

(B) There is a weak negative correlation between higher fines and the number of drivers cited for texting while driving.

(C) There is a strong positive correlation between higher fines and the number of drivers cited for texting while driving.

(D) There is no correlation between higher fines and the number of drivers cited for texting while driving.

15. If the fine for texting while driving was increased to $800, approximately how many citations could be expected to be issued?

(A) 70

(B) 230

(C) 460

(D) 520

Questions 16 and 17 refer to the following information.

$$S(x) = \frac{3}{5}x + 60$$

$$D(x) = 240 - x$$

The quantity of a product supplied to the public and the quantity of a product that is demanded by the public are each functions of the product's price. The functions above model the estimated supply and demand of a particular product. The function $S(x)$ gives the quantity of the product supplied to the market when the price is x dollars and the function $D(x)$ indicates the quantity of the product demanded when its price is x dollars.

16. What will be the effect on the quantity of the product supplied to the market if the price of the product is increased by $15?

(A) The quantity supplied will increase by 9 units.

(B) The quantity supplied will decrease by 9 units.

(C) The quantity supplied will increase by 36 units.

(D) The quantity supplied will increase by 69 units.

17. At what price will the supply of the product be equal to the demand for the product?

(A) $202.50

(B) $180.00

(C) $127.50

(D) $112.50

Questions 18 and 19 refer to the table below.

A recent marathon featured runners of many different ages. The table below shows a listing of the participants as categorized by age and place in the race.

Age	Under 20	20–29	30–39	40–49	50–69	70 and Over	Total
Top 10 finisher	2	6	1	1	0	0	10
Finished in place 11 to 40	11	11	5	3	0	0	30
Finished after 40th place	5	8	23	31	43	12	122
Total	18	25	29	35	43	12	162

18. What percent of the top forty finishers came from the 30 to 39 age group?

    (A) 8%
    (B) 10%
    (C) 15%
    (D) 18%

19. What is the difference between the percent of runners under 20 years of age who finished in places 11 to 40 and the percent of runners aged 40 to 49 who also finished in places 11 through 40?

    (A) 52.5%
    (B) 46.4%
    (C) 34.2%
    (D) 31.1%

x	1	2	3
$g(x)$	3	5	7

x	3	4	5
$h(x)$	8	16	24

20. Values for $g(x)$ and $h(x)$ are listed above. What is the value for the $h(g(2))$?

    (A) 24
    (B) 36
    (C) 48
    (D) 72

21. $|m - 3| = 12$
    $|n + 7| = 22$

    In the equations above, $m < 0$ and $n < 0$. What is the value of $m - n$?

    (A) 14
    (B) 18
    (C) 20
    (D) 24

Questions 22 and 23 refer to the expression below.

22. $\dfrac{3 + 5i}{6 - 3i}$

What must be done to the fraction above to rationalize the denominator? (Note: $i = \sqrt{-1}$)

(A) Multiply both the numerator and the denominator by $6 - 3i$.

(B) Multiply both the numerator and the denominator by $3 - 5i$.

(C) Multiply the denominator by $6 + 3i$ and the numerator by $3 - 5i$.

(D) Multiply both the numerator and the denominator by $6 + 3i$.

23. If the fraction is written in the form of $a + bi$, what is the value of ab?

(A) $\dfrac{13}{225}$

(B) $\dfrac{1}{13}$

(C) $\dfrac{2}{7}$

(D) $\dfrac{14}{15}$

24. Homeowners want to create a circular rock garden that measures 20 feet in diameter. Reference materials state that the space for the garden needs to be 3" deep. The rocks they wish to buy cost $80 per cubic yard and must be purchased in whole cubic yards. How much will they have to spend on rocks?

(A) $480

(B) $400

(C) $320

(D) $240

25. A Boy Scout troop in Des Moines is practicing its marching order in the upcoming Memorial Day parade. The troop leader wants the boys to march in neat rows, the same number in each row. When the leader tries four in a row, the last row has three. When he tries five boys in a row, the last row has four. In desperation, he tries to line up six boys in a row, only to find five in the last row. What is the least number of boys that could be in the troop?

(A) 11

(B) 14

(C) 59

(D) 119

26. Seven students draw numbered cards, each with a value that is a positive integer. The mean of their selections is 14. What is the largest number any student could have drawn?

(A) 92

(B) 70

(C) 28

(D) 14

27. The golden ratio compares dimensions that are appealing to the eye. Sometimes the golden ratio appears in nature but more frequently in painting and architecture. The ratio has been defined as $\dfrac{1 + \sqrt{5}}{2}$:1, which corresponds to length:width.

A new downtown cultural center is being planned for construction in 2017. The city planners hope to construct the main amphitheater using the golden ratio. If the proposed width of the amphitheater is to be 87 meters, what will be its length? (Round your answer to the nearest meter.)

(A) 211

(B) 176

(C) 157

(D) 141

Questions 28 and 29 refer to the data below.

	BMI
Underweight	Below 18.5
Normal	18.5–24.9
Overweight	25.0–29.9
Obesity	30.0 and above

Body Mass Index is a calculation that measures obesity and the potential for serious health risks such as strokes and heart attacks. The BMI can be found by using the following formula:

$$\frac{\text{weight (pounds)}}{\text{height}^2 \text{ (inches)}} \times 703$$

28. What is the category of BMI of a patient who weighs 182 pounds and is 5′10″?

   (A) Underweight
   (B) Normal
   (C) Overweight
   (D) Obesity

29. What is the weight of a patient who is 6 feet tall and has the lowest BMI that is categorized as obese? (Round to the nearest pound.)

   (A) 194
   (B) 221
   (C) 231
   (D) 241

30. A large snowball is in the shape of a sphere. At 10:00 A.M., the radius of the snowball is 2 feet. The radius grows 6 inches every 10 minutes it is rolled in the snow. If the snowball is continuously rolled, how much greater, in cubic feet, is the snowball at 11:30 A.M. than it is at 10:00 A.M.? (Round your answer to the nearest cubic foot.)

   (A) 1,150
   (B) 1,117
   (C) 167
   (D) 34

4   4

Grid-in Response Directions

In questions 31–38, first solve the problem, and then enter your answer on the grid provided on the answer sheet. The instructions for entering your answers follow.

- First, write your answer in the boxes at the top of the grid.
- Second, grid your answer in the columns below the boxes.
- Use the fraction bar in the first row or the decimal point in the second row to enter fractions and decimals.

Write your answer in the boxes

Grid in your answer

Answer: $\frac{8}{15}$ Answer: 1.75   Answer: 100

Either position is acceptable

- Grid only one space in each column.
- Entering the answer in the boxes is recommended as an aid in gridding but is not required.
- The machine scoring your exam can read only what you grid, so you **must grid-in your answers correctly to get credit**.
- If a question has more than one correct answer, grid-in only one of them.
- The grid does not have a minus sign; so no answer can be negative.
- A mixed number *must* be converted to an improper fraction or a decimal before it is gridded.

  Enter $1\frac{1}{4}$ as $\frac{5}{4}$ or 1.25; the machine will interpret 11/4 as $\frac{11}{4}$ and mark it wrong.

- **All decimals must be entered as accurately as possible.** Here are three acceptable ways of gridding

$$\frac{3}{11} = 0.272727\ldots$$

- Note that rounding to .273 is acceptable because you are using the full grid, but you would receive **no credit** for .3 or .27, because they are less accurate.

31. Alina has $7.50 to spend on tomatoes and avocados. Tomatoes cost $.55 each, and avocados cost $.95 each. If she buys 7 tomatoes, what is the maximum number of avocados Alina can purchase? (Note: taxes are excluded)

	7th grade	8th grade	9th grade
Girls	191	215	174
Boys	162	219	181

32. The data above represent students categorized by gender and grade at a local middle school. If a student is selected at random, what is the probability the student is not an eighth-grade girl (round your answer to the nearest hundredth)?

33. A furniture manufacturer of office chairs uses the following profit function:

$P(x) = -.08x^2 + 23.1x + 500$, where x represents the number of chairs that are manufactured and $P(x)$ is profit in dollars. What is the most profitable number of chairs to manufacture? (Round your answer to the nearest whole number.)

$$\left(\frac{1}{3}\right)^{x-2} = (27)^{3-x}$$

34. Given the equation above, what is the value of $2x + 11$?

35. A small wooden bridge has a maximum carrying capacity of 15,000 pounds. Three cars are currently crossing the bridge, each with a mean weight of 3,250 pounds. What is the greatest weight a fourth car or truck can have and still cross the bridge safely?

36. Students at a local art school wish to create a Styrofoam pyramid. The pyramid will have a rectangular base that measures 6 feet by 8 feet and will have a height that measures 12 feet. If each cubic foot weighs 4 ounces and the cost per pound of Styrofoam is $.50 per pound, what will be the cost to create the pyramid? (Note: 16 ounces = 1 pound) (Ignore the $ sign)

Questions 37 and 38 refer to the information below.

Objects above the Earth's surface weigh less than objects on the Earth's surface due to the effects of gravity. Scientists use the following formula when considering the weight of satellites orbiting Earth.

$$W(h) = m\left(\frac{4000}{4000 + h}\right)^2$$

where m equals the weight of an object at sea level and h is its height in miles above sea level.

37. A NOAH weather satellite is in a decaying orbit around Earth. In anticipation of this development, the engineers that built the satellite created the vehicle to be light enough to completely disintegrate as it descended to Earth. Thus, the scientists created the weather satellite to weigh 50 pounds when it orbited at 22,000 miles. What was the weight of the satellite on Earth before it was launched into space? (Round your answer to the nearest pound.)

38. Susan is flying in a military test jet that can fly several miles higher than a passenger jet. At sea level, she weighs 120 pounds. At what height will she weigh 119.5 pounds? (Round your answer to the nearest hundredth of a mile.)

STOP   If there is still time remaining, you may review your answers.

ANSWER KEY
Practice Test 3

Section 1: Reading

1. **D**	14. **D**	27. **A**	40. **A**
2. **A**	15. **C**	28. **A**	41. **A**
3. **B**	16. **C**	29. **D**	42. **A**
4. **A**	17. **C**	30. **A**	43. **C**
5. **C**	18. **C**	31. **A**	44. **B**
6. **B**	19. **C**	32. **C**	45. **A**
7. **C**	20. **C**	33. **B**	46. **C**
8. **C**	21. **B**	34. **A**	47. **A**
9. **A**	22. **C**	35. **A**	48. **C**
10. **B**	23. **B**	36. **D**	49. **B**
11. **A**	24. **C**	37. **C**	50. **D**
12. **C**	25. **D**	38. **B**	51. **D**
13. **B**	26. **D**	39. **D**	52. **A**

Number Correct _____

Number Incorrect _____

Section 2: Writing and Language

1. **D**	12. **C**	23. **A**	34. **C**
2. **B**	13. **D**	24. **C**	35. **A**
3. **B**	14. **B**	25. **B**	36. **C**
4. **D**	15. **D**	26. **C**	37. **C**
5. **C**	16. **B**	27. **D**	38. **D**
6. **C**	17. **C**	28. **C**	39. **D**
7. **C**	18. **B**	29. **B**	40. **B**
8. **C**	19. **A**	30. **A**	41. **B**
9. **D**	20. **D**	31. **C**	42. **D**
10. **C**	21. **A**	32. **C**	43. **A**
11. **D**	22. **B**	33. **A**	44. **B**

Number Correct _____

Number Incorrect _____

ANSWER KEY
Practice Test 3

Section 3: Math (No Calculator)

1. **A**	5. **A**	9. **B**	13. **D**
2. **B**	6. **A**	10. **A**	14. **C**
3. **C**	7. **C**	11. **D**	15. **B**
4. **D**	8. **A**	12. **B**	

16. **200**

17. **3/2 or 1.5**

or

18. **5/8 or .625**

19. **870**

or

ANSWER KEY
Practice Test 3

20. **3/2 or 1.5**

or

Number Correct _____

Number Incorrect _____

Section 4: Math (Calculator)

1. **D**	9. **C**	17. **D**	25. **C**
2. **D**	10. **B**	18. **C**	26. **A**
3. **A**	11. **A**	19. **A**	27. **D**
4. **D**	12. **B**	20. **A**	28. **C**
5. **A**	13. **A**	21. **C**	29. **B**
6. **C**	14. **B**	22. **D**	30. **B**
7. **B**	15. **B**	23. **A**	
8. **B**	16. **A**	24. **D**	

31. **3**   32. **.81**   33. **144**   34. **18**

ANSWER KEY
Practice Test 3

35. **5,250**

36. **24.0 or 24**

or

37. **2,113**

38. **8.02**

Number Correct _____

Number Incorrect _____

SCORE ANALYSIS

Reading and Writing Test

Section 1: Reading _____ = _____ (A)
             # correct   raw score

Section 2: Writing _____ = _____ (B)
             # correct   raw score

To find your Reading and Writing test scores, consult the chart below; find the ranges in which your raw scores lie and read across to find the ranges of your test scores.

_____ + _____ = _____ (C)
range of Reading   range of Writing   range of Reading + Writing
test scores   test scores   test scores

To find the range of your Reading and Writing Scaled Score, multiply (C) by 10.

Test Scores for the Reading and Writing Sections

Reading Raw Score	Writing Raw Score	Test Score
44–52	39–44	35–40
36–43	33–38	31–34
30–35	28–32	28–30
24–29	22–27	24–27
19–23	17–21	21–23
14–18	13–16	19–20
9–13	9–12	16–18
5–8	5–8	13–15
less than 5	less than 5	10–12

Math Test

Section 3: _____ = _____ (D)
         # correct   raw score

Section 4: _____ = _____ (E)
         # correct   raw score

Total Math raw score: (D) + (E) = _____

To find your Math Scaled Score, consult the chart below; find the range in which your raw score lies and read across to find the range for your scaled score.

Scaled Scores for the Math Test

Raw Score	Scaled Score	Raw Score	Scaled Score
50–58	700–800	20–25	450–490
44–49	650–690	15–19	400–440
38–43	600–640	11–14	350–390
32–37	550–590	7–10	300–340
26–31	500–540	less than 7	200–290

Answer Explanations

Section 1: Reading Test

1. **(D)** The author says that Boers had "a dour fatalistic Old Testament religion" (lines 20–21). The word *dour* means "stern and gloomy."

2. **(A)** In lines 30–34 the author is comparing Napoleon's troops with Boer soldiers, so in context this phrase refers to the fact that the Boer soldiers were harder for the British to defeat than Napoleon's troops.

3. **(B)** As discussed in lines 22–26, the author says the Boers were very difficult foes on the battlefield, so it makes sense that they would have very effective rifles. The word *inconveniently* is used humorously, referring to the word *ancient* in the phrase "ancient theology" (line 30).

4. **(A)** The author says "cold and poverty and storm are the nurses of the qualities which make for empire" (lines 62–63). Clearly he means that cold, poverty, and hardship fostered these characteristics in the Boer. In these lines he explains this: "It . . . climate" (lines 64–67).

5. **(C)** In lines 59–67 ("But it was . . . that robust climate"), the author explains why the Dutch succeeded where the Portuguese had not.

6. **(B)** Throughout the passage the writer has an admiring attitude toward the Boers. This is well illustrated in the first paragraph, in which the author describes the origin and qualities of the Boers.

7. **(C)** *Temper* in context means "resilience."

8. **(C)** *Consuming* in context means "deeply felt."

9. **(A)** All of the other characteristics are either mentioned or implied. However, there is no suggestion that the modern Boers are willing to compromise.

10. **(B)** The author mainly recounts events in the course of describing the history of the Boers.

11. **(A)** *Unique* means "one of a kind." It is clear from the author's description of periodical cicadas that they are one of a kind.

12. **(C)** The cicada nymphs are described as *patiently* sucking the juice from the tree roots. Attributing patience to a non-human can be described as *anthropomorphic*.

13. **(B)** The likely intended audience is laypersons interested in biology because it describes an interesting theory in biology. It is a bit informal and not highly technical, so (A) can be ruled out. It is too advanced for (C) children. There is no reason to think (D) journalists in particular would be interested in it.

14. **(D)** The theory is outlined in lines 17–35.

15. **(C)** We can infer this from the theory described in lines 17–35. As described in the theory, the parasite must keep extending its life cycle to keep up with the cicada's increasing life cycle. The parasite thus must have become extinct after *Magicicada tredecim's* life cycle became 13 years.

16. **(C)** This is not true because, according to the theory described in the passage, the longer the cicada's life cycle is, the more difficult it will be for its parasite to survive.

17. **(C)** The author says that the cicadas' best strategy for avoiding their parasites is to have a long life cycle. This contradicts the statement in choice (C) from question 16 that the parasite benefits from the fact that the cicadas have a long life cycle. Thus, (C) provides the best evidence to answer question 17.

18. **(C)** The theory explains the phenomenon very well. The fact that the parasite has not been found (lines 50–51) suggests that it does not exist but does not provide what scientists consider to be empirical evidence because they believe that a lack of evidence should not be considered evidence.

19. **(C)** As mentioned in question 8, the fact that the parasite has not been found provides good support for the theory. The discovery of the parasite would be strong evidence against the theory, but it would not invalidate it because it is possible that the parasite survived even though it had to make it through the difficult 272-year period mentioned in line 60 without a cicada to parasitize.

20. **(C)** The passage does not cite scientific studies. It does all of the others.

21. **(B)** The phrase "for possible future uses" (line 10) signals that *values* (which means "uses") in the future are being referred to.

22. **(C)** "They can be continually recycled" (lines 23–24) signals that land can be used successively for an infinite number of purposes. "Does not mean they are infinite in amount" (lines 24–25) indicates that the amount of land cannot be increased.

23. **(B)** "Once dedicated, [a river system] cannot be used again without disturbing the constituencies that use its features" (lines 44–46).

24. **(C)** This provides good evidence. The sentence says that once a river system is dedicated, it cannot be used for other purposes without affecting those already using it.

25. **(D)** In context, *perverse* means "arising from obstinate persistence in an error." The author is saying that often unsustainable resource use is encouraged by policies that continue despite evidence that they do not work.

26. **(D)** The author uses groundwater resources in the U.S. as an example of a situation in which there exist "perverse institutional or legal incentives" (lines 61–62). The phrase "use it or lose it" (line 68) immediately after "a lack of tradable rights to water" (lines 67–68) signals that the author is saying that because people can't trade water rights they have an incentive to use the water they have before others gain access to it and use it through digging wells.

27. **(A)** The author cites the example of cattle to illustrate the principle that private ownership often results in more effective conservation of resources than public ownership. We can infer that the author believes that cattle might become scarce if they were owned in common because individuals would have little incentive to care for cattle and limit the number of cattle they consume. (In fact, the author might argue that people would have an incentive to kill as many cattle as they can before others do.)

28. **(A)** The author argues throughout the passage that in many cases assigning ownership rights is the most effective way to conserve unsustainable resources. In lines 98–99 he says, "Getting the incentives right" should mean chiefly assigning property rights to environmental goods.

29. **(D)** This is the most accurate characterization of each passage.

30. **(A)** The author of Passage 1 says, "Air and water are particularly susceptible to pollutants because of the ease with which they can be used as open-access resources for receiving and disseminating waste" (lines 28–32). Thus, he would probably argue for close monitoring of the result of assigning ownership rights. In his discussion of the example of a river system, the author stresses that the various uses it is put to can have a great effect on other uses it has, on the system itself, and on things outside the system related to it. Thus, it is likely he would be concerned about the effects of the activity of one owner on the parts of the ocean owned by others.

31. **(A)** The author of Passage 1 does not discuss the value of a market-based approach, but there is no reason to think that he would rule out some use of a market-based approach if the results achieved by it were carefully monitored and the approach helped to effectively sustain renewable resources. However, he would also be likely to say that granting ownership rights cannot be the sole solution in the case of resources that have many, and often competing, uses, such as a river system. He says (in lines 55–58), "Policy for renewable . . . or irreversible loss."

32. **(C)** The author says Stephen Sondheim "zeroes in on the *essential* differences between the art of the lyricist and that of the poet" (lines 2–3) but he also says, "And yet, the line between song and poem is not as firm as Sondheim suggests" (lines 8–9).

33. **(B)** The author says, "[Blake's *Songs of Innocence* and *Songs of Experience* and Whitman's 'Song of Myself' straddle] the line between genres" (lines 13–14). He then quotes from *Songs of Innocence* and says the lines "practically [beg] to be set to music" (line 19).

34. **(A)** The author says, "Whereas poetry is aimed almost exclusively at a limited number of fellow poets, hundreds of millions of men and women listen to songs . . . " (lines 31–33).

35. **(A)** This is the best choice because it provides clear evidence for the answer to the previous question. It is reasonable to infer that material written for a small, specialized audience will have less appeal than material written for a broad audience.

36. **(D)** As it is used in line 61, *eschew* means "avoid" and *programmatically* means "following a set system." The writer is saying that many poets follow a set system of avoiding the use of memory cues that songwriters employ.

37. **(C)** Robert Fenton is suggesting that writing students tend to be one "person"—that is, think in a certain way—when listening to music and another "person" when writing poems, and thus do not apply what they know about music to their writing of poetry.

38. **(B)** In context, "schizophrenic" refers to taste that is divided by two antagonistic qualities. One of these qualities is a liking for rhyme, meter, and other "musical" qualities in poetry, and the other is a dislike for these qualities. A clue to the meaning is Robert Fenton's reference to "the person" in lines 67–68 and "the same person" in line 69, suggesting a division in taste in one person.

39. **(D)** The expression "elephant in the room" is a (C) *colorful* and (A) *metaphorical* idiom meaning *an obvious truth that is being ignored*. The author's adjective "singing" is a (B) *jocular* (joking) reference to the idea that it's the music, not the lyric, that makes a person want to hear a song again. (D) *Elegiac* (related to an elegy or mourning) is the correct answer because the expression has nothing to do with an elegy or mourning.

40. **(A)** The author says, "Poets cannot rely on actual musical tones; still the poems I love . . . have a quasi-melodic structure that has an effect not unlike melody proper" (lines 85–88). The author is saying that some poems have an effect that is very similar to musical melody.

41. **(A)** In the sentence preceding the last line ("At a time . . . not be denied;" lines 95–99) the author says that poets are no longer using repetition and melody, but that songwriters continue to use these techniques, which help make their songs popular. It makes sense, therefore, that in the last sentence the author is suggesting that to become more widely popular poets should use some of the techniques of their "big sister" (line 102)—that is, songwriting.

42. **(A)** One of the author's main points is that poets can use some of the techniques of songwriters to make their poems more popular. There is nothing in the passage to suggest that the author believes that a poem cannot be both excellent and popular.

43. **(C)** In lines 16–18 the author mentions, "the region of space dominated by Saturn's magnetic field, called its magnetosphere." In line 63 he mentions, "our planet's powerful magnetic field."

44. **(B)** As mentioned in the explanation to the previous question, these lines tell us that Earth and Saturn have a magnetosphere.

45. **(A)** In line 40 the author mentions, "a powerful outburst of solar activity," from which we can infer that the strength of the solar wind varies. Also, in lines 41–42 he mentions, "The strong surge in the solar wind."

46. **(C)** Of the choices given, this sentence provides the best evidence.

47. **(A)** The author summarizes a theory based on observations. Both the observations and the theory are elaborated upon in the rest of the passage.

48. **(C)** The possible solution discussed can be described as "elegant" because it does not require a "unique approach" (lines 73–74) to explain Titan's response to the solar wind. Scientists typically describe an approach as elegant when it offers an ingenious solution that is simple yet can be applied to complex and varied phenomena.

49. **(B)** The arrows in the diagram depict the intense burst of solar wind compressing Saturn's normal magnetosphere so that Titan is outside of Saturn's magnetosphere.

50. **(D)** The adjective "naked" refers to the fact that sometimes Titan is not within Saturn's magnetosphere and thus is unprotected from the solar wind. Using the word *naked* instead of *unprotected* helps make the occurrence seem more dramatic, in part because Titan is also a god.

51. **(D)** The author does not use any rhetorical questions.

52. **(A)** We can infer that Titan may have a magnetic field because the author says Cassini has only observed Titan when it was within Saturn's powerful magnetosphere. The fact that a magnetic field coming from Titan has not been found does not mean it does not exist. Titan may have a magnetic field that is relatively weak and thus difficult to detect due to interference from Saturn's powerful magnetic field. The author does not mention whether Cassini looked for a magnetic field coming from Titan when Titan was outside Saturn's magnetic field, but presumably the intense solar wind that existed at this time would have made the detection of a weak magnetic field difficult.

Section 2: Writing and Language Test

1. **(D)** This is the correct choice because it creates a grammatical sentence that follows logically from the preceding sentence. In this choice "they" refers to the "Egyptian masters" in the previous sentence. Both sentences are correctly cast in the past tense. The other choices do not create grammatical sentences that make good sense.

2. **(B)** This choice creates a grammatical sentence that makes good sense. Note that the infinitive phrase "to reduce them to a system," like the preceding infinitive phrase "to tabulate those properties," is the object of the verb "troubled." None of the other choices creates a grammatical sentence.

3. **(B)** The adjective prepositional phrase "in what remains to us of their work" modifies the noun "nothing," which is the subject of the sentence. "Justifies" is the correct verb form because it agrees in number with the subject, "nothing."

4. **(D)** The past tense is correct because the sentence is describing what the pupils did in the past. "Were copied" agrees with the subject, "models," in number.

5. **(C)** In context *rendered* means "represented in drawing." This makes sense because this sentence, like the previous sentence, is describing how the students improved their ability to depict things.

6. **(C)** This is the only choice that creates a grammatical sentence. The participial phrase "having neither pencil nor stylus" modifies the noun "they," creating a clear sentence that makes good sense.

7. **(C)** This choice creates the phrasal preposition "in which," which refers to the object of the preceding prepositional phrase, "groove." A grammatical and coherent sentence is created.

8. **(C)** Choice (A) is incorrect because a semicolon can only join two independent clauses, and in this case the part of the sentence after the semicolon is not an independent clause. Choice (B) is not grammatical. Choice (D) makes little sense. Choice (C) is correct because a dash can be used to introduce additional information about a topic, which in this case is "ink." Note that the words after the dash do not have to create an independent clause as they must after a semicolon.

9. **(D)** This is the correct answer because this sentence is not relevant to the subject being described, which is how students learned to draw. The sentence immediately preceding describes the apparatus used, and the sentence following describes how the apparatus was used. Inserting this sentence makes no sense because it is not directly relevant to either of the surrounding sentences.

10. **(C)** Past action is being described, so the past tense "squatted" is correct. A subject of the verb "squatted" is needed. Choice (B) provides this subject—"he."

11. **(D)** This is the correct choice because the context requires the phrasal verb *looked over*, which means "examined."

12. **(C)** This is the best choice because Jon *advocates* (supports) that the body is interconnected by practicing acupuncture, which is based on this idea.

13. **(D)** This is the only grammatically correct choice. It corrects the run-on sentence by creating a new sentence. Note that "it's" is the contraction of "it is."

14. **(B)** This is grammatical and makes good sense. Choice (A) and choice (C) create run-on sentences. Choice (D) is not grammatical.

15. **(D)** The present tense is correct because recommending treatment is something that Jon does regularly.

16. **(B)** This choice creates an effective sentence in which the practice of needling is clearly explained. The colon is used appropriately to set off the explanation of an important procedure.

17. **(C)** This is the only choice that creates a grammatical sentence. Choice (A) and choice (B) are incorrect because they do not create an independent clause, which is necessary before the semicolon. Choice (D) does not make sense.

18. **(B)** This choice is the best choice because it makes sense that the reason Jon gives patients an explanation of Oriental medicine is to help them understand the treatment.

19. **(A)** As mentioned in the correct answer, this sentence provides a logical link between the previous sentence and the following sentence. It describes the principle of Oriental medicine, which makes sense because in the previous sentence the writer says, "Jon usually gives a brief description of Oriental medicine." The following sentence describes how illnesses occur when the processes this principle describes are disrupted.

20. **(D)** This is the best choice because the first sentence of the paragraph says that visits to practitioners of alternative medicine increased.

21. **(A)** This is the standard expression in this context. Choice (D) is acceptable but somewhat awkward; it is also rather ambiguous because "with licenses" could mean they have a license for some other activity or field.

22. **(B)** This makes the best sense because it is an effective topic sentence for the paragraph, which is about the increasing popularity of acupuncture and other forms of traditional Oriental medicine.

23. **(A)** This is the correct answer because paragraph 1 serves as an introduction to the passage. It introduces the topic of stained glass and how it is produced. The following three paragraphs elaborate on this topic.

24. **(C)** As mentioned in the correct answer, this sentence is necessary for the sentence following it to make good sense.

25. **(B)** This is the only choice that is grammatical and makes sense. The passage is about what the author calls the "gorgeous" (line 5) stained glass of the thirteenth or fourteenth century, so it makes sense that he would describe the color effects very favorably.

26. **(C)** This is the only choice that is grammatical. The participial phrase "being built up" modifies *window*, the object of the prepositional phrase beginning with "by."

27. **(D)** Parallelism requires that the verb "fit" be in the present tense. This can be seen by looking at the two preceding verbs in the series: "the artist must *choose* . . . [and] *cut*."

28. **(C)** In context *amuse* means "provide interesting occupation." This makes good sense because it would amuse the reader to make the calculations mentioned.

29. **(B)** This is the correct choice because it is grammatical and makes sense.

30. **(A)** The present tense is correct in context because a statement of fact is being made.

31. **(C)** The given sentence is a run-on sentence. This choice corrects the error and is the only choice that makes sense in context.

32. **(C)** *Its* is correct because the context requires the possessive form of the personal pronoun *it*. Choice (A) is incorrect because *its'* is not how the possessive form of *it* is formed. Choice (B) is incorrect because *it's* is the contracted form of *it is*, which makes no sense in context. Similarly, choice (D) is incorrect.

33. **(A)** This is the correct choice because the context requires the adverb *otherwise*, which here means "under other circumstances."

34. **(C)** This can be seen in the bar graph. The precise percentage is given on the left side of each bar.

35. **(A)** This is stated in the first paragraph of explanation of the bar graph.

36. **(C)** This is the best choice. It makes sense because only one literacy rate is given for the category "Latin America and the Caribbean," so there is no way to determine the literacy rate in each separate area.

37. **(C)** *Respectively* is used correctly to tell us that 99% applies to Central and Eastern Europe and that 100% applies to Central Asia.

38. **(D)** This is the only choice that is grammatical and makes good sense.

39. **(D)** This is the best choice because sentence 2 provides more detailed information about literacy rates in Latin America and the Caribbean, which is the subject of sentence 5.

40. **(B)** This can be seen both in the bar graph and in the paragraph in which this question appears.

41. **(B)** This information is given in the bar graph.

42. **(D)** This is the best choice in context. The first sentence of the paragraph says that literacy rates are "projected to increase in all regions." The second sentence says that Central and Eastern Europe is "an exception," so it makes sense that there are projections of "a small drop in adult literacy."

43. **(A)** The answer to this question can be arrived at by a process of elimination. Choices (B), (C), and (D) can be eliminated because the sentence says, "South and West Asia is projected to *also* come below the target for 2015." This means that sub-Saharan Africa is also predicted to come below the target.

44. **(B)** This is the only choice that makes sense in context.

Section 3: Math Test (No Calculator)

1. **(A)** Substitute 4 for *y* and solve for *x*.

$$\frac{x+1}{4} = 4$$
$$x + 1 = 16$$
$$x = 15$$

2. **(B)** Factor and cancel as needed.

$$-2\left(\frac{x^2 - 8x - 180}{x + 10}\right) =$$

$$-2\left(\frac{(x + 10)(x - 18)}{x + 10}\right) =$$

$$-2(x - 18) = -2x + 36$$

3. **(C)** Find the value of n^2 by completing the square in $x^2 + 19x + n^2$.

Multiply 19 by $\frac{1}{2}$ and square the product.

$$x^2 + 19x + n^2 = x^2 + 19x + \left(\frac{19}{2}\right)^2 = x^2 + 19x + \frac{361}{4}$$

$$n^2 = \frac{361}{4}$$

Choice (B) can be eliminated at once since the denominator, 2, is not a perfect square.

4. **(D)** Find the x-intercept(s) by letting $y = 0$.

Choice (A):

$$x^2 + 2x - 48 = 0$$
$$(x + 8)(x - 6) = 0$$
$$x = -8 \quad \text{and} \quad x = 6$$

There are two x-intercepts.

Choice (B):

$$x^2 + 11x + 30 = 0$$
$$(x + 6)(x + 5) = 0$$
$$x = -6 \quad \text{and} \quad x = -5$$

There are two x-intercepts.

Choice (C):

$$x^2 - 6x + 8 = 0$$
$$(x - 4)(x - 2) = 0$$
$$x = 4 \quad \text{and} \quad x = 2$$

There are two x-intercepts.

Choice (D):

$$x^2 + 6x + 9 = 0$$
$$(x + 3)^2 = 0$$
$$x = -3$$

There is only one x-intercept.

5. **(A)** The prime numbers less than 25 are: 2, 3, 5, 7, 11, 13, 17, 19, 23. There are nine prime numbers less than 25, so $M = 9$. Find the range of this set of numbers by subtracting the lowest value from the highest.

$$23 - 2 = 21$$

The range of the numbers is 21, so $r = 21$

$$2M - r = 2(9) - 21 = -3$$

6. **(A)** Parallel lines have the same slope but different y-intercepts. The slope of $y = -\frac{5}{8}x + 3$ is $-\frac{5}{8}$ and the y-intercept is 3. Transform each of the answer choices into slope-intercept form to assess slopes and y-intercepts.

Choice (A) is $5x + 8y = 48$. Begin the transformation by isolating y.

$$5x + 8y = 48$$
$$8y = -5x + 48$$
$$y = -\frac{5}{8}x + 6$$

Rewriting $5x + 8y = 48$ in slope-intercept form yields the same slope, $-\frac{5}{8}$, but a different y-intercept, 6. So choice (A) is parallel to the given equation.

7. **(C)** Separate $g(f(4))$ into its two parts.

$$f(4) = 2 \text{ so } g(f(4)) = g(2)$$
$$g(2) = 6$$

8. **(A)** Although this system of equations can be solved via the substitution or elimination method, it is much easier to add the two equations together.

$$2x + 3y = 17$$
$$+\ 5x - 7y = 31$$
$$\overline{7x - 4y = 48}$$

$$\frac{7x - 4y}{8} = \frac{48}{8} = 6$$

9. **(B)** Factoring $16x^2 - 9y^2$ gives $(4x + 3y)(4x - 3y)$. The area of a rectangle is given by the formula Area = (length)(width) or $A = lw$. Since $4x - 3y$ is the width, $4x + 3y$ is the length. The perimeter of a rectangle is found by using perimeter = $2l + 2w$.

$$2(4x + 3y) + 2(4x - 3y) = 8x + 6y + 8x - 6y = 16x$$

10. **(A)** The intersections of two lines, parabolas, etc. are those points that satisfy both equations. In this case, the parabola $y = (x - 6)^2$ intersects the horizontal line $y = 36$. Since both equations are equal to y, set each of them equal to one another.

$$36 = (x - 6)^2$$

Solve this equation by finding the square root of each side of the equation.

$$36 = (x - 6)^2$$
$$\sqrt{36} = \sqrt{(x - 6)^2}$$
$$\pm 6 = x - 6$$
$$x = 12 \quad \text{or} \quad x = 0$$

The points of intersection are (12, 36) and (0, 36). Although we can use the distance formula to find the distance between these two points, intuitively, they lie along the line $y = 36$. Subtract the x-coordinates to find the distance between the two points.

$$12 - 0 = 12$$

The length of AB, then, is 12.

11. **(D)** Square $EFGH$ has an area that measures 64 square units, which means each side is 8 units. All four of the triangles are isosceles right triangles with hypotenuse 8. Using the formula for a 45-45-90 triangle, both legs of each right triangle are therefore $4\sqrt{2}$ units. Each side of square $ABCD$, then, is $8\sqrt{2}$ units long. The formula for the area of a square is Area $= s^2$, where s is the measure of a side.

$$\text{Area} = s^2$$
$$\text{Area} = (8\sqrt{2})^2 = 128$$

The figures can be assumed to be to scale as there is no note indicating otherwise. We therefore can deduce square $ABCD$ is larger than square $EFGH$. Thus, choices (A) 36 and (B) 64 can be immediately eliminated.

12. **(B)** A total of 8 outcomes are possible when guessing among 3 questions:
Let C = the answers guessed correctly
Let I = the answers guessed incorrectly

CCC, CCI, CIC, CII, ICC, ICI, IIC, and III

Of the 8 possible outcomes, 3 contain exactly two correct guesses (and therefore one incorrect guess). Therefore, the probability of guessing correctly on exactly two of the three questions among questions 6 through 8 is $\frac{3}{8}$.

13. **(D)** Substitute $4x$ for y in $2x^2 + y^2 = 360$.

$$2x^2 + (4x)^2 = 360$$
$$2x^2 + 16x^2 = 360$$
$$18x^2 = 360$$
$$x^2 = 20$$

14. **(C)** Divide both sides of the equation by 2, the GCF of $2x^2 + 8x - 12$.

$$(2x^2 + 8x - 12) \div 2 = 0 \div 2$$
$$x^2 + 4x - 6 = 0$$

The equation does not factor so solve by using the quadratic equation.

$$x = \frac{-b \pm \sqrt{b^2 - 4ac}}{2a}$$
$$a = 1 \quad b = 4 \quad c = -6$$
$$x = \frac{-4 \pm \sqrt{(4)^2 - 4(1)(-6)}}{2(1)}$$
$$x = \frac{-4 \pm \sqrt{40}}{2}$$
$$x = \frac{-4 \pm 2\sqrt{10}}{2}$$
$$x = -2 \pm \sqrt{10}$$

15. **(B)**

$$(ax - 7)(bx + 5) = 6x^2 + cx - 35$$

Solve for a or b in $a - b = -1$ and create a system of equations.

$$a - b = -1 \text{ so } a = b - 1$$

Substitute $b - 1$ for a in $ab = 6$.

$$(b - 1)b = 6$$
$$b^2 - b = 6$$
$$b^2 - b - 6 = 0$$

Factor and solve for b.

$$(b + 2)(b - 3) = 0$$
$$b + 2 = 0 \text{ or } b - 3 = 0$$
$$b = -2 \text{ or } b = 3$$

Find a when $b = 3$ or $b = -2$.

$$ab = 6$$
$$3a = 6$$
$$a = 2$$

When $b = 3$, $a = 2$

$$ab = 6$$
$$-2a = 6$$
$$a = -3$$

When $b = -2$, $a = -3$

Solve for c when a and b are 2 and 3, respectively.

$$(2x - 7)(3x + 5) = 6x^2 - 11x - 35$$
$$c = -11$$

Solve for c when a and b are -3 and -2, respectively.

$$(-3x - 7)(-2x + 5) = 6x^2 - x - 35$$
$$c = -1$$

You only have to solve for one of the values of c. Choice (B) is the only one that has either of the correct solutions to the question.

16. **200** Let $x = $ the number of miles for the two trailer rental costs to be equal.

$$40 + 0.20x = 30 + 0.25x$$
$$40 + 0.20x - 0.20x = 30 + 0.25x - 0.20x$$
$$40 = 30 + 0.05x$$
$$10 = 0.05x$$
$$200 = x$$

17. $\frac{3}{2}$ **or 1.5** The graph of an absolute value function is in the form $f(x) = a|x - h| + k$ where (h, k) is the vertex. In the function $f(x) = -2|x - m| + n$, $m = h$ and $n = k$. The graph shows the vertex is $(3, -2)$ so $m = 3$ and $n = -2$. Therefore, $-mn^{-1} = -(3)\left(-\frac{1}{2}\right) = \frac{3}{2}$.

18. $\frac{5}{8}$ **or .625** By the complementary angle relationship for sine and cosine, $\sin(x°) = \cos(90° - x°)$. Therefore, $\cos(90° - x°) = \frac{5}{8}$.

Either the fraction $\frac{5}{8}$ or its decimal equivalent, .625, may be gridded in as the correct answer.

19. **870** Add the equations together and divide by 10.

$$
\begin{array}{r}
6x + 4y = 1{,}200 \\
+\ 4x + 6y = 1{,}700 \\
\hline
10x + 10y = 2{,}900
\end{array}
$$

$$\frac{10x + 10y}{10} = \frac{2{,}900}{10}$$
$$x + y = 290$$

Multiply $x + y = 290$ by 3 to arrive at $3x + 3y$.

$$(3)(x + y = 290) = 3x + 3y = 870$$

20. $\frac{3}{2}$ **or 1.5** If the system of equations has infinite solutions, they are equations that represent the same line. Multiply the top equation by 6 to ensure that the constant terms are the same in both equations.

$$6(ax + by = 8) = 6ax + 6by = 48$$

The system of equations now appears as follows:

$$6ax + 6by = 48$$
$$4x + 6y = 48$$

We can now conclude that $6ax = 4x$ and $6by = 6y$.

$$\frac{6ax}{6x} = \frac{4x}{6x}$$
$$a = \frac{2}{3}$$
$$\frac{6by}{6y} = \frac{6y}{6y}$$
$$b = 1$$

Now find $\frac{b}{a}$.

$$\frac{b}{a} = \frac{1}{\frac{2}{3}} = \frac{3}{2}$$

The correct answer can also be entered as 1.5.

Section 4: Math Test (Calculator)

1. **(D)** Let x equal the number of movies rented by Warren in the past month.

$$2.25x + 4 = 24.25$$
$$2.25x = 20.25$$

Divide both sides of the equation by 2.25.

$$\frac{2.25x}{2.25} = \frac{20.25}{2.25}$$
$$x = 9$$

2. **(D)** Use the proportion $\dfrac{\text{map distance}}{\text{actual distance}} = \dfrac{\text{map distance}}{\text{actual distance}}$ to answer the question.

$$\frac{1}{80} = \frac{5.05}{d}$$
$$1 \times d = 80 \times 5.05$$
$$d = 404$$

The distance between Hartford and Roanoke is 404 miles.

Choice (A) can be immediately eliminated; 1 inch = 80 miles and the map shows 5.05 inches.

3. **(A)** The density of an object is equal to the mass of the object divided by the volume of the object, which can be expressed as density = mass/volume. Thus, if an object has a density of 4 grams per milliliter and a mass of 48 grams, the equation becomes:

$$4 = \frac{48}{V}$$
$$4V = 48$$
$$V = 12$$

The volume, then, is 12 milliliters/gram.

4. **(D)** If 1 in 8 callers were solicited for the survey, then one-eighth of the callers were asked to participate. Thus, one-eighth of 400 callers is 50 callers. Since 20% of the callers consented to the survey, then 80% did not want to take part. Find 80% of 50 by multiplying 50 by .8.

$$50 \times .8 = 40$$

5. **(A)** Begin to isolate b_1 by multiplying the area formula by 2.

$$A = \frac{1}{2}(h)(b_1 + b_2)$$
$$(2)A = \frac{1}{2}(h)(b_1 + b_2)(2)$$
$$2A = (h)(b_1 + b_2)$$

Divide both sides of the equation by h, the height of the trapezoid.

$$\frac{2A}{h} = \frac{(h)(b_1 + b_2)}{h}$$
$$\frac{2A}{h} = b_1 + b_2$$

Subtract b_2 from both sides of the equation.

$$\frac{2A}{h} - b_2 = b_1$$

6. **(C)** Since the number of classes the student took is unknown, let x equal that value. Adding the monthly cost we get the following equation:

$$5.75x + 11.50 = 51.75$$

Subtract 11.50 from both sides.

$$5.75x + 11.50 - 11.50 = 51.75 - 11.50$$
$$5.75x = 40.25$$

Divide each side of the equation by 5.75 to isolate x.

$$5.75x \div 5.75 = 40.25 \div 5.75$$
$$x = 7$$

7. **(B)** Solve $2p - 4 \geq 6$ and assess its least value.

$$2p - 4 + 4 \geq 6 + 4$$
$$2p \geq 10$$
$$p \geq 5$$

Substitute 5 into the expression $2p + 4$ to calculate its least value.

$$2(5) + 4 = 14$$

8. **(B)** Use the distance formula to find the distance from the center to point A.

$$d = \sqrt{(x_1 - x_2)^2 + (y_1 - y_2)^2}$$
$$d = \sqrt{(4 - 7)^2 + (-2 - 3)^2} = \sqrt{34}$$

The formula for the area of a circle is $A = \pi r^2$. Replace r with $\sqrt{34}$ to find the area of the circle.

$$A = \pi(\sqrt{34})^2 = 34\pi$$

9. **(C)** The greatest drop, as a percentage, occurred between years 4 and 5.

Year 4: $20
Year 5: $5

Use the formula $\dfrac{\text{decrease}}{\text{original}} = \dfrac{n}{100}$ to find the percent decrease.

$$\frac{15}{20} = \frac{n}{100}$$
$$20n = 1{,}500$$
$$n = 75\%$$

10. **(B)** In year 3, the internet plan price was $50. In year 4, the plan price decreased to $20.

$$50 - 20 = 30$$

11. **(A)** Stack the equations vertically.

$$4a - 3b = 12$$
$$6a + 8b = 17$$

Although the system of equations can be solved via the substitution or elimination methods, it is easier to simply add the two equations.

$$4a - 3b = 12$$
$$\underline{+\ 6a + 8b = 17}$$
$$10a + 5b = 29$$

Divide the sum by 5.

$$\frac{10a}{5} + \frac{5b}{5} = \frac{29}{5}$$
$$2a + b = \frac{29}{5}$$

12. **(B)** Let m equal the number of miles. Multiply m by the cost per mile, and add the fixed charge of $1.50 per transaction.

$$.55m + 1.50$$

This amount can be no more than $11 since that is all the money that Mustafa has.

$$.55m + 1.50 \leq 11$$

Choices (C) and (D) can immediately be eliminated as they express inequalities permitting costs no lower than $11. Mustafa has only $11 to spend.

13. **(A)** Because Pham surveyed a random sample of the students in her school, her sample was representative of the entire high school. Thus, the percent of students in the entire high school expected to prefer starting a 4H Club is appropriately estimated by the percent of students who preferred it in the sample, 31.5%. Thus, of the 1,145 students in the high school, approximately $1,145 \times 0.315 = 360.7$ students would be expected to prefer starting the 4H Club. Of the choices given, this is closest to 360.

14. **(B)** Although the number of students cited for texting while driving is reduced slightly as higher fees are levied, a line of best fit would show only a mild negative slope. Thus, there is a weak negative correlation between higher fines and the number of students cited for texting while driving.

15. **(B)** The data points in the graph indicate a modest decrease in the number of citations issued as the cost of fines increases. Thus, we expect the number of citations to be fewer than 300. We can eliminate answer choices (C) and (D).

Pick two data points to find a line of best fit, such as (100, 350) and (400, 300).

Start to create an equation for the line of best fit by first finding the slope.

$$m = \frac{300 - 350}{400 - 100} = -\frac{1}{6}$$
$$y = -\frac{1}{6}x + b$$

Select one of the points to calculate b, the y-intercept.

$$300 = -\frac{1}{6}(400) + b$$
$$367 \approx b$$
$$y = -\frac{1}{6}x + 367$$

Replace x with 800 to estimate the number of citations issued when the fine is $800.

$$y = -\frac{1}{6}(800) + 367$$
$$y = 233$$

Answer choice (B), 230, is closest to this estimate.

16. **(A)** The quantity of the product supplied to the public is modeled by the function $S(x) = \frac{3}{5}x + 60$. If the price of the product is increased by $15, the function becomes $S(x + 15) = \frac{3}{5}(x + 15) + 60$. To find the impact of increasing the price of the product by $15, subtract $S(x)$ from $S(x + 15)$.

$$S(x + 15) = \frac{3}{5}x + 9 + 60$$
$$= \frac{3}{5}x + 69$$
$$S(x) = \frac{3}{5}x + 60$$
$$S(x + 15) - S(x) = \left(\frac{3}{5}x + 69\right) - \left(\frac{3}{5}x + 60\right) = 9$$

An increase of $15 in the price of the product yields an increase of 9 units of the product that is supplied to the public.

17. **(D)**

$$S(x) = \frac{3}{5}x + 60$$
$$D(x) = 240 - x$$

To find the price of the product in which its demand equals supply, set the supply and demand functions equal to one another and solve for x.

$$\frac{3}{5}x + 60 = 240 - x$$
$$\frac{8}{5}x = 180$$
$$x = \$112.50$$

Choices (A), (B), and (C) yield prices in which the supply and demand functions are not equal.

18. **(C)** Of the runners who placed in the top 40, 6 were in the age group of 30 to 39. One runner in that age group finished in the top 10 and 5 others finished somewhere in places between 11 and 40. Divide 6 by 40 to get .15, which, when expressed as a percent, is 15%.

19. **(A)** The number of runners under 20 years of age who placed in positions 11 through 40 was 11. Given that the total number of runners in that age group was 18, the percent who finished in places 11 through 40 is 61.1%. The number of runners between the ages of 40 and 49 who also finished in places 11 through 40 was 3. Given that a total of 35 runners were in this category, the percent of those runners who finished in places 11 through 40 was 8.6%. The difference between 61.1% and 8.6% is 52.5%.

20. **(A)** Using the values chart, note that when $x = 2$, $g(2) = 5$. Now, check the $h(x)$ values chart for $x = 5$. We find $h(5) = 24$. Therefore, $h(g(2)) = 24$.

21. **(C)** Solve each absolute value equation:

$$|m - 3| = 12$$

Therefore:

$$m - 3 = 12 \text{ or } m - 3 = -12$$
$$m = 15 \text{ or } m = -9$$

Therefore:

$$|n + 7| = 22$$
$$n + 7 = 22 \text{ or } n + 7 = -22$$
$$n = 15 \text{ or } n = -29$$

Since m and n are both less than 0, select -9 and -29 for m and n, respectively.

$$m - n = -9 - (-29) = 20$$

22. **(D)** Rationalizing the fraction means eliminating the imaginary component from the denominator. Multiply both the numerator and the denominator by $6 + 3i$, which is the conjugate of $6 - 3i$. Remember that $i^2 = -1$.

$$\frac{3 + 5i}{6 - 3i} \times \frac{6 + 3i}{6 + 3i} =$$

$$\frac{18 + 39i + 15i^2}{36 + 18i - 18i - 9i^2} =$$

$$\frac{3 + 39i}{45} =$$

$$\frac{1 + 13i}{15}$$

23. **(A)** Multiply both the numerator and the denominator by $6 + 3i$, which is the conjugate of $6 - 3i$.

$$\frac{3 + 5i}{6 - 3i} \times \frac{6 + 3i}{6 + 3i} =$$

$$\frac{18 + 39i + 15i^2}{36 + 18i - 18i - 9i^2} =$$

$$\frac{3 + 39i}{45} =$$

$$\frac{1 + 13i}{15}$$

Rewrite the fraction in the form of $a + bi$.

$$\frac{1}{15} + \frac{13i}{15}$$

We find $a = \frac{1}{15}$ and $b = \frac{13}{15}$ so ab equals $\left(\frac{1}{15}\right)\left(\frac{13}{15}\right) = \frac{13}{225}$.

24. **(D)** Convert everything into yards.

$$3 \text{ inches} = .08 \text{ yards}$$
$$10 \text{ foot radius} = 3.33 \text{ yards}$$
$$\pi = 3.14$$

Use the formula $V = \pi r^2 h$, the volume of a cylinder, to determine how much rock is needed if 3.33 yards is the radius and .08 yards is the height.

$$3.14 \times 3.33^2 \times .08 = 3.14 \times 11.09 \times .08 = 2.79 \text{ cubic yards}$$

Rounding to the nearest cubic yard, the homeowners must purchase 3 cubic yards of rock.

$$3 \text{ cubic yards} \times \$80 = \$240$$

25. **(C)** Whether the rows contained 4, 5, or 6 boys, the last row was always one short. Suppose the number of boys in the group is r, then $r + 1$ would be the quantity that is divisible by 4, 5, and 6. Find the least common multiple of 4, 5, and 6 and set the value equal to $r + 1$. The least common multiple of 4, 5, and 6 is 60, so $r + 1 = 60$. Therefore, r must be 59, the least number of boys that could be in the Boy Scout troop.

26. **(A)** Find the sum of the cards by multiplying the mean by the number of cards:

$$7 \times 14 = 98$$

To maximize the value of a single card, minimize the value of the other cards by assigning each a value of 1:

$$1 + 1 + 1 + 1 + 1 + 1 + 92 = 98$$

27. **(D)** Use a proportion to find the length of the proposed amphitheater in the downtown cultural center. This operation can be facilitated by approximating the length in decimal form. $\frac{1 + \sqrt{5}}{2} : 1$ is approximately equal to 1.62 : 1. Use this ratio substituting 87 for the width.

$$\frac{1.62}{1} = \frac{x}{87}$$

Cross-multiply and solve for x.

$$x = (1.62)(87) = 140.94$$

140.94 rounded to the nearest meter is 141.

Choice (A) can be eliminated quickly (and possibly choice (B) as well). Once it is determined that the golden ratio is about 1.62:1, 211 would surely seem more than twice as large as 87.

28. **(C)** Use the BMI formula with the provided data to assess the patient's BMI number. Remember to convert the height to inches: 5 feet 10 inches equals 70 inches.

$$\frac{182}{70^2} \times 703 = 26.11$$

A patient with a BMI of 26.11 is classified as overweight.

29. **(B)** Use the BMI formula using the provided data to assess the patient's BMI weight. Remember to convert the height to inches: 6 feet equals 72 inches. The lowest BMI categorized as obese is 30.0.

Let $x =$ the patient's weight.

$$\frac{x}{72^2} \times 703 = 30$$
$$.136x = 30$$
$$x \approx 221$$

30. **(B)** Find the difference between the volume of the snowball at 10:00 A.M. and at 11:30 A.M. At 10:00 A.M., the radius of the snowball is 2 feet, so input that value into the volume formula of a sphere.

$$V = \frac{4}{3}\pi r^3 = \frac{4}{3}\pi(2)^3 \approx 33.5 \text{ ft}^3$$

Every 10 minutes, the radius of the snowball grows 6 inches, which is 0.5 feet. There are nine 10-minute intervals between 10:00 A.M. and 11:30 A.M., so multiply 9 by 0.5 to find how much the snowball's radius increased.

$$(9)(0.5) = 4.5$$

Add 4.5 feet to 2 feet to get a final radius of 6.5 feet. Replace r with 6.5 in the volume formula.

$$V = \frac{4}{3}\pi(6.5)^3 \approx 1,150.3 \text{ ft}^3$$

Subtract 33.5 from 1,150.3 to find the increase in the snowball's volume.

$$1,150.3 - 33.5 \approx 1,117$$

31. **3** Find the cost of the tomatoes, and subtract that amount from $7.50.

$$7.50 - 7(.55) = 3.65$$

Divide $3.65 by $.95, which is the cost of a single avocado.

$$3.65 \div .95 = 3.84$$

Fruits must be sold in whole units, so Alina can purchase 3 avocados.

32. **.81** Find the probability that the student selected is an eighth-grade girl and subtract that value from 1.0.

$$\frac{\text{eighth-grade girl}}{\text{all students}} = \frac{215}{1142} = .188$$

Subtract .188 from 1.0 to find the probability that the student selected is not an eighth-grade girl.

$$1.0 - .188 = .812$$

The answer, .812, rounds to .81.

33. **144** The profit function, $P(x) = -.08x^2 + 23.1x + 500$, is a parabola that opens down. The vertex is a maximum with the x-coordinate representing the most profitable number of chairs to manufacture. Find the x-coordinate by using the formula for finding the axis of symmetry, $x = -\frac{b}{2a}$.

$$a = -.08 \quad b = 23.1$$

$$x = -\frac{23.1}{2(-.08)} = 144.375 \approx 144$$

34. **18** Solve for x by changing each base to 3.

$$\left(\frac{1}{3}\right)^{x-2} = (27)^{3-x}$$

$$(3^{-1})^{x-2} = (3^3)^{3-x}$$

$$-x + 2 = 9 - 3x$$

$$-7 = -2x$$

$$\frac{7}{2} = x$$

or

$$3.5 = x$$

Substitute 3.5 for x in $2x + 11$.

$$(2)(3.5) + 11 = 18$$

35. **5,250 pounds** Find the weight of the three cars currently crossing the bridge. Subtract that sum from 15,000, the carrying capacity of the bridge. Since the average weight of the three cars is 3,250 pounds, multiply that value by 3 to find the weight of all three.

$$3 \times 3,250 = 9,750$$

Subtract 9,750 from 15,000 to find the maximum allowable weight for a fourth car or truck.

$$15,000 - 9,750 = 5,250$$

36. **24.0 or 24** Find the volume of the pyramid using the formula $V = \frac{1}{3}Bh$, where B is the base area of the pyramid and h is its height.
Use the formula Area = (length)(width) to find the base area.

$$\text{Area} = 6 \times 8 = 48 \text{ square feet}$$

Replace B with 48 in the volume formula.

$$V = \left(\frac{1}{3}\right)(48)(12) = 192$$

The pyramid has a volume that measures 192 cubic feet. Since each cubic foot weighs 4 ounces, multiply 192 by 4 to find its weight in ounces.

$$192 \times 4 = 768$$

Divide 768 by 16, the number of ounces in a pound, to find the weight of the pyramid in pounds.

$$768 \div 16 = 48$$

Multiply 48 by .50 to find the cost for the Styrofoam to make the pyramid.

$$48 \times \$.50 = \$24.00$$

37. **2,113** Replace $W(h)$ with 50 and h with 22,000 in $W(h) = m\left(\dfrac{4000}{4000 + h}\right)^2$

$$50 = m\left(\dfrac{4000}{26000}\right)^2$$

$$50 = m\left(\dfrac{2}{13}\right)^2$$

$$\left(\dfrac{169}{4}\right)50 = m\left(\dfrac{\cancel{4}}{\cancel{169}}\right)\left(\dfrac{\cancel{169}}{\cancel{4}}\right)$$

$$2,112.5 = m$$

The question asks to round to the nearest pound, so the answer is 2,113 pounds.

38. **8.02** Substitute Susan's sea level weight, 120 pounds, for m and her weight in the jet, $W(h)$, with 119.5.

$$119.5 = 120\left(\dfrac{4000}{4000 + h}\right)^2$$

Divide both sides of the equation by 120.

$$.996 = \left(\dfrac{4000}{4000 + h}\right)^2$$

Find the square root of both sides of the equation.

$$.998 = \dfrac{4000}{4000 + h}$$

Begin to solve for h.

$$.998(4000 + h) = 4,000$$
$$3,992 + .998h = 4,000$$
$$.998h = 8$$
$$h = 8.02$$

ANSWER SHEET
Practice Test 4

Section 1: Reading

1. Ⓐ Ⓑ Ⓒ Ⓓ
2. Ⓐ Ⓑ Ⓒ Ⓓ
3. Ⓐ Ⓑ Ⓒ Ⓓ
4. Ⓐ Ⓑ Ⓒ Ⓓ
5. Ⓐ Ⓑ Ⓒ Ⓓ
6. Ⓐ Ⓑ Ⓒ Ⓓ
7. Ⓐ Ⓑ Ⓒ Ⓓ
8. Ⓐ Ⓑ Ⓒ Ⓓ
9. Ⓐ Ⓑ Ⓒ Ⓓ
10. Ⓐ Ⓑ Ⓒ Ⓓ
11. Ⓐ Ⓑ Ⓒ Ⓓ
12. Ⓐ Ⓑ Ⓒ Ⓓ
13. Ⓐ Ⓑ Ⓒ Ⓓ

14. Ⓐ Ⓑ Ⓒ Ⓓ
15. Ⓐ Ⓑ Ⓒ Ⓓ
16. Ⓐ Ⓑ Ⓒ Ⓓ
17. Ⓐ Ⓑ Ⓒ Ⓓ
18. Ⓐ Ⓑ Ⓒ Ⓓ
19. Ⓐ Ⓑ Ⓒ Ⓓ
20. Ⓐ Ⓑ Ⓒ Ⓓ
21. Ⓐ Ⓑ Ⓒ Ⓓ
22. Ⓐ Ⓑ Ⓒ Ⓓ
23. Ⓐ Ⓑ Ⓒ Ⓓ
24. Ⓐ Ⓑ Ⓒ Ⓓ
25. Ⓐ Ⓑ Ⓒ Ⓓ
26. Ⓐ Ⓑ Ⓒ Ⓓ

27. Ⓐ Ⓑ Ⓒ Ⓓ
28. Ⓐ Ⓑ Ⓒ Ⓓ
29. Ⓐ Ⓑ Ⓒ Ⓓ
30. Ⓐ Ⓑ Ⓒ Ⓓ
31. Ⓐ Ⓑ Ⓒ Ⓓ
32. Ⓐ Ⓑ Ⓒ Ⓓ
33. Ⓐ Ⓑ Ⓒ Ⓓ
34. Ⓐ Ⓑ Ⓒ Ⓓ
35. Ⓐ Ⓑ Ⓒ Ⓓ
36. Ⓐ Ⓑ Ⓒ Ⓓ
37. Ⓐ Ⓑ Ⓒ Ⓓ
38. Ⓐ Ⓑ Ⓒ Ⓓ
39. Ⓐ Ⓑ Ⓒ Ⓓ

40. Ⓐ Ⓑ Ⓒ Ⓓ
41. Ⓐ Ⓑ Ⓒ Ⓓ
42. Ⓐ Ⓑ Ⓒ Ⓓ
43. Ⓐ Ⓑ Ⓒ Ⓓ
44. Ⓐ Ⓑ Ⓒ Ⓓ
45. Ⓐ Ⓑ Ⓒ Ⓓ
46. Ⓐ Ⓑ Ⓒ Ⓓ
47. Ⓐ Ⓑ Ⓒ Ⓓ
48. Ⓐ Ⓑ Ⓒ Ⓓ
49. Ⓐ Ⓑ Ⓒ Ⓓ
50. Ⓐ Ⓑ Ⓒ Ⓓ
51. Ⓐ Ⓑ Ⓒ Ⓓ
52. Ⓐ Ⓑ Ⓒ Ⓓ

Section 2: Writing and Language

1. Ⓐ Ⓑ Ⓒ Ⓓ
2. Ⓐ Ⓑ Ⓒ Ⓓ
3. Ⓐ Ⓑ Ⓒ Ⓓ
4. Ⓐ Ⓑ Ⓒ Ⓓ
5. Ⓐ Ⓑ Ⓒ Ⓓ
6. Ⓐ Ⓑ Ⓒ Ⓓ
7. Ⓐ Ⓑ Ⓒ Ⓓ
8. Ⓐ Ⓑ Ⓒ Ⓓ
9. Ⓐ Ⓑ Ⓒ Ⓓ
10. Ⓐ Ⓑ Ⓒ Ⓓ
11. Ⓐ Ⓑ Ⓒ Ⓓ

12. Ⓐ Ⓑ Ⓒ Ⓓ
13. Ⓐ Ⓑ Ⓒ Ⓓ
14. Ⓐ Ⓑ Ⓒ Ⓓ
15. Ⓐ Ⓑ Ⓒ Ⓓ
16. Ⓐ Ⓑ Ⓒ Ⓓ
17. Ⓐ Ⓑ Ⓒ Ⓓ
18. Ⓐ Ⓑ Ⓒ Ⓓ
19. Ⓐ Ⓑ Ⓒ Ⓓ
20. Ⓐ Ⓑ Ⓒ Ⓓ
21. Ⓐ Ⓑ Ⓒ Ⓓ
22. Ⓐ Ⓑ Ⓒ Ⓓ

23. Ⓐ Ⓑ Ⓒ Ⓓ
24. Ⓐ Ⓑ Ⓒ Ⓓ
25. Ⓐ Ⓑ Ⓒ Ⓓ
26. Ⓐ Ⓑ Ⓒ Ⓓ
27. Ⓐ Ⓑ Ⓒ Ⓓ
28. Ⓐ Ⓑ Ⓒ Ⓓ
29. Ⓐ Ⓑ Ⓒ Ⓓ
30. Ⓐ Ⓑ Ⓒ Ⓓ
31. Ⓐ Ⓑ Ⓒ Ⓓ
32. Ⓐ Ⓑ Ⓒ Ⓓ
33. Ⓐ Ⓑ Ⓒ Ⓓ

34. Ⓐ Ⓑ Ⓒ Ⓓ
35. Ⓐ Ⓑ Ⓒ Ⓓ
36. Ⓐ Ⓑ Ⓒ Ⓓ
37. Ⓐ Ⓑ Ⓒ Ⓓ
38. Ⓐ Ⓑ Ⓒ Ⓓ
39. Ⓐ Ⓑ Ⓒ Ⓓ
40. Ⓐ Ⓑ Ⓒ Ⓓ
41. Ⓐ Ⓑ Ⓒ Ⓓ
42. Ⓐ Ⓑ Ⓒ Ⓓ
43. Ⓐ Ⓑ Ⓒ Ⓓ
44. Ⓐ Ⓑ Ⓒ Ⓓ

ANSWER SHEET
Practice Test 4

Section 3: Math (No Calculator)

1. Ⓐ Ⓑ Ⓒ Ⓓ 5. Ⓐ Ⓑ Ⓒ Ⓓ 9. Ⓐ Ⓑ Ⓒ Ⓓ 13. Ⓐ Ⓑ Ⓒ Ⓓ
2. Ⓐ Ⓑ Ⓒ Ⓓ 6. Ⓐ Ⓑ Ⓒ Ⓓ 10. Ⓐ Ⓑ Ⓒ Ⓓ 14. Ⓐ Ⓑ Ⓒ Ⓓ
3. Ⓐ Ⓑ Ⓒ Ⓓ 7. Ⓐ Ⓑ Ⓒ Ⓓ 11. Ⓐ Ⓑ Ⓒ Ⓓ 15. Ⓐ Ⓑ Ⓒ Ⓓ
4. Ⓐ Ⓑ Ⓒ Ⓓ 8. Ⓐ Ⓑ Ⓒ Ⓓ 12. Ⓐ Ⓑ Ⓒ Ⓓ

16. 17. 18.

19. 20.

ANSWER SHEET
Practice Test 4

Section 4: Math (Calculator)

1. Ⓐ Ⓑ Ⓒ Ⓓ 9. Ⓐ Ⓑ Ⓒ Ⓓ 17. Ⓐ Ⓑ Ⓒ Ⓓ 25. Ⓐ Ⓑ Ⓒ Ⓓ
2. Ⓐ Ⓑ Ⓒ Ⓓ 10. Ⓐ Ⓑ Ⓒ Ⓓ 18. Ⓐ Ⓑ Ⓒ Ⓓ 26. Ⓐ Ⓑ Ⓒ Ⓓ
3. Ⓐ Ⓑ Ⓒ Ⓓ 11. Ⓐ Ⓑ Ⓒ Ⓓ 19. Ⓐ Ⓑ Ⓒ Ⓓ 27. Ⓐ Ⓑ Ⓒ Ⓓ
4. Ⓐ Ⓑ Ⓒ Ⓓ 12. Ⓐ Ⓑ Ⓒ Ⓓ 20. Ⓐ Ⓑ Ⓒ Ⓓ 28. Ⓐ Ⓑ Ⓒ Ⓓ
5. Ⓐ Ⓑ Ⓒ Ⓓ 13. Ⓐ Ⓑ Ⓒ Ⓓ 21. Ⓐ Ⓑ Ⓒ Ⓓ 29. Ⓐ Ⓑ Ⓒ Ⓓ
6. Ⓐ Ⓑ Ⓒ Ⓓ 14. Ⓐ Ⓑ Ⓒ Ⓓ 22. Ⓐ Ⓑ Ⓒ Ⓓ 30. Ⓐ Ⓑ Ⓒ Ⓓ
7. Ⓐ Ⓑ Ⓒ Ⓓ 15. Ⓐ Ⓑ Ⓒ Ⓓ 23. Ⓐ Ⓑ Ⓒ Ⓓ
8. Ⓐ Ⓑ Ⓒ Ⓓ 16. Ⓐ Ⓑ Ⓒ Ⓓ 24. Ⓐ Ⓑ Ⓒ Ⓓ

31. 32. 33. 34.

35. 36. 37. 38.

1   1   1

Practice Test 4

READING TEST

65 MINUTES, 52 QUESTIONS

Turn to Section 1 of your answer sheet to answer the questions in this section.

> **DIRECTIONS:** Following each of the passages (or pairs of passages) below are questions about the passage (or passages). Read each passage carefully. Then, select the best answer for each question based on what is stated in the passage (or passages) and in any graphics that may accompany the passage.

Questions 1–10 are based on the following passage.

This passage is from John Okada, *No-No Boy*, published by the University of Washington Press, Copyright © 2001.

First, the real Japanese-Japanese were rounded up. These real Japanese-Japanese were Japanese nationals who had the misfortune to be diplomats and businessmen and visiting professors.
(5) They were put on a boat and sent back to Japan.

Then the alien Japanese, the ones who had been in America for two, three, or even four decades, were screened, and those found to be too actively Japanese were transported to the
(10) hinterlands and put in a camp.

The security screen was sifted once more and, this time, the lesser lights were similarly plucked and deposited. An old man, too old, too feeble, and too scared, was caught in the
(15) net. In his pocket was a little, black book. He had been a collector for the Japan-Help-the-Poor-and-Starving—and Flooded-Out-and-Homeless-and-Crippled-and-What-Have-You Fund. "Yamada-san, 50 American cents; Okada-
(20) san, two American dollars; Watanabe-san, 24 American cents; Takizaki-san, skip this month because boy broke leg"; and so on down the

page. Yamada-san, Okada-san, Watanabe-san, Takizaki-san, and so on down the page were
(25) whisked away from their homes while weeping families wept until the tears must surely have been wept dry, and then wept some more.

By now, the snowball was big enough to wipe out the rising sun. The big rising sun would take
(30) a little more time, but the little rising sun which was the Japanese in countless Japanese communities in the coastal states of Washington, Oregon, and California presented no problem. The whisking and transporting of Japanese and
(35) the construction of camps with barbed wire and ominous towers supporting fully armed soldiers in places like Idaho and Wyoming and Arizona, places which even Hollywood scorned for background, had become skills which demanded
(40) the utmost of America's great organizing ability.

And so, a few months after the seventh day of December of the year nineteen forty-one, the only Japanese left on the west coast of the United States was Matsusaburo Inabukuro who, while
(45) it has been forgotten whether he was Japanese-American or American-Japanese, picked up an "I am Chinese"—not American or American-Chinese or Chinese-American but "I am Chinese"—button and got a job in a California shipyard.

(50)   Two years later a good Japanese-American who had volunteered for the army sat smoking in the belly of a B-24 on his way back to Guam from a reconnaissance flight to Japan. His job was to listen through his earphones, which (55) were attached to a high-frequency set, and jot down air-ground messages spoken by Japanese-Japanese in Japanese planes and in Japanese radio shacks.

The lieutenant who operated the radar-(60) detection equipment was a blond giant from Nebraska.

The lieutenant from Nebraska said: "Where you from?"

The Japanese-American who was an (65) American soldier answered: "No place in particular."

"You got folks?"

"Yeah, I got folks."

"Where at?"

(70)   "Wyoming, out in the desert."

"Farmers, huh?"

"Not quite."

"What's that mean?"

"Well, it's this way . . . ." And then the (75) Japanese-American whose folks were still Japanese-Japanese, or else they would not be in a camp with barbed wire and watchtowers with soldiers holding rifles, told the blond giant from Nebraska about the removal of the Japanese (80) from the Coast, which was called the evacuation, and about the concentration camps, which were called relocation centers.

The lieutenant listened and he didn't believe it. He said: "That's funny. Now, tell me again."

(85)   The Japanese-American soldier of the American army told it again and didn't change a word.

The lieutenant believed him this time. "Hell's bells," he exclaimed, "if they'd done that to me,

(90)   I wouldn't be sitting in the belly of a broken-down B-24 going back to Guam from a reconnaissance mission to Japan."

"I got reasons," said the Japanese-American soldier soberly.

1. As it is used in line 10 *hinterlands* most nearly means

    (A) lands outside the continental United States
    (B) a special area outside the border of the United States
    (C) camps within the United States for housing people displaced by order of the United States government
    (D) a region remote from urban areas

2. As it is used in line 12 *lights* most nearly means

    (A) enemy soldiers
    (B) notable people
    (C) rebels
    (D) inspiring speakers

3. The *snowball* mentioned in line 28 most likely refers to

    (A) the accumulating tears of Japanese family members who have seen their relatives moved to relocation camps
    (B) the steadily increasing, accumulating efforts of Americans to defeat the Japanese
    (C) the steadily growing efforts of Americans to relocate Japanese aliens living in America
    (D) the steadily accumulating efforts of Japanese aliens living in America to return to Japan to fight for their country

4. Which of the following words best describes the author's tone in lines 34–40?

"The whisking and transporting of Japanese and the construction of camps with barbed wire and ominous towers supporting fully armed soldiers in places like Idaho and Wyoming and Arizona, places which even Hollywood scorned for background, had become skills which demanded the utmost of America's great organizing ability."

(A) jocular
(B) sarcastic
(C) apologetic
(D) solemn

5. We can infer that the "I am Chinese" button that Matsusaburo Inabukuro wore helped him get a job because

(A) people believed that he wasn't Japanese
(B) people thought he was a Japanese person trying to make people believe he was a Chinese person
(C) people believed that a Chinese person in America was likely to be an American citizen
(D) people thought that he was a Chinese alien

6. The author would be most likely to describe the term "relocation centers" (line 82) as

(A) hyperbole
(B) an understatement
(C) a euphemism
(D) a cliché

7. As it is used in line 84 *funny* most nearly means

(A) strange
(B) exaggerated
(C) humorous
(D) not true

8. The author uses all of the following *except*

(A) irony
(B) humor
(C) metaphor
(D) extrapolation

9. At the time of this account the narrator's parents are

(A) living on their farm in Wyoming
(B) living in Japan
(C) living in a relocation camp in Wyoming
(D) deceased

10. Which of the following provides evidence for the answer to the previous question?

(A) "By . . . problem." (lines 28–33)
(B) "The . . . ability." (lines 34–40)
(C) "'You . . . centers.'" (lines 67–82)
(D) "'The . . . Japan.'" (lines 88–92)

1   1   1

Questions 11–21 are based on the following passage.

This passage is from Freeman Dyson, *Disturbing the Universe.* Copyright © 1979 by Freeman J. Dyson.

There are some striking examples in the laws of nuclear physics of numerical accidents that seem to conspire to make the universe habitable. The strength of the attractive nuclear
(5) force is just sufficient to overcome the electrical repulsion between the positive charges in the nuclei of ordinary atoms such as oxygen or iron. But the nuclear forces are not quite strong enough to bind together two protons
(10) (hydrogen nuclei) into a bound system which would be called a diproton if it existed. If the nuclear forces had been slightly stronger than they are, the diproton would exist and almost all the hydrogen in the universe would have been
(15) combined into diprotons and heavier nuclei. Hydrogen would be a rare element, and stars like the sun, which live for a long time by the slow burning of hydrogen in their cores, could not exist. On the other hand, if the nuclear
(20) forces had been substantially weaker than they are, hydrogen could not burn at all and there would be no heavy elements. If, as seems likely, the evolution of life requires a star like the sun, supplying energy at a constant rate for billions
(25) of years, then the strength of nuclear forces had to lie within a rather narrow range to make life possible.

A similar but independent numerical accident appears in connection with the weak inter-
(30) action by which hydrogen actually burns in the sun. The weak interaction is millions of times weaker than the nuclear force. It is just weak enough so that the hydrogen in the sun burns at a slow and steady rate. If the weak interaction
(35) were much stronger or much weaker, any forms of life dependent on sunlike stars would again be in difficulties.

The facts of astronomy include some other numerical accidents that work to our advan-
(40) tage. For example, the universe is built on such a scale that the average distance between stars in an average galaxy like ours is about twenty million million miles—an extravagantly large distance by human standards If a scientist
(45) asserts that the stars at these immense distances have a decisive effect on the possibility of human existence, he will be suspected of being a believer in astrology. But it happens to be true that we could not have survived if the
(50) average distance between stars were only two million million miles instead of twenty. If the distances had been smaller by a factor of ten, there would have been a high probability that another star, at some time during the four bil-
(55) lion years that the earth has existed, would have passed by the sun close enough to disrupt with its gravitational field the orbits of the planets. To destroy life on earth, it would not be necessary to pull the earth out of the solar system. It would
(60) be sufficient to pull the earth into a moderately eccentric elliptical orbit.

All the rich diversity of organic chemistry depends on a delicate balance between electrical and quantum-mechanical forces. The bal-
(65) ance exists only because the laws of physics include an "exclusion principle" which forbids two electrons to occupy the same state. If the laws were changed so that electrons no longer excluded each other, none of our essential
(70) chemistry would survive. There are many other

lucky accidents in atomic physics. Without such
accidents, water could not exist as a liquid,
chains of carbon atoms could not form complex
organic molecules, and hydrogen atoms could
(75) not form breakable bridges between molecules.

I conclude from the existence of these accidents of physics and astronomy that the universe is an unexpectedly hospitable place for
living creatures to make their home. Being a
(80) scientist, trained in the habits of thought and
language of the twentieth century rather than
the eighteenth, I do not claim that the architecture of the universe proves the existence of
God. I claim only that the architecture of the
(85) universe is consistent with the hypothesis that
mind plays an essential role in its functioning.

11. According to the author, if the nuclear forces in
atoms had been slightly stronger than they are

(A) there would be many more stars like the Sun
than there are
(B) the universe would be made up of over 99%
hydrogen
(C) most of the hydrogen in the universe would
have burned up
(D) stars like the Sun would not exist

12. As it is used in line 43 *extravagantly* most nearly
means

(A) erroneously
(B) imprudently
(C) incomprehensibly
(D) in a way that exceeds a reasonable amount

13. The author most likely refers to astrology in line
48 to

(A) show that he is familiar with ways of thinking
outside of conventional science
(B) support his assertion that stars greatly affect
human beings
(C) emphasize how remarkable it is that faraway
stars affect life on Earth
(D) support his contention that faraway stars can
come near the Sun and disrupt the Earth's
orbit around it

14. As it is used in line 46 *decisive* most nearly means

(A) resolute
(B) important
(C) extreme
(D) conclusive

15. According to the author, which of the following
does not contribute to making the universe "an
unexpectedly hospitable place for living creatures
to make their home" (lines 78–79)?

(A) The "exclusion principle" forbids two
electrons to occupy the same state.
(B) The strength of the attractive nuclear force
lies within a narrow range.
(C) Hydrogen atoms cannot form breakable
bridges between molecules.
(D) The average distance between stars in
galaxies like the Milky Way is about twenty
million million miles rather than only two
million million miles.

16. Which of the following provides the evidence to answer the previous question?

    (A) "If . . . nuclei." (lines 11–15)
    (B) "On . . . elements." (lines 19–22)
    (C) "If . . . difficulties." (lines 34–37)
    (D) "Without . . . molecules." (lines 71–75)

17. The phrase "habits of thought" as it is used in line 80 most nearly means

    (A) recurrent patterns of thinking
    (B) scientific thinking
    (C) unconscious thinking
    (D) philosophical thinking

18. The author's tone in the passage is most accurately described as

    (A) measured and reasonable
    (B) mildly amused
    (C) deeply skeptical
    (D) indignant

19. Which of the following, if it occurred, would support the conclusion reached by the author?

    (A) the discovery of a diproton
    (B) proof that no organic compounds exist on planets in several nearby solar systems
    (C) the discovery of life on a planet in orbit around another star in our galaxy
    (D) the discovery that stars like the Sun are burning hydrogen at a rapidly increasing rate

20. The author would be most likely to agree that the argument he makes in this passage

    (A) shows conclusively that the universe was designed by some super-human agency
    (B) offers good but far from decisive support for philosophers who argue that the highly ordered structure of the universe proves the existence of God
    (C) demonstrates the futility of speculating about how and why the universe was created
    (D) strongly suggests that life exists on some planets in solar systems near to Earth

21. Which of the following does the author make use of in his argument?

    (A) paradox
    (B) understatement
    (C) inductive reasoning
    (D) concession

Questions 22–32 are based on the following passage.

This passage is from Lewis Thomas, *The Medusa and the Snail*, copyright ©1974.

It is customary to place the date for the beginnings of modern medicine somewhere in the mid-1930s, with the entry of sulfonamides and penicillin into the pharmacopoeia, and it
(5) is usual to ascribe to these events the force of a revolution in medical practice. This is what things seemed like at the time. Medicine was upheaved, revolutionized indeed. Therapy had been discovered for great numbers of patients
(10) whose illnesses had previously been untreatable. Cures were now available. It seemed a totally new world. Doctors could now cure disease, and this was astonishing, most of all to the doctors themselves.
(15) It was a major occurrence in medicine, and a triumph for biological science applied to medicine but perhaps not a revolution after all, looking back from this distance. For the real revolution in medicine, which set the stage
(20) for antibiotics and whatever else we have in the way of effective therapy today, had already occurred one hundred years before penicillin. It did not begin with the introduction of science into medicine. That came years later. Like
(25) a good many revolutions this one began with the destruction of dogma. It was discovered, sometime in the 1830s, that the greater part of medicine was nonsense.

The history of medicine has never been a
(30) particularly attractive subject in medical education, and one reason for this is that it is so unrelievedly deplorable a story. For century after century, all the way into the remote millennia of its origins, medicine got along by sheer
(35) guesswork and the crudest sort of empiricism. It is hard to conceive of a less scientific enterprise among human endeavors. Virtually anything that could be thought up for treatment of disease was tried out at one time or another, and

(40) once tried, lasted decades or even centuries before being given up. It was, in retrospect, the most frivolous and irresponsible kind of human experimentation, based on nothing but trial and error, and usually resulting in pre-
(45) cisely that sequence. Bleeding, purging, cupping, the administration of infusions of every known plant, solutions of every known metal, every conceivable diet including total fasting, most of these based on the weirdest imaginings
(50) about the cause of disease, concocted out of nothing but thin air—this was the heritage of medicine until a little over a century ago. It is astounding that the profession survived so long, and got away with so much with so little outcry.
(55) Almost everyone seems to have been taken in. Evidently, one had to be a born skeptic to see through the old nonsense. Most people were convinced of the magical powers of medicine and put up with it.

(60) Then, sometime in the early nineteenth century, it was realized by a few of the leading figures in medicine that almost all of the complicated treatments then available for disease did not really work, and the suggestion was made
(65) by several courageous physicians that most of them actually did more harm than good. Simultaneously, the surprising discovery was made that certain diseases were self-limited, got better by themselves, possessed a "natural
(70) history." It is hard for us now to imagine the magnitude of this discovery and its effect on the practice of medicine. That long habit, extending back into the distant past, had been to treat everything with something, and it was taken
(75) for granted that every disease demanded treatment and might in fact end fatally if not treated. In a sober essay written on this topic in 1876, Professor Edward H. Clarke reviewed what he regarded as the major scientific accomplish-
(80) ment of medicine in the preceding fifty years, which consisted of studies proving that patients with typhoid and typhus fever could recover all

1   1   1

by themselves, without medical intervention, and often did better for being untreated than (85) when they received the bizarre herbs, heavy metal and fomentations that were popular at that time. Delirium tremens, a disorder long believed to be fatal in all cases unless subjected to constant and aggressive medical interven- (90) tion, was observed to subside by itself more readily in patients left untreated, with a substantially improved rate of survival.

Gradually, over succeeding decades, the traditional therapeutic ritual of medicine was (95) given up, and what came to be called the "art of medicine" emerged to take its place. In retrospect, this art was really the beginning of the science of medicine. It was based on meticulous, objective, even cool observations of sick (100) people. From this endeavor we learned the details of the natural history of illness, so that, for example, it came to be understood that typhoid and typhus were really two entirely separate, unrelated disorders, with quite different (105) causes. Accurate diagnosis became the central purpose and justification for medicine, and as the methods for diagnosis improved, accurate prognosis also became possible.

22. As it is used in line 4 *pharmacopoeia* most nearly means

(A) collection of drugs approved by the government for medical use
(B) accepted medical practice
(C) stock of medical drugs
(D) knowledge of doctors

23. Why, according to the author, were doctors astonished around the mid-1930s?

(A) They were amazed that drugs were able to cure diseases.
(B) Cures were becoming available for some illnesses, whereas before these doctors had little capacity to cure illnesses.
(C) The practice of medicine was being revolutionized by a bold young breed of doctors.
(D) They were surprised that people still had so much respect for doctors and medicine.

24. Which of the following is part of the "dogma" referred to in line 26?

(A) Every illness must be treated.
(B) Every illness ends in the patient's death if it is not treated.
(C) Some diseases get better if left untreated.
(D) Accurate diagnosis, not treatment, is the most important purpose of medicine.

25. As it is used in line 35 the phrase "the crudest sort of empiricism" most nearly means

   (A) acquisition of scientific knowledge by careful experimentation
   (B) extremely impolite experimentation on patients
   (C) very unsophisticated use of observation and experimentation to gain knowledge
   (D) the use of powerful drugs without a scientific understanding of their compositions

26. What is the most likely reason that the author says, "It is astounding that the profession survived so long" (lines 52–53)?

   (A) He believes that being a doctor in the time before the development of modern medicine was extremely demanding, and he's amazed that so few doctors left the medical profession.
   (B) He believes it is very surprising that the medical profession was not assimilated into the larger field of biological science, as the latter field made huge advances in the early years of the twentieth century.
   (C) He believes it is remarkable that a profession that was so poor at doing its job was so popular.
   (D) He believes it is amazing that the medical profession was not more appreciated by the public before the mid-1930s.

27. As it is used in line 56 *skeptic* most nearly means

   (A) person of very high intelligence
   (B) cynical person
   (C) person who analyzes things objectively
   (D) person who questions generally accepted ideas

28. It can be inferred that the author describes "several physicians" as "courageous" (line 65) because

   (A) he believes that it took courage for physicians to risk injuring their own health by administering new drugs to patients
   (B) he believes that it took courage for physicians to suggest that the methods used in their profession were almost completely wrong, since doing so would make them unpopular with other members of the profession and possibly endanger their standing in the medical profession
   (C) he believes that it took courage for physicians to suggest that the profession should try new methods of treating patients
   (D) he believes that it took courage for such physicians to admit to their fellow professionals that they had been wrong in their criticism of accepted medical practice

29. The author describes the "discovery" mentioned in line 67 as "surprising" because

   (A) doctors at the time believed that medical intervention in illness was generally unhelpful
   (B) doctors at the time believed that there were some diseases that could not be cured
   (C) most people, including doctors, believed that all illnesses had to be treated
   (D) medicine has advanced so much since the early nineteenth century that it is surprising that such a discovery was made then

1   1   1

30. Which of the following provides evidence for the answer to the previous question?

(A) "Doctors . . . themselves." (lines 12–14)
(B) " Virtually . . . up." (lines 37–41)
(C) "Simultaneously . . . 'history.'" (lines 67–70)
(D) "That . . . treated." (lines 72–76)

31. The word that best describes the "the major scientific accomplishment of medicine in the preceding fifty years" (lines 79–80) is

(A) ironic
(B) unsubstantiated
(C) humorous
(D) unethical

32. As it is used in line 89 *aggressive* most nearly means

(A) dangerous
(B) destructive
(C) very intensive
(D) hostile

Questions 33–42 are based on the following passage.

This passage is from Elizabeth Zubritsky, "NASA Finds Friction from Tides Could Help Distant Earths Survive, and Thrive," NASA's Goddard Space Flight Center.

As anybody who has started a campfire by rubbing sticks knows, friction generates heat. Now, computer modeling by NASA scientists shows that friction could be the key to survival
(5) for some distant Earth-sized planets traveling in dangerous orbits.

The findings are consistent with observations that Earth-sized planets appear to be very common in other star systems. Although heat
(10) can be a destructive force for some planets, the right amount of friction, and therefore heat, can be helpful and perhaps create conditions for habitability.

"We found some unexpected good news
(15) for planets in vulnerable orbits," said Wade Henning, a scientist working at NASA and lead author of the new study. "It turns out these planets will often experience just enough friction to move them out of harm's way and into
(20) safer, more-circular orbits more quickly than previously predicted."

Simulations of young planetary systems indicate that giant planets often upset the orbits of smaller inner worlds. Even if those interactions
(25) aren't immediately catastrophic, they can leave a planet in a treacherous eccentric orbit—a very elliptical course that raises the odds of crossing paths with another body, being absorbed by the host star, or getting ejected from the system.
(30)   Another potential peril of a highly eccentric orbit is the amount of tidal stress a planet may undergo as it draws very close to its star and then retreats away. Near the star, the gravitational force is powerful enough to deform the

planet, while in more distant reaches of the orbit, the planet can ease back into shape. This flexing action produces friction, which generates heat. In extreme cases, tidal stress can produce enough heat to liquefy the planet.

(40)   In this new study Henning and his colleague Terry Hurford explored the effects of tidal stresses on planets that have multiple layers, such as rocky crust, mantle or iron core. One conclusion of the study is that some planets (45) could move into a safer orbit about 10 to 100 times faster than previously expected—in as a little as a few hundred thousand years, instead of the more typical rate of several million years. Such planets would be driven close to the point (50) of melting or, at least, would have a nearly melted layer, similar to the one right below Earth's crust. Their interior temperatures could range from moderately warmer than our planet is today up to the point of having modest-sized (55) magma oceans.

The transition to a circular orbit would be speedy because an almost-melted layer would flex easily, generating a lot of friction-induced heat. As the planet threw off that heat, it would (60) lose energy at a fast rate and relax quickly into a circular orbit. (Later, tidal heating would turn off, and the planet's surface could become safe to walk on.) In contrast, a world that had completely melted would be so fluid that it (65) would produce little friction. Before this study, that is what researchers expected to happen to planets undergoing strong tidal stresses. Cold, stiff planets tend to resist the tidal stress and release energy very slowly. In fact, Henning (70) and Hurford found that many of them actually generate less friction than previously thought. This may be especially true for planets farther from their stars. If these worlds are not crowded by other bodies, they may be stable in their (75) eccentric orbits for a long time. "In this case, the longer, non-circular orbits could increase the 'habitable zone,' because the tidal stress will remain an energy source for longer periods of time," said Hurford. "This is great for dim stars (80) or ice worlds with subsurface oceans."

Surprisingly, another way for a terrestrial planet to achieve high amounts of heating is to be covered in a very thick ice shell, similar to an extreme "snowball Earth." Although a (85) sheet of ice is a slippery, low-friction surface, an ice layer thousands of miles thick would be very springy. A shell like this would have just the right properties to respond strongly to tidal stress, generating a lot of heat. (The high (90) pressures inside these planets could prevent all but the topmost layers from turning into liquid water.)

The researchers found that the very responsive layers of ice or almost-melted material (95) could be relatively thin, just a few hundred miles deep in some cases, yet still dominate the global behavior. The team modeled planets that are the size of Earth and up to two-and-a-half times larger. Henning added that superEarths— (100) planets at the high end of this size range—likely would experience stronger tidal stresses and potentially could benefit more from the resulting friction and heating.

Planets in eccentric orbits can experience powerful tidal forces. A planet covered by a very thick ice shell (left) is springy enough to flex a great deal, generating a lot of internal friction and heat. Some terrestrial planets (right) also will flex, especially with partially molten inner layers.

Credit: NASA's Goodard Space Flight Center

33. The data gathered in the study conducted by Wade Henning and his colleague and described in the passage was obtained by

(A) telescopic observation of planets in orbit around stars

(B) simulations run on computers

(C) a review of past studies

(D) all of the above

34. Which choice provides the best evidence for the answer to the previous question?

(A) lines 3–6 ("Now . . . orbits.")

(B) lines 30–33 ("Another . . . away.")

(C) lines 56–59 ("The . . . heat.")

(D) lines 93–97 (The . . . behavior.")

35. The word *dangerous* in line 6 most nearly means

(A) likely to cause harm

(B) threatening

(C) risky

(D) certain to be destroyed

36. The author most likely refers to making a campfire to

(A) help the reader visualize a phenomenon

(B) show that terrestrial and astronomical phenomena are fundamentally different

(C) create humor

(D) introduce a mystery that will be explained later in the passage

37. Which of the following is the main phenomenon discussed in the passage that may prevent a young planet from developing into a habitable planet?

   (A) tidal stress
   (B) an eccentric orbit
   (C) absorption by a star
   (D) collision or near collision with other bodies

38. Based on the information in the passage, which of the following conclusions would the authors of the study discussed in the passage probably believe to be most likely?

   (A) Nearly all of the Earth-size planets in a typical star system are in a circular orbit.
   (B) Earth-size planets are rare.
   (C) All of the Earth-size planets that exist in other star systems were once in elliptical orbits around their host star.
   (D) Some of the Earth-like planets in other star systems have always been in a circular orbit, while others were previously in elliptical orbits.

39. Which word most accurately describes the phenomenon described in lines 81–89 ("Surprisingly . . . heat.")?

   (A) paradoxical
   (B) inexplicable
   (C) simple
   (D) mysterious

40. Based on the information in the passage, which of the following statements would the authors of the study described in the passage be most likely to agree with?

   (A) The composition of Earth-size planets in other systems is important for scientists to understand and should be investigated further.
   (B) Planets in eccentric orbits can never be habitable.
   (C) Once a planet melts it can never become habitable.
   (D) Tidal friction is the main process driving the formation of Earth-size habitable planets.

41. The most appropriate title for the passage would be

   (A) How Earth-like Planets Are Created
   (B) Evidence Found that Friction from Tides Could Help Earth-like Planets Survive
   (C) The Possibility of Life on Earth-size Planets
   (D) Proof Found that Habitable Earth-size Planets Are Common

42. The study discussed in this passage would be most likely to appear

   (A) in a science magazine for the general public
   (B) in a weekly news magazine
   (C) in a professional astronomy journal
   (D) in a NASA newsletter for high school science students

Questions 43–52 are based on the following passage.

This passage is from John L. O'Sullivan, "The Great Nation of Futurity." It was originally published in 1839.

The American people having derived their origin from many other nations, and the Declaration of National Independence being entirely based on the great principle of human
(5) equality, these facts demonstrate at once our disconnected position as regards any other nation; that we have, in reality, but little connection with the past history of any of them, and still less with all antiquity, its glories, or its
(10) crimes. On the contrary, our national birth was the beginning of a new history, the formation and progress of an untried political system, which separates us from the past and connects us with the future only; and so far as regards the
(15) entire development of the natural rights of man, in moral, political, and national life, we may confidently assume that our country is destined to be the great nation of futurity.

It is so destined because the principle upon
(20) which a nation is organized fixes its destiny, and that of equality is perfect, is universal. It presides in all the operations of the physical world, and it is also the conscious law of the soul—the self-evident dictates of morality, which
(25) accurately defines the duty of man to man, and consequently man's rights as man. Besides, the truthful annals of any nation furnish abundant evidence that its happiness, its greatness, its duration, were always proportionate to the dem-
(30) ocratic equality in its system of government.

What friend of human liberty, civilization, and refinement can cast his view over the past history of the monarchies and aristocracies of antiquity, and not deplore that they ever existed?

(35) What philanthropist can contemplate the oppressions, the cruelties, and injustice inflicted by them on the masses of mankind, and not turn with moral horror from the retrospect?

America is destined for better deeds. It is
(40) our unparalleled glory that we have no reminiscences of battle fields but in defense of humanity, of the oppressed of all nations, of the rights of conscience, the rights of personal enfranchisement. Our annals describe no scenes of
(45) horrid carnage, where men were led on by hundreds of thousands to slay one another, dupes and victims to emperors, kings, nobles, demons in the human form called heroes. We have had patriots to defend our homes, our liberties, but
(50) no aspirants to crowns or thrones; nor have the American people ever suffered themselves to be led on by wicked ambition to depopulate the land, to spread desolation far and wide, that a human being might be placed on a seat
(55) of supremacy.

We have no interest in the scenes of antiquity, only as lessons of avoidance of nearly all their examples. The expansive future is our arena, and for our history. We are entering on
(60) its untrodden space, with the truths of God in our minds, beneficent objects in our hearts, and with a clear conscience unsullied by the past. We are the nation of human progress, and who will, what can, set limits to our onward march?
(65) Providence is with us, and no earthly power can. We point to the everlasting truth on the first page of our national declaration, and we proclaim to the millions of other lands, that "the gates of hell"—the powers of aristocracy and
(70) monarchy—"shall not prevail against it."

The far-reaching, the boundless future will be the era of American greatness. In its

1   1   1

magnificent domain of space and time, the
nation of many nations is destined to manifest
(75) to mankind the excellence of divine principles;
to establish on earth the noblest temple ever
dedicated to the worship of the Most High—the
Sacred and the True.

Its floor shall be a hemisphere—its roof the
(80) firmament of the star-studded heavens, and
its congregation a Union of many Republics,
comprising hundreds of happy millions, calling,
owning no man master, but governed by God's
natural and moral law of equality, the law of
(85) brotherhood—of "peace and good will amongst
men." . . .

We are the nation of progress, of individual
freedom, of universal enfranchisement. We
must onward to the fulfillment of our mission—
(90) to the entire development of the principle of our
organization—freedom of conscience, freedom
of person, freedom of trade and business pursuits, universality of freedom and equality. This
is our high destiny, and we must accomplish it.
(95) All this will be our future history, to establish on
earth the moral dignity and salvation of man—
the immutable truth and beneficence of God.
For this blessed mission to the nations of the
world, which are shut out from the life-giving
(100) light of truth, has America been chosen.

43. The passage can best be described as

(A) a discussion of the historical origins of
American values
(B) an endeavor to reconcile political and reli-
gious ideals
(C) an effort to put America's place in the world
in historical perspective
(D) an attempt to rally readers around a belief

44. The word *suffered* as it is used in line 51 most
nearly means

(A) felt guilty
(B) endured pain
(C) objected to
(D) permitted

45. Which statement would the author be most likely
to agree with?

(A) Democracy is the best form of government.
(B) War is never justified.
(C) Nothing can be learned from history.
(D) Religious ideals have no place in a nation's
politics.

46. Which choice provides the best evidence for the
answer to the previous question?

(A) lines 1–10 ("The . . . crimes.")
(B) lines 31–34 ("What . . . existed?")
(C) lines 26–30 ("Besides . . . government.")
(D) lines 87–88 ("We . . . enfranchisement.")

47. The word *philanthropist* as it is used in
line 35 most nearly means

(A) kind person
(B) person who gives money to help others
(C) historian specializing in the study of
monarchies
(D) lover of humankind

1   1   1

48. Which of the following does the author make use of to persuade the reader of his views?

   (A) rhetorical questions
   (B) quotations from America's Founding Fathers
   (C) studies by political scientists
   (D) careful analysis of the underlying assumptions made in the course of his argument

49. The meaning of the word *objects* as it is used in line 61 most nearly means

   (A) focuses of attention
   (B) things perceptible to the senses
   (C) goals
   (D) gifts

50. Which of the following is the most accurate summary of the main argument of the passage?

   (A) America is destined to be a perfect Republic with freedom and equality for all, something no other nation could achieve.
   (B) America's future greatness is assured, but no one can predict what form this greatness will take.
   (C) Because America is unique in being founded on the principles of freedom and equality it has a sacred duty to manifest them and spread them to other nations.
   (D) Although America is exceptional among nation states in some ways, it cannot escape the ultimate fate of all nations—decline, and, finally, death.

51. The author's tone can most accurately be described as

   (A) ironic and understated
   (B) derisive
   (C) enthusiastic and serious
   (D) dispassionate

52. The most appropriate title for this passage would be

   (A) The Republican Form of Government
   (B) America's Sacred Mission
   (C) Democracy and Equality
   (D) The Influence of Religious Ideas on American Government and Politics

STOP   If there is still time remaining, you may review your answers.

2   2   2

WRITING AND LANGUAGE TEST

35 MINUTES, 44 QUESTIONS

Turn to Section 2 of your answer sheet to answer the questions in this section.

DIRECTIONS: Questions follow each of the passages below. Some questions ask you how the passage might be changed to improve the expression of ideas. Other questions ask you how the passage might be altered to correct errors in grammar, usage, and punctuation. One or more graphics accompany some passages. You will be required to consider these graphics as you answer questions about editing the passage.

There are three types of questions. In the first type, a part of the passage is underlined. The second type is based on a certain part of the passage. The third type is based on the entire passage.

Read each passage. Then, choose the answer to each question that changes the passage so that it is consistent with the conventions of standard written English. One of the answer choices for many questions is "NO CHANGE." Choosing this answer means that you believe the best answer is to make no change in the passage.

Questions 1–11 are based on the following passage and supplementary material.

Toxoplasmosis

Toxoplasmosis is a zoonotic protozoal disease of humans and animals caused by the coccidian parasite *Toxoplasma gondii* (*T. gondii*). Infection by *T. gondii* is widely prevalent in ❶ humans, in spite of nearly one-third of humanity having been exposed to this parasite. Although toxoplasmosis usually does not cause clinical illness in healthy people, it can cause debilitating disease in congenitally infected infants.

[1] Since 1937 *T. gondii* has become recognized as a significant cause of disease in infants and children, as well as adults who may suffer from delayed conditions originating from congenital infections. [2] Because about 90 percent of these infants usually do not show any signs of the disease at birth, the effects of the infection may not be ❷ foreseen until later in childhood

1. For the sake of clarity of meaning and effectiveness of expression, the underlined portion of the sentence should be written as follows:

   (A) NO CHANGE
   (B) humans, despite the fact that one-third of humanity has been exposed
   (C) humans, one-third of humanity exposed
   (D) humans, and nearly one-third of humanity has been exposed

2. (A) NO CHANGE
   (B) disclosed
   (C) recognized
   (D) unveiled

2   2   2

or adulthood. [3] Early identification of infants at risk of infection or disease ❸ is vital except for limiting the financial and social costs of people suffering the effects of the infection. [4] In the United States 400–4,000 infants are born each year with congenital toxoplasmosis. ❹

❺ The organism is transmitted during gestation when the mother becomes infected for the first time while the mother rarely has symptoms of infection. She does have parasites in the blood temporarily. Focal lesions develop in the placenta and the fetus may become infected. At first there is generalized infection in the fetus. Later, infection is cleared from the visceral tissues and may localize in the central nervous system.

3. (A) NO CHANGE
   (B) is vital to limiting
   (C) vitally limited
   (D) vitally has a limit on

4. For the sake of the cohesion of this paragraph, sentence 4 should be placed

   (A) where it is now
   (B) before sentence 1
   (C) before sentence 2
   (D) before sentence 3

5. For the sake of clarity of meaning and effectiveness of expression, the underlined sentences should be written as follows:

   (A) NO CHANGE
   (B) The organism, transmitted during gestation when the mother becomes infected for the first time, rarely has symptoms of infection, but there are parasites in the blood temporarily.
   (C) The organism is transmitted during gestation. Rarely having symptoms of infection, the mother is infected for the first time, but there are parasites in the blood temporarily.
   (D) The organism is transmitted during gestation when the mother becomes infected for the first time. While the mother rarely has symptoms of infection, she does have parasites in the blood temporarily.

2   2   2

Risk of congenital infection and development of clinical signs by duration of gestation at maternal seroconversion.

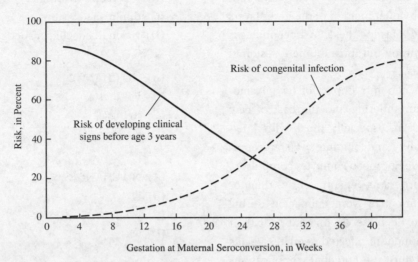

Source: U.S. Geological Survey, Circular 1389, 2014.

The risk of congenital infection is lowest when maternal infection is during the first trimester and highest when infection is during the third trimester. **6** <u>Also, the risk of developing clinical signs before age 3 years is lower when congenital infection occurs during the first trimester than it is when the infection occurs during the third trimester</u> (see graph above).

A wide **7** <u>spectrum</u> of pregnancy outcomes and clinical diseases can occur as a result of congenital toxoplasmosis, including spontaneous abortion and stillbirth, as well as birth defects in live born infants such as hydrocephalus (accumulation of cerebrospinal fluid in the brain), microcephalus (abnormally small

6. Which choice most accurately and effectively represents the information in the graph?

(A) NO CHANGE
(B) However, the risk of developing clinical signs before age 3 years is higher when congenital infection occurs during the first trimester than it is when the infection occurs during the third trimester.
(C) However, the risk of developing clinical signs before age 3 years increases when congenital infection occurs in the second or third trimesters instead of the first trimester.
(D) The risk of developing clinical signs before age 3 is the same whether congenital infection occurs during the first, second, or third trimester.

7. (A) NO CHANGE
(B) catalogue
(C) horizon
(D) panorama

2   2   2

brain for age), intracerebral calcification, convulsions, **8** <u>diminishing of vision</u>, and retinochoroiditis (inflammation of the inner layers of the eye). **9** <u>Listing these</u>, hydrocephalus is the least common but most dramatic lesion of toxoplasmosis.

The socioeconomic impact of toxoplasmosis on human suffering and the cost of care of sick children, especially those with intellectual disability and blindness, **10** <u>are</u> enormous. In some European countries compulsory screening programs ensure early diagnosis and treatment of women infected during pregnancy to decrease **11** <u>migration</u> to their fetuses. Treatment of infected neonates begins at birth to reduce the potential complications of infection.

8. (A) NO CHANGE
   (B) vision diminishing
   (C) diminished vision
   (D) vision that is diminished

9. (A) NO CHANGE
   (B) For these,
   (C) In these,
   (D) Of these,

10. (A) NO CHANGE
    (B) is
    (C) were
    (D) was

11. (A) NO CHANGE
    (B) distribution
    (C) communication
    (D) transmission

2   2   2

Questions 12–22 are based on the following passage and supplementary material.

Aiming for a Ph.D.?

⓬ Desiring a doctorate for thousands of students outweighs concern about the job market that awaits after graduation. Most Ph.D. candidates are willing to ⓭ direct themselves to intensive research and study because they enjoy the subject matter. Statistics also show other, more ⓮ tangible payoffs for Ph.D. recipients when they enter the labor force. Unemployment rates are consistently lower and earnings are significantly higher for people with a Ph.D. degree ⓯ than people with lower levels of educational attainment. Doctoral degree holders in 2001 had an unemployment rate of slightly more than 1 percent and median annual earnings of $66,000—considerably better than the 3.7-percent unemployment rate and $30,300 median earnings of the population aged 25 and older. Prior to embarking on doctoral studies, many students already ⓰ were completing several years of formal study in their chosen field. The Survey of Earned Doctorates shows that in 2000, more than half of all Ph.D. recipients held a bachelor's degree in the same subject as that of their doctoral study—and nearly three-fourths held a master's.

According to the same survey, the total number of new research doctorates awarded each year ⓱ had grown about 10 percent

12. For the sake of clarity of meaning and clarity of expression, the underlined portion of the sentence should be written as follows:

   (A) As it is now
   (B) Thousands of students desire a doctorate, outweighing
   (C) For thousands of students, the desire for a doctorate outweighs
   (D) Thousands of students who desire a doctorate outweigh

13. (A) NO CHANGE
    (B) allocate
    (C) appropriate
    (D) dedicate

14. (A) NO CHANGE
    (B) tactile
    (C) tangential
    (D) corporeal

15. (A) NO CHANGE
    (B) than people having
    (C) than those people with
    (D) than they are for people with

16. (A) NO CHANGE
    (B) have completed
    (C) had completed
    (D) complete

17. Which choice most accurately and effectively represents the information in the graph?

    (A) NO CHANGE
    (B) grew about 20 percent
    (C) grew about 40 percent
    (D) grew about 60 percent

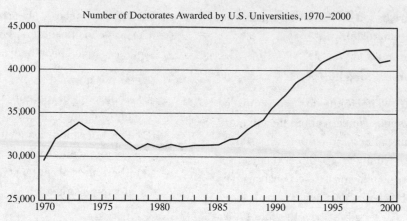

Number of Doctorates Awarded by U.S. Universities, 1970–2000

Source: National Science Foundation/SRS, Survey of Earned Doctorates

between 1970 and 2000 (see graph above). Of these research doctorates, about 95 percent are Ph.D.'s. After rising steadily from **18** the late 1970s into the 1990s, the total number of degrees awarded stabilized.

Between 1970 and 2000, there have been changes by field of study in the numbers of Ph.D. degrees granted. Generally, fields with the greatest increases in the numbers of doctoral degrees **19** awarding also had the most job growth.

[1] In 1999, about 405,000 people held doctorates in the natural sciences and engineering, according to the National Science Foundation's Survey of Doctorate Recipients. [2] **20** Relating to the fields that exhibited gains, biological sciences and health sciences experienced relatively steady increases in the numbers of doctoral degrees awarded. [3] Computer science, first measured in 1978, showed similar increases, **21** and this demonstrated

18. (A) NO CHANGE
    (B) from 1970 to
    (C) from 1980 to
    (D) the late 1980s into

19. (A) NO CHANGE
    (B) award
    (C) awarded
    (D) awards

20. (A) NO CHANGE
    (B) In all
    (C) Speaking of
    (D) Of

21. (A) NO CHANGE
    (B) demonstrated
    (C) demonstrating
    (D) a demonstration of

2   2   2

particularly strong growth from 1980 to 1990. [4] Engineering had large decreases in the number of degrees awarded from 1970 to 1980 but experienced significant increases in the following decades. [5] Between 1970 and 2000, some fields gained a relative share of doctorates awarded; others lost ground. [6] In physics and astronomy, chemistry, and mathematics, the numbers of doctorates awarded in 2000 were below 1970 levels in those fields. **22**

22. For the sake of the logic and cohesion of this paragraph, sentence 5 should be placed

(A) where it is now
(B) after sentence 1
(C) after sentence 2
(D) after sentence 6

2   2   2

Questions 23–33 are based on the following passage.

Sargon the Great

[1] The first great Semitic empire in Babylonia was that founded by the famous Sargon of Akkad. [2] **㉓** As the case with many popular heroes and monarchs whose deeds are remembered in song and story—for example, Perseus, Oedipus, Cyrus, Romulus—the early years of Sargon were passed in **㉔** ambiguity. [3] Sargon is, in fact, one of the "fatal children." [4] He was, legend stated, born in concealment and sent adrift, like Moses, in an ark of bulrushes on the waters of the Euphrates, whence he was rescued and brought up by one Akki, a husbandman. [5] But the time of his recognition at length arrived, and he received the crown of Babylonia. [6] His foreign conquests were extensive. [7] On four successive occasions he invaded Syria and Palestine, which he succeeded in welding into a single empire with Babylonia. [8] **㉕** He, pressing his victories to the margin of the Mediterranean, erected upon its shores statues of himself as a symbol of his conquests. **㉖**

Even at this comparatively early time (3800 B.C.) the resources of the country had been well exploited by its Semitic conquerors, and their absorption of the Sumerian civilization had permitted them to make very considerable progress in the enlightened arts. Some of their work in bas-relief, and even in **㉗** the less if equally difficult craft of gem-cutting, is among

23. (A) NO CHANGE
    (B) As is the case with
    (C) As the case of
    (D) The same as

24. (A) NO CHANGE
    (B) camouflage
    (C) suppression
    (D) obscurity

25. For the sake of clarity of meaning and effectiveness of expression, the sentence should be rewritten as follows:

    (A) NO CHANGE
    (B) He erected upon its shores, pressing his victories to the margin of the Mediterranean, statues of himself as a symbol of his conquests.
    (C) He erected upon its shores statues of himself where he pressed his victories, to the margin of the Mediterranean, as a symbol of his conquests.
    (D) Pressing his victories to the margin of the Mediterranean, he erected upon its shores statues of himself as a symbol of his conquests.

26. For the sake of the cohesion of this paragraph, sentence 3 should be placed

    (A) where it is now
    (B) after sentence 4
    (C) after sentence 5
    (D) after sentence 6

27. (A) NO CHANGE
    (B) the lesser if
    (C) the least if
    (D) at least an

2   2   2

the finest efforts of Babylonian art. Nor were they deficient in more **28** <u>efficient</u> fields. They constructed roads through the most important portions of the empire, **29** <u>along with</u> a service of posts carried messages at stated intervals, the letters conveyed by these being stamped or franked by clay seals, bearing the name of Sargon.

Sargon is also famous as the first founder of a Babylonian library. This library appears to have contained works of a most surprising nature, **30** <u>considering</u> the period at which it was instituted. One of these was entitled The Observations of Bel, and consisted of no less than seventy-two books dealing with astronomical matters of considerable **31** <u>complexity, it registered</u> and described the appearances of comets, conjunctions of the sun and moon, and the phases of the planet Venus, besides recording many eclipses. This wonderful work **32** <u>had been</u> long afterward translated into Greek by the Babylonian historian Berossus, and it demonstrates the great antiquity of Babylonian astronomical science even at this very early epoch. Another famous work contained in the library of Sargon dealt with omens, the manner of casting them, and their interpretation—very important side-issues of Babylonian magico-religious practice. **33**

28. (A) NO CHANGE
(B) realistic
(C) utilitarian
(D) productive

29. (A) NO CHANGE
(B) along this
(C) along which
(D) along

30. (A) NO CHANGE
(B) without considering
(C) in consideration of
(D) in considering

31. (A) NO CHANGE
(B) complexity; it registered
(C) complexity, having been registered
(D) complexity, registered

32. (A) NO CHANGE
(B) has been
(C) was
(D) being

33. Which choice most effectively establishes the main topic of the paragraph?

(A) Babylonian astronomical knowledge
(B) changes in Babylonian science during Sargon's rule
(C) the contents of a library established by Sargon
(D) how Sargon established the first library in Babylonia

2   2   2

Questions 34–44 are based on the following passage.

The Art of Fiction

[1] One is sometimes asked about the "obstacles" that confront young writers who are trying to do good work. [2] I should say the greatest obstacles that writers today have to get over, are the dazzling journalistic successes of twenty years **34** ago, they were stories that surprised and delighted by their sharp photographic detail and that were really nothing more than lively pieces of reporting. [3] The whole aim of that school of writing was novelty —never a very important thing in art. [4] They gave us, altogether, poor standards— taught us to multiply our ideas instead of to condense them. [5] They tried to make a story out of every theme that occurred to them and to get returns on every situation that suggested itself. [6] They got returns, of a kind. [7] But their work, when one **35** was looking back on it, now that the novelty upon which they counted so much is gone, is journalistic and thin. [8] The especial merit of a good reportorial story is that it shall be intensely interesting and **36** apparent today and shall have lost its point by tomorrow. **37**

38 That, indeed, is very nearly the whole of the higher artistic process: finding what conventions of form and what detail one can do without and yet preserve the spirit of the

34. (A) NO CHANGE
    (B) ago. Stories that surprised and delighted
    (C) ago, stories that surprised and delighted
    (D) ago, surprising and delightful stories

35. (A) NO CHANGE
    (B) had looked
    (C) has looked
    (D) looks

36. (A) NO CHANGE
    (B) consequential
    (C) influential
    (D) pertinent

37. For the sake of the logic and cohesion of this paragraph, sentence 6 should be placed

    (A) where it is now
    (B) after sentence 2
    (C) after sentence 4
    (D) after sentence 7

38. At this point, the writer is considering adding the following sentence.

    Art, it seems to me, should simplify.

    Should the writer make this addition here?

    (A) Yes, because this sentence clearly and concisely presents a view of "the higher artistic process" that is at odds with the view of the writer.
    (B) Yes, because the sentence concisely and effectively summarizes the focus of the second paragraph, which is the importance of simplification in art.
    (C) No, because this sentence is a summary of the first paragraph, so it should be the last sentence of that paragraph.
    (D) No, because based on what the writer says in the rest of the passage, this sentence overstates her argument about art.

2   2   2

whole—so that all that one has suppressed and cut away is there to the reader's consciousness as much as if it were **39** in type on the page. Millet had done hundreds of sketches of peasants sowing grain, some of them very complicated and interesting, but when **40** he comes to paint the spirit of them all into one picture, "The Sower," the composition is so simple that it seems inevitable. **41** Previously, all the discarded sketches that went before made the picture what it finally became, and the process was all the time one of simplifying, of sacrificing many conceptions good in themselves for one that was better and more universal.

Any first rate novel or story must have in it the strength of a dozen fairly good stories that **42** have been a sacrifice to it. A good workman can't be a cheap workman; he can't be stingy about wasting material, and he cannot compromise. Writing ought either to be the manufacture of stories for which there is a market demand—a business as safe and commendable as making soap or breakfast foods—or it should be an art, which is always a search for something for which there is no market demand, something new and untried, where the values are **43** introverted and have nothing to do with standardized values. **44**

39. (A) NO CHANGE
(B) a typing on the page.
(C) a type of page.
(D) a page of typing.

40. (A) NO CHANGE
(B) has come
(C) came
(D) is coming

41. (A) NO CHANGE
(B) All the previous sketches, discarded,
(C) All the sketches, previously discarded,
(D) All the discarded sketches that went before

42. (A) NO CHANGE
(B) sacrificing to it
(C) have been sacrificed to it
(D) were made a sacrifice to it

43. (A) NO CHANGE
(B) intrinsic
(C) congenital
(D) ingrained

44. Which choice most effectively establishes the main topic of the paragraph?
(A) techniques of writing
(B) making money as a writer
(C) writing as an art
(D) the writer and her readers

STOP   If there is still time remaining, you may review your answers.

3

3

MATH TEST (NO CALCULATOR)

25 MINUTES, 20 QUESTIONS

Turn to Section 3 of your answer sheet to answer the questions in this section.

DIRECTIONS: For questions 1–15, solve each problem and choose the best answer from the given options. Fill in the corresponding circle on your answer document. For questions 16–20, solve the problem and fill in the answer on the answer sheet grid. Please use scrap paper to work out your answers.

Notes:
- You **CANNOT** use a calculator on this section.
- All variables and expressions represent real numbers unless indicated otherwise.
- All figures are drawn to scale unless indicated otherwise.
- All figures are in a plane unless indicated otherwise.
- Unless indicated otherwise, the domain of a given function is the set of all real numbers x for which the function has real values.

REFERENCE INFORMATION

Area Facts	Volume Facts	Triangle Facts

Area Facts:
$A = \ell w$
$A = \frac{1}{2} bh$
$A = \pi r^2$
$C = 2\pi r$

Volume Facts:
$V = \ell wh$
$V = \pi r^2 h$
$V = \frac{4}{3}\pi r^3$
$V = \frac{1}{3}\pi r^2 h$
$V = \frac{1}{3}\ell wh$

Triangle Facts:
$a^2 + b^2 = c^2$

The arc of a circle contains 360°.
The arc of a circle contains 2π radians.
The sum of the measures of the angles in a triangle is 180°.

1. The product of an integer, n, and 5, increased by 12, is -13. What is the value of n?

   (A) 25
   (B) 5
   (C) $\frac{1}{5}$
   (D) -5

2. If $i = \sqrt{-1}$, what is the value of $(7 - 2i) + (4 - 5i)$?

   (A) $4i$
   (B) $11 - 7i$
   (C) $7 - 11i$
   (D) $-77i^2$

3

3

3. $3x^2 + 3x - 36 = 0$

What are all of the values that satisfy the quadratic equation above?

(A) $x = -3$ and $x = 4$
(B) $x = -4$ and $x = 3$
(C) $x = 3$ and $x = 4$
(D) $x = -3$ and $x = -4$

4. Jorge earns a weekly allowance of \$10, and he gets \$8 for every chore he does at his home. During a recent week, Jorge was paid \$106 for his allowance and chores. How many chores did he do?

(A) 12
(B) 11
(C) 9
(D) 7

5. $-4xy^2 - 2xy + xy - 8mn + mn$

Which of the following is equivalent to the expression above?

(A) $-5x^3y^3 - 8m^2n^2$
(B) $-5x^3y - 7m^2n^2$
(C) $32y - 8$
(D) $-4xy^2 - xy - 7mn$

6. A small city was incorporated in the year Y. Every 15 years, the town doubled in size. How many times larger was the town in year $Y + 90$ than it was in year Y?

(A) 16
(B) 32
(C) 64
(D) It cannot be determined because the initial population is unknown.

7. If $\frac{m}{n} = 7$, what is the value of $\frac{2n}{m}$?

(A) 14
(B) $\frac{7}{2}$
(C) $\frac{2}{7}$
(D) $\frac{1}{7}$

8.
$$y = \frac{2}{5}x - 3$$
$$2x - 5y = 7$$

The linear equations above form lines that are

(A) parallel
(B) perpendicular
(C) parallel and perpendicular
(D) neither parallel nor perpendicular

9. Which of the following is true about the graph of the equation $y = 4(x - 3)^2 + 13$?

(A) The graph is wider than the graph of $y = (x - 3)^2 + 13$.
(B) It has no real roots.
(C) Its minimum value is -3.
(D) Its roots are $x = 3$ and $x = -13$.

10. $V = 7.5 + .75x$

$C = 1.25x$

Sarah is an art teacher who wants to purchase calligraphy pens for her students. Visionary Arts (V) charges a delivery fee of $7.50 plus $.75 for each pen. Cramer's Art Supply charges $1.25 per pen with free delivery. What number of pens would need to be purchased such that the two deals are equivalent?

(A) 8

(B) 10

(C) 15

(D) 20

11. A line in the xy-plane passes through the origin and has a slope of $\frac{1}{9}$. Which of the following points lies on the line?

(A) $(-6, 12)$

(B) $(-4, 36)$

(C) $\left(3, \frac{1}{3}\right)$

(D) $\left(-\frac{1}{3}, 3\right)$

12. Which of the following is equivalent to

$$\dfrac{1}{\dfrac{1}{x+4} + \dfrac{1}{x+6}}?$$

(A) $x^2 + 10x + 24$

(B) $\dfrac{1}{\dfrac{1}{x+12}}$

(C) $\dfrac{x^2 + 10x + 24}{2x + 10}$

(D) $\dfrac{x+4}{x+6}$

13. If $12x - 3y = 5$, what is the value of $\dfrac{16^{3x}}{8^y}$?

(A) 4

(B) 16

(C) 32

(D) 64

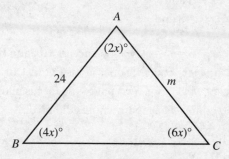

Note: Figure not drawn to scale

14. In $\triangle ABC$, what is the value of m?

(A) 12

(B) $12\sqrt{3}$

(C) $12\sqrt{2}$

(D) $3\sqrt{6}$

15. Which of the following is equal to $\left(\dfrac{m}{2} + n\right)^2$?

(A) $\dfrac{m^2}{2} + n^2$

(B) $\dfrac{m^2}{4} + mn + n^2$

(C) $\dfrac{m^2}{2} + mn + \dfrac{n^2}{4}$

(D) $m + \dfrac{mn}{2} + n$

Grid-in Response Directions

In questions 16–20, first solve the problem, and then enter your answer on the grid provided on the answer sheet. The instructions for entering your answers follow.

- First, write your answer in the boxes at the top of the grid.
- Second, grid your answer in the columns below the boxes.
- Use the fraction bar in the first row or the decimal point in the second row to enter fractions and decimals.

- Grid only one space in each column.
- Entering the answer in the boxes is recommended as an aid in gridding but is not required.
- The machine scoring your exam can read only what you grid, so you **must grid-in your answers correctly to get credit.**
- If a question has more than one correct answer, grid-in only one of them.
- The grid does not have a minus sign; so no answer can be negative.
- A mixed number *must* be converted to an improper fraction or a decimal before it is gridded.

  Enter $1\frac{1}{4}$ as $\frac{5}{4}$ or 1.25; the machine will interpret 11/4 as $\frac{11}{4}$ and mark it wrong.

- **All decimals must be entered as accurately as possible.** Here are three acceptable ways of gridding

$$\frac{3}{11} = 0.272727\ldots$$

- Note that rounding to .273 is acceptable because you are using the full grid, but you would receive **no credit** for .3 or .27, because they are less accurate.

3

3

16. Kareem has purchased a hybrid automobile that has an average fuel efficiency of 40 miles per gallon. He recently filled his 12-gallon tank yesterday but it now registers $\frac{3}{4}$ full. How many miles did Kareem drive if his mileage reflected his average fuel efficiency?

17. $\frac{1}{4}(12x + 2y) = \frac{27}{4}$

    $y = 3x$

    In the system of equations above, what is the value of x?

18. If $\frac{1}{5}x + \frac{5}{8}y = 2$, then $8x + 25y = $?

19. In a right triangle, one angle measures $n°$ where $\sin(n°) = \frac{7}{9}$. What is $\cos(90 - n)°$?

20. New drivers must learn that braking distance is dependent on speed. If you travel x miles per hour, your stopping distance in feet can be approximated by $f(x) = x + \frac{x^2}{20}$. What is the difference in braking distance between a driver traveling at 60 miles per hour and a driver traveling at 40 miles per hour? (Answer in feet.)

STOP   If there is still time remaining, you may review your answers.

MATH TEST (CALCULATOR)

55 MINUTES, 38 QUESTIONS

Turn to Section 4 of your answer sheet to answer the questions in this section.

DIRECTIONS: For questions 1–30, solve each problem and choose the best answer from the given options. Fill in the corresponding circle on your answer document. For questions 31–38, solve the problem and fill in the answer on the answer sheet grid. Please use scrap paper to work out your answers.

Notes:
- The **use of** a calculator on this section IS permitted.
- All variables and expressions represent real numbers unless indicated otherwise.
- All figures are drawn to scale unless indicated otherwise.
- All figures are in a plane unless indicated otherwise.
- Unless indicated otherwise, the domain of a given function is the set of all real numbers x for which the function has real values.

REFERENCE INFORMATION

Area Facts	Volume Facts	Triangle Facts

The arc of a circle contains 360°.
The arc of a circle contains 2π radians.
The sum of the measures of the angles in a triangle is 180°.

Time

1. Thomas rides his bike to the park and then sits down on a bench to rest. After his rest, he jogs several miles. Which part(s) of the graph represents the time he spent sitting on the bench?

   (A) 1 and 2
   (B) 2 only
   (C) 2 and 3
   (D) 3 only

2. If $xy = k$, where k is a constant, when x equals 8 and y equals 10, what is the value of y when $x = 5$?

   (A) 80
   (B) 16
   (C) 8
   (D) 4

3. In the figure above, lines m and n are parallel. If $m\angle 3 = (3x)°$ and $m\angle 4 = (2x)°$, what is the measure of $m\angle 4$?

   (A) 36°
   (B) 48°
   (C) 72°
   (D) 108°

4. If one-half of a number is 5 more than 6, what is the value when the number is tripled?

   (A) 11
   (B) 22
   (C) 33
   (D) 66

5. Which of the following graphs shows a strong positive association between t and w?

(A)

(B)

(C)

(D)

| 1 hectogram = 100 grams |
| 100 centigrams = 1 gram |

6. A popular snack is packaged in 2 hectogram containers. If a customer ate $\frac{1}{4}$ of one of these containers, how many centigrams did he/she consume?

(A) 50
(B) 100
(C) 1,000
(D) 5,000

7. Certain cities in the southwestern United States are experimenting with water-saving plumbing. If the total gallons saved as expressed in the graph above equal 25,000 gallons, what is an appropriate label for the vertical axis?

(A) Gallons saved (in tens)
(B) Gallons saved (in hundreds)
(C) Gallons saved (in thousands)
(D) Gallons saved (in hundred thousands)

8. What value(s) of n satisfies $|n + 11| \geq -12$?

    (A) $-1 \leq n \leq 1$
    (B) $n \geq 11$ or $n \leq -23$
    (C) there is no value n
    (D) all real numbers

Questions 9 and 10 refer to the following information.

An enclosed volume of a certain gas is shown by the following equation:

$$V = \frac{.7T}{P} + 3.77$$

where

$V = $ volume of the gas (in cubic centimeters)
$P = $ pressure (in kilograms per square centimeter)
$T = $ temperature (in degrees Kelvin)

9. Which of the following expresses temperature in terms of volume and pressure?

    (A) $T = (P - V)(.7) - 3.77$
    (B) $T = \frac{P}{.7}(V - 3.77)$
    (C) $T = \frac{(V + 3.77)}{P}$
    (D) $T = \frac{P}{V - 3.77}$

10. Find the temperature (in degrees Kelvin) when the volume of the gas is 8,000 cubic centimeters and the pressure is 1.2 kg/cm^2.

    (A) 7,407
    (B) 8,176
    (C) 13,708
    (D) 16,511

AP Tests Taken

Gender	U.S. History	Literature	French	Total
Male	42	31	12	85
Female	33	42	26	101
Total	75	73	38	186

11. The table above shows the number of 11th-grade students at a local high school who took the following AP tests: U.S. History, Literature, and French. Which category accounts for approximately 17.7% of the test takers?

    (A) males taking the U.S. History test
    (B) males taking the French test
    (C) females taking the Literature test
    (D) females taking the U.S. History test

12. Which of the following is **not** a solution of the inequality $-7x + 4 \leq 4x - 5$?

    (A) 0
    (B) 1
    (C) 3
    (D) 4

13. Two friends are returning home from Vacaville, CA to Carlsbad, CA, a round trip of 984 miles. They would like to stop over in Bakersfield to go to the Museum of Art, free admission on Fridays. They would also like to eat lunch within walking distance of the museum, spending $8 each. This side trip would add 54 miles to the trip. They have designated a budget of $90 for the return trip to Carlsbad. Each gallon of gas costs $3.64 and their car gets 26 miles per gallon. Do they have enough money to take this extra stop?

    (A) Yes, they will have $7.43 extra after the side trip.
    (B) Yes, they will have $4.32 extra after the side trip.
    (C) No, they will need an additional $2.44.
    (D) No, they will need an additional $8.73.

Presidential Candidate	Vice Presidential Candidate	Political Party	Popular Vote		Electoral Vote	
Barack H. Obama	Joseph R. Biden, Jr.	Democratic	65,918,507	51.01%	332	61.7%
Willard Mitt Romney	Paul Ryan	Republican	60,934,407	47.15%	206	38.3%
Gary Johnson	James P. Gray	Libertarian	1,275,923	0.99%	0	0.0%
Jill Stein	Cheri Honkala	Green	469,015	0.36%	0	0.0%
Other (+)	—	—	637,706	0.49%	0	0.0%
Total			129,235,558		538	

14. The results of the 2012 presidential election are listed above. If all of the Libertarian, Green, and Other votes were cast for former governor Romney, what would have been true about the vote difference between Obama and Romney?

    (A) Romney would have earned the presidency by a total of 2,601,456 votes.
    (B) Obama's margin of victory would have been cut by 2,382,644 votes.
    (C) Obama would have won the election by 3,135,721 votes.
    (D) The difference between the candidates' vote totals would have been so slim that a recount would have been in order as had happened in 2000.

15. A large city randomly selected 1,500 residents and surveyed them about their desire to switch to solar power from other power sources. Of the survey respondents, 37% indicated they would strongly consider switching to solar power. Given the results of the survey, which of the following must be true?

    I. 63% of the residents were not strongly considering switching to solar power.

    II. If another 1,500 residents from the same city were randomly surveyed, 37% of the respondents would strongly consider switching to solar power.

    III. If 1,500 residents from another large city were surveyed, 37% of those respondents would strongly consider switching to solar power.

    (A) I only
    (B) II only
    (C) II and III
    (D) None

PRACTICE TEST 4

Questions 16–18 refer to the table below.

Daily Statistics for June 2015											
Day	**Hits**		**Files**		**Pages**		**Visits**		**Sites**		**KBytes**	
1	327	6.35%	274	6.62%	250	7.29%	85	7.58%	60	8.97%	2203	4.87%
2	432	8.39%	383	9.25%	349	10.17%	64	5.71%	57	8.52%	2506	5.54%
3	283	5.49%	235	5.68%	181	5.28%	56	5.00%	50	7.47%	2332	5.15%
4	249	4.83%	208	5.03%	143	4.17%	47	4.19%	56	8.37%	2816	6.22%
5	265	5.14%	164	3.96%	134	3.91%	39	3.48%	44	6.58%	1644	3.63%
6	165	3.20%	142	3.43%	114	3.32%	45	4.01%	42	6.28%	1425	3.15%
7	250	4.85%	155	3.74%	134	3.91%	50	4.46%	51	7.62%	1621	3.58%

The table above is a statistics page for an educational website. The visits, files, and other data are shown for the first week of June 2015. The owner of the educational site is wondering how to effectively reach more viewers.

16. Which of the following can be concluded from the table?

    (A) The number of visits exceeds the number of sites each day.
    (B) On day 7, the ratio of hits to files is greater than the ratio of files to pages.
    (C) The ratio of KBytes to sites is greater on day 6 than on day 1.
    (D) The ratio of pages to visits is never less than $3 : 1$.

17. What is the median number of visits in the first seven days of June 2015?

    (A) 85
    (B) 47
    (C) 56
    (D) 50

18. If R is the range of the File category and r is the range of the KByte category, what is the value of $2r - R$?

    (A) 3,126
    (B) 2,541
    (C) 254
    (D) −249

19. Two brothers remembered their first high school job. In their first week, Rick earned $4.50 per hour while Jay earned $5.25 per hour. They worked a total of 44 hours and their combined wage was $202.50. How many hours did Rick work that week?

    (A) 10
    (B) 17
    (C) 34
    (D) 38

20. Briana bought a pair of running shoes at a 25% discount off of the original price. The total she paid the cashier was *r* dollars, which includes an 8% sales tax on the discounted price. Which of the following represents the original price of the running shoes in terms of *r*?

    (A) .81*r*

    (B) $\dfrac{r}{.75}$

    (C) (.75)(1.08)*r*

    (D) $\dfrac{r}{(1.08)(.75)}$

Questions 21 and 22 refer to the information provided below.

A baseball is thrown into the air with an initial velocity of 64 feet per second. The formula $h(t) = 64t - 16t^2$ provides the height, *h*, of the baseball after *t* seconds.

21. What will be the height of the baseball 2.3 seconds after it was thrown?

    (A) 71.43 feet
    (B) 62.56 feet
    (C) 53.69 feet
    (D) 41.37 feet

22. To the nearest tenth of a second, how much time elapsed when the ball is 41 feet above the ground?

    (A) 3.2
    (B) 2.1 and 3.6
    (C) 0.8
    (D) 0.8 and 3.2

23. A central angle in a circle has a measure of 34.4° and the measure of the area of its sector is 139.6 square units. To the nearest tenth of a unit, what is the measure of the circle's radius?

    (A) 19.4
    (B) 21.6
    (C) 27.3
    (D) 29.7

Questions 24 and 25 refer to the information below.

$$h = -4.9t^2 + 32t$$

The equation above shows the height of a ball thrown upward from ground level with an initial velocity of 32 meters per second.

24. After approximately how many seconds will the ball hit the ground?

    (A) 5.6
    (B) 6.5
    (C) 7.4
    (D) 8.2

25. After how many seconds will the ball be 18 meters in the air?

    (A) 2.2
    (B) 4.3
    (C) .6 and 5.9
    (D) .6 or 6.3

26. Seven people each select an index card. Every card has a positive integer printed on one side. If the mean value of the cards is 15, what is the greatest value any one card can have?

   (A) 69
   (B) 79
   (C) 89
   (D) 99

27. In the xy-plane, the graph of a circle is $2x^2 + 8x + 2y^2 + 12y = 36$. What is the diameter of the circle?

   (A) $\sqrt{31}$
   (B) $2\sqrt{31}$
   (C) $\sqrt{62}$
   (D) $2\sqrt{62}$

28. Which of the following is an equivalent form of the function h, such that the minimum value of h appears as a constant or coefficient?

   $h(x) = (x - 8)(x + 2)$

   (A) $h(x) = x^2 - 6x - 16$
   (B) $h(x) = x^2 + 6x - 16$
   (C) $h(x) = (x - 3)^2 - 25$
   (D) $h(x) = (x + 3)^2 - 25$

29. A circle in the xy-plane has the equation $(x + 2)^2 + (y - 3)^2 = 25$. Which of the following coordinate pairs lies in the interior of the circle?

   (A) $(-3, 2)$
   (B) $(7, -4)$
   (C) $(3, -6)$
   (D) $(0, -11)$

30. Which of the following equations is equivalent to the parabola with equation $y = (x - 4)(x + 6)$?

   (A) $y = (x + 1)^2 - 25$
   (B) $y = (x - 1)^2 + 25$
   (C) $y = (x + 3)(x - 8)$
   (D) $y = (x + 12)(x - 2)$

Grid-in Response Directions

In questions 31–38, first solve the problem, and then enter your answer on the grid provided on the answer sheet. The instructions for entering your answers follow.

- First, write your answer in the boxes at the top of the grid.
- Second, grid your answer in the columns below the boxes.
- Use the fraction bar in the first row or the decimal point in the second row to enter fractions and decimals.

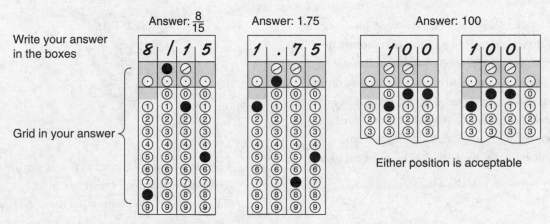

Answer: $\frac{8}{15}$ Answer: 1.75   Answer: 100

Write your answer in the boxes

Grid in your answer

Either position is acceptable

- Grid only one space in each column.
- Entering the answer in the boxes is recommended as an aid in gridding but is not required.
- The machine scoring your exam can read only what you grid, so you **must grid-in your answers correctly to get credit.**
- If a question has more than one correct answer, grid-in only one of them.
- The grid does not have a minus sign; so no answer can be negative.
- A mixed number *must* be converted to an improper fraction or a decimal before it is gridded.

  Enter $1\frac{1}{4}$ as $\frac{5}{4}$ or 1.25; the machine will interpret 11/4 as $\frac{11}{4}$ and mark it wrong.

- **All decimals must be entered as accurately as possible.** Here are three acceptable ways of gridding

$$\frac{3}{11} = 0.272727\ldots$$

- Note that rounding to .273 is acceptable because you are using the full grid, but you would receive **no credit** for .3 or .27, because they are less accurate.

31. A pair of hiking boots sells for $80.00. After one week, the vendor reduced the cost of the boots by 20%. After two weeks, he raised the current price by 20%. What is the cost of the hiking boots after two weeks? (Ignore the $ sign)

32. On July 15, 2015 the New Horizon planet orbiter transmitted its first pictures of minor planet Pluto. Pluto is approximately 3 billion miles distant from Earth. If the transmission of the photographs traveled at light-speed, to the nearest hundredth, how many hours did it take for the Pluto photographs to reach Earth from Pluto? (Note: light travels 186,000 miles per second)

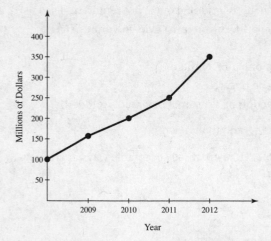

33. The County Education Budget is shown in the graph above. According to the line graph, the budget in 2010 is what fraction of the budget in 2012?

34. The parabola $y = 4x^2 - 15x$ intersects the graph of $y = x$ at point (r, r) and the origin. What is the value of r?

35. A waffle-flavored ice cream cone is pictured above. If the volume of the cone is 14.4π cubic inches, what is the <u>diameter</u> of the cone (in inches)?

36.
$$f(x) = \frac{1}{2(x-3)^2 + 4(x-3) + 2}$$

For what value of x is the function f undefined?

Questions 37 and 38 refer to the information below.

An annuity is a fixed income stream paid out over an agreed upon period of time. A $1,000,000 insurance payment is an annuity if it is paid out over a period of time in fixed installments. The insurance company may offer the payee a lump sum payout called the present value of the annuity. The formula to calculate the present value of an annuity is as follows.

$$P = A\left(1 + \frac{r}{n}\right)^{-nt}$$

P = the present value of the payout
A = the dollars that would have been received over time
t = time in years
r = the interest rate expressed as a decimal
n = compounding periods each year

37. Jorge and his brothers have inherited a pension plan from their grandfather. The plan will pay each grandchild $10,000 over the course of a ten-year period. Jorge chooses to accept the present value of the inheritance at 8% compounded monthly. How much should he expect his payout to be? (Round your answer to the nearest dollar.)

38. Samantha received a cash annuity as a gift for college graduation. The annuity would pay an interest rate of 3.5% over a 5-year period compounded quarterly. Samantha elected to receive the present value of the annuity, which totaled $1,621. To the nearest dollar, what would have been the payout of the annuity if she chose to accept the 5-year payout terms?

STOP If there is still time remaining, you may review your answers.

ANSWER KEY
Practice Test 4

Section 1: Reading

1. **D**	14. **D**	27. **D**	40. **A**
2. **B**	15. **C**	28. **B**	41. **B**
3. **B**	16. **C**	29. **C**	42. **C**
4. **B**	17. **A**	30. **D**	43. **D**
5. **A**	18. **A**	31. **A**	44. **D**
6. **C**	19. **C**	32. **C**	45. **A**
7. **A**	20. **B**	33. **B**	46. **C**
8. **D**	21. **C**	34. **A**	47. **D**
9. **C**	22. **C**	35. **A**	48. **A**
10. **C**	23. **B**	36. **A**	49. **C**
11. **D**	24. **A**	37. **B**	50. **C**
12. **D**	25. **C**	38. **D**	51. **C**
13. **C**	26. **C**	39. **A**	52. **B**

Number Correct   _____

Number Incorrect   _____

Section 2: Writing and Language

1. **D**	12. **C**	23. **B**	34. **C**
2. **C**	13. **D**	24. **D**	35. **D**
3. **B**	14. **A**	25. **D**	36. **D**
4. **C**	15. **D**	26. **A**	37. **A**
5. **D**	16. **B**	27. **B**	38. **B**
6. **B**	17. **C**	28. **C**	39. **A**
7. **A**	18. **D**	29. **C**	40. **C**
8. **C**	19. **C**	30. **A**	41. **D**
9. **D**	20. **D**	31. **B**	42. **C**
10. **A**	21. **C**	32. **C**	43. **B**
11. **D**	22. **B**	33. **C**	44. **C**

Number Correct   _____

Number Incorrect   _____

ANSWER KEY
Practice Test 4

Section 3: Math (No Calculator)

1. **D**
2. **B**
3. **B**
4. **A**

5. **D**
6. **C**
7. **C**
8. **A**

9. **B**
10. **C**
11. **C**
12. **C**

13. **C**
14. **B**
15. **B**

16. **120**

17. **3/2 or 1.5**

 or

18. **80**

19. **7/9**

20. **120**

Number Correct   _____

Number Incorrect   _____

ANSWER KEY
Practice Test 4

Section 4: Math (Calculator)

1. **B**	7. **C**	13. **C**	19. **D**	25. **C**
2. **B**	8. **D**	14. **B**	20. **D**	26. **D**
3. **C**	9. **B**	15. **A**	21. **B**	27. **B**
4. **D**	10. **C**	16. **B**	22. **D**	28. **C**
5. **C**	11. **D**	17. **D**	23. **B**	29. **A**
6. **D**	12. **A**	18. **B**	24. **B**	30. **A**

31. **76.8**   32. **4.48**   33. **4/7**   34. **4**

35. **6**   36. **2**   37. **4,505**   38. **1,930**

Number Correct _____

Number Incorrect _____

SCORE ANALYSIS
Reading and Writing Test

Section 1: Reading   _____ = _____ (A)
                             # correct   raw score

Section 2: Writing   _____ = _____ (B)
                             # correct   raw score

To find your Reading and Writing test scores, consult the chart below; find the ranges in which your raw scores lie and read across to find the ranges of your test scores.

_____ + _____ = _____ (C)

   range of Reading   range of Writing   range of Reading + Writing

       test scores   test scores   test scores

To find the range of your Reading and Writing Scaled Score, multiply (C) by 10.

Test Scores for the Reading and Writing Sections

Reading Raw Score	Writing Raw Score	Test Score
44–52	39–44	35–40
36–43	33–38	31–34
30–35	28–32	28–30
24–29	22–27	24–27
19–23	17–21	21–23
14–18	13–16	19–20
9–13	9–12	16–18
5–8	5–8	13–15
less than 5	less than 5	10–12

Math Test

Section 3:   _____ = _____ (D)
                     # correct   raw score

Section 4:   _____ = _____ (E)
                     # correct   raw score

Total Math raw score: (D) + (E) = _____

To find your Math Scaled Score, consult the chart below; find the range in which your raw score lies and read across to find the range for your scaled score.

Scaled Scores for the Math Test

Raw Score	Scaled Score	Raw Score	Scaled Score
50–58	700–800	20–25	450–490
44–49	650–690	15–19	400–440
38–43	600–640	11–14	350–390
32–37	550–590	7–10	300–340
26–31	500–540	less than 7	200–290

Answer Explanations

Section 1: Reading Test

1. **(D)** *Hinterlands* means "remote country regions" and makes good sense in context because it is likely that these Japanese would have been transported to a remote area.

2. **(B)** *Lights* means "people" in context because the author is describing how Japanese people in America were put in camps.

3. **(B)** Presumably, the image of the snowball was used by the author in an earlier part of the book from which this passage was taken. However, it can be inferred that the "snowball" mentioned in line 28 refers to the accumulating efforts of Americans to destroy the Japanese because the author is describing the steps taken by Americans to prevent Japanese nationals, Japanese aliens, and Japanese-Americans in America from aiding Japan in the war against America. He says, "The snowball was big enough to wipe out the rising sun" (lines 28–29), suggesting that these efforts had stopped the Japanese threat on American soil.

4. **(B)** *Sarcastic* (characterized by words that mean the opposite of what they seem to mean and are intended to mock) is the best choice. It is likely that the author is being sarcastic because it would not require "the utmost of America's great organizing ability" (line 40) to construct camps and put people in them as described in the passage.

5. **(A)** Because America was at war with Japan, it is reasonable to think that some people would hire a person that they believed was Chinese but not a person they believed to be Japanese.

6. **(C)** A *euphemism* (a word or phrase used in place of a term that might be considered too direct, unpleasant, or offensive) is the best choice because "relocation centers" can be seen as a pleasant way of saying "concentration camps" (lines 81–82).

7. **(A)** *Strange* is the best choice because the lieutenant says, "That's funny," after he is told about the removal of the Japanese from the Coast and the construction of relocation centers for them. The narrator says, "He didn't believe it" (lines 83–84), suggesting that the lieutenant thought it was strange that this was being done.

8. **(D)** There is no extrapolation (estimation by projection of known information) in the passage.

9. **(C)** The answer can be inferred from the information in lines 67–82 ("You . . . centers").

10. **(C)** This provides the best evidence for the answer to the previous question because it can be inferred from the conversation between the radio operator and the narrator that the narrator's parents are living in a relocation camp in Wyoming. In response to the radio operator's question "Farmers, huh?" the narrator replies, "Not quite" and then explains how his parents and others have been moved to relocation camps.

11. **(D)** The author says, "If the nuclear forces had been slightly stronger than they are . . . hydrogen would be a rare element, and stars like the sun . . . could not exist" (lines 11–19).

12. **(D)** The author uses the word *extravagantly* to emphasize that the stars in an average galaxy are separated by a distance that is far greater than appears to be necessary.

13. **(C)** After referring to astrology, the author says, "But it happens to be true that we could not have survived if the average distance between stars were only two million million miles instead of twenty" (lines 48–51). It makes sense that the author refers to astrology to stress

how remarkable it is that faraway stars affect life on Earth because astrology also says that faraway stars affect life on Earth.

14. **(D)** The main argument in the passage is that the universe seems designed for life, so it is reasonable that the word *decisive* in line 46 means "conclusive." The author is saying that without the great distances between stars life would be impossible.

15. **(C)** The author says, "Without such accidents . . . hydrogen atoms could not form breakable bridges between molecules" (lines 71–75).

16. **(C)** These lines provide the best evidence. The author is providing an example of an accident that helps make the universe hospitable. He says that the fact that "hydrogen atoms form breakable bridges between molecules" is such an example.

17. **(A)** The author says he is "a scientist, trained in the habits of thought and language of the twentieth century rather than the eighteenth" (lines 79–82). He is contrasting the way a twentieth century scientist is trained to think with the way people were trained to think in the eighteenth century. Such training produces "habits of thought"—that is, recurrent patterns of thinking.

18. **(A)** The author's tone is measured and reasonable. It is not amused, skeptical, or indignant.

19. **(C)** The author says, "I conclude from the existence of these accidents of physics and astronomy that the universe is an unexpectedly hospitable place for living creatures to make their home" (lines 76–79). The discovery of life on a planet of another star in our galaxy would provide evidence that life is not unique to Earth.

20. **(B)** The author says, "I do not claim that the architecture of the universe proves the existence of God. I claim only that the architecture of the universe is consistent with the hypothesis that mind plays an essential role in its functioning" (lines 82–86). The author would probably agree that what he calls the "accidents" of physics and astronomy suggest fairly strongly that the universe was designed, presumably by some powerful agency, such as God.

21. **(C)** Inductive reasoning is the process of deriving general principles from particular facts. The author makes extensive use of this in his argument. He does not use understatement, paradox, or concession.

22. **(C)** The words "the entry of sulfonamides and penicillin" signal that *pharmacopoeia* refers to a stock of medical drugs.

23. **(B)** The author says, "Therapy [new and effective drugs] had been discovered for great numbers of patients whose illnesses had previously been untreatable" (lines 8–11) and "Doctors could now cure disease, and this was astonishing, most of all to the doctors themselves" (lines 12–14).

24. **(A)** The author says, "That long habit . . . had been to treat everything with something" (lines 72–74).

25. **(C)** *Crudest* means "very unsophisticated" and *empiricism* is "the use of observation and experimentation to gain knowledge."

26. **(C)** Before commenting, "It is astounding that the profession survived so long" (lines 52–53), the author describes how medicine was practiced throughout most of history. He describes this practice as "irresponsible" (line 42), as having no scientific basis, and as often harming patients more than helping them.

27. **(D)** A *skeptic* is a person who questions generally accepted ideas. The author says that Montaigne (a sixteenth century French essayist) saw through "the old nonsense" (established medical practice, that is) because he was a skeptic.

28. **(B)** It makes sense that the author believes it took courage for physicians to suggest that their profession was using faulty methods because members of a field who criticize their profession would be likely to be regarded as disloyal by other members of the field.

29. **(C)** The author says, "It is hard for us now to imagine the magnitude of this discovery and its effect on the practice of medicine. That long habit . . . had been to treat everything with something, and it was taken for granted that every disease demanded treatment" (lines 70–76). The discovery that certain diseases are self-limited was surprising because it contradicted what nearly everyone thought.

30. **(D)** These lines provide the best evidence for the answer to the previous question. The discovery that most diseases improve without treatment was surprising because most doctors believed that treatment was necessary for every disease.

31. **(A)** *Ironic* (involving an incongruity between what might be expected and what actually occurs) is the best word to describe the accomplishment because it is ironic that the major scientific accomplishment of medicine, which exists to cure people of disease, is the discovery that patients often are better off without medical treatment.

32. **(C)** In context, *aggressive* refers to "very intensive" medical treatment.

33. **(B)** In line 3 the author refers to "computer modeling by NASA scientists." Also, in line 22 she refers to "simulations of young planetary systems."

34. **(A)** This provides the best evidence for the answer to the previous question.

35. **(A)** In context, *dangerous* means "likely to cause harm." This can be inferred because the sentence in which the word *dangerous* is used is about "the key to survival for some . . . planets" (lines 4–5). A dangerous orbit is one likely to cause harm to the planet in that orbit.

36. **(A)** The reference to a common terrestrial experience helps the reader to visualize a process governed by the same fundamental physical laws but on a far larger scale.

37. **(B)** The passage is about a process (tidal friction) that may help young planets in dangerous orbits achieve a safer orbit. In lines 24–26 the author describes how giant planets can interrupt the orbits of smaller planets and says, "Even if those interactions aren't immediately catastrophic, they can leave a planet in a treacherous eccentric orbit." She then goes on to describe some of the effects on the planet of having an eccentric orbit.

38. **(D)** In lines 8–9 the author says that "Earth-sized planets appear to be very common in other star systems." In lines 22–24 she says, "simulations of young planetary systems indicate that giant planets often upset the orbits of smaller inner worlds." She then goes on to describe a theory that explains how tidal friction may help some Earth-sized planets in elliptical orbits return to circular orbits. We can infer from this information that since their creation some Earth-sized planets have always been in a circular orbit, others have always been in an elliptical orbit, some were once in a circular orbit but are now in an elliptical orbit, and still others once were in an elliptical orbit but have since returned to a circular orbit.

39. **(A)** It can be described as paradoxical because a thick covering of something very cold—ice—helps the planet become warmer.

40. **(A)** Choices (B), (C), and (D) are not supported by information in the passage. It can be inferred that the authors of the study described in the passage would be likely to agree with this statement because much of their study deals with this subject. Further study appears to be important because much of the phenomena described is theoretical and more data are needed to explain it fully.

41. **(B)** This accurately summarizes the main topic of the passage.

42. **(C)** Because the study was by NASA scientists, we can infer that it was technical in nature and written for a specialized journal, such as an astronomy journal, read by professional scientists. The passage itself, in contrast, could have been written by any of the other three choices because the passage describes the scientists' findings and theories in a non-technical way.

43. **(D)** Throughout the passage the author argues for his belief that America "is destined to be the great nation of futurity" (lines 17–18).

44. **(D)** From context, it can be inferred that *suffered* means "permitted." The author is saying what Americans have never permitted themselves to do.

45. **(A)** The author says, "Besides . . . government" (lines 26–30).

46. **(C)** This provides the best evidence. The author says that the more "democratic equality" a country has, the greater it is. We can infer from this that he believes that democracy is the best form of government.

47. **(D)** It is reasonable to think that a lover of mankind would be horrified by the suffering inflicted on people by monarchies and aristocracies.

48. **(A)** The author uses two rhetorical questions in the third paragraph (lines 31–38). The two rhetorical questions in succession are an effective way to advance his argument.

49. **(C)** It makes sense that *objects* means "goals" because the author is discussing America's "expansive future" mentioned in line 58.

50. **(C)** This is the best summary of the passage. A good restatement of it is found in the last paragraph.

51. **(C)** The author is advancing a serious argument with enthusiasm.

52. **(B)** The author's main argument is that America's destiny is to become a great democratic nation, spreading democracy to other countries. As mentioned in the explanation of question 50, a summary of the passage is found in the final paragraph, in which the author discusses America's "blessed mission to the nations of the world."

Section 2: Writing and Language Test

1. **(D)** Choices (A) and (B) do not make sense. Choice (C) is not grammatical. Choice (D) is grammatical and creates a sentence that makes good sense. A clue to the answer is the word *prevalent*.

2. **(C)** Choice (A) makes no sense because the effects of the infection can't be "foreseen" at a "later" time; they can only be foreseen at an earlier time. Choice (B) makes some sense, but the word *disclosed* is used to refer to a situation in which someone knows something but has not said what it is, which is not the case here. Choice (D) has the same meaning as choice (B)

in context, and so also is not correct. Choice (C) makes good sense because the sentence says "about 90 percent of these infants usually do not show any signs of the disease at birth."

3. **(B)** This is the best choice. It is grammatical and makes good sense.

4. **(C)** Sentence 4 follows logically from sentence 1, which says, "*T. gondii* has become recognized as a significant cause of disease in infants and children." Sentence 2 mentions "about 90 percent of these infants," which is a reference to the "400–4,000 infants" mentioned in sentence 4, so sentence 2 follows logically from sentence 4.

5. **(D)** This is the only choice that makes good sense.

6. **(B)** From the graph it can be seen that the risk of developing clinical signs before age 3 is higher when congenital infection occurs during the first trimester than it is when infection occurs during the third trimester. Also, the preceding sentence says that "the risk of congenital infection is *lowest* when maternal infection is during the first trimester and *highest* when infection is during the third trimester." Choice (B) is the correct answer because it describes a contrast (signaled by the word *however*) with what is described in the preceding sentence.

7. **(A)** *Spectrum*, which means "range" in context, is the best choice in context. A clue is the long list of "outcomes" and "diseases" given later in the sentence.

8. **(C)** The outcomes and diseases listed are all nouns (sometimes modified by an adjective), so in order to maintain parallelism, the answer for this blank should also be a noun. The noun *vision* modified by the adjective *diminished* is the best choice.

9. **(D)** This is the correct choice because it signals that one of the diseases listed in the previous sentence will be discussed in the sentence.

10. **(A)** The simple present tense is correct in context because a statement of fact is being made.

11. **(D)** This is the correct choice because it is standard usage in this context.

12. **(C)** Choice (A) makes some sense but creates a very awkward and ambiguous sentence. Choice (B) is grammatical but makes little sense. Choice (D) also is grammatical but makes little sense. Choice (C) is correct because it creates a clear and grammatical sentence.

13. **(D)** *Dedicate*, which in context means "commit oneself to a course of action," is the best choice. A clue is the words "because they enjoy the subject matter," which suggest that the Ph.D. candidates do the research and study more because of this than other motivations.

14. **(A)** *Tangible* (concrete) is the best choice. The author is comparing such "payoffs"—better employment and earning prospects—to the intangible motivations mentioned in the previous sentence.

15. **(D)** The given choice (A) creates a sentence with faulty parallelism because "rates" and "earnings" are compared to "people." Choice (D) corrects this error. In "they are for people with" the pronoun *they* refers to "rates" and "earnings."

16. **(B)** This is the best choice. The present perfect tense is used here because the action ("completing several years of study") was done in the past and continues to be done at present.

17. **(C)** This information is given in the chart.

18. **(D)** This information is given in the chart.

19. **(C)** The participial is the correct choice. It modifies the noun *degrees*, telling us what type of degrees they are.

20. **(D)** This is the best choice because it is idiomatic and makes sense. Choice (C) could be considered acceptable, but it is too informal for the context, which is a formal article.

21. **(C)** This choice creates a grammatical sentence that makes good sense.

22. **(B)** Sentence 5 follows logically from sentence 1 and introduces the topic (gains and losses of shares of doctorates awarded) elaborated on in sentences 2–6.

23. **(B)** This is the standard expression in this sort of context.

24. **(D)** This is the only choice that fits contextually, idiomatically, and grammatically. *Obscurity* in this context means "state of being little known."

25. **(D)** This is the best choice because it is clear and grammatical. The nonrestrictive participial phrase beginning with "Pressing" and ending with "Mediterranean" modifies the pronoun "he." Choice (A) is grammatical but not as effectively expressed as choice (D).

26. **(A)** This is the best choice because sentence 3 helps to link sentence 2 and sentence 4.

27. **(B)** This is the correct choice because in this context *lesser* is an adjective meaning "lower in importance or esteem."

28. **(C)** This is the best choice in context because the author is contrasting "the enlightened arts" discussed in the preceding sentences to practical fields such as road building. In this context *utilitarian* means "practical."

29. **(C)** This is the correct choice because the phrase *along which* begins a prepositional phrase modifying the noun "roads." Note that "through the most important parts of the empire" is also a prepositional phrase modifying the noun "roads." Choice (A) does not create a grammatical sentence because there is not a relative pronoun ("that" or "which") before the verb "carried."

30. **(A)** This is the only choice that is idiomatically correct and makes sense.

31. **(B)** This is the best choice because the independent clause after the semicolon further describes the book mentioned in the independent clause before the semicolon, focusing on the "astronomical matters of considerable complexity" dealt with in the book.

32. **(C)** The simple past tense *was* is correct in context. Choice (A) is incorrect because the work was translated at a time in the past later, not earlier, than the time in the past the author is generally referring to in the paragraph.

33. **(C)** This is the correct answer because most of the paragraph describes the works in the library founded by Sargon. Choice (A) makes some sense because much of the paragraph is about Babylonian astronomical knowledge. However, this knowledge is discussed because it elaborates on the main topic of the paragraph, the contents of the library.

34. **(C)** This choice is correct because it creates a dependent clause providing more information about the "dazzling journalistic successes" mentioned earlier in the sentence.

35. **(D)** The simple present tense is correct in context. The author is making a generalization.

36. **(D)** This is the best choice because in context *pertinent* means "relevant." A clue is the words "shall have lost its point by tomorrow"; "lost its point" means "lost its relevance."

37. **(A)** This is the best choice because sentence 6 follows logically from sentence 5, which describes what the earlier writers attempted to do, providing a link to sentence 7, which evaluates the success of these attempts.

38. **(B)** This sentence is a concise and accurate statement of the view the writer expands on in the second paragraph. It should be added here because it serves as an effective topic sentence of the paragraph.

39. **(A)** This is the correct idiom in context.

40. **(C)** The simple past tense is correct in context because in this sentence the action described moves from an earlier time in the past ("had done," which is cast in the past perfect tense) to a more recent time in the past.

41. **(D)** This is the correct choice. It is clear and grammatical. Choice (A) makes no sense. Choice (C) makes sense and is grammatical; however, it is awkward.

42. **(C)** This is the best choice because it creates a grammatical sentence that makes good sense. Choice (A) and choice (D) are grammatically correct but are not as suitable as choice (C) because they suggest that the "fairly good stories" have been sacrificed to the "first rate novel or story" as an act of devotion.

43. **(B)** *Intrinsic*, which means "inherent" in context, is the best choice. Choices (C) and (D) have similar meanings but are not suitable in context.

44. **(C)** The focus of the paragraph is on writing as an art.

Section 3: Math Test (No Calculator)

1. **(D)** The product of two values is the result of multiplying them. "Increased by" means use addition. We therefore arrive at the equation:

$$5n + 12 = -13$$

Begin isolating the variable by subtracting 12 from both sides of the equation.

$$5n + 12 - 12 = -13 - 12$$
$$5n = -25$$

Complete the problem by dividing both sides of the equation by 5.

$$\frac{5n}{5} = -\frac{25}{5}$$
$$n = -5$$

Check your solution by replacing n with -5 in the equation we have created.

$$5(-5) + 12 = -13$$
$$-25 + 12 = -13$$
$$-13 = -13$$

2. **(B)** Each complex number is expressed in the form $a + bi$ where a is the real component and bi is the imaginary. Add the real components together and then add the imaginary components.

$$(7 - 2i) + (4 - 5i)$$
$$(7 + 4) + (-2i - 5i)$$
$$11 - 7i$$

3. **(B)** Simplify the equation and factor.

$$\tfrac{1}{3}(3x^2 + 3x - 36 = 0)$$
$$x^2 + x - 12 = 0$$
$$(x + 4)(x - 3) = 0$$

Set each factor equal to 0 and solve for x.

$$x + 4 = 0 \quad x - 3 = 0$$
$$x = -4 \quad x = 3$$

4. **(A)** Let n represent the number of chores Jorge performed in the week in which he earned $106. Including Jorge's weekly allowance we come up with the following equation:

$$10 + 8n = 106$$
$$8n = 96$$
$$n = 12$$

Jorge performed 12 chores the week he was paid $106.

5. **(D)** Combine like terms by adding and subtracting the coefficients. Like terms are those that contain the same variable(s) raised to the same power(s). In this example, the following are the like terms:

$$-2xy, xy \text{ and } -8mn, mn$$
$$-4xy^2 - 2xy + xy - 8mn + mn = -4xy^2 - xy - 7mn$$

Remember, a term such as mn is understood to have a coefficient of 1.

6. **(C)** The year $Y + 90$ means 90 years had elapsed since year Y. The town doubled in size every 15 years so it doubled a total of 6 times because $90 \div 15 = 6$. Given that doubling means multiply by 2, the town was 2^6 as large as it was in year Y. $2^6 = 64$, so the town was 64 times larger than it was in year Y. Choice (D) suggests we need to know the original size of the population, but that fact is irrelevant. Whatever its size was in year Y, we only need to know how many times larger it became in year $Y + 90$.

7. **(C)** If $\frac{m}{n} = 7$ then $\frac{n}{m} = \frac{1}{7}$. $\frac{2n}{m}$ can be interpreted as $(2)\left(\frac{n}{m}\right)$. Since $\frac{n}{m} = \frac{1}{7}$, then double that value, $\frac{2n}{m}$, must equal $\frac{2}{7}$.

8. **(A)** Parallel lines have the same slope but different y-intercepts.

$$y = \tfrac{2}{5}x - 3$$
$$2x - 5y = 7$$

Convert the second equation to slope-intercept form to compare the slopes of the equations.

$$2x - 5y = 7$$
$$-5y = -2x + 7$$
$$\frac{-5}{-5}y = \frac{-2}{-5}x + \frac{7}{-5}$$
$$y = \frac{2}{5}x - \frac{7}{5}$$

The slope of both lines is $\frac{2}{5}$ and the y-intercepts are different, so the lines are parallel.

Choice (C) can automatically be eliminated; two lines cannot be both parallel and perpendicular.

9. **(B)** One way to solve this problem is to let $y = 0$. Doing so will let us find the roots of the equation.

$$0 = 4(x - 3)^2 + 13$$
$$-13 = 4(x - 3)^2$$
$$-\frac{13}{4} = (x - 3)^2$$
$$\pm\sqrt{-\frac{13}{4}} = x - 3$$
$$3 \pm \frac{i\sqrt{13}}{2} = x$$

The equation has no real roots, solely imaginary ones. Another way to solve this question is to quickly sketch the graph.

The entire parabola is above the x-axis so its roots are imaginary.

10. **(C)** Set both purchase plans equal to one another to calculate the number of pens that make both deals equal in cost.

$$7.5 + .75x = 1.25x$$
$$7.5 = .5x$$
$$15 = x$$

Purchasing 15 pens gives the same price at Visionary Arts and Cramer's Art Supply. Check your answer.

$$\$7.50 + \$.75(15) = \$18.75$$
$$\$1.25(15) = \$18.75$$

11. **(C)** A line that passes through the origin with a slope of $\frac{1}{9}$ has an equation of $y = \frac{1}{9}x + 0$, or more simply $y = \frac{1}{9}x$. The point $\left(3, \frac{1}{3}\right)$ satisfies the equation.

$$y = \frac{1}{9}x$$
$$\frac{1}{3} = \left(\frac{1}{9}\right)(3)$$
$$\frac{1}{3} = \frac{1}{3}$$

12. **(C)** Multiply $\frac{1}{x+4}$ by $\frac{x+6}{x+6}$ and $\frac{1}{x+6}$ by $\frac{x+4}{x+4}$.

$$\cfrac{1}{\cfrac{1}{x+4} \times \cfrac{(x+6)}{(x+6)} + \cfrac{1}{x+6} \times \cfrac{(x+4)}{(x+4)}} =$$

$$\cfrac{1}{\cfrac{x+6+x+4}{(x+4)(x+6)}} =$$

$$\cfrac{1}{\cfrac{2x+10}{(x+4)(x+6)}} =$$

$$\frac{x^2 + 10x + 24}{2x + 10}$$

13. **(C)** Convert the numerator and the denominator to base 2.

$$\frac{16^{3x}}{8^y} = \frac{(2^4)^{3x}}{(2^3)^y} = \frac{2^{12x}}{2^{3y}}$$

When dividing terms with the same base, subtract the exponents.

$$\frac{2^{12x}}{2^{3y}} = 2^{12x - 3y}$$

Since $12x - 3y = 5$, then $2^{12x - 3y} = 2^5 = 32$.

14. **(B)** Find the measure of each angle by solving for x.

$$6x + 4x + 2x = 180$$
$$12x = 180$$
$$x = 15$$
$$2x = 30$$
$$4x = 60$$
$$6x = 90$$

$\triangle ABC$ is a 30-60-90 triangle. The hypotenuse measures 24 so m measures $12\sqrt{3}$ because it is opposite the 60° angle.

15. **(B)** Use the model $(a + b)^2 = a^2 + 2ab + b^2$ to expand the trinomial $\left(\frac{m}{2} + n\right)^2$.

$$\left(\frac{m}{2}\right)^2 + 2\left(\frac{m}{2}n\right) + (n)^2 = \frac{m^2}{4} + mn + n^2$$

The correct answer could also be found using the FOIL method of multiplication.

$$\left(\frac{m}{2} + n\right)^2 = \left(\frac{m}{2} + n\right) + \left(\frac{m}{2} + n\right)$$

$$= \frac{m^2}{4} + \frac{mn}{2} + \frac{mn}{2} + n^2$$

$$= \frac{m^2}{4} + mn + n^2$$

Choices (A), (C), and (D) are the results of improperly expanding the trinomial $\left(\frac{m}{2} + n\right)^2$.

16. **120** Kareem's gas tank registered $\frac{3}{4}$ full, which means he has used $\frac{1}{4}$ of his full tank, which has a capacity of 12 gallons. Multiply $\frac{1}{4}$ by 12 to find how many gallons Kareem used.

$$\frac{1}{4} \times 12 = 3$$

Kareem used 3 gallons of gas and each gallon provided him 40 miles, so he drove a total of 120 miles.

17. **$\frac{3}{2}$ or 1.5** Multiply both sides of $\frac{1}{4}(12x + 2y) = \frac{27}{4}$ by 4.

$$4\left(\frac{1}{4}(12x + 2y) = \frac{27}{4}\right)$$

$$12x + 2y = 27$$

Substitute $3x$ for y and solve for x.

$$12x + (2)(3x) = 27$$

$$18x = 27$$

$$x = \frac{3}{2}$$

18. **80** Multiply $\frac{1}{5}x + \frac{5}{8}y = 2$ by 40, the least common multiple (LCM) of 5 and 8.

$$(40)\left(\frac{1}{5}x + \frac{5}{8}y = 2\right)$$

$$8x + 25y = 80$$

19. **$\frac{7}{9}$** The acute angles in a right triangle are complementary. The complementary theorem states that $\sin x = \cos(90 - x)$. Since $\sin n° = \frac{7}{9}$ then $\cos(90 - n°)$ also equals $\frac{7}{9}$.

20. **120** Input 60 and 40 for x in the braking distance formula, then find their difference.

$$f(x) = x + \frac{x^2}{20}$$

$$f(60) = 60 + \frac{60^2}{20} = 240$$

$$f(40) = 40 + \frac{40^2}{20} = 120$$

$$240 - 120 = 120$$

Section 4: Math Test (Calculator)

1. **(B)** Part 2 of the graph is flat, indicating that time passed but no additional distance was covered. Sections 1 and 3 show both time and distance were covered over each interval as evidenced by the upward behavior of the graph.

2. **(B)** Input the known data for x and y to find k.

    $$(8)(10) = k$$
    $$80 = k$$

    Replace x with 5 and k with 80 and solve for y.

    $$5y = 80$$
    $$y = 16$$

3. **(C)** $\angle 3$ and $\angle 4$ are consecutive interior angles. When lines are parallel, consecutive interior angles are supplementary. Find their sum and set that value equal to $180°$.

    $$3x + 2x = 180$$
    $$5x = 180$$
    $$x = 36$$

    The measure of $\angle 4$ is $(2x)°$, so replace x with 36 and solve.

    $$(2)(36) = 72$$

    The figure is drawn to scale and angle 4 seems to be acute, so choice (D), $108°$, can be eliminated at once.

4. **(D)** Let $n = $ the number;
    "... one-half of a number is 5 more than 6" translates into the following equation:

    $$\tfrac{1}{2}n = 5 + 6$$

    Solve for n as you normally would.

    $$\tfrac{1}{2}n = 11$$
    $$2\left(\tfrac{1}{2}n = 11\right)2$$
    $$n = 22$$

    The question requires tripling the value of n so multiply 22 by 3.

    $$3 \times 22 = 66$$

5. **(C)** A strong positive association means when t values increase, w values increase. Choice (C) shows this relationship while choice (B) shows a strong negative association. The other two graphs show a weak association and no association.

6. **(D)** One hectogram equals 100 grams, so 2 hectograms equal 200 grams. The customer consumed $\frac{1}{4}$ of one container, so 50 grams of the snack was consumed $\left(\frac{1}{4} \times 200 = 50\right)$. Each gram equals 100 centigrams, so multiply 50 by 100 to find the amount consumed expressed as centigrams.

$$50 \times 100 = 5,000$$

7. **(C)** The sum of the measures of the bars in the graph is 25 units. Given that the four cities saved 25,000 gallons of water, the vertical axis should read *Gallons saved (in thousands)* because $25,000 \div 25 = 1,000$.

8. **(D)** The absolute value of a quantity is greater than or equal to 0. Therefore, any value of n satisfies $|n + 11| \geq -12$. The solution set to the inequality, then, is all real numbers.

9. **(B)** Isolate T by subtracting 3.77 from each side of $V = \frac{.7T}{P} + 3.77$.

$$V = \frac{.7T}{P} + 3.77$$

$$V - 3.77 = \frac{.7T}{P}$$

Multiply both sides of the equation by $\frac{P}{.7}$, the reciprocal of $\frac{.7}{P}$.

$$\left(\frac{P}{.7}\right)(V - 3.77) = \frac{.7T}{P}\left(\frac{P}{.7}\right)$$

$$\left(\frac{P}{.7}\right)(V - 3.77) = T$$

10. **(C)** Use the formula $V = \frac{.7T}{P} + 3.77$ and input 8,000 for V and 1.2 for P.

$$8,000 = \frac{.7T}{1.2} + 3.77$$

$$7996.23 = \frac{.7T}{1.2}$$

Multiply each side of the equation by $\frac{1.2}{.7}$, the reciprocal of $\frac{.7}{1.2}$.

$$\frac{1.2}{.7}\left(7996.23 = \frac{.7T}{1.2}\right)\frac{1.2}{.7}$$

$$13,708 \approx T$$

11. **(D)** Find 17.7% of 186, which is the total number of students who took the AP tests.

$$(.177)(186) = 32.92$$

Females taking the AP U.S. History test numbered 33, which is closest to 32.92.

12. **(A)** Simplify by subtracting $4x$ from both sides of the inequality.

$$-7x + 4 \leq 4x - 5$$
$$-11x + 4 \leq -5$$

Subtract 4 from both sides of the inequality.

$$-11x \leq -9$$

Divide both sides of the inequality by -11, remembering to reverse the direction of the inequality sign.

$$\frac{-11x}{-11} \le \frac{-9}{-11}$$

$$x \ge \frac{9}{11}$$

The answer choice (A), 0, does not satisfy the inequality.

13. **(C)** The return trip from Vacaville to Carlsbad is 492 miles. Add 54 miles to get a total of 546 miles. Divide this number by 26 miles to the gallon, which comes out to 21 gallons. Multiply 21 by $3.64, which comes to $76.44. Add $16 for the two lunches to $76.44, which brings the cost to $92.44. The friends had allocated $90 for the cost of the return trip, so the side trip and the two lunches will exceed their budget by $2.44.

14. **(B)** President Obama's margin of victory over former governor Romney was a total of 4,984,100 votes ($65,918,507 - 60,934,407 = 4,984,100$). However, if all of the other votes, other than those cast for Obama, went to Romney, Romney's new vote total would have been 63,317,051. With this new total, Romney would have earned 2,601,456 fewer votes than the victor. Had Romney accumulated all of the Green, Libertarian, and Other votes, his margin of loss would have been reduced by 2,382,646 because $4,984,100 - 2,601,456 = 2,382,644$.

15. **(A)** Statement I must be true. If 37% of the survey respondents strongly considered switching to solar power, then $100\% - 37\% = 63\%$ of the respondents were **not** strongly considering switching to solar power. Statement II may or may not be true. The statement indicates that 37% of the original surveyed group would consider switching to solar power. However, if 36.9%, not 37%, of the second survey's respondents would switch, then Statement II is not true. Similarly, Statement III considers a survey in another city. Perhaps there are only 30 sunny days a year in that city. So perhaps a number lower than 37%, would switch to solar power. Thus, only Statement I must be true.

16. **(B)** On day 7, the ratio of hits to files is greater than the ratio of files to pages. Note the ratio of hits to files:

$$\frac{250}{155} \approx 1.61$$

The ratio of files to pages is $\frac{155}{134} \approx 1.61$.

$$1.61 > 1.16$$

Choices (A), (C), and (D) cannot be supported by the data in the table.

17. **(D)** The median is the middle value when the numbers are arranged in order. The numbers are arranged in order below.

$$39 \quad 45 \quad 47 \quad 50 \quad 56 \quad 64 \quad 85$$

The value in the middle, 50, is the median.

18. **(B)** The range of a group of numbers is found by finding the difference between the greatest and least values.

The range of the Files is $383 - 142 = 241$.

$$R = 241$$

The range of the KBytes is $2,816 - 1,425 = 1,391$.

$$r = 1,391$$

Find $2r - R$ by substituting 241 and 1,381 for R and r, respectively.

$$(2)(1,391) - 241 = 2,541$$

19. **(D)** Use a system of equations to answer this question.
Let $r =$ Rick's number of hours worked
Let $j =$ Jay's number of hours worked
They worked a total of 44 hours, so $r + j = 44$. Assign the monetary value of each boy's work to get the second equation, $4.5r + 5.25j = 202.5$. Our system of equations, then, is

$$r + j = 44$$
$$4.5r + 5.25j = 202.5$$

Use substitution or elimination to solve for r, Rick's hours worked. Transform $r + j = 44$ to $j = 44 - r$ and substitute the value into the second equation.

$$4.5r + 5.25(44 - r) = 202.5$$
$$4.5r + 231 - 5.25r = 202.5$$
$$-.75r + 231 = 202.5$$
$$-.75r = -28.5$$
$$r = 38$$

20. **(D)** Let x be the original price of the running shoes, in dollars. The discounted price is 25 percent off the original price, so $x - 0.25x = 0.75x$ is the discounted price, in dollars. The tax is 8 percent of the discounted price, so $0.08(0.75x)$ is the tax on the purchase, in dollars. The price r, in dollars, that Briana paid the cashier is the sum of the discounted price and the tax:

$$r = 0.75x + (0.08)(0.75x)$$

which can be rewritten as $r = 1.08(0.75x)$. Therefore, the original price, x, of the running

shoes, in dollars, can be written as $\dfrac{r}{(1.08)(.75)}$.

21. **(B)** Find $h(2.3)$.

$$h(2.3) = (64)(2.3) - (16)(2.3^2) = 62.56 \text{ feet}$$

22. **(D)** Replace $h(t)$ with 41.

$$41 = 64t - 16t^2$$

Set the equation equal to 0 and solve.

$$16t^2 - 64t + 41 = 0$$

$$a = 16 \qquad b = -64 \qquad c = 41$$

$$t = \frac{-b \pm \sqrt{b^2 - 4ac}}{2a}$$

$$t = \frac{64 \pm \sqrt{64^2 - 4(16)(41)}}{32}$$

$$t = 0.8 \text{ and } t = 3.2$$

23. **(B)** The area of a sector is found by using the formula $A = \frac{m}{360}\pi r^2$, where m = measure of the central angle and r = length of the radius. Input the known data and solve for r.

$$139.6 = \frac{34.4}{360}\pi r^2$$

$$465.03 \approx r^2$$

$$21.6 \approx r$$

24. **(B)** The ball hits the ground when the height is 0 feet. Let h equal 0 and solve for t.

$$0 = -4.9t^2 + 32t$$

$$0 = t(-4.9t + 32)$$

$$t = 0 \text{ or } -4.9t + 32 = 0$$

$$t = 0 \text{ or } t = 6.5$$

The initial value of $t = 0$ represents the time before the ball was thrown.

25. **(C)** Replace h with 18 as the height the ball attains. Use the formula $h = -4.9t^2 + 32t$.

$$18 = -4.9t^2 + 32t$$

Set the equation equal to 0 and solve for t.

$$-4.9t^2 + 32t - 18 = 0$$

The equation does not factor, so use the quadratic formula $\frac{-b \pm \sqrt{b^2 - 4ac}}{2a}$.

Let $a = -4.9 \quad b = 32 \quad c = -18$

After using the quadratic formula, we arrive at two different answers, .6 and 5.9. We get two different answers because after .6 seconds the ball attains a height of 18 meters and rises higher. As the ball returns to earth, it reaches 18 meters high again, 5.9 seconds after it was thrown into the air.

26. **(D)** Since seven cards have a mean value of 15, their sum is 105 because $7 \times 15 = 105$. If six of the cards have the number 1 on them, then one card would have 99 because $105 - (6 \times 1) = 99$.

27. **(B)** The graphing form of a circle is $(x - h)^2 + (y - k)^2 = r^2$ where:

(h, k) is the center of the circle

r is the radius of the circle

Divide by 2 to simplify the equation:

$$(2x^2 + 8x + 2y^2 + 12y) \div 2 = 36 \div 2$$
$$x^2 + 4x + y^2 + 6y = 18$$

Next, complete the square for both the x and y components of the equation.

$$x^2 + 4x + 4 + y^2 + 6y + 9 = 18 + 4 + 9$$

Factor the left side of the equation and simplify the left.

$$(x + 2)^2 + (y + 3)^2 = 31$$

In this circle, $r^2 = 31$ so $r = \sqrt{31}$. The question requires the diameter of the circle, so multiply the radius by 2.

$$2 \times \sqrt{31} = 2\sqrt{31}$$

28. **(C)** Transform $h(x) = (x - 8)(x + 2)$ to graphing form by multiplying the parentheses.

$$h(x) = (x - 8)(x + 2) = x^2 - 6x - 16$$

Move -16 to the far right of the equation as you complete the square. Remember as you add a value to complete the square, that same value must be subtracted from -16.

$$h(x) = x^2 - 6x - 16$$
$$h(x) = x^2 - 6x + 9 - 16 - 9$$
$$h(x) = (x - 3)^2 - 25$$

The vertex of the parabola is $(3, -25)$ and the minimum value is -25.

29. **(A)** In order for a point to lie in the interior of $(x + 2)^2 + (y - 3)^2 = 25$, its coordinates must satisfy $(x + 2)^2 + (y - 3)^2 < 25$. Substitute choice (A), $(-3, 2)$, into the inequality.

$$(-3 + 2)^2 + (2 - 3)^2 < 25$$
$$2 < 25$$

An alternate way to answer the question is by sketching a graph.

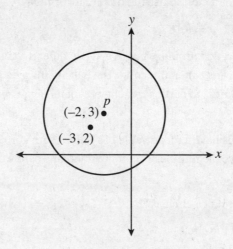

30. **(A)** Transform the equation to graphing form $y = (x - h)^2 + k$, where (h, k) represents the parabola's vertex.

$$y = (x - 4)(x + 6)$$
$$y = x^2 + 2x - 24$$

Move -24 to the far right of the equation.

$$y = x^2 + 2x - 24$$

Complete the square by dividing b by 2 and squaring that quantity.

$$b = 2 \text{ so } \left(\frac{2}{2}\right)^2 = 1$$

Add 1 to $2x$, remembering to subtract 1 from -24.

$$y = (x^2 + 2x + 1) - 24 - 1$$

Factor and combine like terms.

$$y = (x + 1)^2 - 25$$

Looking at the graph, we could also have identified the vertex as $(-1, -25)$, which confirms that choice (A) is the correct answer.

31. **76.8** Find the cost of the boots after one week:

$$\$80.00 - (.20)(\$80.00) = \$64.00$$

Add 20% to $64.00 to find the cost after two weeks.

$$\$64.00 + (.20)(\$64.00) = \$76.80$$

32. **4.48** Find the quotient of 3 billion and 186,000 to find the number of seconds elapsed between the transmission and reception of the photos (these are known as "light seconds").

$$3,000,000,000 \div 186,000 = 16,129 \text{ seconds}$$

There are 60 seconds in a minute and 60 minutes in an hour, so there are 3,600 seconds in one hour ($60 \times 60 = 3,600$). Divide 16,129 by 3,600 to find the number of hours needed to successfully transmit photographs from Pluto to Earth.

$$16,129 \div 3,600 = 4.48 \text{ hours}$$

33. $\frac{4}{7}$ The County Education Budget for 2010 was \$200,000,000. By 2012, the budget had increased to \$350,000,000. Divide \$200,000,000 by \$350,000,000 to find what fraction 2010's figure is of 2012's: $\frac{200,000,000}{350,000,000} = \frac{4}{7}$.

34. **4** The parabola $y = 4x^2 - 15x$ intersects the graph of $y = x$. At that point of intersection, both x and y have the same value. Thus, substitute x for y to get $x = 4x^2 - 15x$. Then solve for x.

$$x = 4x^2 - 15x$$
$$0 = 4x^2 - 16x$$
$$0 = 4x(x - 4)$$
$$4x = 0 \qquad x - 4 = 0$$
$$x = 0 \quad x = 4$$

We know the graph also intersects the origin $(0, 0)$, so discount that solution. The value of r is 4.

35. **6** The volume of a cone is found by using the formula $V = \frac{1}{3}\pi r^2 h$, where r is the radius of the circular base and h is the height. Input the known data and solve for r.

$$14.4\pi = \frac{1}{3}\pi r^2(4.8)$$
$$14.4 = 1.6r^2$$
$$9 = r^2$$
$$3 = r$$

The question asks for the diameter, so multiply the radius, 3, by 2.

$$2 \times 3 = 6$$

36. **2** Simplify the denominator.

$$f(x) = \frac{1}{2(x-3)^2 + 4(x-3) + 2}$$
$$f(x) = \frac{1}{2x^2 - 12x + 18 + 4x - 12 + 2}$$
$$f(x) = \frac{1}{2x^2 - 8x + 8}$$
$$f(x) = \frac{1}{2(x - 4x + 4)}$$
$$f(x) = \frac{1}{2(x-2)^2}$$

Division by 0 is not allowed. Set $x - 2$ equal to 0 to find the restriction on

$$x - 2 = 0$$
$$x = 2$$

37. **4,505** Use the present value formula and input the known information.

$$P = A\left(1 + \frac{r}{n}\right)^{-nt}$$

$$P = 10{,}000\left(1 + \frac{.08}{12}\right)^{(-12)(10)} = 4{,}505$$

Jorge can expect to receive $4,505 as the present value of his $10,000 ten-year annuity.

38. **1,930** Input the known information into the present value formula and solve for A.

$$P = A\left(1 + \frac{r}{n}\right)^{-nt}$$

$$1{,}621 = A\left(1 + \frac{.035}{4}\right)^{(-4)(5)}$$

$$1{,}621 = .84A$$

$$1{,}930 = A$$

Samantha would have earned $1,930 if she had elected to receive her gift as an annuity.

ANSWER SHEET
Practice Test 5

Section 1: Reading

1. Ⓐ Ⓑ Ⓒ Ⓓ
2. Ⓐ Ⓑ Ⓒ Ⓓ
3. Ⓐ Ⓑ Ⓒ Ⓓ
4. Ⓐ Ⓑ Ⓒ Ⓓ
5. Ⓐ Ⓑ Ⓒ Ⓓ
6. Ⓐ Ⓑ Ⓒ Ⓓ
7. Ⓐ Ⓑ Ⓒ Ⓓ
8. Ⓐ Ⓑ Ⓒ Ⓓ
9. Ⓐ Ⓑ Ⓒ Ⓓ
10. Ⓐ Ⓑ Ⓒ Ⓓ
11. Ⓐ Ⓑ Ⓒ Ⓓ
12. Ⓐ Ⓑ Ⓒ Ⓓ
13. Ⓐ Ⓑ Ⓒ Ⓓ

14. Ⓐ Ⓑ Ⓒ Ⓓ
15. Ⓐ Ⓑ Ⓒ Ⓓ
16. Ⓐ Ⓑ Ⓒ Ⓓ
17. Ⓐ Ⓑ Ⓒ Ⓓ
18. Ⓐ Ⓑ Ⓒ Ⓓ
19. Ⓐ Ⓑ Ⓒ Ⓓ
20. Ⓐ Ⓑ Ⓒ Ⓓ
21. Ⓐ Ⓑ Ⓒ Ⓓ
22. Ⓐ Ⓑ Ⓒ Ⓓ
23. Ⓐ Ⓑ Ⓒ Ⓓ
24. Ⓐ Ⓑ Ⓒ Ⓓ
25. Ⓐ Ⓑ Ⓒ Ⓓ
26. Ⓐ Ⓑ Ⓒ Ⓓ

27. Ⓐ Ⓑ Ⓒ Ⓓ
28. Ⓐ Ⓑ Ⓒ Ⓓ
29. Ⓐ Ⓑ Ⓒ Ⓓ
30. Ⓐ Ⓑ Ⓒ Ⓓ
31. Ⓐ Ⓑ Ⓒ Ⓓ
32. Ⓐ Ⓑ Ⓒ Ⓓ
33. Ⓐ Ⓑ Ⓒ Ⓓ
34. Ⓐ Ⓑ Ⓒ Ⓓ
35. Ⓐ Ⓑ Ⓒ Ⓓ
36. Ⓐ Ⓑ Ⓒ Ⓓ
37. Ⓐ Ⓑ Ⓒ Ⓓ
38. Ⓐ Ⓑ Ⓒ Ⓓ
39. Ⓐ Ⓑ Ⓒ Ⓓ

40. Ⓐ Ⓑ Ⓒ Ⓓ
41. Ⓐ Ⓑ Ⓒ Ⓓ
42. Ⓐ Ⓑ Ⓒ Ⓓ
43. Ⓐ Ⓑ Ⓒ Ⓓ
44. Ⓐ Ⓑ Ⓒ Ⓓ
45. Ⓐ Ⓑ Ⓒ Ⓓ
46. Ⓐ Ⓑ Ⓒ Ⓓ
47. Ⓐ Ⓑ Ⓒ Ⓓ
48. Ⓐ Ⓑ Ⓒ Ⓓ
49. Ⓐ Ⓑ Ⓒ Ⓓ
50. Ⓐ Ⓑ Ⓒ Ⓓ
51. Ⓐ Ⓑ Ⓒ Ⓓ
52. Ⓐ Ⓑ Ⓒ Ⓓ

Section 2: Writing and Language

1. Ⓐ Ⓑ Ⓒ Ⓓ
2. Ⓐ Ⓑ Ⓒ Ⓓ
3. Ⓐ Ⓑ Ⓒ Ⓓ
4. Ⓐ Ⓑ Ⓒ Ⓓ
5. Ⓐ Ⓑ Ⓒ Ⓓ
6. Ⓐ Ⓑ Ⓒ Ⓓ
7. Ⓐ Ⓑ Ⓒ Ⓓ
8. Ⓐ Ⓑ Ⓒ Ⓓ
9. Ⓐ Ⓑ Ⓒ Ⓓ
10. Ⓐ Ⓑ Ⓒ Ⓓ
11. Ⓐ Ⓑ Ⓒ Ⓓ

12. Ⓐ Ⓑ Ⓒ Ⓓ
13. Ⓐ Ⓑ Ⓒ Ⓓ
14. Ⓐ Ⓑ Ⓒ Ⓓ
15. Ⓐ Ⓑ Ⓒ Ⓓ
16. Ⓐ Ⓑ Ⓒ Ⓓ
17. Ⓐ Ⓑ Ⓒ Ⓓ
18. Ⓐ Ⓑ Ⓒ Ⓓ
19. Ⓐ Ⓑ Ⓒ Ⓓ
20. Ⓐ Ⓑ Ⓒ Ⓓ
21. Ⓐ Ⓑ Ⓒ Ⓓ
22. Ⓐ Ⓑ Ⓒ Ⓓ

23. Ⓐ Ⓑ Ⓒ Ⓓ
24. Ⓐ Ⓑ Ⓒ Ⓓ
25. Ⓐ Ⓑ Ⓒ Ⓓ
26. Ⓐ Ⓑ Ⓒ Ⓓ
27. Ⓐ Ⓑ Ⓒ Ⓓ
28. Ⓐ Ⓑ Ⓒ Ⓓ
29. Ⓐ Ⓑ Ⓒ Ⓓ
30. Ⓐ Ⓑ Ⓒ Ⓓ
31. Ⓐ Ⓑ Ⓒ Ⓓ
32. Ⓐ Ⓑ Ⓒ Ⓓ
33. Ⓐ Ⓑ Ⓒ Ⓓ

34. Ⓐ Ⓑ Ⓒ Ⓓ
35. Ⓐ Ⓑ Ⓒ Ⓓ
36. Ⓐ Ⓑ Ⓒ Ⓓ
37. Ⓐ Ⓑ Ⓒ Ⓓ
38. Ⓐ Ⓑ Ⓒ Ⓓ
39. Ⓐ Ⓑ Ⓒ Ⓓ
40. Ⓐ Ⓑ Ⓒ Ⓓ
41. Ⓐ Ⓑ Ⓒ Ⓓ
42. Ⓐ Ⓑ Ⓒ Ⓓ
43. Ⓐ Ⓑ Ⓒ Ⓓ
44. Ⓐ Ⓑ Ⓒ Ⓓ

ANSWER SHEET
Practice Test 5

Section 3: Math (No Calculator)

1. (A) (B) (C) (D)   5. (A) (B) (C) (D)   9. (A) (B) (C) (D)   13. (A) (B) (C) (D)

2. (A) (B) (C) (D)   6. (A) (B) (C) (D)   10. (A) (B) (C) (D)   14. (A) (B) (C) (D)

3. (A) (B) (C) (D)   7. (A) (B) (C) (D)   11. (A) (B) (C) (D)   15. (A) (B) (C) (D)

4. (A) (B) (C) (D)   8. (A) (B) (C) (D)   12. (A) (B) (C) (D)

16. [grid-in answer grid]   17. [grid-in answer grid]   18. [grid-in answer grid]

19. [grid-in answer grid]   20. [grid-in answer grid]

ANSWER SHEET
Practice Test 5

Section 4: Math (Calculator)

1. Ⓐ Ⓑ Ⓒ Ⓓ
2. Ⓐ Ⓑ Ⓒ Ⓓ
3. Ⓐ Ⓑ Ⓒ Ⓓ
4. Ⓐ Ⓑ Ⓒ Ⓓ
5. Ⓐ Ⓑ Ⓒ Ⓓ
6. Ⓐ Ⓑ Ⓒ Ⓓ
7. Ⓐ Ⓑ Ⓒ Ⓓ
8. Ⓐ Ⓑ Ⓒ Ⓓ

9. Ⓐ Ⓑ Ⓒ Ⓓ
10. Ⓐ Ⓑ Ⓒ Ⓓ
11. Ⓐ Ⓑ Ⓒ Ⓓ
12. Ⓐ Ⓑ Ⓒ Ⓓ
13. Ⓐ Ⓑ Ⓒ Ⓓ
14. Ⓐ Ⓑ Ⓒ Ⓓ
15. Ⓐ Ⓑ Ⓒ Ⓓ
16. Ⓐ Ⓑ Ⓒ Ⓓ

17. Ⓐ Ⓑ Ⓒ Ⓓ
18. Ⓐ Ⓑ Ⓒ Ⓓ
19. Ⓐ Ⓑ Ⓒ Ⓓ
20. Ⓐ Ⓑ Ⓒ Ⓓ
21. Ⓐ Ⓑ Ⓒ Ⓓ
22. Ⓐ Ⓑ Ⓒ Ⓓ
23. Ⓐ Ⓑ Ⓒ Ⓓ
24. Ⓐ Ⓑ Ⓒ Ⓓ

25. Ⓐ Ⓑ Ⓒ Ⓓ
26. Ⓐ Ⓑ Ⓒ Ⓓ
27. Ⓐ Ⓑ Ⓒ Ⓓ
28. Ⓐ Ⓑ Ⓒ Ⓓ
29. Ⓐ Ⓑ Ⓒ Ⓓ
30. Ⓐ Ⓑ Ⓒ Ⓓ

31. 32. 33. 34.

35. 36. 37. 38.

Practice Test 5

READING TEST

65 MINUTES, 52 QUESTIONS

Turn to Section 1 of your answer sheet to answer the questions in this section.

> **DIRECTIONS:** Following each of the passages (or pairs of passages) below are questions about the passage (or passages). Read each passage carefully. Then, select the best answer for each question based on what is stated in the passage (or passages) and in any graphics that may accompany the passage.

Questions 1–10 are based on the following passage.

This passage is from Henry Van Dyke, *The Americanism of Washington*. It was originally published in 1906.

"Professedly prudent" is the phrase that I have chosen to apply to Benjamin Franklin. For the one thing that is clear, as we turn to look at him and the other men who stood
(5) with Washington, is that, whatever their philosophical professions may have been, they were not controlled by prudence. They were really imprudent, and at heart willing to take all risks of poverty and death in a struggle whose cause
(10) was just though its issue was dubious. If it be rashness to commit honor and life and property to a great adventure for the general good, then these men were rash to the verge of recklessness. They refused no peril, they withheld no
(15) sacrifice, in the following of their ideal.

I hear John Dickinson saying: "It is not our duty to leave wealth to our children, but it is our duty to leave liberty to them. We have counted the cost of this contest, and we find nothing
(20) so dreadful as voluntary slavery." I see Samuel Adams, impoverished, living upon a pittance, hardly able to provide a decent coat for his back, rejecting with scorn the offer of a profitable office, wealth, a title even, to win him from
(25) his allegiance to the cause of America. I see Robert Morris, the wealthy merchant, opening his purse and pledging his credit to support the Revolution, and later devoting all his fortune and his energy to restore and establish
(30) the financial honor of the Republic, with the memorable words, "The United States may command all that I have, except my integrity." I hear the proud John Adams saying to his wife, "I have accepted a seat in the House of Representatives,
(35) and thereby have consented to my own ruin, to your ruin, and the ruin of our children;" and I hear her reply, with the tears running down her face, "Well, I am willing in this cause to run all risks with you, and be ruined with you, if you are
(40) ruined." I see Benjamin Franklin, in the Congress of 1776, already past his seventieth year, prosperous, famous, by far the most celebrated man in America, accepting without demur the difficult and dangerous mission to France, and whisper-
(45) ing to his friend, Dr. Rush, "I am old and good for nothing, but as the store-keepers say of their remnants of cloth, 'I am but a fag-end, and you may have me for what you please.'"

1

1

1

Here is a man who will illustrate and prove,
(50) perhaps better than any other of those who
stood with Washington, the point at which
I am aiming. There was none of the glam-
our of romance about old Ben Franklin. He
was shrewd, canny, humorous. The chivalric
(55) Southerners disliked his philosophy, and the
solemn New-Englanders mistrusted his jokes.
He made no extravagant claims for his own
motives, and some of his ways were not dis-
tinctly ideal. He was full of prudential proverbs,
(60) and claimed to be a follower of the theory of
enlightened self-interest. But there was not a
faculty of his wise old head which he did not
put at the service of his country, nor was there a
pulse of his slow and steady heart which did not
(65) beat loyal to the cause of freedom.

He forfeited profitable office and sure prefer-
ment under the crown, for hard work, uncertain
pay, and certain peril in behalf of the colonies.
He followed the inexorable logic, step by step,
(70) which led him from the natural rights of his
countrymen to their liberty, from their liberty
to their independence. He endured with a grim
humor the revilings of those whom he called
"malevolent critics and bug-writers." He broke
(75) with his old and dear associates in England,
writing to one of them, "You and I were long
friends; you are now my enemy and I am Yours,
B. Franklin."

1. In applying the term "professedly prudent"
   (line 1) to Benjamin Franklin, the author is
   suggesting that

   (A) Benjamin Franklin claimed to be prudent but
       in many ways was not
   (B) Benjamin Franklin did not claim to be
       prudent
   (C) historians are unsure whether Benjamin
       Franklin was prudent or not
   (D) Benjamin Franklin was prudent in profes-
       sional matters

2. As it is used in line 6 *professions* most nearly
   means

   (A) fields of study
   (B) misgivings
   (C) occupations
   (D) avowals of belief

3. As it is used in line 10 *issue* most nearly means

   (A) offspring
   (B) moral principle
   (C) outcome
   (D) controversial topic

4. The author most likely quotes Robert Morris's
   words, "The United States may command all that I
   have, except my integrity" (lines 31–32) to suggest
   that Robert Morris

   (A) had no integrity
   (B) was not loyal to the United States
   (C) was a person of both great integrity and great
       patriotism
   (D) was not completely reliable

5. As it is used in line 42 *celebrated* most nearly
   means

   (A) iconoclastic
   (B) highly decorated for military service
   (C) intrepid
   (D) known and praised widely

6. Based on the information in the passage, which of
   the following is *not* true of Benjamin Franklin?

   (A) He was wise.
   (B) He believed deeply in natural rights and
       liberty.
   (C) He never went to Europe.
   (D) He was widely admired in his country.

7. According to the information given in the passage, Benjamin Franklin said that he

(A) was motivated by what would benefit him

(B) was motivated to action by the highest ideals

(C) was chivalrous

(D) was the most useful person that his country could send on a mission to France

8. The most appropriate title of this passage would be

(A) Ben Franklin: A Study in Prudence

(B) Benjamin Franklin: An American Hero

(C) John Dickinson, Robert Morris, John Adams, and Benjamin Franklin: Flawed Heroes of the American Revolution

(D) Benjamin Franklin's Theory of Enlightened Self-interest

9. The quotation from Benjamin Franklin's letter in lines 76–77 ("You and I were long friends; you are now my enemy and I am Yours") is primarily intended to show

(A) how upset Benjamin Franklin was after his decision to support American independence

(B) that Benjamin Franklin was a less than perfect man

(C) that some of Benjamin Franklin's friends in England did not have a good character

(D) that Benjamin Franklin was so patriotic that he sacrificed friendships for his love of country

10. The author makes use of all of the following *except*

(A) quotations

(B) understatement

(C) description

(D) assertion of fact

Questions 11–20 are based on the following passage.

This passage is from Suparna Choudhury, "Culturing the adolescent brain: what can neuroscience learn from anthropology?" in *Social Cognitive and Affective Neuroscience*, 2010.

If we assume that a transitional period of the life cycle, akin to adolescence, organized around puberty and of variable length, exists almost universally, the next question is what
(5) forms it takes and whether its features, too, are universal. Ethnographic research in Samoa conducted by anthropologist Margaret Mead brought the issue of cultural difference in the experience of adolescence to the fore. Her book,
(10) *Coming of Age in Samoa,* famously challenged Hall's "storm and stress" model and argued that Samoan culture influenced psychological development of girls in such a way that the transition from childhood to adulthood was smooth
(15) and lacked the "natural" turbulence with which it had been characterized by the evolutionary view. Unlike American culture, Samoan culture, she argued, did not place judgments and pressures on adolescents and was more relaxed, for
(20) example, in its views about sexuality.

All of these factors were thought to make Samoan adolescence relatively tranquil and enjoyable and led to Mead's assertion of the primacy of nurture over nature. While Derek
(25) Freeman later critiqued Mead's culturally deterministic approach for a number of methodological reasons her ethnographic approach has been important for subsequent cross-cultural approaches to adolescence. Since then, a size-
(30) able literature in psychology and anthropology has developed which has addressed cross-cultural differences in adolescence.

Schlegel and Barry's cross-cultural study of adolescents in tribal and traditional societies
(35) using data collected from over 175 societies

around the world demonstrated that adolescence as a distinctive, socially marked stage of life is ubiquitous. These researchers put forward a biosocial theory, arguing that the
(40) social stage of adolescence is a response to the development of the reproductive capacity. Most notably, however, these cross-cultural studies challenge the notion that features of "storm and stress" and a period of psychological crisis
(45) are universal inevitabilities in adolescence. For example, while mild forms of antisocial behavior were present in some societies, it was certainly not generalizable as a feature. Similarly, aggressive and violent behavior occurred in
(50) a minority of cultures and when present was heavily gendered with aggression in girls being particularly low. Cross-cultural researchers stress that the *meanings* of developmental tasks associated with adolescence such as the estab-
(55) lishment of independence or autonomy may differ according to culture, and may be subject to change over time. For example, developing independence in some cultures may mean taking on duties to care for siblings or elders,
(60) and not necessarily separating from adults and orienting towards peers. Based on a study comparing five cultures that could be contrasted as "traditional" and "modern" or "collectivistic" and "individualistic," Trommsdorff suggested
(65) that "turbulent" features such as intergenerational conflict stem from the focus on attaining independence from parents during this period and are linked to cultural values of individualism in Western societies. Certainly, in many
(70) cultures, particularly in pre-industrial societies, adolescence is not marked by such a characterization or psychological turmoil, and thus, both the characterization and length of this life stage vary according to culture. Puberty, too, which
(75) is clearly grounded in biology across cultures, interacts with the local environment. Menarche, which marks the beginning of puberty in girls, is occurring increasingly early in industrialized countries such as Japan or the USA. This finding

(80) may be connected to changes in dietary intake. Even if puberty could be the biological marker of the start of adolescence in every culture, the end point is less clear.

In summary, adolescence conceptualized
(85) as a prolonged period of identity development linked to increased autonomy, intergenerational conflict, peer-relatedness and social psychological anxieties, is not the norm across cultures.
(90) Indeed, these features seem to depend on degrees of individualism, social/economic role expectations, gender and class. A historical appreciation of adolescence as a category of science as well as cross-cultural investigations
(95) of the experience of adolescence demonstrates that characteristics associated with this developmental stage may not only have biological bases but also social and cultural origins.

11. As it is used in line 25 *critiqued* most nearly means

(A) criticized
(B) extolled
(C) evaluated objectively
(D) imitated

12. According to the author of the passage, from her observation that adolescence in Samoa is different from adolescence in America, Margaret Mead argued that

(A) Samoan culture is different from American culture
(B) culture has a larger part in shaping human behavior than does genetics
(C) girls are treated better in Samoa than they are in America
(D) people go through the same basic life experiences in all societies but do so at different times in their lives

1   1   1

13. According to the author, Schlegel and Barry's cross-cultural study of adolescents in tribal and traditional societies showed that

  (A) the phenomenon of adolescence is found everywhere
  (B) adolescence is a time of great conflict in every society
  (C) antisocial behavior always increases during adolescence
  (D) adolescent boys become aggressive in every society

14. In line 45 *inevitabilities* most nearly means

  (A) stages of life
  (B) assumptions
  (C) unavoidable occurrences
  (D) rare happenings

15. In line 51 *gendered* most nearly means

  (A) free of bias toward either males or females
  (B) based on genetics
  (C) characteristic of one gender
  (D) seen from a male perspective

16. Trommsdorff, whose study is cited in the passage, would most likely agree that

  (A) modern cultures are "collectivistic"
  (B) individualistic cultures are "traditional" cultures
  (C) adolescents in "collectivist" cultures do not argue with their parents as much as adolescents in "individualistic" cultures do
  (D) adolescents in "collectivist" societies never become fully adult because they never achieve independence from their parents

17. Which of the following lines offers the best evidence for the answer to question 16?

  (A) "Schlegel . . . ubiquitous." (lines 33–38)
  (B) "Cross-cultural . . . time." (lines 52–57)
  (C) "Based . . . societies." (lines 61–69)
  (D) "In . . . cultures." (lines 84–89)

18. Based on what is said in the passage, it can be inferred that its author most likely believes that

  (A) one of the main features of adolescence everywhere is rebellion by young people against parental authority
  (B) adolescence as a distinct period of life is unique to industrialized societies
  (C) adolescence occurs in every culture (or at least nearly every culture), but the form that it takes varies from culture to culture
  (D) adolescence as a distinct period of life occurs only in "individualistic" societies

19. The point of view of the author of the passage is that of

  (A) a proponent of the view that nature is predominant in human development
  (B) an objective commentator on an important issue in social science
  (C) a strong critic of the view that a young person's culture largely determines his or her experience of adolescence
  (D) an advocate for the rights of people in pre-industrial societies

20. The author makes use of all of the following *except*

  (A) assumption
  (B) qualification
  (C) citing of research
  (D) humor

1   1   1

Questions 21–31 are based on the following passage.

This passage is from Gilbert Highet, *The Art of Teaching*, copyright 1950 by Gilbert Highet.

The first professional higher educators in the Western world were the group of brilliant talkers and keen thinkers who appeared in Greece during the fifth century B.C. They were called
(5)   "sophists."

They were exclusively lecturers. All that we hear of them shows them as phenomenally graceful and subtle talkers, usually to fairly large audiences. In that they are the direct ancestors
(10)   of the modern "authority" who tours the large cities giving a carefully prepared speech in which his own personal power or charm is combined with well-spaced jokes and memorable epigrams, the whole varying very little from one
(15)   repetition to another. Like him, they were highly paid and widely advertised and welcomed by a reception committee and entertained by ambitious hosts. But unlike him, some of them professed to be authorities on everything. They said
(20)   they could lecture on any subject under the sun. Often they were challenged to speak on odd and difficult topics, and accepted the dare. However, they did not pretend to know more facts than others, but rather to be able to think and talk
(25)   better. In that, perhaps, they are the ancestors of the modern journalists who have the knack of turning out a bright and interesting article on any new subject, without using special or expert information. The sophists dazzled everyone
(30)   without convincing anyone of anything positive. They argued unsystematically and unfairly, but painted over the gaps in their reasoning with glossy rhetoric. They had few constructive ideas, and won most applause by taking tradi-
(35)   tional notions and showing they were based on convention rather than logic. They demonstrated that almost anything could be proved by a fast talker—sometimes they made a powerful speech on one side of a question in the morn-

(40)   ing, and an equally powerful speech on the opposite side in the afternoon.

To some of his contemporaries Socrates looked like a sophist. But he distrusted and opposed the sophists wherever possible. They
(45)   made carefully prepared continuous speeches; he only asked questions. They took rich fees for their teaching; he refused regular payment, living and dying poor. They were elegantly dressed, with secretaries and servants. Socrates wore the
(50)   workingman's clothes, bare feet and smock. They spoke in specially prepared lecture-halls; he talked to people at street-corners and in the gymnasium, where every afternoon the young men exercised, and old men talked. Socrates
(55)   said he trained people to think. The sophists said they knew everything and were ready to explain it. Socrates said he knew nothing and was trying to find out.

The sophists were the first lecturers. Socrates
(60)   was the first tutor. His invention was more radical than theirs. Speeches such as they delivered could be heard elsewhere—in the new democratic law-courts, where clever orators tried to sway large juries by dozens of newly developed
(65)   oratorical tricks, and in the theaters, where tragic kings, queens, gods, and heroes accused and defied one another in mortal tirades, and in the assemblies of the people, where any citizen could speak on the destinies of Athens. And
(70)   traveling virtuosi like the sophists were fairly common in other fields—touring musicians, painters, and eminent poets, were all welcome in Greek cities and at the rich court of the "tyrants." It was not too hard, then for the soph-
(75)   ists to work out a performance of their own, as brilliant and sometimes as impermanent as a harpist's recital. The innovations Socrates made were to use ordinary conversation as a method of teaching, and to act on one society only, his
(80)   own city of Athens, instead of detaching himself and traveling. And he made the other fellow do most of the talking. He merely asked questions.

1   1   1

But anyone who has watched a cross-examination in court knows that this is more (85) difficult than making a prepared speech. Socrates questioned all sorts, from schoolboys to elderly capitalists, from orthodox middle-of-the-road citizens to extremists, friends and enemies, critics and admirers, the famous and (90) the obscure, prostitutes and politicians, average Athenians and famous visitors. It was incredibly difficult for him to adapt himself to so many different characters and outlooks, and yet we know that he did. Socrates looked ugly. He had (95) good manners, but no aristocratic polish. Yet he was able to talk to the cleverest and the toughest minds of this age and to convince them that they knew no more than he did. His methods were, first, the modest declaration of his own (100) ignorance—which imperceptibly flattered the other man and made him eager to explain to such an intelligent but naive inquirer; second, his adaptability—which showed him the side on which each man could be best approached; (105) and, third, his unfailing good humor—which allowed him always to keep the conversation going and at crises, when the other lost his temper, to dominate it.

21. The author would be most likely to say that modern journalists often produce articles that are

(A) not authoritative
(B) poorly written
(C) insipid
(D) not understandable by readers who are not experts in the subject of the article

22. The phrase "glossy rhetoric" as it is used in line 33 most nearly means

(A) colorful language
(B) elaborate language with little meaning
(C) specious conclusions
(D) fascinating but distracting details

23. According to the author all of the following were true about the sophists *except*

(A) they made speeches that had been prepared in advance
(B) they were well paid
(C) some of them said that they were experts on everything
(D) they were always scrupulously fair in argument

24. It can be inferred that the author believes that Socrates "opposed the sophists wherever possible" (line 44) because he believes that Socrates

(A) was seeking the truth, whereas the sophists had little concern for the truth
(B) resented the popularity of the sophists
(C) believed that emphasizing his rivalry with the sophists would help make him popular
(D) tended to attack anyone with views and methods different from his own

25. According to the author, all of the following contributed to the acceptance and success of the sophists *except*

(A) they were articulate
(B) speeches of high quality by others besides sophists were common in Athens
(C) they and similar traveling virtuosos were welcomed by the wealthy rulers
(D) they offered people clear and profound new answers to their philosophical perplexities

26. The most appropriate title for this passage would be

(A) The Sophists and Socrates
(B) The Greek World at the Time of Socrates
(C) The Influence of the Sophists on Socrates
(D) Socrates: A Man in Search of Truth

27. Based on the information in the passage, which of the following statements would Socrates have been *least* likely to agree with?

    (A) It is more important to seek the truth than to impress other people.
    (B) The truth is often hidden by language.
    (C) Many people do not carefully examine their beliefs and assumptions.
    (D) Most truths have already been discovered.

28. The word *naive* as it is used in line 102 most nearly means

    (A) innocent
    (B) guileless
    (C) uninformed
    (D) credulous

29. It can be inferred that people with whom Socrates was discussing ideas sometimes lost their temper because

    (A) they became frustrated at their inability to refute Socrates's arguments
    (B) they regarded Socrates's debating tactics as unfair
    (C) they became upset because Socrates could not understand their argument
    (D) Socrates continually insulted them

30. Based on the author's description of Socrates, it can be inferred that Socrates possessed which of the following qualities not mentioned in the passage?

    (A) the ability to write entertaining dramatic literature
    (B) an excellent understanding of human nature
    (C) an ability to charm women
    (D) great legal acumen

31. Which of the following provides evidence for the answer to the previous question?

    (A) "Socrates . . . out." (lines 54–58)
    (B) "The . . . only" (lines 77–79)
    (C) "And . . . talking." (lines 81–82)
    (D) "It . . . did." (lines 91–94)

Questions 32–42 are based on the following passage.

This passage is from Milton Friend, "Why bother about wildlife disease?" U.S. Geological Survey Circular 1401, 2014.

The animal life of urban environments varies greatly from one geographic area to another and with season of the year. Nevertheless, it is useful to consider the general composition
(5) of urban fauna and their disease dynamics. For free-ranging wild birds, there is considerable interfacing between resident and transient populations during seasonal migration periods. Spring dispersal of wild mammals may also
(10) result in some infusion of dispersed young into and through urban areas. This interfacing of previously disparate cohorts of the same and other wildlife species provides fresh opportunities for pathogen transfers resulting in disease
(15) events. Furthermore, the infection of transient cohorts by their resident urban cohorts can facilitate disease transfer to other areas as those migrants continue their journey. The spread of West Nile virus (see map on page 318) is a
(20) graphic example of the ability of birds to expand the enzootic* range of infectious disease great distances.

Duck plague first appeared in North America in 1967 as the cause for a major epizootic** in
(25) the Long Island, New York white Pekin duck industry. The subsequent eradication of duck plague from the commercial duck industry of the United States has been followed by numerous duck plague epizootics in urban, migratory,
(30) and other waterfowl flocks across the nation. In addition, there have been two large-scale epizootics involving migratory waterfowl.

*maintained in the population without the need for external inputs
** a disease that appears as new cases in a given animal population, during a given period, at a rate that substantially exceeds what is expected based on recent experience

Aggressive actions taken to combat urban waterfowl duck plague epizootics may have
(35) contributed to the rare documentation of duck plague in migratory waterfowl populations despite recurring outbreaks in a variety of urban and suburban captive and free ranging wildlife populations. However, in some instances the
(40) culling of urban waterfowl collections infected by duck plague has been vigorously opposed by various segments of society. That opposition highlights one of the difficulties associated with wildlife disease management within urban
(45) environments; companion animal status conferred upon these waterfowl by segments of the public may interfere with needed disease control actions and facilitate disease establishment and spread when eradication was possible.
(50) Another disease dynamic of increased importance within urban environments is the transfer of pathogens between wildlife and companion animals (dogs and cats). A recent study of urban areas in California has disclosed
(55) that domestic cats, wild bobcats and mountain lions that live in the same area share the same diseases. The passage of those pathogens from wildlife to domestic cats provides a vehicle for bringing those diseases into the home, thereby
(60) bridging an "infection gap" between people and wildlife. Rabies, plague, and tularemia are among the diseases of wildlife that cats and dogs have brought into the home. There is also potential for companion animals to transmit
(65) their pathogens to free-ranging wildlife. The establishment of parvovirus and heartworm infections in wolves and wildlife rabies in the United States are examples of disease transfers from infected dogs to wild mammals.
(70) Pathogen-laden feces are a common means for disease transmission. Infection of the southern sea otter with toxoplasmosis is an example of the transfer of an infectious pathogen from the domestic cat to a marine mammal (via run-
(75) off into the nearshore environment with contaminated cat feces). In addition, during 2008

1   1   1

PRACTICE TEST 5

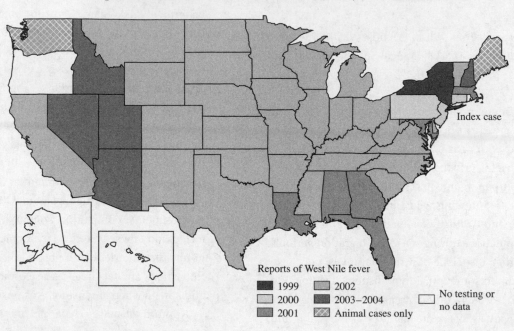

Reports of West Nile Fever in the United States, 1999–2003

Index case

Reports of West Nile fever

	1999		2002		No testing or no data
	2000		2003–2004		
	2001		Animal cases only		

Source: U.S. Geological Survey Circular 1401

an *Escherichia coli* outbreak among a cluster of children was traced to elk droppings on football fields near Denver, Colorado and resulted in a
(80) decision to cancel football games on fields close to where elk graze. Urban waterfowl commonly litter park areas and golf courses with their feces. That type of contamination periodically results in public health agencies closing pub-
(85) lic swimming areas because of *E. coli* from waterfowl feces. An extremely hazardous feces shed parasite is *Echinococcus multilocularis*, a tapeworm of foxes. People who accidentally ingest the eggs of this parasite may develop
(90) alveolar hydatid disease. Because dogs and cats can also become infected and serve as defini- tive hosts, usually by feeding on infected small rodents (intermediate hosts), they can bring the parasite to one's home as well as to public
(95) areas where companion animals are walked or allowed to roam.

Urban environments are important wild- life habitats and need to be managed in ways

that benefit free-ranging wildlife. Furthermore,
(100) human attitudes towards wildlife will increas- ingly be shaped by human experiences in urban environments, because this is where most with- in urbanized society now interface with wildlife. Thus, it is imperative that wildlife disease be
(105) adequately addressed in these environments so that wildlife continue to be cherished.

32. Which of the following would be an appropriate title for this passage?

(A) Managing the Urban Wildlife Habitat
(B) Urban and Suburban Diseases
(C) Diseases in Urban Areas
(D) Urban Fauna and Disease

33. The word *dynamics* as it is used in line 5 most nearly means

    (A) variations in intensity
    (B) the forces and motions that characterize a system
    (C) continuous changes
    (D) powerful forces

34. The "aggressive actions taken to combat urban waterfowl duck plague epizootics" (lines 33–34) most likely included

    (A) prohibiting people from photographing waterfowl in urban environments
    (B) culling of at least some of the infected animals
    (C) tagging waterfowl to track their movements
    (D) encouraging people to care for such waterfowl, and, if possible, keep them as pets

35. Which of the following provides evidence for the answer to the previous question?

    (A) "The . . . nation." (lines 26–30)
    (B) "Aggressive . . . populations." (lines 33–39)
    (C) "However . . . society." (lines 39–42)
    (D) "That . . . possible." (lines 42–49)

36. According to the author, a difficulty faced by authorities in charge of wildlife management in urban areas is that

    (A) people in urban areas often have little interest in wildlife
    (B) many people in urban areas take action to destroy non-indigenous wildlife
    (C) quite a few people can become quite emotionally attached to animals and seek to protect them despite the need for disease control measures
    (D) the interests of fishermen, hunters, and wildlife conservationists seldom coincide

37. Which of the following provides evidence for the answer to the previous question?

    (A) "For . . . periods." (lines 6–8)
    (B) "Furthermore . . . distances." (lines 15–22)
    (C) "That . . . possible." (lines 42–49)
    (D) "Furthermore . . . wildlife." (lines 99–103)

38. The word *interfacing* as it is used in line 7 most nearly means

    (A) interfering
    (B) fighting
    (C) mating
    (D) interacting

39. According to the author, pet dogs and cats in urban areas

    (A) are immune to the diseases of wildlife in their area
    (B) are rapidly beginning to share the characteristics of wildlife in their area
    (C) frequently bring disease-causing agents from wildlife into homes but never bring disease-causing agents to wildlife
    (D) sometimes bring diseases into homes and can also bring their disease-causing agents to wildlife

1   1   1

40. Based on the information in the passage, which of the following statements would the author be likely to agree with?

   (A) Based on past experience in urban areas, there is little that wildlife managers and public health officials can do to stop the spread of disease between animals and humans.

   (B) As the world becomes more urbanized it is important for wildlife managers and public health professionals to work closely together to monitor and control human and animal disease.

   (C) Zoos must be abolished to reduce the spread of disease from captive animals to wild animals.

   (D) The health of resident wildlife in urban environments has little to do with the health of free-ranging wildlife.

41. According to the map, in what year(s) was the spread of West Nile fever the most extensive in the United States?

   (A) 2000
   (B) 2001
   (C) 2002
   (D) 2003–2004

42. The author does all of the following *except*

   (A) cite studies
   (B) provide examples
   (C) quote recognized experts
   (D) describe processes

Questions 43–52 are based on the following passage.

This passage is from Charles Darwin, *The Autobiography of Charles Darwin*, originally published in 1887.

In one respect my mind has changed during the last twenty or thirty years. Up to the age of thirty, poetry of many kinds gave me great pleasure, and even as a schoolboy I took intense
(5) delight in Shakespeare. Formerly, pictures gave me considerable, and music very great delight. But now for many years I cannot endure to read a line of poetry: I have tried lately to read Shakespeare, and found it intolerably dull. I
(10) have also almost lost my taste for pictures. On the other hand, novels which are works of the imagination, though not of a very high order, have been for years a wonderful pleasure to me, and I often bless all novelists. I like all if moder-
(15) ately good, and if they do not end unhappily— against which a law ought to be passed.

This lamentable loss of the higher aesthetic tastes is all the odder, as books on history, biographies, and travels (independently of any
(20) scientific facts which they may contain), and essays on all sorts of subjects interest me as much as ever they did. My mind seems to have become a kind of machine for grinding general laws out of large collections of facts, but why
(25) this should have caused the atrophy of that part of the brain alone, on which the higher tastes depend, I cannot conceive. A man with a mind more highly organized or better constituted than mine, would not, I suppose, have thus suf-
(30) fered; and if I had to live my life again, I would have made a rule to read some poetry and listen to some music at least once every week; for perhaps the parts of my brain now atrophied would thus have been kept active through use.
(35)   I have no great quickness of apprehension or wit which is so remarkable in some clever men. I am therefore a poor critic: a paper or book,

when first read, generally excites my admiration, and it is only after considerable reflection
(40) that I perceive the weak points. My power to follow a long and purely abstract train of thought is very limited; and therefore I could never have succeeded with metaphysics or mathematics. My memory is extensive, yet hazy: it suffices to
(45) make me cautious by vaguely telling me that I have observed or read something opposed to the conclusion which I am drawing, or on the other hand in favor of it; and after a time I can generally recollect where to search for my
(50) authority.

Some of my critics have said, "Oh, he is a good observer, but he has no power of reasoning!" I do not think that this can be true, for *The Origin of Species* is one long argument from the
(55) beginning to the end, and it has convinced not a few able men. No one could have written it without having some power of reasoning. I have a fair share of invention, and of common sense, but not in any higher degree.

(60) On the favorable side of the balance, I think that I am superior to the common run of men in noticing things which easily escape attention, and in observing them carefully. My industry has been nearly as great as it could have been
(65) in the observation and collection of facts. From my early youth I have had the strongest desire to understand or explain whatever I observed,— that is to group all facts under some general laws. These causes combined have given me the
(70) patience to reflect or ponder for any number of years over any unexplained problem. I am not apt to follow blindly the lead of other men. I have steadily endeavored to keep my mind free so as to give up any hypothesis, however
(75) much beloved (and I cannot resist forming one on every subject), as soon as facts are shown to be opposed to it. Indeed, I have had no choice but to act in this manner, for with the exception of the Coral Reefs, I cannot remember a single
(80) first-formed hypothesis which had not after a time to be given up or greatly modified. This has

naturally led me to distrust greatly deductive reasoning in the mixed sciences. On the other hand, I am not very skeptical,—a frame of mind
(85) which I believe to be injurious to the progress of science. A good deal of skepticism in a scientific man is advisable to avoid much loss of time, but I have met with not a few men, who have often thus been deterred from experiment or obser-
(90) vations, which would have proved directly or indirectly serviceable.

43. When the author writes "against which a law ought to be passed" (line 16), he is most likely being

(A) satirical
(B) serious
(C) jocular
(D) sarcastic

44. Which of the following would the author probably have most enjoyed doing when he was the age at which he wrote this passage?

(A) reading a poem by William Wordsworth
(B) reading a play by William Shakespeare
(C) reading an essay on English history
(D) studying advanced mathematics

45. The author says "independently of any scientific facts which they may contain" (lines 19–20). This is most likely intended to make clear that

(A) he is interested in reading books on history, biographies, and travels for their intrinsic merit and not only for the scientific facts they may contain
(B) he is interested in reading books on history, biographies, and travels only for the scientific facts they contained
(C) books on history, biographies, and travels do not contain any scientific facts
(D) facts found in books on history, biographies, and travels cannot be related to the facts found by science

46. The author believes that he has considerable ability in all of the following areas *except*

    (A) thinking independently
    (B) evaluating the worth of hypotheses he has formed
    (C) quickly evaluating the worth of a book or paper written by someone else
    (D) observing carefully

47. Which of the following provides evidence for the answer to the previous question?

    (A) "My . . . conceive." (lines 22–27)
    (B) "I . . . points." (lines 35–40)
    (C) "On . . . carefully." (lines 60–63)
    (D) "On . . . science." (lines 83–86)

48. Which of the following best characterizes the main process the author says he employs in his study of nature?

    (A) skepticism
    (B) deduction
    (C) induction
    (D) impartiality

49. The word *apprehension* as it is used in line 35 most nearly means

    (A) trepidation
    (B) diligence
    (C) understanding
    (D) anticipation

50. The author believes that

    (A) the more skeptical a scientist is, the better the scientist he or she will be
    (B) a scientist must be somewhat skeptical but not excessively so
    (C) skepticism has no place in science
    (D) skepticism is irrelevant to the pursuit of scientific research

51. Which of the following provides evidence for the answer to the previous question?

    (A) "My . . . mathematics." (lines 40–43)
    (B) "I . . . degree." (lines 57–59)
    (C) "I . . . men." (lines 71–72)
    (D) "On . . . serviceable." (lines 83–91)

52. The word *invention* as it is used in line 58 most nearly means

    (A) discovery
    (B) mechanical aptitude
    (C) insight
    (D) creativity

STOP If there is still time remaining, you may review your answers.

2   2   2

WRITING AND LANGUAGE TEST

35 MINUTES, 44 QUESTIONS

Turn to Section 2 of your answer sheet to answer the questions in this section.

DIRECTIONS: Questions follow each of the passages below. Some questions ask you how the passage might be changed to improve the expression of ideas. Other questions ask you how the passage might be altered to correct errors in grammar, usage, and punctuation. One or more graphics accompany some passages. You will be required to consider these graphics as you answer questions about editing the passage.

There are three types of questions. In the first type, a part of the passage is underlined. The second type is based on a certain part of the passage. The third type is based on the entire passage.

Read each passage. Then, choose the answer to each question that changes the passage so that it is consistent with the conventions of standard written English. One of the answer choices for many questions is "NO CHANGE." Choosing this answer means that you believe the best answer is to make no change in the passage.

Questions 1–11 are based on the following passage and supplementary material.

Millions of Jobs in Healthcare

In career news, healthcare is everywhere. ❶ Because the healthcare industry is projected to add more jobs—over 4 million—than any other industry between 2012 and 2022, according to the U.S. Bureau of Labor Statistics (BLS). And it is projected to be among the fastest-growing industries in the economy.

In 2013, there were more than 15.8 million jobs in healthcare industries, according to BLS. Hospitals ❷ purported the largest number of jobs in healthcare, about 39 percent of total healthcare employment in 2013.

1. (A) NO CHANGE
   (B) That's because
   (C) The cause of this is that
   (D) This is caused by the fact that

2. (A) NO CHANGE
   (B) explained
   (C) accounted for
   (D) professed

2 2 2

PRACTICE TEST 5

Total Nonfarm Employment and Healthcare and Related Employment, January 2004–14 (in Thousands)

—— Total Nonfarm – – – – Healthcare and Related

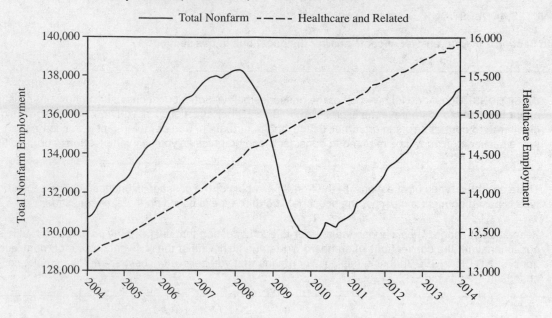

Note: Healthcare and related include series CEU6562000101, CEU9091622001, CEU9092262201, and CEU9093262201; January 2014 data are preliminary.
Source: U.S. Bureau of Labor Statistics, Current Employment Statistics (wage and salary employment, seasonally adjusted).

Offices of health practitioners made up about 26 percent, **❸** <u>only</u> nursing and residential care facilities made up about 20 percent of healthcare jobs. Home healthcare services, and outpatient, laboratory, and other **❹** <u>ambulatory</u> care services each had about 8 percent of healthcare jobs in 2013.

Employment in the healthcare industry **❺** <u>will be growing</u> steadily for years, BLS data show (see graph). This growth is due, in part, to people depending on health services no matter what the economic climate. Even when total U.S. employment fell during the 2007–09

3. (A) NO CHANGE
   (B) at the same time
   (C) yet
   (D) while

4. (A) NO CHANGE
   (B) itinerant
   (C) roving
   (D) migratory

5. Which choice most accurately and effectively represents the information in the graph?

   (A) NO CHANGE
   (B) has been growing
   (C) is to grow
   (D) was grown

2   2   2

recession, for example, healthcare employ-ment ❻ had only a slight fall. And because healthcare-related jobs often require personal interaction, they are difficult to outsource or replace with automation, as happens in some other industries. ❼ "Jobs being stable is one of the best parts about any healthcare career," says pharmacist Jennifer Adams, a senior direc-tor at the American Association of Colleges of Pharmacy.

[1] Because hospitals make up a big portion of all healthcare employment, however, the number of new jobs in hospitals is still expected to be large over the decade. [2] Each area of healthcare is expected to offer many career opportunities through 2022. [3] Offices of health practitioners are projected to add more jobs—1.2 million—than any other type of healthcare employer. [4] Some of this increase reflects expected cost-cutting efforts to shift demand for health services away from ❽ hospitals being relatively expensive. ❾

Home healthcare services ❿ are projected to be the fastest growing detailed industry in the economy, with employment projected to increase by almost 60 percent between 2012 and 2022. As greater numbers of older people seek care that allows them to stay in their homes and maintain their independence, the need for workers in home healthcare services is expected to ⓫ extend.

6. Which choice most accurately represents the information in the graph?

(A) NO CHANGE
(B) remained stable
(C) continued to rise
(D) experienced a lull

7. (A) NO CHANGE
(B) That jobs have stability
(C) That the jobs are stable
(D) Job stability

8. (A) NO CHANGE
(B) hospitals, which are
(C) hospitals, and these are
(D) hospitals, they are

9. For the sake of the cohesion of this paragraph, sentence 1 should be placed

(A) where it is now
(B) after sentence 2
(C) after sentence 3
(D) after sentence 4

10. (A) NO CHANGE
(B) will project to be
(C) were projected to be
(D) is projected to be

11. (A) NO CHANGE
(B) elevate
(C) amplify
(D) expand

2   2   2

Questions 12–22 are based on the following passage.

Ohiyesa: The Winner

The author of this book was born in a teepee of buffalo hide near Redwood Falls, Minnesota, during the winter of 1858. **12** His father was a full-blooded Sioux called "Many Lightnings," his mother, the granddaughter of Chief "Cloud Man" of the Sioux and daughter of a well-known army officer, she died shortly after his birth. He was named Ohiyesa (The Winner).

[1] The knowledge thus gained of life's realities and the secrets of nature, as well as of the idealistic philosophy of the Indian, has always been regarded by the author as a most valuable part of his education. [2] The baby was reared to boyhood by the care of his grandmother. [3] When he was four years old, the so-called "Minnesota massacre" of 1862 separated him from his father and elder brothers and only sister, and drove him with a **13** residue of the eastern Sioux into exile in Manitoba. [4] For more than ten years, he lived the original nomadic life of his people in the family of an uncle, from whom he received the Spartan training of an Indian youth of that day. **14**

12. Select from the following the choice that forms two distinct sentences that make sense:

(A) His father, a full-blooded Sioux, was called "Many Lightnings." His mother was the granddaughter of Chief "Cloud Man" of the Sioux, and she was also the daughter of a well-known army officer, she died shortly after his birth.

(B) His father was a full-blooded Sioux. He was called "Many Lightnings" and his mother was the granddaughter of Chief "Cloud Man" of the Sioux and daughter of a well-known army officer who died shortly after birth.

(C) His father, he was a full-blooded Sioux called "Many Lightnings" and his mother was the granddaughter of Chief "Cloud Man" of the Sioux. She was also the daughter of a well-known army officer, dying shortly after his birth.

(D) His father was a full-blooded Sioux called "Many Lightnings." His mother, the granddaughter of Chief "Cloud Man" of the Sioux and daughter of a well-known army officer, died shortly after his birth.

13. (A) NO CHANGE
(B) remnant
(C) shred
(D) trace

14. For the sake of the cohesion of this paragraph, sentence 1 should be placed

(A) where it is now
(B) after sentence 2
(C) after sentence 3
(D) after sentence 4

2   2   2

When Ohiyesa had reached the age of fifteen years, and had been presented with a flint-lock musket in token of his arrival at the estate of young manhood, he was astonished by the reappearance of the father whose **⓯** considered death at the hands of white men he had been taught that he must some day avenge. He learned that this father had adopted the religion and customs of the hated **⓰** race, and had come to take home his youngest son.

Ohiyesa's new home was a pioneer log cabin on a farm at Flandreau, Dakota Territory, **⓱** that a small group of progressive Indians had taken up homesteads like white men **⓲** and had earnings of an independent livelihood. His long hair was cropped, he was put into a suit of citizen's clothing and sent off to a mission day school. **⓳** First he was reluctant, he soon became interested, and two years later voluntarily walked 150 miles to attend a larger and better school at Santee, Nebraska, where he made rapid progress under the veteran missionary educator, Dr. Alfred L. Riggs, and was soon advanced to the preparatory department of Beloit College, Wisconsin. **⓴** Although the boy named himself Charles Alexander, his father had adopted his wife's English name of Eastman.

15. (A) NO CHANGE
    (B) regarded
    (C) implied
    (D) supposed

16. (A) NO CHANGE
    (B) race and comes
    (C) race, being come
    (D) race, and would come

17. (A) NO CHANGE
    (B) where
    (C) whereby
    (D) from this

18. (A) NO CHANGE
    (B) whose earnings were
    (C) and were earning
    (D) so that they earned

19. (A) NO CHANGE
    (B) Being that he was first reluctant,
    (C) At first reluctant,
    (D) Reluctant first,

20. For the sake of clarity of meaning and effectiveness of expression, the sentence should be rewritten as follows:

    (A) NO CHANGE
    (B) His father had adopted his wife's English name of Eastman, and the boy named himself Charles Alexander.
    (C) The boy named himself Charles Alexander, the father having adopted his wife's English name of Eastman.
    (D) His father had adopted his wife's English name, Eastman, the boy having named himself Charles Alexander.

After two years at Beloit, young Eastman went on to Knox College, Illinois; then east to Kimball Union Academy in New Hampshire, and to Dartmouth College, where Indians had found a special welcome since colonial days. He was graduated from Dartmouth in 1887, and went immediately to Boston University, where he took the medical course, and was graduated in **㉑** 1890 as orator of his class. The entire time spent in primary, preparatory, college, and professional education, including the **㉒** ability of the English language, was seventeen years, or about two years less than is required by the average white youth.

21. (A) NO CHANGE
    (B) 1890 orator
    (C) 1890 by orator
    (D) 1890 with orator

22. (A) NO CHANGE
    (B) mastery
    (C) agility
    (D) digestion

Questions 23–33 are based on the following passage.

Exploration of Cuba

23 For a considerable time after the last visit of Columbus, Cuba was strangely neglected by the enterprising explorers and conquistadors of Spain. Hispaniola became the chief colony and centre of Spanish authority in the **24** Antilles. It for many years was far outranking Cuba in interest and importance. It does not appear that for more than a dozen years after the last visit of Columbus any attempt whatever was made to colonize or to explore the great island, if indeed it was so much as voluntarily visited. **25** Frequently doubtless navigators passed near its shores, on their way to and from Darien and the Venezuelan coast, and occasionally stress of weather on the "stormy Caribbean" or actual shipwreck compelled some to land upon it. Such involuntary landings were presumably made either in the neighborhood of the Zapata Peninsula, or, still more probably, not exactly upon Cuba at all but upon the southern shore of the tributary Isle of Pines. **26** In spite of this, the voyagers carried back to Hispaniola or to Spain the not unnatural report that Cuba consisted of nothing but

23. The writer is considering deleting the underlined sentence. Should the writer do this?

(A) Yes, because this sentence focuses on Cuba, whereas the rest of the passage largely focuses on Hispaniola.

(B) Yes, because no evidence is cited to support the claim that "Cuba was strangely neglected by the enterprising explorers and conquistadors of Spain."

(C) No, because this sentence is a concise and accurate statement of the main topic of the passage, which is how and why "Cuba was strangely neglected by the enterprising explorers and conquistadors of Spain."

(D) No, because this sentence introduces the main topic of the passage, which is the conquistadors of Spain.

24. Which choice most effectively combines the sentences at the underlined portion?

(A) Antilles—far outranked Cuba for many years
(B) Antilles, and it for many years far outranked Cuba
(C) Antilles, it was for many years far outranking Cuba
(D) Antilles in which, for many years, it was far out outranking Cuba

25. (A) NO CHANGE
(B) Frequently navigators without doubts passed
(C) Navigators, frequently doubtless, passed
(D) Navigators doubtless frequently passed

26. (A) NO CHANGE
(B) In such a case
(C) In consequence
(D) In like fashion

swamps; this report of course did not inspire others with zeal to visit so unfavorable a place.

[1] For a similar space of time, too, the delusion that Cuba was a part of the continent generally prevailed. [2] It is true that on a map of Juan de la Cosa's, to which the date of 1500 **㉗** attributed, Cuba is indicated to be an island. [3] But the date is not certain, by any means; and it is notorious that more than one early cartographer drew upon imagination as well as upon **㉘** ascertained geographical facts. [4] There is no proof, however, that this **㉙** has been more than a rumor. [5] Somewhat more significant is the fact that Peter Martyr spoke of Cuba as an island, and said that some sailors pretended to have circumnavigated it. [6] What seems certain is that as late as 1508 the best authorities were ignorant whether Cuba was an island or mainland, and that not until that time was the question settled. **㉚**

Columbus **㉛** had succeeded in authority in Hispaniola by Francisco de Bobadilla, and the latter in turn had in 1501 given way to Nicholas de Ovando. It does not appear that Ovando sought to colonize Cuba. But he did wish to determine its extent, and whether it was insular or continental, and he commissioned Sebastian de Ocampo to explore the coasts of the country and, if he found it to be an island, to circumnavigate it. **㉜** This was done by Ocampo, returning to Hispaniola in the fall of 1508 with the report that he had sailed completely round Cuba. On the way, he said, he had made occasional landings, and **㉝** founded the whole island to be inhabited by a kindly and intelligent people, well disposed toward Spain.

27. (A) NO CHANGE
    (B) is attributed
    (C) attributes
    (D) was attributing

28. (A) NO CHANGE
    (B) classified
    (C) resolved
    (D) pinpointed

29. (A) NO CHANGE
    (B) should be
    (C) is
    (D) was

30. For the sake of clarity of meaning and effectiveness of expression, sentence 4 should be placed

    (A) where it is now
    (B) after sentence 5
    (C) after sentence 1
    (D) after sentence 2

31. (A) NO CHANGE
    (B) succeeded
    (C) had been succeeded
    (D) had been succeeding

32. (A) NO CHANGE
    (B) This Ocampo, he did it, and returned
    (C) This Ocampo did, returning
    (D) This Ocampo did, he returned

33. (A) NO CHANGE
    (B) finding
    (C) finds
    (D) had found

2   2   2

Questions 34–44 are based on the following passage.

Hydro-meteorological Hazards in Indonesia

[1] ㉞ Indonesia lies between the Indian Ocean and the Pacific Ocean, positioned on the equator, and has more than 13,000 islands, most of which are small islands. [2] Although the typhoons rarely hit these areas directly, the effects they generate around the ocean are still powerful enough to have adverse impacts on these communities. [3] The majority of the population is made up of coastal and small island communities, which are exposed to a number of hydro-meteorological hazards, such as sea storms (cyclones and typhoons), coastal abrasion, strong winds, floods, droughts, and climate change impacts. [4] Coastal areas around Aceh, Southern Java, the north coast of Sulawesi and Eastern Nusa Tenggara ㉟ have an experience with a number of typhoons every year. ㊱

In the last decades, the combination of land subsidence and sea level rise has been observed in several places in Indonesia. One of the areas most affected by the sea level rise is the north coast of Central ㊲ Java: with the impacts of sea level rise also observed in several coastal villages in Eastern Nusa Temggara. Unlike the city of Jakarta in Central Java, which is constructing giant sea walls to ㊳ mollify the increasing sea level, other areas in Indonesia are far from ready to cope with the effects of climate change.

34. For the sake of clarity of meaning and effectiveness of expression, the underlined portion of the sentence should be written as follows:

   (A) as it is now
   (B) Positioned on the equator, Indonesia lies between the Indian Ocean and the Pacific Ocean and has
   (C) Indonesia lies, positioned on the equator, between the Indian Ocean and the Pacific Ocean and has
   (D) Indonesia's position lies on the equator between the Indian Ocean and the Pacific Ocean, having

35. (A) NO CHANGE
   (B) had experienced
   (C) have the experience of
   (D) experience

36. For the sake of the cohesion of this paragraph, sentence 2 should be placed

   (A) where it is now
   (B) before sentence 1
   (C) after sentence 3
   (D) after sentence 4

37. (A) NO CHANGE
   (B) Java, with the impacts
   (C) Java; with the impacts
   (D) Java, the impacts

38. (A) NO CHANGE
   (B) allay
   (C) mitigate
   (D) temper

2   2   2

Bedono village, located on the north coast of Central Java Province, is an example which illustrates the vulnerability of coastal communities to hydro-meteorological hazards and the impacts of climate ❸❾ change before 1995. Most people in this village cultivated rice on paddy fields. However, in the past ten years, all the paddy fields have been submerged by intruding sea water, forcing people to change their land into fish ponds. The villagers have also had to elevate their houses to avoid sea water at every high tide.

The Pulo Aceh islands are located on the northern tip of Sumatra Island in Aceh province, which is prone to hydro-meteorological hazards and the impacts of climate change. Between 2002 and 2011, 25 cases of extreme waves and coastal erosion, and 49 cases of strong winds were reported in the province. Pulo Aceh islanders have had to adapt and ❹⓿ entertain sea ❹❶ storms, and strong winds are generated around the Andaman Sea and the Indian Ocean. Extreme sea weather often disrupts transportation between the islands and mainland Sumatra, cutting communities off from the ❹❷ mainland and they leave them isolated for several days. Inadequate communication and transportation infrastructure also contributes to the difficulties faced by these communities. They do have their own local and indigenous knowledge to anticipate hydro-meteorological hazards, ❹❸ some of which is similar to knowledge found in other parts of Indonesia. ❹❹

39. (A) NO CHANGE
    (B) change: before 1995, most
    (C) change. Before 1995, most
    (D) change; before 1995, most

40. (A) NO CHANGE
    (B) assume
    (C) conjecture
    (D) anticipate

41. (A) NO CHANGE
    (B) storms, and strong winds generate
    (C) storms and strong winds generated
    (D) storms and strong winds generate

42. (A) NO CHANGE
    (B) mainland and leaving them
    (C) mainland, they are left
    (D) mainland, left

43. (A) NO CHANGE
    (B) similarly
    (C) being similar
    (D) of which is similar

44. Which choice most effectively establishes the main point of the paragraph?

    (A) The Pulo Aceh islands are often cut off from mainland Indonesia.
    (B) The Pulo Aceh islands are subject to a variety of extreme weather events that make life difficult for people there.
    (C) The Pulo Aceh islands on Sumatra Island, Indonesia, have poor transportation and communication facilities, making life difficult for residents during severe storms.
    (D) The devastating impact of climate change is seen clearly in the Pulo Aceh islands illustrated by numerous examples.

STOP If there is still time remaining, you may review your answers.

3   3

MATH TEST (NO CALCULATOR)

25 MINUTES, 20 QUESTIONS

Turn to Section 3 of your answer sheet to answer the questions in this section.

DIRECTIONS: For questions 1–15, solve each problem and choose the best answer from the given options. Fill in the corresponding circle on your answer document. For questions 16–20, solve the problem and fill in the answer on the answer sheet grid. Please use scrap paper to work out your answers.

Notes:
- You **CANNOT** use a calculator on this section.
- All variables and expressions represent real numbers unless indicated otherwise.
- All figures are drawn to scale unless indicated otherwise.
- All figures are in a plane unless indicated otherwise.
- Unless indicated otherwise, the domain of a given function is the set of all real numbers x for which the function has real values.

REFERENCE INFORMATION

Area Facts	Volume Facts	Triangle Facts

$A = \ell w$

$A = \frac{1}{2} bh$

$A = \pi r^2$

$C = 2\pi r$

$V = \ell w h$

$V = \pi r^2 h$

$V = \frac{4}{3}\pi r^3$

$V = \frac{1}{3}\pi r^2 h$

$V = \frac{1}{3}\ell w h$

$a^2 + b^2 = c^2$

The arc of a circle contains 360°.
The arc of a circle contains 2π radians.
The sum of the measures of the angles in a triangle is 180°.

1. If $7n = 42$, what is the value of $4n - 11$?

   (A) 13
   (B) 16
   (C) 17
   (D) 19

2. Which of the following is equal to $(m^{\frac{1}{3}})^2$?

   (A) $\sqrt{m^{\frac{1}{6}}}$
   (B) $\sqrt[3]{m^2}$
   (C) $\sqrt{m^3}$
   (D) $m\sqrt{m}$

3 3

3. A marathon runner can run m miles at d miles per hour in h hours. The formula for the distance she runs is $hd = m$. If m is a constant, which of the following conclusions is correct?

(A) when d increases, h increases
(B) when d decreases, h decreases
(C) as h increases, d decreases
(D) d will never increase but m can increase or decrease

4. If the area of a square is doubled, how many times longer is a side of the larger square than is the length of the smaller square?

(A) 4
(B) 2
(C) $\sqrt{3}$
(D) $\sqrt{2}$

5. If $\dfrac{6}{n} = \dfrac{18}{n+24}$, what is the value of $\dfrac{n}{12}$?

(A) 1
(B) 1.5
(C) 2
(D) 4.5

$$3x + 6y = 14$$
$$2x + 5y = -11$$

6. If (x, y) is a solution to the system of equations above, what is the value of $x + y$?

(A) 3
(B) 17.5
(C) 24
(D) 25

x	$f(x)$
0	5
2	3
4	1
5	0
8	-2

7. The function f is defined by a polynomial. Some values of x and $f(x)$ are shown in the table above. Which of the following must be a factor of $f(x)$?

(A) x
(B) $x - 3$
(C) $x - 5$
(D) $x - 8$

8. In the diagram above, $r \parallel t \parallel s$ and $m \parallel n$. If the measure of $\angle 3 = (2m + 18)°$ and the measure of $\angle 2 = (4m + 42)°$, what is the measure of $\angle 18$?

(A) 122°
(B) 61°
(C) 58°
(D) 20°

3

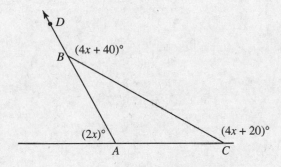

$$5x + 3y = -10$$
$$bx - 4.5y = 13.5$$

9. In the system of equations above, b is a constant and x and y are variables. For what value of b will the system of equations have no solution?

    (A) -10
    (B) -7.5
    (C) 2.5
    (D) 4

10. What is the measure of $\angle ABC$?

    (A) 20
    (B) 40
    (C) 65
    (D) 70

$$y = m(x + 3)(x - 5)$$

11. In the quadratic function above, m is a non-zero constant. The graph of the equation in the xy-plane has vertex (e, f). Which of the following is the value of f?

    (A) $16m$
    (B) $4m$
    (C) $-4m$
    (D) $-16m$

12. What is the value of x if $x = \dfrac{w^2 + 2w + 1}{\dfrac{w + 1}{3}}$?

    (A) $\dfrac{3}{w + 1}$
    (B) $3(w + 1)$
    (C) $\dfrac{1}{3w + 1}$
    (D) $\dfrac{\frac{1}{w}}{3 + w}$

13. Which of the following is equivalent to $25^{\frac{3}{4}}$?

    (A) $5\sqrt{5}$
    (B) $\sqrt[3]{25}$
    (C) $5\sqrt[3]{25}$
    (D) 37.5

3

3

$$F = \frac{9}{5}C + 32$$

14. The equation above shows how a temperature, C, measured in degrees Celsius, relates to a temperature, F, in degrees Fahrenheit. Based on the equation, which of the following must be true?

   I. An increase in temperature of 1 degree Celsius is equivalent to an increase of 1.8 degrees Fahrenheit.

  II. A temperature of 5°F is equivalent to -15°C.

 III. A temperature of 20°C is equivalent to 62°F.

(A) I only
(B) I and II
(C) I and III
(D) III only

15. The expression $\frac{4n + 6}{n - 4}$ is equivalent to which of the following?

(A) $-\frac{4 + 6}{4}$

(B) $4 - \frac{6}{4}$

(C) $4 + \frac{6}{n - 4}$

(D) $4 + \frac{22}{n - 4}$

Grid-in Response Directions

In questions 16–20, first solve the problem, and then enter your answer on the grid provided on the answer sheet. The instructions for entering your answers follow.

- First, write your answer in the boxes at the top of the grid.
- Second, grid your answer in the columns below the boxes.
- Use the fraction bar in the first row or the decimal point in the second row to enter fractions and decimals.

Write your answer in the boxes

Grid in your answer

Answer: $\frac{8}{15}$ Answer: 1.75   Answer: 100   Answer: 100

Either position is acceptable

- Grid only one space in each column.
- Entering the answer in the boxes is recommended as an aid in gridding but is not required.
- The machine scoring your exam can read only what you grid, so you **must grid-in your answers correctly to get credit**.
- If a question has more than one correct answer, grid-in only one of them.
- The grid does not have a minus sign; so no answer can be negative.
- A mixed number *must* be converted to an improper fraction or a decimal before it is gridded.

  Enter $1\frac{1}{4}$ as $\frac{5}{4}$ or 1.25; the machine will interpret 11/4 as $\frac{11}{4}$ and mark it wrong.

- **All decimals must be entered as accurately as possible.** Here are three acceptable ways of gridding

$$\frac{3}{11} = 0.272727\ldots$$

- Note that rounding to .273 is acceptable because you are using the full grid, but you would receive **no credit** for .3 or .27, because they are less accurate.

3

3

16. If $m^2 - 6m + 8 = 0$, what is *one* possible value of $\frac{1}{m}$?

Cost per Lure

17. What is the radius of the circle whose equation is $x^2 + 6y + y^2 - 4x = 12$?

19. The bar graph above represents the fishing lures sold in a sales competition sponsored by the seller.

What is the median cost of the lures sold?

18. What is *one* possible value for the compound inequality $-8 \leq 2x - 8 < 8$?

20. An academic quiz show features local high school students. Each correctly answered question nets the team one point and an incorrectly answered question results in a two-point deduction. If a team scored 38 points on a fifty-question quiz, how many questions did it answer incorrectly?

STOP   If there is still time remaining, you may review your answers.

MATH TEST (CALCULATOR)

55 MINUTES, 38 QUESTIONS

Turn to Section 4 of your answer sheet to answer the questions in this section.

DIRECTIONS: For questions 1–30, solve each problem and choose the best answer from the given options. Fill in the corresponding circle on your answer document. For questions 31–38, solve the problem and fill in the answer on the answer sheet grid. Please use scrap paper to work out your answers.

Notes:
- The **use of** a calculator on this section IS permitted.
- All variables and expressions represent real numbers unless indicated otherwise.
- All figures are drawn to scale unless indicated otherwise.
- All figures are in a plane unless indicated otherwise.
- Unless indicated otherwise, the domain of a given function is the set of all real numbers x for which the function has real values.

REFERENCE INFORMATION

The arc of a circle contains 360°.
The arc of a circle contains 2π radians.
The sum of the measures of the angles in a triangle is 180°.

4

4

1. If $\frac{3x}{5} = 12$, what is the value of x?

   (A) 15

   (B) 20

   (C) 30

   (D) 60

	Boy	Girl	Total
Swim	12	14	26
Water Polo	16	15	31
Total	28	29	57

2. The above chart represents the students who are members of a high school's swim and water polo teams.

   The water polo and swim teams are having a Spring Banquet. One of the team members will be chosen as athlete of the year. What is the probability the person chosen will be a member of the water polo team or a boy?

   (A) $\frac{31}{57}$

   (B) $\frac{43}{57}$

   (C) $\frac{52}{57}$

   (D) $\frac{55}{57}$

Questions 3 and 4 refer to the information below.

The graph below shows the number of domestic bee farms in the metropolitan Atlanta area from 2005 to 2010.

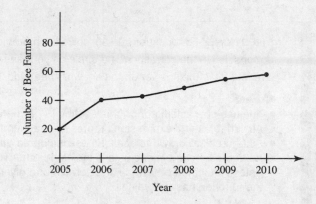

3. Based on the graph, which of the following describes the trend in the number of domestic bee farms in the Atlanta area?

   (A) exponential growth between 2005 and 2010

   (B) continued but modest growth after 2006

   (C) an increase until 2007 followed by a gradual decline after that year

   (D) a dramatic decrease after 2008

4. If each bee farm harvests 11,000 gallons of honey annually, which of the following is closest to the number of gallons collected in 2006?

   (A) 110,000

   (B) 220,000

   (C) 440,000

   (D) 660,000

n	1	2	3	4
$r(n)$	−1	1	3	5

5. The table above shows some values of the linear function r. Which of the following defines r?

(A) $r(n) = 2n + 3$
(B) $r(n) = 3n - 5$
(C) $r(n) = n - 3$
(D) $r(n) = 2n - 3$

$$4x^2 + 5x - 6$$
$$3x^2 + x - 11$$

6. Which of the following is the sum of the polynomials above?

(A) $x^2 + 4x + 5$
(B) $x^2 + 6x - 17$
(C) $7x^2 + 6x - 17$
(D) $7x^4 + 6x^2 - 17$

7. If $\frac{5}{9}n = \frac{7}{20}$, what is the value of n?

(A) $\frac{16}{25}$

(B) $\frac{27}{50}$

(C) $\frac{17}{25}$

(D) $\frac{63}{100}$

8. $x - 2 = \dfrac{4}{x - 2}$

Which of the following is the solution to the equation above?

(A) −4
(B) 0
(C) 0, 4
(D) 2, −2

9. Gina runs 28 meters in 4.7 seconds. If she continues to run at this rate, which of the following is the closest to the distance (in meters) she will run in 2.4 minutes?

(A) 269 meters
(B) 542 meters
(C) 653 meters
(D) 858 meters

Questions 10 and 11 refer to the information below.

The following table represents federal spending for NASA for the years 1958 through 1963.

NASA Spending Since 1958

Year	NASA Fed Outlay, $ in Millions	Total US Fed Spending, $ in Millions	NASA as % of US Spending	President	Party
1958	89	71,936	0.1	Dwight D. Eisenhower	Rep
1959	145	80,697	0.2	Dwight D. Eisenhower	Rep
1960	401	76,539	0.5	Dwight D. Eisenhower	Rep
1961	744	81,515	0.9	John F. Kennedy	Dem
1962	1,257	106,821	1.18	John F. Kennedy	Dem
1963	2,552	111,316	2.28	Lyndon B. Johnson	Dem

10. Which of the following can be concluded about the information portrayed in the table?

(A) From 1958 until 1963, spending on NASA as a percentage of the US budget increased nearly 2,200%.

(B) Between 1962 and 1963, spending on NASA virtually tripled.

(C) In 1963, real spending on NASA exceeded the $1 billion mark for the first time.

(D) The total dollars spent each year from 1958 to 1963 decreased.

11. Total US spending in 1962 was about how many times larger than the NASA budget in 1958?

(A) 77 times
(B) 88 times
(C) 650 times
(D) 1,200 times

4

4

Questions 12 and 13 refer to the following information.

An investment of $7,500 in a certain piece of artwork has depreciated in value. The investor uses the following formula to calculate the value of her investment.

$$A = P(1 - r)^t$$

where

A = the accumulated value over time
P = the initial price of the artwork
r = rate of decrease expressed as a decimal
t = time in years

12. Which of the following equations models the value of the artwork if it has devalued at 4.6% annually for 3.5 years?

    (A) $A = 7,500(.965)^{3.5}$
    (B) $A = 7,500(1.035)^{3.5}$
    (C) $A = 7,500(1.046)^{3.5}$
    (D) $A = 7,500(.954)^{3.5}$

13. Three years after the purchase date, the value of the artwork had declined to $6,511.88. If the depreciation has occurred at a 4.6% annual rate, what was its value five years later?

    (A) $5,145.75
    (B) $5,337.62
    (C) $5,476.39
    (D) $6,126.63

14. A clinical study was devised to see if a new procedure was an effective early detector of skin cancer. A group of 500 patients participated but only 250, group A, received the treatment. The other 250 participants, group B, received the standard procedure, which is 45% effective. Group A was treated with the new procedure, resulting in 79% effectiveness. Based on the design and results of the study, which of the following is an appropriate conclusion?

    (A) The study size was too small to make a conclusion.
    (B) The new early detection program is better than any other available program.
    (C) The new early detection program was more effective than the current standard procedure.
    (D) The new procedure will help all patients in danger of skin cancer.

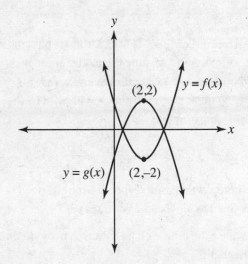

15. Graphs of the functions f and g are shown in the xy-plane. What is the value of $f(2) + g(2)$?

    (A) 0
    (B) 1
    (C) 2
    (D) 3

4   4

Questions 16 and 17 refer to the information below.

The term *light-year* refers to the distance light travels in one year.

16. If light travels 186,000 miles per second, which of the following is closest to the distance from Earth to Sirius, 8 light-years distant?

   (A) 47 billion miles
   (B) 198 billion miles
   (C) 9 trillion miles
   (D) 50 trillion miles

17. If light travels 186,000 miles per second, how far does light travel in one-billionth of a second? (Note: 1 mile = 5,280 feet)

   (A) 10 miles
   (B) 1 mile
   (C) 1 foot
   (D) 0.01 feet

18. An airline company is calculating its passenger cost for a trans-Atlantic flight. The plane flies approximately 3,000 miles at an average air speed of 500 miles per hour. The cost is given by the following function.

$$C(x) = 100 + \frac{x}{10} + \frac{36,000}{x}$$

where x is the ground speed. Ground speed is defined as air speed ± wind speed.

What is the airline's cost if there is no wind during the flight?

   (A) $176
   (B) $222
   (C) $358
   (D) $422

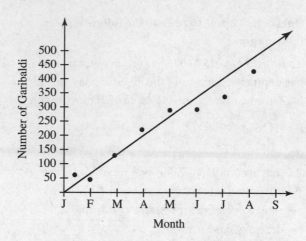

19. Garibaldi are bright orange fish that are closely related to goldfish. They are frequently found in the waters of the eastern Pacific Ocean. In different coastal California lagoons, researchers counted the number of Garibaldi found per cubic mile of ocean. The graph of that study is shown above along with a line of best fit.

In August, what was the difference between the number predicted by the line of best fit and the actual number of Garibaldi that were counted?

   (A) 120
   (B) 100
   (C) 60
   (D) 50

20. The sum of three numbers is 780. One of the numbers, n, is 50% more than the sum of the other two numbers. What is the value of n?

   (A) 144
   (B) 312
   (C) 424
   (D) 468

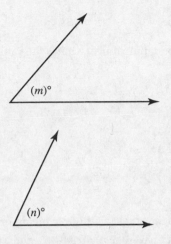

Note: Figures not drawn to scale

Height of Cylinder: 12'

Radius of Cylinder: 8'

Radius of Cone: 8'

Height of Cone: 8'

21. The angles shown above are complementary and $\sin(m°) = \cos(n°)$. If $m = (3x - 12)°$ and $n = (6x - 18)°$, what is the value of x?

(A) $13.\overline{3}$
(B) 20.6
(C) 30.25
(D) 40.3

22. Ms. Garcia has a jar containing m milliliters of a solution for her chemistry class. If she gives 8 milliliters to each student, she will have 6 milliliters left over. If she provides 10 milliliters to each student, she will need an additional 16 milliliters. How many students are in her class?

(A) 10
(B) 11
(C) 17
(D) 22

23. The diagram above represents a grain silo with a right cylindrical base and a top in the shape of a right cone. The owner believes he needs a new silo, which will store 10% more grain than his existing silo. Which of the following represents the volume of the new silo (in cubic feet)?

(A) 2,123
(B) 2,678
(C) 2,948
(D) 3,243

24. In the xy-plane, the line determined by $(6, m)$ and $(m, 54)$ passes through the origin. Which of the following could be the value of m?

(A) 2
(B) 18
(C) 36
(D) 48

4   4

x	$f(x)$
-2	-2.2
0	-3
6	-5.4
7	-5.8

25. Some values of the linear function f are shown in the table. What is the value of $f(8)$?

(A) $-.6$
(B) -1.8
(C) -3.2
(D) -6.2

26. $x^2 + y^2 - 12x + 3y = -7$

The equation above models a circle in the xy-plane. What is the measure of the diameter of the circle?

(A) $\frac{5\sqrt{5}}{2}$
(B) $5\sqrt{5}$
(C) $10\sqrt{5}$
(D) $10\sqrt{10}$

27. $g(x) = (x + 4)(x - 8)$

Which of the following shows an equivalent form of the function g so that a minimum value of $g(x)$ appears as a constant or coefficient?

(A) $g(x) = x^2 - 32$
(B) $g(x) = (x^2 - 4x - 32)$
(C) $g(x) = (x - 2)^2 - 36$
(D) $g(x) = (x - 4)^2 - 32$

$$2x^{\frac{2}{3}} = 6^{\frac{1}{2}}$$

28. In the equation above, what is the value of x?

(A) $\frac{27}{8}$
(B) $\left(\frac{27}{8}\right)^{\frac{1}{4}}$
(C) $\left(\frac{8}{27}\right)^{\frac{1}{4}}$
(D) $\frac{16}{27}$

29. If x is the average (arithmetic mean) of $2p$ and 12, y is the average of $5p$ and 18, and z is the average of $8p - 6$, what is the average of x, y, and z in terms of p?

(A) $5p + 8$
(B) $3p + 6$
(C) $p + 12$
(D) $p + 6$

Year	Hits
2015	2,150
2016	3,230

30. Steve's website statistics page shows the number of hits the website received in 2015 and 2016 as shown in the table above. He believes the percentage increase from 2015 to 2016 will be triple the percentage increase from 2016 to 2017. If Steve is correct, which of the following is closest to the website's projected hits in 2017?

(A) 1,925
(B) 2,150
(C) 3,770
(D) 4,430

Grid-in Response Directions

In questions 31–38, first solve the problem, and then enter your answer on the grid provided on the answer sheet. The instructions for entering your answers follow.

- First, write your answer in the boxes at the top of the grid.
- Second, grid your answer in the columns below the boxes.
- Use the fraction bar in the first row or the decimal point in the second row to enter fractions and decimals.

- Grid only one space in each column.
- Entering the answer in the boxes is recommended as an aid in gridding but is not required.
- The machine scoring your exam can read only what you grid, so you **must grid-in your answers correctly to get credit.**
- If a question has more than one correct answer, grid-in only one of them.
- The grid does not have a minus sign; so no answer can be negative.
- A mixed number *must* be converted to an improper fraction or a decimal before it is gridded.

  Enter $1\frac{1}{4}$ as $\frac{5}{4}$ or 1.25; the machine will interpret 11/4 as $\frac{11}{4}$ and mark it wrong.

- **All decimals must be entered as accurately as possible.** Here are three acceptable ways of gridding

  $$\frac{3}{11} = 0.272727\ldots$$

- Note that rounding to .273 is acceptable because you are using the full grid, but you would receive **no credit** for .3 or .27, because they are less accurate.

4

4

PRACTICE TEST 5

31. Belts cost $11 and blouses cost $18. If Kara spends at least $51 but no more than $62 for x belts and one blouse, what is *one* possible value of x?

$$(-8x^2 + 15x - 2) - 3(2x^2 + 4x - 2)$$

32. If the expression above is written in the form of $ax^2 + bx + c$, where a, b, and c are constants, what is the value of b?

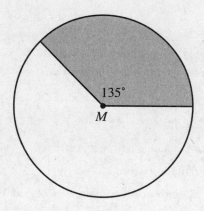

33. Point M is the center of the circle shown above. The shaded area is what fraction of the area of the circle?

34. A new movie recently scored an average rating of 4.3 stars out of 5 from its first 12 reviewers. If the next two reviewers each give the movie a 5-star review, what will the new average rating be?

$$A = 25m + 275$$

35. Terrence has made an initial deposit into his bank account. Each month after his initial deposit he has deposited a fixed amount into the account. The equation above represents the amount, A, he has in dollars after he has made m monthly deposits. According to this equation, what was the initial deposit Terrence made into his account?

36. The points $(2, 7)$ and $(-3, 37)$ lie on the graph of $y = ax^2 - 4x + 7$. What is the value of a?

Questions 37 and 38 refer to the following information.

The theory of special relativity suggests that an observer moving at great speed experiences the flow of time much more slowly than an observer on Earth. The following formula is used to calculate what is known as time dilation.

$$F(t) = \frac{t}{\sqrt{1 - v^2}}$$

In the formula, t represents some unit of time and v represents velocity as some fraction of light-speed. For example, an observer counts one second in a rocket ship traveling at 60% of the speed of light while an observer on Earth measures 1.25 seconds.

37. If an observer traveling at 80% the speed of light counts off one second, how many seconds will be counted by an observer on Earth?

38. An observer on Earth measures 2 seconds, while an observer traveling at a fraction of light-speed measures 1 second. What fraction of light-speed was the moving observer traveling?

STOP If there is still time remaining, you may review your answers.

ANSWER KEY
Practice Test 5

Section 1: Reading

1.	A	14.	C	27.	D	40.	B
2.	D	15.	C	28.	C	41.	C
3.	C	16.	C	29.	A	42.	C
4.	C	17.	C	30.	B	43.	C
5.	D	18.	C	31.	D	44.	C
6.	C	19.	B	32.	D	45.	A
7.	A	20.	D	33.	B	46.	C
8.	B	21.	A	34.	B	47.	B
9.	D	22.	B	35.	B	48.	C
10.	B	23.	D	36.	C	49.	C
11.	A	24.	A	37.	C	50.	B
12.	B	25.	D	38.	D	51.	D
13.	A	26.	A	39.	D	52.	D

Number Correct _____

Number Incorrect _____

Section 2: Writing and Language

1.	B	12.	D	23.	C	34.	B
2.	C	13.	B	24.	B	35.	D
3.	D	14.	D	25.	D	36.	D
4.	A	15.	D	26.	C	37.	B
5.	B	16.	A	27.	B	38.	C
6.	C	17.	B	28.	A	39.	C
7.	D	18.	C	29.	D	40.	D
8.	B	19.	C	30.	B	41.	C
9.	D	20.	B	31.	C	42.	B
10.	D	21.	A	32.	C	43.	A
11.	D	22.	B	33.	D	44.	B

Number Correct _____

Number Incorrect _____

ANSWER KEY
Practice Test 5

Section 3: Math (No Calculator)

1. **A**	5. **A**	9. **B**	13. **A**
2. **B**	6. **D**	10. **A**	14. **B**
3. **C**	7. **C**	11. **D**	15. **D**
4. **D**	8. **A**	12. **B**	

16. **1/4 or 1/2**

17. **5**

18. **Answers may vary.**

$$0 \le x < 8$$

or

19. **5**

20. **4**

Number Correct _____

Number Incorrect _____

ANSWER KEY
Practice Test 5

Section 4: Math (Calculator)

1. **B**	9. **D**	17. **C**	25. **D**
2. **B**	10. **A**	18. **B**	26. **B**
3. **B**	11. **D**	19. **D**	27. **C**
4. **C**	12. **D**	20. **D**	28. **B**
5. **D**	13. **A**	21. **A**	29. **A**
6. **C**	14. **C**	22. **B**	30. **C**
7. **D**	15. **A**	23. **D**	
8. **C**	16. **D**	24. **B**	

31. **3 or 4**

or

32. **3**

33. **3/8**

or

34. **4.4**

35. **275**

36. **2**

.375

ANSWER KEY
Practice Test 5

37. **1.66 or 1.67 or 5/3**

or   or

38. **.866**

Number Correct   _____

Number Incorrect   _____

SCORE ANALYSIS
Reading and Writing Test

Section 1: Reading   _____ = _____ (A)
             # correct   raw score

Section 2: Writing   _____ = _____ (B)
             # correct   raw score

To find your Reading and Writing test scores, consult the chart below; find the ranges in which your raw scores lie and read across to find the ranges of your test scores.

_____ + _____ = _____ (C)
range of Reading   range of Writing   range of Reading + Writing
test scores   test scores   test scores

To find the range of your Reading and Writing Scaled Score, multiply (C) by 10.

Test Scores for the Reading and Writing Sections

Reading Raw Score	Writing Raw Score	Test Score
44–52	39–44	35–40
36–43	33–38	31–34
30–35	28–32	28–30
24–29	22–27	24–27
19–23	17–21	21–23
14–18	13–16	19–20
9–13	9–12	16–18
5–8	5–8	13–15
less than 5	less than 5	10–12

Math Test

Section 3:   _____ = _____ (D)
          # correct   raw score

Section 4:   _____ = _____ (E)
          # correct   raw score

Total Math raw score: (D) + (E) = _____

To find your Math Scaled Score, consult the chart below; find the range in which your raw score lies and read across to find the range for your scaled score.

Scaled Scores for the Math Test

Raw Score	Scaled Score	Raw Score	Scaled Score
50–58	700–800	20–25	450–490
44–49	650–690	15–19	400–440
38–43	600–640	11–14	350–390
32–37	550–590	7–10	300–340
26–31	500–540	less than 7	200–290

Answer Explanations

Section 1: Reading Test

1. **(A)** The author says, "Whatever their [Franklin's and the other men's who stood with Washington] philosophical professions may have been, they were not controlled by prudence" (lines 5–7). The word *professions* in this context means "avowals of belief." The phrase "professedly prudent" means that Franklin professed—that is, *avowed*—to be *prudent* (cautious and sensible).

2. **(D)** As stated in the previous explanation, *professions* in this context means "avowals of belief."

3. **(C)** The author says, "They were . . . willing to take all risks . . . in a struggle whose course was just though its issue was dubious" (lines 7–10). It makes sense that the word *issue* means "outcome" here because a struggle results in an outcome.

4. **(C)** It can be inferred that the author quotes these words to show that Robert Morris had great integrity and patriotism because Morris said he will do anything asked of him by his country unless it would mean a loss of his integrity.

5. **(D)** In context, the word *celebrated* means "known and praised widely."

6. **(C)** The author says, "I see Benjamin Franklin . . . accepting without demur the difficult and dangerous mission to France" (lines 40–44).

7. **(A)** The author says that Benjamin Franklin "claimed to be a follower of the theory of enlightened self-interest" (lines 60–61).

8. **(B)** This is the best title because the passage concentrates on the important role Benjamin Franklin had in American history and the sacrifices he made for America.

9. **(D)** The quotation referred to is in the last sentence of a paragraph (lines 66–78; "He . . . Franklin") describing the great sacrifices that Benjamin Franklin made for his country.

10. **(B)** The author makes use of all of the choices except *understatement* (intentional lack of emphasis in expression).

11. **(A)** The author says, "While Derek Freeman later critiqued Mead's culturally deterministic approach" (lines 24–26), so we can infer that by *critique* the author means "criticized."

12. **(B)** The author says, "All of these factors were thought to make Samoan adolescence relatively tranquil and enjoyable and led to Mead's assertion of the primacy of nurture over nature" (lines 21–24). "Nurture" refers to cultural influences and "nature" refers to the influence of a person's genetic make-up.

13. **(A)** The author says, "Schlegel and Barry's cross-cultural study of adolescents . . . demonstrated that adolescence . . . is ubiquitous" (lines 33–38). In context, *ubiquitous* means "existing everywhere."

14. **(C)** In context, the word *inevitabilities* (line 45) means "unavoidable occurrences."

15. **(C)** In context, the word *gendered* (line 51) means "characteristic of one gender." The phrase "with aggression in girls being particularly low" (lines 51–52) provides a clue to the meaning.

16. **(C)** According to the author, based on a study, "Trommsdorff suggested that 'turbulent' features such as intergenerational conflict stem from the focus on attaining independence from parents during this period and are linked to cultural values of individualism in Western

societies" (lines 64–69). From this it can be inferred that Trommsdorff would probably agree that adolescents in individualistic cultures would be more likely to argue with their parents than adolescents in collectivistic cultures.

17. **(C)** These lines provide the best evidence because they state what Trommsdorff suggested about adolescence in collectivist and individualistic cultures.

18. **(C)** The author says, "If we assume that a transitional period of the life cycle, akin to adolescence, organized around puberty and of variable length, exists almost universally . . ." (lines 1–6). The author also says, "Adolescence conceptualized as a prolonged period of identity development linked to increased autonomy, intergenerational conflict, peer-relatedness and social psychological anxieties, is not the norm across cultures" (lines 84–89).

19. **(B)** The author objectively evaluates what social science has discovered about adolescence and reaches a conclusion about an important issue concerning it.

20. **(D)** Humor is not used in the passage.

21. **(A)** The author says modern journalists can produce articles "without using . . . expert information" (lines 28–29). Thus, it is probable that he would say that modern journalists often produce articles that are not authoritative because such articles require expert information that journalists normally do not have.

22. **(B)** *Rhetoric* in context means "language that is elaborate but has little meaning." The author says the sophists used rhetoric to hide the gaps in their logic. The adjective *glossy* means "slick or smooth," suggesting that the sophist used rhetoric to, metaphorically, paint over the gaps in their reasoning with slick language.

23. **(D)** The author says the sophists "argued unsystematically and unfairly" (line 31).

24. **(A)** The author believes that Socrates "opposed the sophists wherever possible" because he believes that Socrates, unlike the sophists, was seeking the truth. This can be inferred from what the author says about the sophists and about Socrates. First, the sophists: "The sophists dazzled everyone without convincing anyone of anything positive. They argued unsystematically and unfairly . . . . They had few constructive ideas . . . . They demonstrated that almost anything could be proved by a fast talker" (lines 29–38). Second, Socrates: "He distrusted . . . the sophists (lines 43–44); "He only asked questions" (line 46); "Socrates said he knew nothing and was trying to find out" (lines 57–58). It is thus reasonable that the author believes that Socrates opposed the sophists because he believed that they not only were not seeking the truth, but they were also detrimental to the search for the truth.

25. **(D)** The other choices are mentioned in lines 61–77. It is unlikely that the sophists had new philosophical answers that helped them become successful because the author says that the sophists "dazzled without convincing anyone of anything positive" (lines 29–31) and "had few constructive ideas" (lines 33–34), and generally were not concerned with finding the truth.

26. **(A)** This is the best choice because the passage is mainly concerned with the sophists and Socrates.

27. **(D)** According to the author, "Socrates said he knew nothing and was trying to find out" (lines 57–58). He spent his life questioning all sorts of people "and to convinc[ing] them that they knew no more than he did" (lines 97–98). Thus, it is very unlikely that Socrates would believe that most truths have been discovered.

28. **(C)** In context, the word *naive* means "uninformed." This can be inferred because the author says that Socrates convinced people they "knew no more than he did" (line 98) by first telling them that he knew nothing. This made the person eager to explain to Socrates because they believed he was "intelligent" (line 102) but uninformed.

29. **(A)** The author describes Socrates's "unfailing good humor—which allowed him to . . . keep the conversation going and at crises when the other lost his temper, to dominate it" (lines 105–108).

30. **(B)** The author says that "Socrates questioned all sorts" (line 86) of people and that he adapted to them (lines 91–94; "It . . . did"). He also says that Socrates's "adaptability . . . showed him the side on which each man could be best approached" (lines 103–104). We can infer from this information about Socrates that he had an excellent understanding of human nature because it would have been difficult for him to adapt to so many people without it.

31. **(D)** This provides the best evidence for the answer to the previous question for reasons explained in the explanation to question 30.

32. **(D)** The primary concern of the passage is disease in animals (fauna) in urban areas.

33. **(B)** The author is describing the processes by which diseases are spread among animals as a result of their movement. This system is a dynamic one, with continual changes in the interactions among animals.

34. **(B)** The author is advancing a theory that measures taken to control urban waterfowl duck plague epizootics resulted in very few ("rare"—line 35) cases of duck plague in migratory ducks. In lines 39–42 ("However . . . society"), he discusses "culling" of urban waterfowl.

35. **(B)** As discussed in the explanation of the answer to the previous question, the author is suggesting that culling of infected waterfowl in urban waterfowl populations resulted in fewer occasions for the spread of disease to migratory waterfowl.

36. **(C)** In lines 45–46 the author says that some people living in urban areas regard resident waterfowl as companions ("companion animal status [is] conferred"). We can infer from this that many of these people would actively oppose the culling of resident waterfowl because of their emotional attachment to these animals, making wildlife management and disease control difficult.

37. **(C)** These lines provide the best evidence for the answer to the previous question because they describe a difficulty sometimes encountered in managing wildlife in urban areas.

38. **(D)** The author is discussing disease "dynamics" (line 5) in urban fauna. These dynamics involve the movement of animals, resulting in interaction between different populations of animals.

39. **(D)** The author describes these processes in lines 50–65.

40. **(B)** The author would agree with this statement because throughout the passage he describes some of the complex interactions in urban areas among various animal populations and between animal populations and humans that sometimes result in the spread of disease. In lines 97–106 ("Urban . . . cherished"), he stresses the importance of managing wildlife in urban areas. We can therefore infer that he would agree that increased urbanization requires effective cooperation between wildlife managers and public health officials.

41. **(C)** West Nile fever spread to more states in 2002 than in the other years.

42. **(C)** The author does not quote "recognized experts."

43. **(C)** The author says he has liked the novels that have been read to him "if they do not end unhappily" (line 15). He is most likely being *jocular* (humorous) because it is very unlikely that he would believe that a law should be passed against novels ending unhappily.

44. **(C)** The author says that he still enjoys "books on history, biographies, and travels . . . and essays on all sorts of subjects" (lines 18–21). It is thus likely that the author would enjoy reading an essay on English history. He says he no longer enjoys choices (A) and (B), and it is unlikely that he would enjoy choice (D), *studying advanced mathematics*, because he says, "My power to follow a long and purely abstract train of thought is very limited; and therefore I could never have succeeded with . . . mathematics" (lines 40–43).

45. **(A)** The author's main point in the sentence is that his loss of "the higher aesthetic tastes" is strange in view of the fact that he is still able to appreciate essays on history and so forth. The words in parentheses are thus presumably intended mainly to make it clear that he is interested in such essays for their intrinsic merit and not only for the scientific facts they may contain.

46. **(C)** The author says, "I have no great quickness of apprehension or wit . . . I am therefore a poor critic: a paper or book, when first read, generally excites my admiration, and it is only after considerable reflection that I perceive the weak points" (lines 35–40).

47. **(B)** These lines provide the best evidence for the answer to the previous question.

48. **(C)** Induction is *the process of deriving general principles from particular facts*. The author says that "My mind seems to have become a kind of machine for grinding general laws out of large collections of facts" (lines 22–24). He also says, "I have had the strongest desire to understand or explain whatever I observed,—that is, to group all facts under some general laws" (lines 66–69). Finally, he says, "This has naturally led to distrust greatly deductive reasoning in the mixed sciences" (lines 81–83).

49. **(C)** The author is describing his intellectual abilities, so the meaning he intends by the word "apprehension" must be *understanding*.

50. **(B)** The author says, "I am not very skeptical,—a frame of mind which I believe to be injurious to the progress of science. A good deal of skepticism in a scientific man is advisable to avoid much loss of time, but [some men] have often thus been deterred from experiment or observations, which would have proved directly or indirectly serviceable" (lines 84–91).

51. **(D)** These lines provide the best evidence for the answer to the previous question.

52. **(D)** The writer is describing his intellectual abilities. He has already discussed his "power of reasoning" (line 57), so it is unlikely that "invention" refers to choice (C), logical ability. Therefore, the meaning of the word "invention" as it is used in line 58 is *creativity*.

Section 2: Writing and Language Test

1. **(B)** All of the choices are grammatically correct because they all correct the error, which is that the clause beginning with "Because" and ending with "BLS" is not an independent clause and thus is not a complete sentence. However, choice (B) is the best choice because it is the most clear and concise.

2. **(C)** This is the only choice that makes good sense in context.

3. **(D)** This is the best choice because the context requires a conjunction linking the two parts of the sentences. The second part of the sentence provides more of the same type of information as given in the first part of the sentence, so the word *while* used as a conjunction meaning "and" is correct.

4. **(A)** This is the correct choice because in this context *ambulatory* means "of medical care or services provided on an outpatient basis." "Outpatient care" and "laboratory [care]" are examples of such medical care.

5. **(B)** This is the correct choice. Some form of the past tense is required because growth in the healthcare industry in the past is being discussed. This is confirmed by the data shown in the chart. Choice (D) is a past tense verb but is not a good choice because it makes little sense. Choice (B) is grammatical and makes good sense because the verb is cast in the past progressive tense, which is used to show that some action (in this case, growth in employment) was in process during a period of time in the past.

6. **(C)** It can be seen from the graph that healthcare employment continued to increase steadily between 2007 and 2009.

7. **(D)** All of the choices are grammatically correct and make sense in context. However, this is the best choice because it is clear and concise. In the phrase *job stability* the word *job* functions as an adjective modifying the noun *stability*.

8. **(B)** Choice (A) is grammatical (if *hospitals* was changed to *hospitals'*) but makes little sense. Choice (C) is grammatical but awkward. Choice (D) is incorrect because it creates a run-on sentence. Choice (B) is the best choice because it creates a clear and grammatical sentence: the focus of the sentence is cost-cutting efforts; the nonrestrictive adjective clause beginning with *which* modifies the noun *hospitals*, telling us something about them in relation to cost-cutting.

9. **(D)** This is the best choice because sentence 1 does not make sense as the first sentence of this paragraph because it provides additional information about the topic that sentence 4 is about. Moving sentence 1 so that it comes after sentence 4 makes sentence 2 the first sentence of the paragraph, which makes sense because it is an appropriate topic sentence.

10. **(D)** This is the only choice that is grammatical and makes good sense. Note that the phrase "home healthcare services" is singular because in the context of the passage it is a category within the healthcare industry.

11. **(D)** This is the correct choice because it is standard usage in this context.

12. **(D)** The second sentence in choice (A) is a run-on sentence, so this is incorrect. Choice (B) does not make sense because an army officer cannot die shortly after birth. Choice (C) contains a grammatical error; "His father, he . . . ." Choice (D) is grammatical and clear.

13. **(B)** The correct choice is *remnant*, which in context means "a small surviving group of people." Choice (A) makes sense but *residue* is not used to refer to people.

14. **(D)** This is the correct choice because sentence 4 describes how Ohiyesa "lived the original nomadic life of his people." Sentence 1 follows logically from this because it explains "the knowledge thus gained" from this experience.

15. **(D)** This choice makes good sense because Ohiyesa "was astonished by the reappearance of his father."

16. **(A)** This choice is correct because the present perfect tense is used here correctly to indicate that Ohiyesa's father came home at an earlier point in time than the point in time at which he learned about it.

17. **(B)** In this context, *where* is a conjunction meaning "at which place." It refers to "Flandreau, Dakota Territory."

18. **(C)** This is the correct choice in context because the past progressive tense indicates that the group of Indians were earning their living over a period of time in the past.

19. **(C)** This is the correct choice in context. *At first reluctant* is a standard phrase meaning "Although [he] was reluctant at first." It makes good sense because the sentence goes on to say, "he soon became interested."

20. **(B)** Choices (A) and (C) do not make sense. Choice (D) makes sense but is unclear because it suggests a relationship between the father's action and the boy's action that is not specified. Choice (B) is the best choice because it is clear and grammatical.

21. **(A)** This is the idiomatically correct choice.

22. **(B)** This is the correct choice because it is standard usage in this context.

23. **(C)** This statement clearly summarizes the main subject of the passage, which is that Spanish explorers and conquistadors paid little attention to Cuba.

24. **(B)** This is the only grammatically correct choice. It creates a compound sentence, whereas the other choices do not make a grammatical sentence.

25. **(D)** This is the only choice that is grammatical and makes good sense in context.

26. **(C)** *In consequence* makes the best sense because the sentence that this phrase introduces describes a report brought back to Hispaniola or Spain as a *consequence* of what is described in the previous sentence.

27. **(B)** The linking verb "is" is necessary to create a grammatical sentence. None of the other choices is grammatically correct.

28. **(A)** *Ascertained*, which in context means "determined with certainty," is the correct choice. *Ascertained* in context is a participial adjective modifying the noun "facts."

29. **(D)** The simple past tense is the correct tense in context. The writer is referring to events in the past.

30. **(B)** This is the best placement for sentence 4 because sentence 5 describes "somewhat more significant" evidence in support of the belief that people knew that Cuba was an island. Sentence 4 follows logically from this because it suggests that this evidence may be based on a rumor.

31. **(C)** This is the only choice that is grammatical and makes sense in context. In this context *succeeded* means "came after and took the place of." The past perfect "had been succeeded" is correct because the writer is talking about a time period before the one he was talking about in the previous paragraph. Note that the verb must be in the passive voice (indicated by *been,*

the past participle of *be*) because Francisco de Bobadilla performed the action, as indicated by the preposition "by."

32. **(C)** Choice (B) is grammatically correct, but it creates a clumsy sentence. Choice (C) creates a clear and grammatical sentence.

33. **(D)** This is the correct choice. The past perfect tense is the appropriate tense here because the sentence is recounting what Sebastian de Ocampo *said* (simple past tense; earlier event) he *had found* (past perfect tense; later event).

34. **(B)** Choice (A) creates an ungrammatical sentence. Choice (B) corrects the error by placing the participial phrase "positioned on the equator" in the beginning of the sentence. In addition to being grammatical, this choice puts emphasis on what is in context important—Indonesia's position.

35. **(D)** Choice (B) is incorrect because the past tense is not suitable in this context because a statement of fact is being made, which requires the present tense. Choices (A) and (C) are grammatical but not idiomatic.

36. **(D)** This is the best choice because sentence 2 follows naturally from sentence 4, describing the effects of the typhoons mentioned in sentence 4. Also, sentence 2 makes little sense placed after sentence 1; whereas sentence 3 makes good sense after sentence 1.

37. **(B)** Choice (A) is not correct because it creates an ungrammatical sentence in which the second part of the sentence is a dependent clause rather than an independent clause. Choice (B) corrects this error and creates a grammatically correct sentence. Choice (C) is incorrect because a dependent clause cannot come after a semicolon. Choice (D) is incorrect because a run-on sentence is created.

38. **(C)** *Mitigate* (moderate in force) is the best choice in context. It is unlikely that the sea walls will solve the problem; rather, it is likely that the sea walls will make the effects of the typhoons less damaging.

39. **(C)** Choice (A) makes little sense. Choice (C) is the best choice in context. Although choice (B) and choice (D) each create a grammatical sentence that makes sense, choice (C) is best because the sentence now beginning with "Before . . ." expresses a new idea rather than one closely related to the previous sentence.

40. **(D)** This is the only choice that makes good sense in context and is grammatical. In this context *anticipate* means "act in advance so as to mitigate."

41. **(C)** This is the only choice that creates a grammatical sentence. "Sea storms and strong winds" becomes the object of the verbs "adapt" and "entertain," creating a grammatical sentence.

42. **(B)** Choices (A), (C), and (D) are not grammatical. Choice (B) corrects the error by creating a participial phrase beginning with "cutting."

43. **(A)** Choices (B), (C), and (D) are not grammatical. Choice (A) creates a sentence that is grammatical and makes good sense.

44. **(B)** This is the focus of the paragraph. The other choices are mentioned in relation to this main topic.

Section 3: Math Test (No Calculator)

1. **(A)** Solve for n in $7n = 42$ and replace that value in $4n - 11$.

$$7n = 42$$
$$n = 6$$
$$4(6) - 11 = 13$$

2. **(B)** When raising an exponent to another, multiply the exponents.

$$(m^{\frac{1}{3}})^2 = m^{\frac{2}{3}}$$

Rational exponents can be expressed as radicals: the numerator is the exponent and the denominator is the root.

$$m^{\frac{2}{3}} = \sqrt[3]{m^2}$$

The root, 3, exceeds the exponent, 2, so $\sqrt[3]{m^2}$ is simplified to its lowest term.

3. **(C)** Use simple values for m, d, and h to find the correct conclusion.
   Let $m = 12$
   $hd = m$

h	d
1	12
2	6
3	4
4	3
6	2
12	1

As h increases, d decreases.

4. **(D)** Imagine a square that has an area of 4 square units. Since the area of a square is found by using the formula $A = s^2$ (where s is the length of a side), then each side of the square is 2 because $\sqrt{4} = 2$. If the area of the larger square is double the smaller, then its area must be 8. Find the square root of 8 to find the length of a side.

$$\sqrt{8} = 2\sqrt{2}$$

When the area of a square is doubled, each side length increases by a factor of $\sqrt{2}$.

5. **(A)** Cross-multiply and solve for n.

$$\frac{6}{n} = \frac{18}{n + 24}$$
$$6(n + 24) = (18)(n)$$
$$6n + 144 = 18n$$
$$144 = 12n$$
$$12 = n$$

Find the value of $\frac{n}{12}$ by substituting 12 for n.

$$\frac{12}{12} = 1$$

6. **(D)** Although the system of equations can be solved by using elimination or substitution, it is easier to subtract the equations.

$$3x + 6y = 14$$
$$\underline{-(2x + 5y = -11)}$$
$$x + y = 25$$

7. **(C)** A polynomial has a zero x if $f(x) = 0$. The chart indicates $(5, 0)$ satisfies the function, so $f(5) = 0$ and $x = 5$. Subtracting 5 from both sides of the equation we get $x - 5 = 0$. Therefore, $x - 5$ is a factor of $f(x)$.

8. **(A)** Angle 2 and $\angle 3$ are consecutive interior angles, so their sum is 180°. Solve for m by setting their sum equal to 180.

$$(2m + 18) + (4m + 42) = 180$$
$$6m + 60 = 180$$
$$6m = 120$$
$$m = 20$$

Substitute 20 for m and find the measure of $\angle 2$.

$$(4)(20) + 42 = 122$$

Angle 2 and $\angle 6$ are corresponding angles so their measures are equal. Angle 6 and $\angle 18$ are corresponding angles so their measures are also the same. Using the transitive property, we find that the measure of $\angle 2$ equals the measure of $\angle 6$, which equals the measure of $\angle 18$, which all equal 122°.

There are several alternate ways to solve this problem but the easiest way is visually. The diagram is drawn to scale and $\angle 18$ appears to be obtuse. Solely choice (A), 122°, appears to have a measure greater than 90°.

9. **(B)** A system of equations has no solution when the equations are parallel lines. Parallel lines have the same slope but different y-intercepts. Convert $5x + 3y = -10$ to slope-intercept form to inspect the slope and y-intercept.

$$5x + 3y = -10$$
$$3y = -5x - 10$$
$$y = -\frac{5}{3}x - \frac{10}{3}$$

Substitute -7.5 for b and convert to slope-intercept form.

$$-7.5x - 4.5y = 13.5$$
$$-4.5y = 7.5x + 13.5$$
$$y = -\frac{5}{3}x - 3$$

The equations $y = -\frac{5}{3}x - \frac{10}{3}$ and $y = -\frac{5}{3}x - 3$ are parallel lines because their slopes are the same but the y-intercepts are different. When $b = -7.5$, the system of equations has no solution.

10. **(A)** The sum of the measures of the exterior angles of a polygon is 360°. Add the exterior angles of $\triangle ABC$ and set them equal to 360 to find x.

$$(4x + 40) + (4x + 20) + 2x = 360$$

$$10x + 60 = 360$$

$$10x = 300$$

$$x = 30$$

$\angle DBC$ and $\angle ABC$ are supplementary angles; their sum is 180°.

$$\angle DBC = 4x + 40 = 4(30) + 40 = 160$$

Therefore, $m\angle ABC + 160 = 180$ and $m\angle ABC = 20$.

11. **(D)** Use FOIL to expand the quantities in the parentheses.

$$y = m(x + 3)(x - 5) = m(x^2 - 2x - 15)$$

Multiply each term in the parentheses by m.

$$m(x^2 - 2x - 15) = mx^2 - 2xm - 15m$$

Find the value of e by using the formula $e = -\dfrac{b}{2a}$ (this is also the formula for finding the axis of symmetry of a parabola).

$$e = -\frac{b}{2a} = -\frac{(-2m)}{2m} = 1$$

Find f by replacing x with 1 in $mx^2 - 2xm - 15m$.

$$m(1)^2 - 2(1)m - 15m = -16m$$

The value of f in the vertex is $-16m$.

12. **(B)** Factor the numerator of the complex fraction.

$$\frac{w^2 + 2w + 1}{\dfrac{w + 1}{3}} = \frac{(w + 1)(w + 1)}{\dfrac{w + 1}{3}}$$

When dividing a complex fraction, invert the denominator and multiply that quantity with the numerator.

$$\frac{(w + 1)(w + 1)}{\dfrac{w + 1}{3}} = (w + 1)(w + 1)\left(\frac{3}{w + 1}\right)$$

Cross-divide as needed.

$$(w + 1)(w + 1)\left(\frac{3}{w + 1}\right) = 3(w + 1)$$

13. **(A)** Transform $25^{\frac{3}{4}}$ to $(5^2)^{\frac{3}{4}}$, which equals $5^{\frac{6}{4}} = 5^{\frac{3}{2}}$.

When a number is raised to a rational power, the numerator serves as the power of the number and the denominator is its root. Therefore, raise 5 to the third power and find the square root of that quantity.

$$\sqrt{5^3} = \sqrt{125} = 5\sqrt{5}$$

Choices (B) and (C) are incorrect because $25^{\frac{3}{4}}$ transforms to a square root, not a cube root. Choice (D) is incorrect because it multiplies 25 by $\frac{3}{2}$ rather than raising it to the $\frac{3}{4}$ power.

14. **(B)** Verify the accuracy of the statements.

I. An increase in temperature Celsius is equivalent to an increase of 1.8 degrees Fahrenheit.

Use $C = 1$ and $C = 2$

$$\frac{9}{5}(1) + 32 = 33.8$$

$$\frac{9}{5}(2) + 32 = 35.6$$

$$35.6 - 33.8 = 1.8$$

Statement I is true.

II. A temperature of 5°F is equivalent to -15°C.

$$5 = \frac{9}{5}C + 32$$

$$-27 = \frac{9}{5}C$$

$$-15 = C$$

Statement II is correct.

III. A temperature of 20°C is equivalent to 62°F.

$$\frac{9}{5}(20) + 32 = 68$$

Statement III is incorrect. Statements I and II are correct and statement III is incorrect.

15. **(D)** Use long division to assess the equivalent statement.

$$
\begin{array}{r}
4 + \dfrac{22}{n-4} \\[4pt]
n-4\overline{)\,4n+6} \\[2pt]
\underline{4n-16} \\[2pt]
22
\end{array}
$$

$4 + \dfrac{22}{n-4}$ is equivalent to $\dfrac{4n+6}{n-4}$.

16. $\dfrac{1}{4}$ **or** $\dfrac{1}{2}$

Solve for m.

$$m^2 - 6m + 8 = 0$$
$$(m-4)(m-2) = 0$$
$$m - 4 = 0 \text{ or } m - 2 = 0$$
$$m = 4 \text{ or } m = 2$$

$\dfrac{1}{m}$ equals $\dfrac{1}{4}$ or $\dfrac{1}{2}$.

17. **5** Complete the square for both x and y:

$$x^2 + 6y + y^2 - 4x = 12$$
$$x^2 - 4x + y^2 + 6y = 12$$
$$x^2 - 4x + 4 + y^2 + 6y + 9 = 12 + 4 + 9$$
$$(x-2)^2 + (y+3)^2 = 25$$

The graphing form of a circle is $(x-h)^2 + (y-k)^2 = r^2$. Since $r^2 = 25$, $r = 5$.

18. **Answers may vary.** $0 \leq x < 8$

Solve the compound inequality by writing it as two separate inequalities.

$$-8 \leq 2x - 8 \qquad and \qquad 2x - 8 < 8$$
$$0 \leq 2x \qquad\qquad\qquad\qquad 2x < 16$$
$$0 \leq x \qquad\qquad\qquad\qquad\quad x < 8$$
$$0 \leq x < 8$$

19. **5** The median of a data set is the middle value when data are arranged in order. Array the number of lures sold; there are four $2 lures, five $5 lures, and three $10 lures.

$$2 \quad 2 \quad 2 \quad 2 \quad 5 \quad 5 \quad 5 \quad 5 \quad 5 \quad 10 \quad 10 \quad 10$$

The middle numbers are both 5's, so find their mean.

$$(5 + 5) \div 2 = 5$$

20. **4** There are two ways this question can be solved.

Method 1: System of equations.

Let x = questions answered correctly
Let y = questions answered incorrectly

There are 50 questions, so the first equation is $x + y = 50$. Since two points are deducted for each incorrect answer, we get $x - 2y = 38$. Solve by subtracting the equations.

$$x + y = 50$$
$$\underline{- (x - 2y = 38)}$$
$$3y = 12$$
$$y = 4$$

There were 4 incorrectly answered questions.

An alternate method to solve the problem is by using trial and error. Suppose 40 questions were answered correctly and 10 questions were answered incorrectly.

$40(1) - 10(2) = 20$; too many incorrect answers.

Try 48 questions answered correctly and 2 questions answered incorrectly.

$48(1) - 2(2) = 44$; too few questions answered incorrectly.

Try the correct answer 46 questions answered correctly and 4 questions answered incorrectly.

$$46(1) - 4(2) = 38$$

Section 4: Math Test (Calculator)

1. **(B)** Multiply both sides of the equation by $\frac{5}{3}$ to isolate x.

$$\left(\frac{5}{3}\right)\left(\frac{3x}{5}\right) = (12)\left(\frac{5}{3}\right)$$
$$x = 20$$

2. **(B)** Find the probability that the athlete will be a boy or a water polo member. Avoid double counting by subtracting the boys who are on the water polo team.

$$\text{boys: } \frac{28}{57} \qquad \text{water polo members: } \frac{31}{57}$$

$$\text{boys on the water polo team: } \frac{16}{57}$$

$$\frac{28}{57} + \frac{31}{57} - \frac{16}{57} = \frac{43}{57}$$

3. **(B)** From 2005 to 2006, there was a 100% growth (from 20 to 40). After 2006, however, the graph shows about a 5% increase per year.

4. **(C)** The graph indicates that approximately 40 bee farms were operating in 2006. Multiply 40 by 11,000 to find the 2006 yield of honey.

$$40 \times 11{,}000 = 440{,}000$$

5. **(D)** Use the formula $\frac{\text{rise}}{\text{run}}$ to find the slope of the linear function. As n increases by 1, $r(n)$ increases by 2. Thus, $r(n) = 2n + b$ with b representing the y-intercept. Input any of the points to calculate b.

$$(4, 5)$$
$$5 = 2(4) + b$$
$$5 = 8 + b$$
$$-3 = b$$
$$r(n) = 2n - 3$$

6. **(C)** Polynomials are added by combining like terms. Like terms have the same variable(s) raised to equivalent exponents.

$$\begin{array}{r} 4x^2 + 5x - 6 \\ + \ 3x^2 + \ x - 11 \\ \hline 7x^2 + 6x - 17 \end{array}$$

Note that when like terms are added, coefficients are combined but the exponents remain the same.

7. **(D)** Isolate n by multiplying both sides of the equation by $\frac{9}{5}$.

$$\frac{9}{5}\left(\frac{5}{9}n\right) = \left(\frac{7}{20}\right)\frac{9}{5}$$

$$n = \frac{63}{100}$$

8. **(C)** Some test takers may find that a plug-and-check strategy is best for them. If you solve the question correctly and quickly, using that method is fine. Here is the math needed to solve this equation. Multiply both sides of the equation by $x - 2$.

$$(x - 2)(x - 2) = \left(\frac{4}{x - 2}\right)(x - 2)$$

$$(x - 2)^2 = 4$$

Find the square root of both sides of the equation.

$$\sqrt{(x - 2)^2} = \sqrt{4}$$

$$x - 2 = \pm 2$$

$$x = 4 \qquad x = 0$$

Check for extraneous solutions.

$$0 - 2 = \frac{4}{0 - 2}$$

$$-2 = -2$$

$$4 - 2 = \frac{4}{4 - 2}$$

$$2 = 2$$

Neither 4 nor 0 is an extraneous solution. So both 4 and 0 are solutions to the equation.

9. **(D)** Use the proportion $\frac{\text{distance}}{\text{time}} = \frac{\text{distance}}{\text{time}}$ to find how far Gina will run in 2.4 minutes. Since the original ratio is stated in seconds, convert 2.4 minutes into seconds. 2.4 minutes $= 2.4(60) = 144$ seconds.

$$\frac{28}{4.7} = \frac{n}{144}$$

$$4.7n = (144)(28)$$

$$4.7n = 4,032$$

$$n \approx 858$$

10. **(A)** The percent of the U.S. budget was .1% in 1958. By 1963, the percentage of the U.S. budget rose to 2.28%. Use the formula $\frac{\text{increase}}{\text{original}} = \frac{n}{100}$ to find the percent increase. Increase $= 2.28 - .1 = 2.18$

$$\frac{2.18}{.1} = \frac{n}{100}$$

$$218 = .1n$$

$$n = 2,180\%$$

Choice (A), 2,200%, is the closest to this figure.

11. **(D)** U.S. spending in 1962 was $106,821,000,000. The NASA budget in 1958 was $89,000,000. Divide 106,821,000 by 89,000,000 to calculate how many times larger the 1962 U.S. spending was than the 1958 NASA budget.

$$106,821,000,000 \div 89,000,000 = 1,200.23$$

Choice (D), 1,200, is the closest.

12. **(D)** Use $7500(.954)^{3.5}$ to represent the depreciated value of the artwork. Each year the piece loses 4.6% of its value, so place $1 - .046$ in the parentheses, which simplifies to .954. Show 3.5 years of compounding decline by placing 3.5 in the exponential position. Choices (B) and (C) can be eliminated immediately because each demonstrates growth, not depreciation.

13. **(A)** Five years after the three-year value is a total of eight years beyond the purchase date. Let $t = 8$

$$A = 7500(.954)^8 = \$5,145.75$$

14. **(C)** The study size, 250 per group, is large enough to conclude that the new early detection program is more effective than the standard procedure. However, since the new procedure compared its results to solely the standard procedure, no conclusion can be made about alternate procedures for early detection of skin cancer.

15. **(A)** From the graph, $g(2)$ yields a value of 2 while $f(2)$ yields a value of -2. In other words:

$$f(2) = -2$$
$$g(2) = 2$$

Thus, $f(2) + g(2) = -2 + 2 = 0$.

16. **(D)** Find the number of seconds in one year.

(365 days) $\times$ (24 hours in a day) $\times$ (60 minutes in an hour) $\times$ (60 seconds in a minute) = 31,536,000 seconds in one year

Next, find the product of 31,536,000 and 186,000 to find how many miles light travels in one year.

$$186,000 \times 31,536,000 = 5,860,000,000,000 \text{ (about 6 trillion miles)}$$

Multiply 5,860,000,000,000 by 8 to find the number of miles to Sirius.

$$5,860,000,000,000 \times 8 = 46.9 \text{ trillion}$$

Choice (D), 50 trillion, was the closest to this figure.

17. **(C)** Divide 186,000 miles by one billion. Scientific notation will facilitate this process.

$$\frac{1.86 \times 10^5}{1 \times 10^9} = 1.86 \times 10^{-4} = .000186$$

In one billionth of a second, light travels .000186 miles. Multiply .000186 by 5,280 feet, the number of feet in a mile.

$$.000186 \times 5,280 = .98 \text{ feet}$$

.98 feet is closest to choice (C), 1 foot.

18. **(B)** Ground speed is defined as air speed $\pm$ wind speed. If there is no wind, then the ground speed is the air speed because $500 \pm 0 = 500$.

$$C(500) = 100 + \frac{500}{10} + \frac{36,000}{500} = 222$$

19. **(D)** The line of best fit predicts 450 Garibaldi would be counted per cubic mile in August. The actual number that was counted, however, was 400. Find the difference by subtracting 400 from 450.

$$450 - 400 = 50$$

20. **(D)** If n is the largest of the three numbers, then $780 - n$ is the sum of the other two. Since n is 50% greater than the sum of the smaller numbers, we arrive at:

$$n = 1.5(780 - n)$$
$$n = 1170 - 1.5n$$
$$2.5n = 1170$$
$$n = 468$$
$$(.6)(780) = 468$$

21. **(A)** Since the angles are complementary and $\sin(m°) = \cos(n°)$, it follows from the complementary angle property of sines and cosines that $m + n = 90$. Substituting $3x - 12$ for m and $6x - 18$ for n gives $(3x - 12) + (6x - 18) = 90$, which simplifies to $9x - 30 = 90$. Therefore, $9x = 120$, and $x = 13.\overline{3}$.

22. **(B)** Let x equal the number of students in the chemistry class. When providing 8 milliliters per student we get $m = 8x + 6$. This reflects the fact that 6 milliliters are left over from the jar containing m milliliters. When Ms. Garcia wished to provide 10 milliliters per student, she required an additional 16 milliliters to ensure each student had the same amount. This situation is represented by the equation $m = 10x - 16$. Since $8x + 6$ and $10x - 16$ both equal m, set each expression equal to one another.

$$10x - 16 = 8x + 6$$
$$2x = 22$$
$$x = 11$$

There are 11 students in Ms. Garcia's chemistry class.

23. **(D)** Find the volume of the cylinder and the cone and add 10% to that sum.
Volume of a cylinder, $\pi r^2 h$: $\pi(8^2)(12) = 2{,}412$

Volume of a cone, $\frac{1}{3}\pi r^2 h = \frac{1}{3}\pi(8^2)(8) = 536$

Add the two quantities to find the volume of the silo.

$$2{,}412 + 536 = 2{,}948$$

The farmer needs 10% more space so find 10% of 2,948 and add it to 2,948.

$$2{,}948 + (.10)(2{,}948) = 3{,}243$$

Once the volume of the silo has been determined to be 2,948 you don't need to finish the calculation. Only choice (D), 3,243, is larger than 2,948.

24. **(B)** In order for the line containing $(6, m)$ and $(m, 54)$ to pass through the origin, each point must share the slope that connects it to the origin. Use the formula $\frac{\text{rise}}{\text{run}}$ for both points and set the quantities equal.

$$\frac{m}{6} = \frac{54}{m}$$

Cross-multiply and solve for m.

$$m^2 = 324$$
$$m = 18 \text{ or } m = -18$$

Although both 18 and -18 are solutions to the equation, only 18 was provided as an answer choice.

25. **(D)** Find the slope of $f(x)$ by selecting values from the table, such as $(-2, -2.2)$ and $(0, -3)$.

$$m = \frac{-3 - (-2.2)}{0 - (-2)} = -0.4$$

The table shows the coordinates $(0, -3)$, which means that the y-intercept is -3. Thus, the linear function f is defined as $f(x) = -.4x - 3$.

Substitute 8 for x.

$$f(8) = -.4(8) - 3$$
$$f(8) = -6.2$$

26. **(B)** Calculate the length of the diameter by first finding the radius. Use completing the square to transform the equation from standard form to graphing form.

$$x^2 + y^2 - 12x + 3y = -7$$
$$x^2 - 12x \quad + y^2 + 3y \quad = -7$$
$$x^2 - 12x + 36 + y^2 + 3y + \frac{9}{4} = -7 + 36 + \frac{9}{4}$$
$$(x-6)^2 + \left(y + \frac{3}{2}\right)^2 = \frac{125}{4}$$

The graphing form of a circle is $(x-h)^2 + (y-k)^2 = r^2$ in which (h, k) are the coordinates of the center and r is the length of the radius. Find r.

$$r^2 = \frac{125}{4}$$
$$r = \frac{5\sqrt{5}}{2}$$

Multiply the radius by 2 to find the measure of the diameter.

$$d = (2)\left(\frac{5\sqrt{5}}{2}\right) = 5\sqrt{5}$$

27. **(C)** The vertex, or graphing, form of a parabola shows the vertex. Because the leading coefficient of $g(x) = (x+4)(x-8)$ is positive, the parabola opens up and its vertex is a minimum. Follow these steps to transform the equation from factored form to vertex form.

$$g(x) = (x+4)(x-8)$$
$$g(x) = x^2 - 4x - 32$$
$$g(x) = x^2 - 4x \quad - 32$$
$$g(x) = x^2 - 4x + 4 - 32 - 4$$
$$g(x) = (x-2)^2 - 36$$

The vertex of $g(x) = (x+4)(x-8)$ is $(2, -36)$.

28. **(B)** Begin isolating x by raising both sides of the equation to the sixth power.

$$2x^{\frac{2}{3}} = 6^{\frac{1}{2}}$$
$$(2x^{\frac{2}{3}})^6 = (6^{\frac{1}{2}})6$$
$$64x^4 = 6^3$$
$$64x^4 = 216$$

Divide both sides of the equation by 64.

$$\frac{64x^4}{64} = \frac{216}{64}$$
$$x^4 = \frac{27}{8}$$

Raise both sides of the equation to the $\frac{1}{4}$th power.

$$(x^4)^{\frac{1}{4}} = \left(\frac{27}{8}\right)^{\frac{1}{4}}$$
$$x = \left(\frac{27}{8}\right)^{\frac{1}{4}}$$

29. **(A)** Find the average of x, y, and z by calculating their sum and dividing by 3.

$$\frac{(2p + 12) + (5p + 18) + (8p - 6)}{3} = \frac{15p + 24}{3} = 5p + 8$$

30. **(C)** Find the percent increase of hits from 2015 to 2016.

$$\frac{\text{increase}}{\text{original}} = \frac{x}{100}$$

Find the increase from 2015 to 2016.

$$3{,}230 - 2{,}150 = 1{,}080$$

$$\frac{1{,}080}{2{,}150} = \frac{x}{100}$$

$$x = 50.2\%$$

Steve believes the 50.2% increase is triple the projected increase from 2016 to 2017. Thus, divide 50.2% by 3 to get the expected increase from those years.

$$50.2\% \div 3 = 16.7\%$$

Multiply the 2016 figure by 1.167 to find the expected hits on the website in 2017.

$$3{,}230 \times 1.167 = 3{,}769$$

Choice (C), 3,770, is the closest to this answer.

31. **3 or 4** Subtract $18 from $51 and $62 to find the amount of money Kara may have spent on belts.

$$51 - 18 = 33$$

$$62 - 18 = 44$$

Kara may have spent between $33 and $44 for belts. Given that each belt cost $11, Kara could have purchased 3 or 4 belts.

32. **3** Multiply $2x^2 + 4x - 2$ by 3.

$$3(2x^2 + 4x - 2) = 6x^2 + 12x - 6$$

Subtract $6x^2 + 12x - 6$ from $-8x^2 + 15x - 2$.

$$(-8x^2 + 15x - 2) - (6x^2 + 12x - 6) = -14x^2 + 3x + 4$$

$3x$ represents the bx term in $ax^2 + bx + c$ so $b = 3$.

33. **$\frac{3}{8}$ or .375** The shaded area has a central angle that measures 135°. Therefore, the shaded area is $\frac{135}{360}$ of the circle. Reduce $\frac{135}{360}$ to $\frac{3}{8}$ or express it as the decimal .375.

34. **4.4** Find the total points amassed by the first 12 reviews by multiplying 12 by the 4.3, the average review.

$$12 \times 4.3 = 51.6$$

Add 10 to 51.6 to include the two additional 5-star reviews.

$$51.6 + 10 = 61.6$$

Divide 61.6 by 14, the total number of reviewers.

$$61.6 \div 14 = 4.4$$

35. **275** After his initial deposit, Terrence made fixed monthly deposits. Consider the initial deposit to have occurred in month zero, prior to the start of the monthly deposits.

$$\text{Let } m = 0$$
$$A = 25(0) + 275$$
$$A = 275$$

Terrence made an initial deposit of $275.

36. **2** Substitute either $(2, 7)$ or $(-3, 37)$ for x and y and solve for a.

$$7 = (a)(2)^2 - (4)(2) + 7$$
$$7 = 4a - 8 + 7$$
$$8 = 4a$$
$$2 = a$$

37. **1.66 or 1.67 or $\frac{5}{3}$** Input 80% for v into the formula of special relativity.

$$F(t) = \frac{t}{\sqrt{1 - v^2}}$$
$$F(1) = \frac{1}{\sqrt{1 - .8^2}} = 1.\overline{66}$$

38. **.866** Input 1 and 2 for t and $F(t)$, respectively, into the special relativity formula.

$$F(t) = \frac{t}{\sqrt{1 - v^2}}$$
$$2 = \frac{1}{\sqrt{1 - v^2}}$$
$$2(\sqrt{1 - v^2}) = 1$$
$$\sqrt{1 - v^2} = .5$$
$$(\sqrt{1 - v^2})^2 = (.5)^2$$
$$1 - v^2 = .25$$
$$-v^2 = -.75$$
$$v = .866$$

ANSWER SHEET
Practice Test 6

Section 1: Reading

1. Ⓐ Ⓑ Ⓒ Ⓓ
2. Ⓐ Ⓑ Ⓒ Ⓓ
3. Ⓐ Ⓑ Ⓒ Ⓓ
4. Ⓐ Ⓑ Ⓒ Ⓓ
5. Ⓐ Ⓑ Ⓒ Ⓓ
6. Ⓐ Ⓑ Ⓒ Ⓓ
7. Ⓐ Ⓑ Ⓒ Ⓓ
8. Ⓐ Ⓑ Ⓒ Ⓓ
9. Ⓐ Ⓑ Ⓒ Ⓓ
10. Ⓐ Ⓑ Ⓒ Ⓓ
11. Ⓐ Ⓑ Ⓒ Ⓓ
12. Ⓐ Ⓑ Ⓒ Ⓓ
13. Ⓐ Ⓑ Ⓒ Ⓓ

14. Ⓐ Ⓑ Ⓒ Ⓓ
15. Ⓐ Ⓑ Ⓒ Ⓓ
16. Ⓐ Ⓑ Ⓒ Ⓓ
17. Ⓐ Ⓑ Ⓒ Ⓓ
18. Ⓐ Ⓑ Ⓒ Ⓓ
19. Ⓐ Ⓑ Ⓒ Ⓓ
20. Ⓐ Ⓑ Ⓒ Ⓓ
21. Ⓐ Ⓑ Ⓒ Ⓓ
22. Ⓐ Ⓑ Ⓒ Ⓓ
23. Ⓐ Ⓑ Ⓒ Ⓓ
24. Ⓐ Ⓑ Ⓒ Ⓓ
25. Ⓐ Ⓑ Ⓒ Ⓓ
26. Ⓐ Ⓑ Ⓒ Ⓓ

27. Ⓐ Ⓑ Ⓒ Ⓓ
28. Ⓐ Ⓑ Ⓒ Ⓓ
29. Ⓐ Ⓑ Ⓒ Ⓓ
30. Ⓐ Ⓑ Ⓒ Ⓓ
31. Ⓐ Ⓑ Ⓒ Ⓓ
32. Ⓐ Ⓑ Ⓒ Ⓓ
33. Ⓐ Ⓑ Ⓒ Ⓓ
34. Ⓐ Ⓑ Ⓒ Ⓓ
35. Ⓐ Ⓑ Ⓒ Ⓓ
36. Ⓐ Ⓑ Ⓒ Ⓓ
37. Ⓐ Ⓑ Ⓒ Ⓓ
38. Ⓐ Ⓑ Ⓒ Ⓓ
39. Ⓐ Ⓑ Ⓒ Ⓓ

40. Ⓐ Ⓑ Ⓒ Ⓓ
41. Ⓐ Ⓑ Ⓒ Ⓓ
42. Ⓐ Ⓑ Ⓒ Ⓓ
43. Ⓐ Ⓑ Ⓒ Ⓓ
44. Ⓐ Ⓑ Ⓒ Ⓓ
45. Ⓐ Ⓑ Ⓒ Ⓓ
46. Ⓐ Ⓑ Ⓒ Ⓓ
47. Ⓐ Ⓑ Ⓒ Ⓓ
48. Ⓐ Ⓑ Ⓒ Ⓓ
49. Ⓐ Ⓑ Ⓒ Ⓓ
50. Ⓐ Ⓑ Ⓒ Ⓓ
51. Ⓐ Ⓑ Ⓒ Ⓓ
52. Ⓐ Ⓑ Ⓒ Ⓓ

Section 2: Writing and Language

1. Ⓐ Ⓑ Ⓒ Ⓓ
2. Ⓐ Ⓑ Ⓒ Ⓓ
3. Ⓐ Ⓑ Ⓒ Ⓓ
4. Ⓐ Ⓑ Ⓒ Ⓓ
5. Ⓐ Ⓑ Ⓒ Ⓓ
6. Ⓐ Ⓑ Ⓒ Ⓓ
7. Ⓐ Ⓑ Ⓒ Ⓓ
8. Ⓐ Ⓑ Ⓒ Ⓓ
9. Ⓐ Ⓑ Ⓒ Ⓓ
10. Ⓐ Ⓑ Ⓒ Ⓓ
11. Ⓐ Ⓑ Ⓒ Ⓓ

12. Ⓐ Ⓑ Ⓒ Ⓓ
13. Ⓐ Ⓑ Ⓒ Ⓓ
14. Ⓐ Ⓑ Ⓒ Ⓓ
15. Ⓐ Ⓑ Ⓒ Ⓓ
16. Ⓐ Ⓑ Ⓒ Ⓓ
17. Ⓐ Ⓑ Ⓒ Ⓓ
18. Ⓐ Ⓑ Ⓒ Ⓓ
19. Ⓐ Ⓑ Ⓒ Ⓓ
20. Ⓐ Ⓑ Ⓒ Ⓓ
21. Ⓐ Ⓑ Ⓒ Ⓓ
22. Ⓐ Ⓑ Ⓒ Ⓓ

23. Ⓐ Ⓑ Ⓒ Ⓓ
24. Ⓐ Ⓑ Ⓒ Ⓓ
25. Ⓐ Ⓑ Ⓒ Ⓓ
26. Ⓐ Ⓑ Ⓒ Ⓓ
27. Ⓐ Ⓑ Ⓒ Ⓓ
28. Ⓐ Ⓑ Ⓒ Ⓓ
29. Ⓐ Ⓑ Ⓒ Ⓓ
30. Ⓐ Ⓑ Ⓒ Ⓓ
31. Ⓐ Ⓑ Ⓒ Ⓓ
32. Ⓐ Ⓑ Ⓒ Ⓓ
33. Ⓐ Ⓑ Ⓒ Ⓓ

34. Ⓐ Ⓑ Ⓒ Ⓓ
35. Ⓐ Ⓑ Ⓒ Ⓓ
36. Ⓐ Ⓑ Ⓒ Ⓓ
37. Ⓐ Ⓑ Ⓒ Ⓓ
38. Ⓐ Ⓑ Ⓒ Ⓓ
39. Ⓐ Ⓑ Ⓒ Ⓓ
40. Ⓐ Ⓑ Ⓒ Ⓓ
41. Ⓐ Ⓑ Ⓒ Ⓓ
42. Ⓐ Ⓑ Ⓒ Ⓓ
43. Ⓐ Ⓑ Ⓒ Ⓓ
44. Ⓐ Ⓑ Ⓒ Ⓓ

Section 3: Math (No Calculator)

1. Ⓐ Ⓑ Ⓒ Ⓓ   5. Ⓐ Ⓑ Ⓒ Ⓓ   9. Ⓐ Ⓑ Ⓒ Ⓓ   13. Ⓐ Ⓑ Ⓒ Ⓓ
2. Ⓐ Ⓑ Ⓒ Ⓓ   6. Ⓐ Ⓑ Ⓒ Ⓓ   10. Ⓐ Ⓑ Ⓒ Ⓓ   14. Ⓐ Ⓑ Ⓒ Ⓓ
3. Ⓐ Ⓑ Ⓒ Ⓓ   7. Ⓐ Ⓑ Ⓒ Ⓓ   11. Ⓐ Ⓑ Ⓒ Ⓓ   15. Ⓐ Ⓑ Ⓒ Ⓓ
4. Ⓐ Ⓑ Ⓒ Ⓓ   8. Ⓐ Ⓑ Ⓒ Ⓓ   12. Ⓐ Ⓑ Ⓒ Ⓓ

16.

17.

18.

19.

20.

ANSWER SHEET
Practice Test 6

Section 4: Math (Calculator)

1. Ⓐ Ⓑ Ⓒ Ⓓ 9. Ⓐ Ⓑ Ⓒ Ⓓ 17. Ⓐ Ⓑ Ⓒ Ⓓ 25. Ⓐ Ⓑ Ⓒ Ⓓ
2. Ⓐ Ⓑ Ⓒ Ⓓ 10. Ⓐ Ⓑ Ⓒ Ⓓ 18. Ⓐ Ⓑ Ⓒ Ⓓ 26. Ⓐ Ⓑ Ⓒ Ⓓ
3. Ⓐ Ⓑ Ⓒ Ⓓ 11. Ⓐ Ⓑ Ⓒ Ⓓ 19. Ⓐ Ⓑ Ⓒ Ⓓ 27. Ⓐ Ⓑ Ⓒ Ⓓ
4. Ⓐ Ⓑ Ⓒ Ⓓ 12. Ⓐ Ⓑ Ⓒ Ⓓ 20. Ⓐ Ⓑ Ⓒ Ⓓ 28. Ⓐ Ⓑ Ⓒ Ⓓ
5. Ⓐ Ⓑ Ⓒ Ⓓ 13. Ⓐ Ⓑ Ⓒ Ⓓ 21. Ⓐ Ⓑ Ⓒ Ⓓ 29. Ⓐ Ⓑ Ⓒ Ⓓ
6. Ⓐ Ⓑ Ⓒ Ⓓ 14. Ⓐ Ⓑ Ⓒ Ⓓ 22. Ⓐ Ⓑ Ⓒ Ⓓ 30. Ⓐ Ⓑ Ⓒ Ⓓ
7. Ⓐ Ⓑ Ⓒ Ⓓ 15. Ⓐ Ⓑ Ⓒ Ⓓ 23. Ⓐ Ⓑ Ⓒ Ⓓ
8. Ⓐ Ⓑ Ⓒ Ⓓ 16. Ⓐ Ⓑ Ⓒ Ⓓ 24. Ⓐ Ⓑ Ⓒ Ⓓ

31. 32. 33. 34.

35. 36. 37. 38.

1   1   1

Practice Test 6

READING TEST

65 MINUTES, 52 QUESTIONS

Turn to Section 1 of your answer sheet to answer the questions in this section.

DIRECTIONS: Following each of the passages (or pairs of passages) below are questions about the passage (or passages). Read each passage carefully. Then, select the best answer for each question based on what is stated in the passage (or passages) and in any graphics that may accompany the passage.

Questions 1– 11 are based on the following passages.

Passage 1 is from "Hotspots: Mantle Thermal Plumes" in *This Dynamic Earth: The Story of Plate Tectonics* by Jacqueline Kious and Robert I. Tilling, U.S. Geological Survey, 1996.

Passage 2 is from "Scientists Locate Deep Origins of Hawaiian Hotspots," press release 09-232, December 3, 2009, National Science Foundation.

PASSAGE 1

The vast majority of earthquakes and volcanic eruptions occur near tectonic plate boundaries, but there are some exceptions. For example, the Hawaiian Islands, which are entirely of volcanic
(5) origin, have formed in the middle of the Pacific Ocean more than 3,200 km from the nearest plate boundary. How do the Hawaiian Islands and other volcanoes that form in the interior of plates fit into the plate-tectonics picture?
(10) In 1963, J. Tuzo Wilson came up with an ingenious idea that became known as the "hotspot" theory. Wilson noted that in certain locations around the world, such as Hawaii, volcanism has been active for very long periods

(15) of time. This could only happen, he reasoned, if relatively small, long-lasting, and exceptionally hot regions—called hotspots—existed below the plates that would provide localized sources of high heat energy (thermal plumes) to sus-
(20) tain volcanism. Wilson hypothesized that the distinctive linear shape of the Hawaiian Island-Emperor Seamounts chain resulted from the Pacific Plate moving over a deep, stationary hotspot in the mantle, located beneath the
(25) present-day position of the Island of Hawaii. Heat from this hotspot produced a persistent source of magma by partly melting the overriding Pacific Plate. The magma, which is lighter than the surrounding solid rock, then rises
(30) through the mantle and crust to erupt onto the seafloor, forming an active seamount. Over time, countless eruptions cause the seamount to grow until it finally emerges above sea level to form an island volcano. Continuing plate move-
(35) ment eventually carries the island beyond the hotspot, cutting it off from the magma source, and volcanism ceases. As one island volcano becomes extinct, another develops over the hotspot, and the cycle is repeated. This process

(40) of volcano growth and death, over many millions of years, has left a long trail of volcanic islands and seamounts across the Pacific Ocean floor.

According to Wilson's hotspot theory, the (45) volcanoes of the Hawaiian chain should get progressively older and become more eroded the farther they travel beyond the hotspot. The oldest volcanic rocks on Kauai, the northwesternmost inhabited Hawaiian island, are (50) about 5.5 million years old and are deeply eroded. By comparison, on the "Big Island" of Hawaii—southeasternmost in the chain—the oldest exposed rocks are less than 0.7 million years old and new volcanic rock is continually (55) being formed.

PASSAGE 2

The Hawaiian Islands are one of the outstanding volcanic features on Earth, but their origins have been shrouded in mystery. Still in debate has been a theory proposed 40 years ago, which (60) states that mid-tectonic plate hotspots such as Hawaii are generated by upwelling plumes of lava from the base of Earth's lower mantle.

A team of scientists put the theory to the test. They deployed a large network of sea-floor (65) seismometers in Hawaii, through an expedition called the Plume-Lithosphere Undersea Melt Experiment (PLUME), opening up a window into the Earth. PLUME allowed scientists to obtain the best picture yet of a mantle plume (70) originating from the lower mantle, and revealed Hawaii's deep roots.

"The hypothesis that hotspots like Hawaii originate from mantle plumes is one of the longest-standing and most controversial top-(75) ics in geology," says Dr. Robert Detrick. "This experiment combining large numbers of broadband seismometers on the seafloor with instruments on land has provided the most persuasive evidence yet for the existence of a mantle (80) plume extending into the lower mantle beneath Hawaii."

The project involved four oceanographic research cruises to deploy and recover ocean bottom seismometers at 73 sites, and a concur-(85) rent deployment of land seismometers on the main Hawaiian Islands. The large seafloor network yielded unprecedented results in a remote oceanic region. The seismometers were used to record the timing of seismic shear waves from (90) large earthquakes around the world. This information was used to determine whether seismic waves travel more slowly through hot rock as they pass beneath Hawaii.

Combining the timing measurements from (95) earthquakes recorded on many seismometers allowed scientists to construct a sophisticated 3-dimensional image of the Hawaiian mantle. In the upper mantle, the Hawaiian Islands are underlain by low shear-wave velocities, linked (100) with hotter-than-average material from an upwelling plume. Low velocities continue down into the Earth's transition zone, at 410 to 660 km depth, and extend even deeper into the Earth's lower mantle down to at least 1,500 km depth.

(105) The location of the Hawaiian Islands in the middle of the Pacific Ocean had hampered past efforts to resolve its deep structure. Seismometer deployments limited to land sites on the islands did not provide sufficient coverage for high-(110) resolution imaging, and Hawaii is also far from the most active circum-Pacific zones of earthquakes. Therefore, scientists turned to a more technologically challenging, marine approach by placing temporary instrumentation on the (115) seafloor to record seismic waves.

Results of the project make a strong case for the existence of a deep mantle plume.

1. Passage 1 provides information explaining all of the following *except*

   (A) the process by which an island is formed over a hotspot
   (B) the cause of hotspots
   (C) why volcanic rocks on Kauai are deeply eroded, whereas those on the Big Island are not
   (D) why the volcanoes of the Hawaiian chain become progressively older as one moves north along the chain

2. According to J. Tuzo Wilson's "hotspot" theory, the fact that volcanic rock is regularly being formed on the "Big Island" suggests that

   (A) the "Big Island" is situated over a hotspot
   (B) the reason that the "Big Island" is larger than the other islands in the Hawaiian Island chain is that it alone was formed as a result of a hotspot
   (C) volcanism is a relatively recent phenomenon on the "Big Island"
   (D) the Pacific Plate is much nearer to the ocean surface in the area of the "Big Island" than it is in the areas of the other Hawaiian Islands

3. Which of the following is true about J. Tuzo Wilson's "hotspot" theory?

   (A) There is no place in it for the mechanism of plate tectonics.
   (B) It incorporates some features of plate tectonics but largely supersedes it as a theory explaining the cause of volcanoes around the world.
   (C) It envisions hotspots as occurring only in the area of the Hawaiian Island-Emperor Seamounts chain.
   (D) It does not claim to explain the origin of all volcanoes in the world.

4. Which of the following sequences best describes the chronological order of the thought process by which J. Tuzo Wilson most likely came up with the "hotspot" theory?

   (A) observation, deduction, formation of hypothesis
   (B) observation, induction, formation of hypothesis
   (C) observation, formation of hypothesis, testing of hypothesis
   (D) formation of hypothesis, deduction, observation

5. According to the "hotspot" theory, the reason that some Hawaiian Islands are older than other Hawaiian Islands is that

   (A) hotspots move steadily below the Earth's crust, creating island volcanoes at different times
   (B) the Pacific tectonic plate continuously moves, causing one island volcano to form over a hotspot, then another, and so on
   (C) erosion has worn away much of the material from the older islands, such as Kauai
   (D) there are several hotspots, of varying ages, below the Pacific tectonic plate in the area of the Hawaiian Islands; the oldest islands were created by the oldest hotspots and the youngest islands were created by the youngest hotspots

6. Which choice provides the best evidence for the answer to the previous question?

   (A) "For . . . picture?" (lines 3–9)
   (B) "Wilson . . . volcanism" (lines 10–14)
   (C) "The . . . volcano." (lines 28–34)
   (D) "Continuing . . . repeated." (lines 34–39)

7. In line 67, the word *window* is used

(A) hyperbolically
(B) literally
(C) ironically
(D) metaphorically

8. It can be inferred that the earthquakes mentioned in line 95

(A) were caused by the eruption of volcanoes in the Hawaiian Islands
(B) were caused by mid-tectonic hotspots
(C) were largely or entirely unrelated to geological activity on or near the Hawaiian Islands
(D) occurred simultaneously

9. The word *resolve* as it is used in line 107 most nearly means

(A) speculate about
(B) to render visible and distinct
(C) scientifically establish the facts about
(D) solve

10. Both passages are primarily concerned with the question of

(A) what causes deep mantle plumes
(B) what causes volcanic islands to form in the middle of tectonic plates
(C) what caused volcanism to occur in the area of the Hawaiian Islands
(D) what caused the "Big Island" of Hawaii to form

11. Which best describes the relationship between Passage 1 and Passage 2?

(A) Passage 1 describes a theory in detail and provides some evidence for it; Passage 2 describes two experiments that have been done to test the theory described in Passage 1.
(B) Passage 1 describes two competing theories and the evidence for one of them; Passage 2 evaluates the two theories described in Passage 1 and reaches a conclusion about which one is better supported by the evidence.
(C) Passage 1 describes the main geological processes involved in creating the Hawaiian Islands; Passage 2 describes an experiment done to gather information about these processes.
(D) Passage 1 describes a theory in considerable detail and provides some evidence for it; Passage 2 describes an experiment that produced good evidence supporting the theory described in Passage 1.

1 1 1

Questions 12–21 are based on the following passage.

This passage is from W. E. B. Du Bois, *The Souls of Black Folk*, originally published in 1903.

Being a problem is a strange experience,—
peculiar even for one who has never been
anything else, save perhaps in babyhood and in
Europe. It is in the early days of rollicking boy-
(5) hood that the revelation first bursts upon one,
all in a day, as it were. I remember well when
the shadow swept across me. I was a little thing,
away up in the hills of New England, where the
dark Housatonic winds between Hoosac and
(10) Taghkanic to the sea. In a wee wooden school-
house, something put it into the boys' and girls'
heads to buy gorgeous visiting-cards—ten cents
a package—and exchange. The exchange was
merry, till one girl, a tall newcomer, refused my
(15) card,—refused it peremptorily, with a glance.
Then it dawned upon me with a certain sud-
denness that I was different from the others;
or like, mayhap, in heart and life and longing,
but shut out from their world by a vast veil. I
(20) had thereafter no desire to tear down that veil,
to creep through; I held all beyond it in common contempt, and lived above it in a region
of blue sky and great wandering shadows. That
sky was bluest when I could beat my mates at
(25) examination-time, or beat them at a foot-race,
or even beat their stringy heads. Alas, with the
years all this fine contempt began to fade; for
the words I longed for, and all their dazzling
opportunities, were theirs, not mine. But they
(30) should not keep these prizes, I said; some, all,
I would wrest from them. Just how I would do
it I could never decide: by reading law, by healing the sick, by telling the wonderful tales that
swam in my head,—some way. With other black

(35) boys the strife was not so fiercely sunny: their
youth shrunk into tasteless sycophancy, or into
silent hatred of the pale world about them and
mocking distrust of everything white; or wasted
itself in a bitter cry, Why did God make me an
(40) outcast and a stranger in mine own house? The
shades of the prison-house closed round about
us all: walls strait and stubborn to the whitest,
but relentlessly narrow, tall, and unscalable to
sons of night who must plod darkly on in res-
(45) ignation, or beat unavailing palms against the
stone, or steadily, half hopelessly, watch the
streak of blue above.

After the Egyptian and Indian, the Greek
and Roman, the Teuton and Mongolian, the
(50) Negro is a sort of seventh son, born with a veil,
and gifted with second-sight in this American
world,—a world which yields him no true self-
consciousness, but only lets him see himself
through the revelation of the other world. It is a
(55) peculiar sensation, this double-consciousness,
this sense of always looking at one's self through
the eyes of others, of measuring one's soul by
the tape of a world that looks on in amused contempt and pity. One ever feels his twoness,—an
(60) American, a Negro; two souls, two thoughts,
two unreconciled strivings; two warring ideals
in one dark body, whose dogged strength alone
keeps it from being torn asunder.

The history of the American Negro is the
(65) history of this strife,—this longing to attain
self-conscious manhood, to merge his double
self into a better and truer self. In this merging
he wishes neither of the older selves to be lost.
He would not Africanize America, for America
(70) has too much to teach the world and Africa. He
would not bleach his Negro soul in a flood of
white Americanism, for he knows that Negro

blood has a message for the world. He simply wishes to make it possible for a man to be both
(75) a Negro and an American, without being cursed and spit upon by his fellows, without having the doors of Opportunity closed roughly in his face.

This, then, is the end of his striving: to be a co-worker in the kingdom of culture, to escape
(80) both death and isolation, to husband and use his best powers and his latent genius.

12. The word *revelation* in line 5 refers to

(A) the author's realization that despite their different skin color whites and blacks are fundamentally the same
(B) the author's realization that blacks are not part of the white people's world
(C) the author's learning that not everyone is kind
(D) the author's realization that he could beat his white classmates at examinations and in a foot-race

13. From his experience with the visiting-cards the narrator learns that

(A) as a black man he is fundamentally different from white people
(B) white people accept all blacks except him
(C) he is fundamentally the same as white people but separated from them by their attitudes toward blacks
(D) white boys but not white girls accept him

14. According to the narrator, the other black boys at his school

(A) were largely unaware of the attitude of white people toward blacks
(B) often reacted violently to their bad treatment by white people
(C) came to either kowtow to white people, hate the world of white people, or become bitter
(D) learned to accept that they were different and would never have the opportunities that white people did

15. Which choice provides the best evidence for the answer to the previous question?

(A) "It . . . were." (lines 4–6)
(B) "I . . . shadows." (lines 19–23)
(C) "With . . . house?" (lines 34–40)
(D) "The . . . above." (lines 40–47)

16. The author's use of the word *stubborn* in line 42 suggests that he believed that

(A) there were more obstacles for white people than there were for black people
(B) black people were, in general, more stubborn than white people in following the accepted way of thinking of the time
(C) white people were generally more stubborn than black people in following the accepted way of thinking of the time
(D) white people were confined by prevailing attitudes and limited opportunities, but could overcome these with sufficient effort

1   1   1

17. The phrase "second-sight" in line 51 refers to

(A) the unique ability of Negroes to visualize future events

(B) an awareness of the injustice of how the whites treat Negroes

(C) the whites' view of the world

(D) a mystical ability to perceive reality directly

18. The word *end* as it is used in line 78 most nearly means

(A) conclusion

(B) closing stages

(C) result

(D) goal

19. The author makes use of all of the following except

(A) rhetorical question

(B) symbolism

(C) anecdote

(D) appeal to authority

20. The most appropriate title of this passage would be

(A) Blacks Can Never Be Fully American

(B) Blacks Must Give Up Their Heritage to Be Truly American

(C) The Problem of Black Identity in America

(D) The Black Experience in America

21. Which of the following phrases is not used symbolically in the passage?

(A) "vast veil" (line 19)

(B) "blue sky" (line 23)

(C) "prison-house" (line 41)

(D) "latent genius" (line 81)

Questions 22– 31 are based on the following passage.

This passage is from Joseph Conrad, *Lord Jim*, originally published in 1917.

He was an inch, perhaps two, under six feet, powerfully built, and he advanced straight at you with a slight stoop of the shoulders, head forward, and a fixed from-under stare which
(5) made you think of a charging bull. His voice was deep, loud, and his manner displayed a kind of dogged self-assertion which had nothing aggressive in it. It seemed a necessity, and it was directed apparently as much at himself as
(10) at anybody else. He was spotlessly neat, appareled in immaculate white from shoes to hat, and in the various Eastern ports where he got his living as a ship-chandler's water-clerk he was very popular.
(15)   A water-clerk need not pass an examination in anything under the sun, but he must have Ability in the abstract and demonstrate it practically. His work consists in racing under sail, steam, or oars against other water-clerks
(20) for any ship about to anchor, greeting her captain cheerily, forcing upon him a card—the business card of the ship-chandler—and on his first visit on shore piloting him firmly but without ostentation to a vast, cavern-like shop
(25) which is full of things that are eaten and drunk on board ship; where you can get everything to make her seaworthy and beautiful, from a set of chain-hooks for her cable to a book of gold-leaf for the carvings of her stern; and where her
(30) commander is received like a brother by a ship-chandler he has never seen before. There is a cool parlor, easy-chairs, bottles, cigars, writing implements, a copy of harbor regulations, and a warmth of welcome that melts the salt of a three
(35) months' passage out of a seaman's heart. The connection thus begun is kept up, as long as the ship remains in harbor, by the daily visits of the water-clerk. To the captain he is faithful like a friend and attentive like a son, with the patience
(40) of Job, the unselfish devotion of a woman, and

the jollity of a boon companion. Later on the bill is sent in. It is a beautiful and humane occupation. Therefore good water-clerks are scarce. When a water-clerk who possesses Ability in (45) the abstract has also the advantage of having been brought up to the sea, he is worth to his employer a lot of money and some humoring. Jim had always good wages and as much humoring as would have bought the fidelity of (50) a fiend. Nevertheless, with black ingratitude he would throw up the job suddenly and depart. To his employers the reasons he gave were obviously inadequate. They said 'Confounded fool!' as soon as his back was turned. This was their (55) criticism on his exquisite sensibility.

To the white men in the waterside business and to the captains of ships he was just Jim—nothing more. He had, of course, another name, but he was anxious that it should not be (60) pronounced. His incognito, which had as many holes as a sieve, was not meant to hide a personality but a fact. When the fact broke through the incognito he would leave suddenly the seaport where he happened to be at the time and (65) go to another—generally farther east. He kept to seaports because he was a seaman in exile from the sea, and had Ability in the abstract, which is good for no other work but that of a water-clerk. He retreated in good order towards the rising (70) sun, and the fact followed him casually but inevitably. Thus in the course of years he was known successively in Bombay, in Calcutta, in Rangoon, in Penang, in Batavia—and in each of these halting-places was just Jim the water-(75) clerk. Afterwards, when his keen perception of

the Intolerable drove him away for good from seaports and white men, even into the virgin forest, the Malays of the jungle village, where he had elected to conceal his deplorable faculty, (80) added a word to the monosyllable of his incognito. They called him Tuan Jim: as one might say—Lord Jim.

22. The word *humoring* as it is used in lines 47–48 most nearly means

(A) amusing
(B) teasing
(C) entertaining
(D) indulging

23. The phrase "fidelity of a fiend" (lines 49–50) most nearly means

(A) loyalty of a devil
(B) faithfulness of a fanatic
(C) respect and love of a good woman
(D) devotion of a friend

24. Commenting on Jim's occupation, the author says "It is a beautiful and humane occupation. Therefore good water-clerks are scarce" (lines 42–43).

Which of the following words most accurately describes this comment?

(A) exaggerated
(B) tongue-in-cheek
(C) dryly humorous
(D) fatuous

25. Why does Jim regularly give up the job he has in a particular port and move to another port to take up a similar position?

    (A) He becomes tired of living under a false name.
    (B) A secret about him becomes known in the area.
    (C) He wants to advance his career.
    (D) When his real identity becomes known, people shower him with honors (such as calling him "Lord"), which he finds so embarrassing that he has to leave.

26. Which of the following lines provide the best evidence for the answer to the previous question?

    (A) "He . . . popular." (lines 1–14)
    (B) "Nevertheless . . . depart." (lines 50–51)
    (C) "When . . . east." (lines 62–65)
    (D) "Thus . . . water-clerk." (lines 71–75)

27. What does the author mean by "His incognito . . . had as many holes as a sieve" (lines 60–61)?

    (A) Jim often lets his real identity leak out deliberately.
    (B) Jim's false name was able to hide his real personality effectively because it was open to many interpretations.
    (C) Jim's false identity was able to keep "the fact" (line 62) but not his real name secret.
    (D) Jim's false identity did a poor job of keeping people from learning his real identity.

28. The "fact" mentioned in lines 62 and 70 most likely refers to

    (A) something disreputable that Jim did
    (B) Jim's real name
    (C) the fact that Jim had no formal qualification for the position of water-clerk
    (D) the fact that Jim had been exiled from the sea

29. According to the passage, Jim is

    (A) effeminate and extremely neat in appearance
    (B) lonely and aggressive
    (C) powerfully built and popular
    (D) academically gifted, especially in abstract subjects

30. Which of the following lines provides the best evidence for the answer to the previous question?

    (A) "His . . . it." (lines 5–8) and "To . . . companion." (lines 38–41)
    (B) "He . . . built" (lines 1–2) and "He . . . popular." (lines 10–14)
    (C) "Jim . . . fiend." (lines 48–50) and "To . . . more." (lines 56–58)
    (D) "When . . . humoring." (lines 44–48) and "He . . . pronounced." (lines 58–60)

31. The word *casually* as it is used in line 70 most nearly means

    (A) lazily
    (B) cautiously
    (C) unobtrusively
    (D) informally

Questions 32–41 are based on the following passage.

This passage is from Charles A. Eastman (Ohiyesa), *The Indian Today: The Past and Future of The First American*, originally published in 1915.

The original attitude of the American Indian toward the Eternal, the "Great Mystery" that surrounds and embraces us, was as simple as it was exalted. To him it was the supreme concep-
(5)   tion, bringing with it the fullest measure of joy and satisfaction possible in this life.

The worship of the "Great Mystery" was silent, solitary, free from all self-seeking. It was silent, because all speech is of necessity feeble
(10)   and imperfect; therefore the souls of my ancestors ascended to God in wordless adoration. It was solitary, because they believed that He is nearer to us in solitude, and there were no priests authorized to come between a man and
(15)   his Maker. None might exhort or confess or in any way meddle with the religious experience of another. Among us all men were created sons of God and stood erect, as conscious of their divinity. Our faith might not be formulated in
(20)   creeds, nor forced upon any who were unwilling to receive it; hence there was no preaching, proselytizing, nor persecution, neither were there any scoffers or atheists.

There were no temples or shrines among
(25)   us save those of nature. Being a natural man, the Indian was intensely poetical. He would deem it sacrilege to build a house for Him who may be met face to face in the mysterious, shadowy aisles of the primeval forest, or
(30)   on the sunlit bosom of virgin prairies, upon dizzy spires and pinnacles of naked rock, and yonder in the jeweled vault of the night sky! He who enrobes Himself in filmy veils of cloud,

there on the rim of the visible world where
(35)   our Great-Grandfather Sun kindles his evening camp-fire, He who rides upon the rigorous wind of the north, or breathes forth His spirit upon aromatic southern airs, whose war-canoe is launched upon majestic rivers and inland
(40)   seas—He needs no lesser cathedral!

That solitary communion with the Unseen which was the highest expression of our religious life is partly described in the word *bambeday*, literally "mysterious feeling," which has
(45)   been variously translated "fasting" and "dreaming." It may better be interpreted as "consciousness of the divine."

The first bambeday, or religious retreat, marked an epoch in the life of the youth. Having
(50)   first prepared himself by means of the purifying vapor-bath, and cast off as far as possible all human or fleshly influences, the young man sought out the noblest height, the most commanding summit in all the surrounding region.
(55)   Knowing that God sets no value upon material things, he took with him no offerings or sacrifices other than symbolic objects, such as paints and tobacco. Wishing to appear before Him in all humility, he wore no clothing save
(60)   his moccasins and loincloth. At the solemn hour of sunrise or sunset he took up his position, overlooking the glories of earth and facing the "Great Mystery," and there he remained, naked, erect, silent, and motionless, exposed
(65)   to the elements and forces of His arming, for a night and a day to two days and nights. In this holy trance or ecstasy the Indian mystic found his highest happiness and the motive power of his existence.

(70)   The native American has been generally despised by his white conquerors for his pov-

1   1   1

erty and simplicity. They forget, perhaps, that his religion forbade the accumulation of wealth and the enjoyment of luxury. To him, as to other
(75) single-minded men in every age and race, from Diogenes to the brothers of Saint Francis, the love of possessions has appeared a snare, and the burdens of a complex society a source of needless peril and temptation. Furthermore, it
(80) was the rule of his life to share the fruits of his skill and success with his less fortunate brothers. Thus he kept his spirit free from the clog of pride, cupidity, or envy, and carried out, as he believed, the divine decree—a matter pro-
(85) foundly important to him.

It was not, then, wholly from ignorance or improvidence that he failed to establish permanent towns and to develop a material civilization. To the untutored sage, the concentration
(90) of population was the prolific mother of all evils, moral no less than physical. He argued that food is good, while surfeit kills; that love is good, but lust destroys; and not less dreaded than the pestilence following upon crowded
(95) and unsanitary dwellings was the loss of spiritual power inseparable from too close contact with one's fellow men. All who have lived much out of doors know that there is a magnetic and nervous force that accumulates in solitude and
(100) that is quickly dissipated by life in a crowd; and even his enemies have recognized the fact that for a certain innate power and self-poise, wholly independent of circumstances, the American Indian is unsurpassed among men.

32. In lines 10–11 the author says, "the souls of my ancestors ascended to God in wordless adoration." What does he most likely mean by this?

(A) that the souls of his dead ancestors went to be with God in heaven
(B) that the souls of his dead ancestors could not communicate their experience of God to others upon their return from heaven
(C) that his dead ancestors worshipped God using no language and that their souls grew closer to God
(D) that no one can describe God because He is beyond human understanding

33. We can reasonably infer that the author uses the word *original* (line 1) to suggest that

(A) the early attitudes of American Indians toward the "Great Mystery" was not as truly spiritual as it later became
(B) the attitudes of American Indians toward the "Great Mystery" cannot be described in words
(C) the attitudes of American Indians toward the "Great Mystery" was very creative
(D) American Indians' view of the "Great Mystery" changed from what it was earlier

34. The most likely reason the author uses a variety of capitalized names for God is to

   (A) communicate the idea that God cannot be assigned any one name and that humans conceive of God in a variety of ways
   (B) show that American Indians' idea of God was not sophisticated
   (C) remind the reader that the word "God" is different in the languages of the various Indian tribes
   (D) convince the reader of his view that because American Indians had many different names for God they did not truly understand him

35. The second paragraph of the passage (lines 7–23) can most accurately be regarded as containing

   (A) a thinly disguised attack on religion in all its forms
   (B) a defense of all traditional religious beliefs and practices
   (C) an implicit criticism of organized religions such as Christianity
   (D) a call to American Indians to abandon their traditional religious beliefs

36. The author most likely uses exclamation marks in the third paragraph (lines 24–40) to

   (A) convey a sense of religious ecstasy
   (B) convince the reader that he is correct in his description of the religious views of American Indians
   (C) break up the monotony created by ending sentences with a period
   (D) alert the reader that his view might contain exaggerations

37. The language of the third paragraph of the passage (lines 24–40) can most accurately be described as

   (A) understated
   (B) euphemistic
   (C) ironic
   (D) rhapsodic

38. The word *epoch* as it is used in line 49 most nearly means

   (A) a past event
   (B) a historical event
   (C) an important event
   (D) an important period of time in the past

39. Which of the following would the author of the passage be most likely to agree with?

   (A) Native Americans were conquered by white people because they lacked courage in battle.
   (B) Native Americans alone possess true spirituality.
   (C) Native Americans did not develop complex technology because they lacked the intelligence to do so.
   (D) There is much to admire about Native Americans.

40. Which of the following provides the best evidence for the answer to the above question?

   (A) "Our . . . atheists." (lines 19–23)
   (B) "Wishing . . . loincloth." (lines 58–60)
   (C) "The . . . simplicity." (lines 70–72)
   (D) "and . . . men." (lines 100–104)

1   1   1

41. The phrase "untutored sage" (line 89) most nearly means

(A) a wise person who lacks formal education
(B) a wise person who has not received religious instruction from tribal elders
(C) a teacher pretending to be knowledgeable who in reality has little knowledge
(D) a foolish person

Questions 42– 52 are based on the following passage.

This passage is from Anne Fadiman, *Ex Libris: Confessions of a Common Reader.*
Copyright © 1998 by Anne Fadiman.

I call the "to each his own" quandary the His'er Problem, after a solution originally proposed by Chicago school superintendent Ella Young in 1912: "To each his'er own." I'm sorry.
(5) I just can't. My reactionary self has aesthetic as well as grammatical standards, and *his'er* is hideous. Unlike *Ms., his'er* could never become reflexive. (I might interject here that when I posed the His'er Problem to my brother, who
(10) was raised in the same grammatical hothouse as I, he surprised me by saying, "I won't say *his'er*. That would be a capitulation to barbarism. But I would be willing to consider a more rhythmically acceptable neologism such as *hyr*
(15) or *hes*, which would be preferable to having to avoid *his* by plotting each sentence in advance like a military campaign.")

What about "to each his or her own"? I do resort to that construction occasionally, but I
(20) find the double pronoun an ungainly burden. More frequently I recast the entire sentence in the plural, although "to all their own" is slightly off pitch. Even a phrase that is not stylistically disfigured—for example, "all writers worth their
(25) salt," which is only marginally more lumpish than "every writer worth his salt"—loses its specificity, that fleeting moment in which the reader conjures up an individual writer instead of a faceless throng.
(30) But I can't go back. I said "to each his own" until about five years ago, believing what my sixth-grade grammar textbook, *Easy English Exercises*, had told me: that "or her" was "understood," just as womankind was understood to
(35) be lurking somewhere within "mankind." I no longer understand. The other day I came across the following sentence by my beloved role model, E.B. White: "There is one thing the essayist cannot do—he cannot indulge himself

PRACTICE TEST 6

(40) in deceit or concealment, for he will be found out in no time." I felt the door slamming in my face so fast I could feel the wind against my cheek. "But he meant to include you!" some of you may be murmuring. "It was understood!"

(45) I don't think so. Long ago, my father wrote something similar: "The best essays [do not] develop original themes. They develop original men, their composers." Since my father, unlike E.B. White, is still around to testify, I called (50) him up last night and said, "Be honest. What was really in your mind when you wrote those sentences?" He replied, "Males. I was thinking about males. I viewed the world of literature— indeed, the entire world of artistic creation—as (55) a world of males, and so did most writers. Any writer of fifty years ago who denies that is lying. Any male writer, I mean."

I believe that although my father and E.B. White were not misogynists, they didn't real- (60) ly see women, and their language reflected and reinforced that blind spot. Our invisibil- ity was brought home to me fifteen years ago, after *Thunder Out of China,* a 1946 best-seller about China's role in the Second World War, (65) was reissued in paperback. Its co-authors were Theodore H. White and Annalee Jacoby, my mother. In his foreword to the new edition, Harrison Salisbury mentioned White nineteen times and my mother once.

(70) For as long as anyone can remember, my father has called every woman who is more than ten years his junior a girl. Since he is now ninety-one, that covers a lot of women. He would never call a man over the age of eighteen (75) a boy. I have tried to persuade him to mend his

ways, but the word is ingrained, and he means it gallantly. He truly believes that inside every stout, white-haired woman of eighty there is the glimmer of that fresh and lissome thing, a girl.

(80) If my father were still writing essays, every full-grown "girl" would probably be trans- formed by an editor's pencil into a "woman." The same thing would happen to E.B. White. In an essay called "The Sea and the Wind That (85) Blows," White described a small sailing craft as "shaped less like a box than like a fish or a bird or a girl." I don't think he meant a ten-year-old girl. I think he meant a girl old enough to be called a woman. But if he had compared that (90) boat to a woman, his slim little craft, as well as his sentence, would have been forever slowed.

What I am saying here is very simple. Changing our language to make men and women equal has a cost. That doesn't mean it (95) shouldn't be done. High prices are attached to many things that are on the whole worth doing. It does mean that the loss of our heedless grace should be mourned, and then accepted with all the civility we can muster, by every writer worth (100) his'er salt.

42. The author says that she and her brother were "raised in the same grammatical hothouse" (line 10). By this she most likely means to suggest that

   (A) as children she and her brother continually fought with each other about questions of grammar
   (B) she and her brother were sent to schools that emphasized the importance of correct grammar
   (C) she and her brother were brought up by parents who were very concerned with correct grammar and did everything they could to make sure that their children knew and cared about correct grammar
   (D) she and her brother were raised in a family that placed so much emphasis on grammar that it ruined their ability to appreciate beautiful prose

43. The most likely reason that the author was "surprised" (line 11) by her brother's response when she posed the His'er Problem to him is that

   (A) she did not believe that he would object to saying "his'er"
   (B) she thought he was not concerned with the issue because it mainly concerns women
   (C) she thought he would object to saying "hyr" or "hes" because they sound bad
   (D) she thought he would object to using any new word

44. The word *neologism* as it is used in line 14 most nearly means

   (A) new word
   (B) contraction
   (C) pronoun
   (D) correct word

45. The phrase "see women" as it is used in line 60 most nearly means

   (A) regard women as human beings
   (B) notice women
   (C) take women seriously
   (D) have women as friends

46. The author's "reactionary self" (line 5) would most likely write

   (A) "her book"
   (B) "his book"
   (C) "his or her book"
   (D) "his'er book"

1   1   1

47. The author comments on a sentence E.B. White wrote in an essay: "But if he had compared that boat to a woman, his slim little craft, as well as his sentence, would have been forever slowed" (lines 89–91). The author most likely means to suggest by this comment that if E.B. White had written "woman" instead of "girl"

(A) his sentence would have illustrated clearly that he was not sexist

(B) his sentence would have illustrated the truth of the view that although changing language to make it gender neutral has a cost, the cost is worth it

(C) his sentence would not have been as graceful and as effective at conveying its meaning

(D) like the boat in his sentence, his career as a writer would have been slowed

48. The phrase "heedless grace" (line 97) refers to

(A) elegant writing that is not concerned with treating women as the equals of men

(B) awkward language

(C) writing that appears to be aesthetically pleasing but that is really ugly

(D) refusal to be concerned with sexist language

49. The phrase "all the civility we can muster" (lines 98–99) suggests that

(A) writers are essentially selfish in that all they really care about is writing well

(B) female writers will be able to adapt more easily than male writers to using gender-neutral language

(C) few writers will be able to write well using gender-neutral language

(D) it will not be easy for writers to accept the need to change their writing habits to avoid sexist language

50. The most likely reason that the author uses the expression "his'er" in line 100 is to

(A) use some humor to remind the reader of the ongoing difficulties writers face in deciding how to deal with the His'er Problem

(B) demonstrate that the only solution to the His'er Problem is to use clumsy, unappealing language

(C) show that she agrees with Ella Young's suggestion about how to deal with the His'er Problem after all

(D) show that it doesn't really matter whether we say *he or she* or *his'er* or *hyr* or *hes* or any of the other suggestions that have been made about how to deal with the His'er Problem

51. Which of the following statements would the author of the passage be most likely to agree with?

(A) The need to use the English language in a gender-neutral way has imposed an unfair and unnecessary burden on writers.

(B) The English language should not be used to promote social or political objectives.

(C) Writers should make some effort to use gender-neutral language, but should not let it significantly affect the style of their writing.

(D) Writers should make every effort to use language that treats men and women equally, even if their writing loses much of its grace as a result.

52. Based on what she says in the passage, the author would be most likely to believe that the best way to change the sentence "Every writer should watch his P's and Q's when referring to male and female human beings" to make it gender neutral would be

(A) all writers, regardless of his or her gender, should watch his or her P's and Q's when referring to male and female human beings

(B) all writers should watch their P's and Q's when referring to male and female human beings

(C) every writer should watch his'er P's and Q's when referring to male and female human beings

(D) every writer should watch her P's and Q's when referring to male and female human beings

STOP If there is still time remaining, you may review your answers.

PRACTICE TEST 6

WRITING AND LANGUAGE TEST

35 MINUTES, 44 QUESTIONS

TURN TO SECTION 2 OF YOUR ANSWER SHEET TO ANSWER THE QUESTIONS IN THIS SECTION.

> **DIRECTIONS:** Questions follow each of the passages below. Some questions ask you how the passage might be changed to improve the expression of ideas. Other questions ask you how the passage might be altered to correct errors in grammar, usage, and punctuation. One or more graphics accompany some passages. You will be required to consider these graphics as you answer questions about editing the passage.
>
> There are three types of questions. In the first type, a part of the passage is underlined. The second type is based on a certain part of the passage. The third type is based on the entire passage.
>
> Read each passage. Then, choose the answer to each question that changes the passage so that it is consistent with the conventions of standard written English. One of the answer choices for many questions is "NO CHANGE." Choosing this answer means that you believe the best answer is to make no change in the passage.

Questions 1–11 are based on the following passage and supplementary material.

Malaria in the United States

[1]

Malaria in humans is caused by infection with one or more of several species of ❶ *Plasmodium,* the infection is being transmitted by the bite of an infective female *Anopheles* mosquito. *P. falciparum* and *P. vivax* species ❷ cause the most infections worldwide.

[2]

The majority of reported malaria cases diagnosed each year in the United States are imported from regions where malaria transmission is known to occur, ❸ since congenital infections and infections resulting from exposure to blood or blood products also are reported.

1. For the sake of clarity of expression and meaning the underlined portion of the sentence should be written as follows:

   (A) *Plasmodium.* The infection has its transmission

   (B) *Plasmodium,* the infection being transmitted

   (C) *Plasmodium.* The infection is transmitted

   (D) *Plasmodium,* it is transmitted

2. (A) NO CHANGE
   (B) causes
   (C) causing
   (D) being causes of

3. (A) NO CHANGE
   (B) in fact
   (C) and therefore
   (D) although

2   2   2

[3]

In 2010, the Centers for Disease Control and Prevention (CDC) received 1,691 ❹ <u>reports. They are concerning</u> cases of malaria among persons in the United States, representing a 14% increase from the 1,484 cases reported with onset of symptoms in 2009. Additionally, the number of cases reported in 2010 are the largest number of malaria cases that have been reported in the United States since 1980 (N = 1,864). In 2010, a total of 1,131 cases ❺ <u>will have occurred</u> among U.S. residents, 368 cases among foreign residents, and 192 cases among patients with unknown or unreported resident status.

[4]

Among the 1,691 reported cases, 1,688 were classified as imported cases; one transfusion-related case and two ❻ <u>unaccustomed</u> cases were reported. Information on region of ❼ <u>procurement</u> was known for 88% of the imported cases. Of 1,479 imported cases for which the region of acquisition was known, 959 (65%) were acquired in Africa, 285 (19%) in Asia, 230 (15%) in the Americas, and five (0.3%) in Oceania. The majority of cases reported in the United States among persons who indicated travel to Africa

4. Rewrite the underlined portion of the two sentences to form one complete sentence that makes sense.

  (A) reports, these concern
  (B) reports which are concerning
  (C) reports concerning
  (D) reports, and they concern

5. (A) NO CHANGE
  (B) occurred
  (C) occur
  (D) would occur

6. (A) NO CHANGE
  (B) serious
  (C) cryptic
  (D) veiled

7. (A) NO CHANGE
  (B) accession
  (C) accretion
  (D) acquisition

2   2   2

Number of Malaria Cases, by Region and Month, 2010

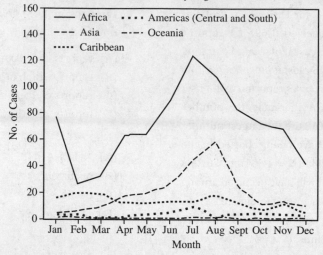

Source: Centers for Disease Control and Prevention, "Malaria Surveillance—United States, 2010."

peaked in ❽ February and July (see above graph). These peaks likely correlated with peak travel times to African destinations related to winter and early summer holidays. The majority of cases reported in the United States among those who indicated travel to Asia (most of whom had traveled to India) peaked in August, followed by a smaller peak in ❾ December (see above graph).

[5]

Among the 1,388 imported malaria cases with an identified *Plasmodium* species, the interval between both the date of arrival in the United States and onset of illness was known for 1,002 cases. Onset of symptoms began before arrival in the United States for 109 ❿ patients; the remaining 893 patients experienced malaria symptoms on or after arrival to the United States. ⓫

8. Which choice most accurately represents the information in the graph?

(A) NO CHANGE
(B) January
(C) June
(D) November

9. (A) NO CHANGE
(B) October
(C) November
(D) February

10. (A) NO CHANGE
(B) patients: the remaining
(C) patients, there remained
(D) patients, the remainder of

Think about the passage as a whole as you answer question 11.

11. To make the passage most logical, paragraph 5 should be placed

(A) where it is now
(B) before paragraph 2
(C) before paragraph 3
(D) before paragraph 4

PRACTICE TEST 6

2   2   2

Questions 12–22 are based on the following passage and supplementary material.

Wanted: Trained Teachers

Universal primary education (UPE) will remain a distant dream for millions of **12** <u>living children</u> in countries without enough teachers in classrooms. Current discussions of the post-2015 development agenda include a target to **13** <u>brace</u> the supply and training of teachers as part of efforts to ensure that every child learns in a stimulating and supportive classroom environment.

14 <u>In help to</u> formulate and monitor possible post-2015 education targets, the Unesco Institute of Statistics (UIS) has released a new set of projections of the demand and supply of primary teachers at the global and national levels. According to the data, countries needed to recruit a total of 4 million teachers to achieve universal primary education by 2015 (see graph below). **15** <u>Of this total 4 million, it</u> will replace teachers who retire,

12. (A) NO CHANGE
    (B) children alive
    (C) children living
    (D) children, and they live

13. (A) NO CHANGE
    (B) cushion
    (C) base
    (D) bolster

14. (A) NO CHANGE
    (B) To help
    (C) When it helps to
    (D) And a help to

15. Which choice most accurately and effectively represents the information in the graph?

    (A) NO CHANGE
    (B) In total 4 million, it
    (C) Of this total 2.6 million, it
    (D) Of this total, 2.6 million will

Total Number of Teachers Needed to Achieve Universal Primary Education by 2015, 2020, 2025, and 2030

Source: UNESCO Institute for Statistics database

change occupations or leave the workforce due to illness or death. The remaining 1.4 million will be needed to universalize access to primary education and underwrite quality by ensuring that there are not more than 40 students for every teacher.

[1] For this reason, the analysis presented in this paper determines how many teachers would be needed if the goal of achieving UPE was shifted to ⑯ 2020 or 2030. [2] UPE will not be achieved by 2015, however, as 58 million children are still out of school. [3] To achieve UPE by 2020, for example, countries will need to recruit a total of 12.6 million primary teachers. [4] This includes the creation of about 2.4 million new teaching positions and the replacement of ⑰ 17.5 million teachers expected to leave the profession due to attrition. By 2030, the total demand for teachers would rise to ⑱ 27.3 million, with about 23.9 million new posts needed for UPE and the remaining 3.4 million to compensate for attrition. ⑲

The region facing the greatest challenges by a large margin is sub-Saharan Africa, which makes up more than one-half (63%) of the additional

16. (A) NO CHANGE
    (B) 2025 or 2035
    (C) 2025 or 2040
    (D) 2020 or 2040

17. Which choice most accurately represents the information in the graph?

    (A) NO CHANGE
    (B) 2.6 million
    (C) 23.9 million
    (D) 10.2 million

18. Which choice most accurately represents the information in the graph?

    (A) NO CHANGE
    (B) 27.3 million, with about 3.4 million new posts needed for UPE and the remaining 23.9
    (C) 12 million, with about 3.4 million new posts needed for UPE and the remaining 23.9
    (D) 20 million, with about 23.9 million new posts needed for UPE and the remaining 3.4

19. For the sake of the cohesion of this paragraph, sentence 2 should be placed

    (A) where it is now
    (B) after sentence 3
    (C) before sentence 1
    (D) after sentence 4

teachers needed to achieve UPE by 2015 or two-thirds (67%) by **20** <u>2030 in the region with</u> more than 7 in 10   countries are faced with an acute shortage of teachers. And the situation in many countries may **21** <u>depreciate</u> as governments struggle with overcrowded classrooms and the rising demand for education from growing school-age **22** <u>populations: for</u> every 100 children in 2012, there will be 147 primary school-age children in 2030. Sub-Saharan Africa alone will need to create 2.3 million new teaching positions by 2030, while filling about 3.9 million vacant positions due to attrition.

20. The underlined portion of the sentence should be written as follows:

(A) NO CHANGE
(B) 2030, regionally
(C) 2030. Across the region,
(D) 2030. Regionally

21. (A) NO CHANGE
(B) dissolve
(C) wither
(D) deteriorate

22. (A) NO CHANGE
(B) populations, for
(C) populations; for
(D) populations for

2   2   2

Questions 23–33 are based on the following passage.

The following is an excerpt from President Franklin Delano Roosevelt's Message to Congress on the State of the Union, January 11, 1944.

It is our duty now to begin to lay the plans and determine the strategy for the winning of a lasting peace and the establishment of an American standard of living higher than ever before known. We cannot be content, no matter how high that general standard of living **㉓ was**, if some fraction of our people—whether it be one-third or one-fifth or one-tenth—is ill-fed, ill-clothed, ill housed, and insecure.

This Republic **㉔ with its beginning,** and grew to its present strength, under the protection of certain inalienable political rights—among them the right of free speech, free press, free worship, trial by jury, freedom from unreasonable searches and **㉕ seizures, these were** our rights to life and liberty.

As our Nation has grown in size and stature, **㉖ however**—as our industrial economy expanded—these political rights proved inadequate to assure us equality in the pursuit of happiness.

23. (A) NO CHANGE
    (B) may be
    (C) were
    (D) had been

24. (A) NO CHANGE
    (B) begun,
    (C) begins,
    (D) had its beginning,

25. (A) NO CHANGE
    (B) seizures being
    (C) seizures. They were
    (D) seizures. It was all of them that were

26. (A) NO CHANGE
    (B) moreover
    (C) especially
    (D) specifically

2   2   2

27 "Necessitous men are not free men." People who are hungry and out of a job are the stuff of which dictatorships are made.

In our day these economic truths have become accepted as self-evident. We have accepted, so to speak, a second Bill of Rights under which a new basis of security and prosperity **28** can establish for all regardless of station, race, or creed.

27. At this point the writer is considering adding the following sentence:

We have come to a clear realization of the fact that true individual freedom cannot exist without economic security and independence.

Should the writer make this addition here?

(A) Yes, because this sentence provides support for the main point of the passage, which is that economic equality must be attained in America before people can be allowed "inalienable rights," such as free speech.

(B) Yes, because this sentence is a concise statement of the writer's main idea, which is that economic rights are as important as political rights and go hand-in-hand with them. This is an appropriate place for this statement because in the previous sentence the writer said that political rights alone are not sufficient.

(C) No, because this sentence is not consistent with the view expressed elsewhere in the passage that while the standard of living is important it must always be regarded as secondary in importance to individual political freedom.

(D) No, because such a sweeping contention should be put in the conclusion of the passage, not in the middle of the passage.

28. (A) NO CHANGE
(B) will establish
(C) can be established
(D) established

2   2   2

Among these are:

The right to a useful and **㉙** solvent job in the industries or shops or farms or mines of the Nation;

The right to earn enough to provide adequate food and clothing and recreation;

The right of every farmer to raise and sell his products at a return which will give him and his family a decent living;

The right of every businessman, large and small, to trade in an atmosphere of freedom from unfair competition and **㉚** dominating by monopolies at home or abroad;

The right of every family to a decent home;

The right to adequate medical care and the opportunity to achieve and enjoy good health;

The right to adequate protection from the economic fears of old age, sickness, accident, and unemployment;

The right to a good education.

㉛ All of these rights spell security, after this war is won we must be prepared to move forward, in the implementation of these rights, to new goals of human happiness and well-being.

America's own rightful place in the world depends in large part upon how fully these and similar rights **㉜** are carrying into practice for our citizens. **㉝** Nevertheless there is security here at home there cannot be lasting peace in the world.

29. (A) NO CHANGE
    (B) remunerative
    (C) viable
    (D) monetary

30. (A) NO CHANGE
    (B) being dominated
    (C) a dominating by
    (D) domination

31. Rewrite the underlined portion of the sentence for clarity of meaning and expression.
    (A) All of these rights spell security. Since after
    (B) All of these rights spell security. And after
    (C) All of these rights spell security that after
    (D) Being that these rights spell security, after

32. (A) NO CHANGE
    (B) will carry
    (C) have been carried
    (D) had been carried

33. (A) NO CHANGE
    (B) For unless
    (C) In spite of
    (D) However little

2   2   2

Questions 34–44 are based on the following passage.

A Letter from Japan

[1] The Doctor took us on Sunday afternoon to his club— **34** which name I think means the perfume of the maple—to see and to listen to some Japanese plays which are given in the club theater **35** building for the purpose. [2] We went there in the afternoon, passing by the Shiba temples, and our carriages were drawn up at one end of the buildings. [3] There everything was Japanese, though I hear stories of the other club and its ultra-European ways—brandies-and-sodas, single eyeglasses, etc. [4] We sat on the steps and had our shoes taken off, according to the Japanese fashion, so as not to injure mats, and we **36** have heard during the operation long wailings, high notes, and the piercing sound of flutes and stringed instruments; the curiously sad rhythm mingled with a background of high, distinct **37** declamation. [5] We walked in with careful attention to make no noise, **38** we forgot that in our stocking-feet we could have made none had we wished, and we found the Doctor's place in a box reserved for him and us, and marked with his name, written large. [6] However that may be, on this side we were in Japan without mistake. [7] Other low boxes, with sides no higher than our elbows as we sat on the mats, divided the sloping floor down to the stage. **39**

The stage was a pretty little **40** building projecting into the great hall from its long side. It had its own roof, and connected with a long gallery or bridge, along which the actors moved, as they came on or disappeared, in a manner new to us, **41** neither did it give a certain natural sequence and made a beginning and an end,—a dramatic introduction and conclusion,—and added greatly to the picture when

34. (A) NO CHANGE
    (B) the
    (C) that
    (D) whose

35. (A) NO CHANGE
    (B) and it had been built
    (C) built
    (D) having built

36. (A) NO CHANGE
    (B) have been hearing
    (C) may hear
    (D) could hear

37. (A) NO CHANGE
    (B) accentuation
    (C) pronunciation
    (D) remarks

38. (A) NO CHANGE
    (B) we had forgot
    (C) forgotten
    (D) forgetting

39. For the sake of the cohesion of this paragraph, sentence 6 should be placed

    (A) where it is now
    (B) after sentence 1
    (C) after sentence 3
    (D) after sentence 4

40. (A) NO CHANGE
    (B) building project
    (C) projected building
    (D) project building

41. (A) NO CHANGE
    (B) not that it gave
    (C) despite that it gave
    (D) but which gave

the magnificent dresses of stiff brocade dragged slowly along **42** <u>over</u> the cadence of the music.

43 <u>The boxes were mostly occupied, and by a distinguished-looking audience. And this is because the *N*, as this operatic acting is called, being a refined, classical drama, is looked upon differently from the more or less disreputable theater.</u> Hence the large proportion of ladies, to whom the theater is forbidden. Hence, also, owing to its antiquity and the character of its style, a difficulty of comprehension for the general public that explained the repeated **44** <u>crackle</u> of the books of the opera which most of the women held, whose leaves turned over at the same moment, just as ours used to do at home when we were favored by French tragedy.

42. (A) NO CHANGE
    (B) to
    (C) beside
    (D) below

43. Rewrite these two sentences to make one distinct sentence that makes sense:

    (A) The boxes were mostly occupied, and by a distinguished-looking audience, the *N*, as this operatic acting is called, is a refined, classical drama, and looked upon differently from the more or less disreputable theater.

    (B) The boxes were mostly occupied, and by a distinguished-looking audience: the *N*, as this operatic acting is called, is a refined, classical drama, and looked upon differently from the more or less disreputable theater.

    (C) The boxes were mostly occupied, and by a distinguished-looking audience; the *N*, as this operatic acting is called, is a refined, classical drama, and looked upon differently from the more or less disreputable theater.

    (D) The boxes were mostly occupied, and by a distinguished-looking audience that is the *N*, as this operatic acting is called, being a refined, classical drama, and looked upon differently from the more or less disreputable theater.

44. (A) NO CHANGE
    (B) rustle
    (C) rumple
    (D) crimple

STOP   If there is still time remaining, you may review your answers.

3   3

MATH TEST (NO CALCULATOR)

25 MINUTES, 20 QUESTIONS

Turn to Section 3 of your answer sheet to answer the questions in this section.

DIRECTIONS: For questions 1–15, solve each problem and choose the best answer from the given options. Fill in the corresponding circle on your answer document. For questions 16–20, solve the problem and fill in the answer on the answer sheet grid. Please use scrap paper to work out your answers.

Notes:

- You **CANNOT** use a calculator on this section.
- All variables and expressions represent real numbers unless indicated otherwise.
- All figures are drawn to scale unless indicated otherwise.
- All figures are in a plane unless indicated otherwise.
- Unless indicated otherwise, the domain of a given function is the set of all real numbers x for which the function has real values.

REFERENCE INFORMATION

| Area Facts | Volume Facts | Triangle Facts |

$A = \ell w$

$A = \frac{1}{2} bh$

$A = \pi r^2$

$C = 2\pi r$

$V = \ell wh$

$V = \pi r^2 h$

$V = \frac{4}{3}\pi r^3$

$V = \frac{1}{3}\pi r^2 h$

$V = \frac{1}{3}\ell wh$

$a^2 + b^2 = c^2$

The arc of a circle contains 360°.
The arc of a circle contains 2π radians.
The sum of the measures of the angles in a triangle is 180°.

3

3

1. $2n + n + n + n - 6 = 4 + n - 2n$

   What is the value of n in the equation above?

   (A) $-\frac{3}{4}$

   (B) $-\frac{2}{3}$

   (C) $\frac{5}{4}$

   (D) $\frac{5}{3}$

2. If $\frac{2k}{7} = 30$, what is the value of $2k + 7$?

   (A) 105
   (B) 179
   (C) 217
   (D) 287

3. Line A is perpendicular to a line that is parallel to $y = \frac{5}{9}x + 7$. What is the slope of line A?

   (A) $\frac{9}{5}$

   (B) $\frac{5}{9}$

   (C) $-\frac{5}{9}$

   (D) $-\frac{9}{5}$

4. Tina repairs sinks in a large housing development. Each month, the number of sinks she has to repair is represented by the following equation:

   $$B = 360 - 88w$$

   where B is the balance of sinks left to repair and w is the number of weeks she has worked in a certain month. What is the meaning of 360 in the equation $B = 360 - 88w$?

   (A) Tina will repair 360 sinks each week.
   (B) Tina starts each month with 360 sinks to repair.
   (C) Tina repairs 360 sinks a year, almost one per day.
   (D) Tina will repair 360 sinks daily.

   $$(-4x^3y - xy^3 + 4x) - (7x - 4xy^3 + 2x^2)$$

5. Which of the following is equivalent to the expression above?

   (A) $-4x^3y + 3xy^3 - 2x^2 - 3x$
   (B) $6x^3y^3 - 3x$
   (C) $-4x^3y + 3xy^3 + 2x^2 - 11x$
   (D) $-9x^3y^3 + 3x$

6. The specific gravity of a substance is the ratio of the weight of the substance compared to the volume of an equal weight of water. If water weighs 62.5 pounds per cubic foot, what is the weight in pounds per cubic foot of a liquid that has a specific gravity of 3?

   (A) .047
   (B) 130
   (C) 187.5
   (D) 260

3   **3**

7. If $a^{\frac{3}{2}} = 64$, what is the value of $\sqrt{a}$?

    (A) 2
    (B) 4
    (C) $2\sqrt{2}$
    (D) 8

x	$g(x)$
0	6
−2	2
−3	0
−4	−2

8. The function g is defined by a certain polynomial. Some of the values of $g(x)$ are shown in the table above. Which of the following must be a factor of $g(x)$?

    (A) $x - 6$
    (B) $x - 3$
    (C) $x + 3$
    (D) $x + 6$

9. If $\dfrac{m^{x^1}}{m^{y^2}} = m^{36}$, $m > 1$, and $x + y = 9$, what is the value of $x - y$?

    (A) 4
    (B) 6
    (C) 9
    (D) 16

10. Sean owed p dollars for a loan he secured for college expenses. He promised to pay off the debt in monthly installments, each installment equal to 20% of the existing debt. After two monthly payments, which expression reflects the balance due on his loan?

    (A) $.8p$
    (B) $.64p$
    (C) $.6p$
    (D) $.48p$

11. $\dfrac{5 + 2i}{7 - 4i}$

    Which of the following complex numbers is equivalent to the fraction shown above? (Note: $i = \sqrt{-1}$)

    (A) $\dfrac{27}{65} - \dfrac{34i}{65}$
    (B) $\dfrac{27}{65} + \dfrac{34i}{65}$
    (C) $\dfrac{12}{65} - \dfrac{8i}{65}$
    (D) $\dfrac{43}{65} - \dfrac{34i}{65}$

12. What is the sum of all values of x that satisfy $4x^2 - 2x - 6 = 0$?

    (A) $-\dfrac{\sqrt{2}}{2}$
    (B) $-\dfrac{1}{2}$
    (C) $2\sqrt{2}$
    (D) $\dfrac{1}{2}$

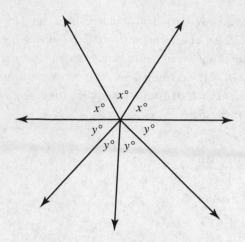

13. In the figure above, what is the value of $(x + y) \div 2(x - y)$?

    (A) 3
    (B) 3.5
    (C) 4
    (D) 5.5

$$\frac{6 - 4i}{2 + 4i}$$

14. If the expression above is rewritten in the form of $a + bi$, what is the value of $a - 2b$?

    (A) $4 + 2i$
    (B) $4 - 2i$
    (C) $\frac{8}{5}$
    (D) 3

15. $y = x^2 + 5x + 8$
    $y + 7x + 28 = 0$

    The system of equations above has how many solutions?

    (A) exactly 3 solutions
    (B) exactly 2 solutions
    (C) exactly 1 solution
    (D) the system of equations has no solutions.

Grid-in Response Directions

In questions 16–20, first solve the problem, and then enter your answer on the grid provided on the answer sheet. The instructions for entering your answers follow.

- First, write your answer in the boxes at the top of the grid.
- Second, grid your answer in the columns below the boxes.
- Use the fraction bar in the first row or the decimal point in the second row to enter fractions and decimals.

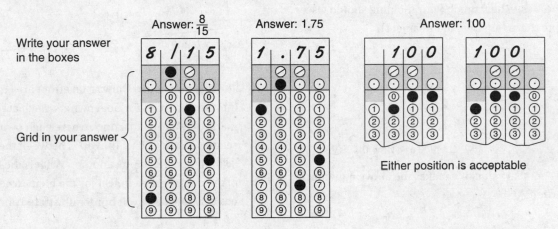

- Grid only one space in each column.
- Entering the answer in the boxes is recommended as an aid in gridding but is not required.
- The machine scoring your exam can read only what you grid, so you **must grid-in your answers correctly to get credit**.
- If a question has more than one correct answer, grid-in only one of them.
- The grid does not have a minus sign; so no answer can be negative.
- A mixed number *must* be converted to an improper fraction or a decimal before it is gridded.

  Enter $1\frac{1}{4}$ as $\frac{5}{4}$ or 1.25; the machine will interpret 11/4 as $\frac{11}{4}$ and mark it wrong.

- **All decimals must be entered as accurately as possible**. Here are three acceptable ways of gridding

$$\frac{3}{11} = 0.272727\ldots$$

- Note that rounding to .273 is acceptable because you are using the full grid, but you would receive **no credit** for .3 or .27, because they are less accurate.

3

3

16. Oscar wants to place molding surrounding the floor in his study room that is in the shape of a rectangle. He remembers that the area of the room is 180 square feet and that the width of the room is 12 feet. However, he does not know the measure of the length of the room. His tape measure is out in the car, but Oscar thinks he can solve the problem with simple algebra. Assuming no waste, how much floor molding should Oscar purchase (answers in linear feet)?

$$x^3 - 6x^2 + 2x - 12 = 0$$

17. What real value of x makes the above equation true?

19. The diagram above shows a lakefront area divided into small parcels for boat owners. Each area is marked by a rope to a dock where each owner secures his/her boat. The ropes between the parcels are parallel to one another. What is the length of the docking area in feet for the boat owner who has a 30 foot lakefront border illustrated above?

$$mx + ny = 8$$
$$2x + 8y = 64$$

18. In the system of equations above, m and n are constants. If the system of equations has infinitely many solutions, what is the value of $\frac{n}{m}$?

20. If $f(x) = 2x + 3$ and $f(2x + 3) = 5x$, what is the value of $3x^2$?

STOP   If there is still time remaining, you may review your answers.

MATH TEST (CALCULATOR)

55 MINUTES, 38 QUESTIONS

Turn to Section 4 of your answer sheet to answer the questions in this section.

DIRECTIONS: For questions 1–30, solve each problem and choose the best answer from the given options. Fill in the corresponding circle on your answer document. For questions 31–38, solve the problem and fill in the answer on the answer sheet grid. Please use scrap paper to work out your answers.

Notes:

- The **use of** a calculator on this section IS permitted.
- All variables and expressions represent real numbers unless indicated otherwise.
- All figures are drawn to scale unless indicated otherwise.
- All figures are in a plane unless indicated otherwise.
- Unless indicated otherwise, the domain of a given function is the set of all real numbers x for which the function has real values.

REFERENCE INFORMATION

| Area Facts | Volume Facts | Triangle Facts |

$A = \ell w$

$A = \frac{1}{2} bh$

$A = \pi r^2$
$C = 2\pi r$

$V = \ell w h$

$V = \pi r^2 h$

$V = \frac{4}{3}\pi r^3$

$V = \frac{1}{3}\pi r^2 h$

$V = \frac{1}{3}\ell w h$

$a^2 + b^2 = c^2$

The arc of a circle contains 360°.
The arc of a circle contains 2π radians.
The sum of the measures of the angles in a triangle is 180°.

4

4

1. A pound of flour costs $1.50 per pound. What is the cost, in dollars, of $(2x + 6)$ pounds of flour? (Ignore the $ sign)

   (A) $\dfrac{2x + 6}{1.50}$

   (B) $2x + 7.50$

   (C) $\dfrac{1.5}{2x + 6}$

   (D) $3x + 9$

2. Gina is saving money for a cross-country road trip with two of her friends. She currently has $240 saved for the excursion and can save $125 each month in the future. Which of the following expressions represents the amount of money Gina will save after m months?

   (A) $365m$

   (B) $125 + 240m$

   (C) $240 + 125m$

   (D) $365m + 240$

3. Jake has five 12-packs of juice for his school's summer picnic. If all of the juice containers are divided into 3 main groups and each group is then divided into 5 smaller groups, how many juice containers are in each of these smaller groups?

   (A) 2

   (B) 4

   (C) 5

   (D) 10

4. Connor surveyed a random sample of 80 students in his class regarding the need for additional crosswalks at the school. Only 15.6% of the students felt they were necessary. Of the 320 students in his sophomore class, about how many would favor additional crosswalks?

   (A) 50

   (B) 58

   (C) 71

   (D) 74

5. The density of an object is found by dividing the object's mass by its volume. If the density of an object is 4 grams per milliliter and its mass is 30 grams, what is the volume in milliliters of the object?

   (A) 4.8

   (B) 6.1

   (C) 7.5

   (D) 9.2

6. Virginia and Chad were performing community service hours for their high school graduation requirement. Chad served three more hours than Virginia did this week and their combined hours were 47. How many hours did Chad work?

   (A) 22

   (B) 25

   (C) 27

   (D) 31

$$y = x^2 - 8x + 15$$

7. The equation above represents a graph of a parabola in the xy-plane. Which of the following equivalent forms of the graph show the parabola's x-intercepts as coefficients or constants?

(A) $y - 15 = x^2 - 8x$
(B) $y + 1 = (x - 4)^2$
(C) $y = x(x - 8) + 15$
(D) $y = (x - 5)(x - 3)$

$$(4 - 3i)(6 + 5i)$$

8. The above expression can be expressed in the form of $a + bi$. What is the value of b in the expression?
(Note: $i = \sqrt{-1}$)

(A) 41
(B) 39
(C) 2
(D) −2

9. The linear function f has values $f(4) = -14$ and $f(-3) = 14$. What would be the value of $f(7)$?

(A) 37.4
(B) 17.28
(C) −26.0
(D) −28.6

Questions 10 and 11 refer to the following information.

Roasted asparagus (134 grams) provides the following percentages of these minimum daily nutritional requirements.

Nutrient	Percentage of Daily Requirement
Vitamin A	20
Calcium	3
Vitamin D	0
Vitamin B$_{12}$	0
Vitamin C	12
Iron	16
Vitamin B$_6$	5
Magnesium	5
Protein	9

10. A red bell pepper (92 grams) provides approximately 123% of the daily minimum requirement of vitamin C. Which of the following is closest to the number of grams of roasted asparagus that is equivalent to this amount?

(A) 1,600
(B) 1,400
(C) 1,200
(D) 1,000

11. Which of the following is closest to the number of grams of roasted asparagus needed to fulfill a person's minimum daily requirement of iron?

(A) 800
(B) 1,000
(C) 1,200
(D) 1,600

Time (A.M.)

When a comet passes by the sun, it leaves a trail of rocks, ice, and dust. As Earth passes through this trail, some of the particles enter Earth's atmosphere, manifesting as meteorites or "shooting stars." The graph above is the line of best fit of a meteor shower that took place in November 2014.

12. Which of the following can be deduced about the line of best fit and the actual number of meteors seen per minute at 3:00 A.M.?

  (A) The line of best fit predicted 4 fewer meteors per minute than were actually witnessed.
  (B) The line of best fit predicted 5 more meteors per minute than were actually witnessed.
  (C) There were fewer meteors witnessed at 3:00 A.M. than there were at 2:00 A.M..
  (D) The line of best fit and the actual number of meteors witnessed at 3:00 A.M. were equivalent.

13. Modern television screens are categorized by the lengths of their diagonals. Ethan was watching a show on his 32" screen in which a truck appeared to be 11" long. Had he watched that show on a television that had a 44" inch diagonal, to the nearest inch, how long would the truck appear to be?

  (A) 8"
  (B) 15"
  (C) 27"
  (D) 38"

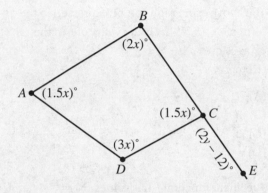

Note: Figure not drawn to scale

14. In the diagram above, what is the measure of y?

  (A) 112.5
  (B) 90
  (C) 62.25
  (D) 45

4 **4**

15. If $m - n = 18$ and $\frac{n}{3} = 6$, what is the value of $\frac{m}{n}$?

    (A) 0
    (B) 2
    (C) 9
    (D) 18

$$5x + 13y = 17$$
$$bx + 54.6y = 37$$

16. In the system of equations above, b is a constant. If there is no solution to the system, what is the value of b?

    (A) 17.4
    (B) 19.6
    (C) 21.0
    (D) 27.3

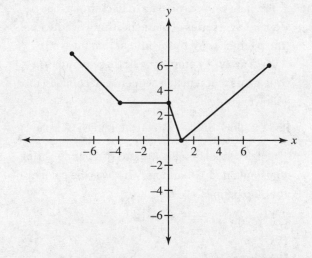

17. The complete graph of the function g is shown in the xy-plane above. What value of x yields the minimum value of $g(x)$?

    (A) 0
    (B) 1
    (C) 2
    (D) 5

18. Swimmers who participate in backstroke races depend on a series of banners strung overhead. The banners warn the swimmer that the wall is 5 yards away. A company sells these banners in long cords that repeat a sequence of colors in the following order:

Red   Yellow   Blue   Green   Orange   Purple

If a high school bought 40 yards of a banner string that contained 75 banners, what was the color of the 59th banner?

(A) yellow
(B) green
(C) orange
(D) purple

19. A food stand sells Mexican fare. Tacos cost $2.00 each and enchiladas cost $4.50 each. On a certain day, revenue from tacos and enchiladas was $198.00 and the number of tacos and enchiladas sold was 54. How many enchiladas were sold?

(A) 54
(B) 36
(C) 27
(D) 18

$$x^2 + y^2 + 6x - 8y = 12$$

20. The equation of a circle in the xy-plane is provided above. What is the radius of the circle?

(A) 5
(B) $3\sqrt{3}$
(C) 6
(D) $\sqrt{37}$

Percent of Homeowners Using Solar Power Fort Myers, Florida

District	Percent of Homeowners Using Solar Power
1	28.1
2	13.6
3	38.3
4	17.9
5	11.6
6	17.4
7	22.0

21. An analysis of all homeowners in Fort Myers, Florida was conducted to determine the percentage of those who use solar power for their electrical needs. The city has 27 districts, of which 7 are listed in the table above. The median percent of all homeowners who use solar power in Fort Myers is 16.8%. What is the difference between the median of the 7 districts listed above and the median percent of the entire city?

(A) 26.7%
(B) 4.5%
(C) 2.3%
(D) 1.1%

$$C(x) = x^3 + 5x^2 + 5x - 2$$

22. In the function above, which of the following can be assumed?

(A) $x + 3$ is a factor
(B) $x + 2$ is a factor
(C) $x - 5$ is a factor
(D) $x + 4$ is a factor

4 4

23. A can of tennis balls is in the shape of a right cylinder. The can contains three tennis balls of equal size. The radius of one of the tennis balls is 1.25 inches. The three stacked tennis balls determine the height of the can, and a single tennis ball determines its diameter. Which of the following is closest to the measure of the volume of the space in the can **not** taken up by the tennis balls?

(A) 18.6 cubic inches
(B) 12.3 cubic inches
(C) 9.8 cubic inches
(D) 4.9 cubic inches

24. Two types of peaches, classified as A and B, are being cultivated. An estimate of the number of peaches of type A, after a 30-day experiment, is approximately 5,200. If type A peaches grew 30% more quickly than type B, what is the estimated count of the type B peaches at the same 30-day mark?

(A) 3,900
(B) 4,000
(C) 4,200
(D) 4,500

Questions 25 and 26 refer to the following information.

A theater group began with a budget from the city of $1.5 million. However, the group had seen its annual funding decline by 6.8% per year. By January 1, 2000, its annual budget was $975,000.

25. What function models the declining balance of annual funding provided by the city?

(A) $f(x) = 1,500,000(1.068)^t$
(B) $f(x) = 1,500,000(.932)^t$
(C) $f(x) = 1,500,000(.068)^t$
(D) $f(x) = 1,500,000(-.068)^t$

26. Due to decreasing budgets, the city council sought to combine its theater group with another city's group on 1/1/2004. If the 6.8% decline in annual budget funds continued, and the two cities needed to have at least $1.2 million, how much did the neighboring city have to provide to the budget?

(A) $684,442
(B) $521,862
(C) $484,324
(D) $464,356

27. The figure above is a regular hexagon with sides of length m and a square with sides of length m as well. If the area of the hexagon is $324\sqrt{3}$ square inches, what is the area of the square in square inches?

(A) 108
(B) 216
(C) 256
(D) 324

$$3x + m = 5x - 6$$
$$3y + n = 5y - 6$$

28. In the equations shown above, m and n are constants. If $m = n + \frac{1}{2}$ which of the following statements is true?

(A) x is y plus $\frac{1}{4}$

(B) x is y minus $\frac{1}{4}$

(C) x is y minus 1

(D) x is y plus 1

29. The distance between the points $(7, 5)$ and $(x, 4)$ is 8. What is/are the coordinate(s) of x?

(A) $7 + 3\sqrt{7}$
(B) $7 - 3\sqrt{7}$
(C) $3 \pm \sqrt{7}$
(D) $7 \pm 3\sqrt{7}$

30. A scuba diving instructor charges $75 per lesson plus an additional fee for the use of her boat. The charge for the use of her boat varies directly with the square root of the time the boat is used. If a lesson plus 25 minutes of boat time costs $110, what is the total amount charged for a lesson that uses the boat for 36 minutes?

(A) $117
(B) $122
(C) $127
(D) $133

Grid-in Response Directions

In questions 31–38, first solve the problem, and then enter your answer on the grid provided on the answer sheet. The instructions for entering your answers follow.

- First, write your answer in the boxes at the top of the grid.
- Second, grid your answer in the columns below the boxes.
- Use the fraction bar in the first row or the decimal point in the second row to enter fractions and decimals.

Write your answer in the boxes

Grid in your answer

Answer: $\frac{8}{15}$ Answer: 1.75   Answer: 100

Either position is acceptable

- Grid only one space in each column.
- Entering the answer in the boxes is recommended as an aid in gridding but is not required.
- The machine scoring your exam can read only what you grid, so you **must grid-in your answers correctly to get credit**.
- If a question has more than one correct answer, grid-in only one of them.
- The grid does not have a minus sign; so no answer can be negative.
- A mixed number *must* be converted to an improper fraction or a decimal before it is gridded.

  Enter $1\frac{1}{4}$ as $\frac{5}{4}$ or 1.25; the machine will interpret 11/4 as $\frac{11}{4}$ and mark it wrong.

- **All decimals must be entered as accurately as possible.** Here are three acceptable ways of gridding

$$\frac{3}{11} = 0.272727\ldots$$

- Note that rounding to .273 is acceptable because you are using the full grid, but you would receive **no credit** for .3 or .27, because they are less accurate.

4   4

31. The moon's gravity is $\frac{1}{6}$ of the gravitational force exerted by Earth. If a rock on the moon weighs 73 pounds, what would the rock weigh, in pounds, on Earth?

Age	Target HR Zone 50–85%	Average Maximum Heart Rate, 100%
20 years	100–170 beats per minute	200 beats per minute
30 years	95–162 beats per minute	190 beats per minute
35 years	93–157 beats per minute	185 beats per minute
40 years	90–153 beats per minute	180 beats per minute

32. The chart above indicates data relating to heart beat rates for adults between the ages of 20 and 40 as put forth by the American Medical Association. If a woman aged 35 has a heart rate that is the mean of the extremes of the Target HR Zone for her age, what percent of the maximum heart rate is that measure (round to the nearest tenth of a percent)?

33. If the height of a cylinder is doubled and the length of its radius is tripled, how many times greater is the volume of the larger cylinder compared to the volume of the original?

34. In the xy-plane, the point $(-4, 8)$ lies on the graph of the function g. If $g(x) = 2b + x^3$, where b is a constant, what is the value of b?

$$f(x) = \frac{1}{(x-3)^2 + 6(x-3) + 9}$$

35. For what value of x is the above function f undefined?

36. A supermarket chain received an average grade (arithmetic mean) of 65% customer satisfaction from 10 recent customer surveys. The chain manager wants to earn at least an 80% rating from its first 20 customer surveys. What is the lowest score the 17th survey can receive and still achieve the 80% satisfaction rate from its first 20 surveys? (Omit percent sign)

4

4

Questions 37 and 38 refer to the information below.

Nutritionists recommend daily consumption of 4,700 milligrams of potassium. Men generally consume 3,200 milligrams per day and women consume about 2,300 milligrams per day. Below is a list of potassium-rich foods as recommended by nutritional experts.

Foods with Potassium	Serving Size	Potassium (mg)
Apricots, dried	10 halves	407
Avocados, raw	1 ounce	180
Bananas, raw	1 cup	594
Beets, cooked	1 cup	519
Brussel sprouts, cooked	1 cup	504
Cantaloupe	1 cup	494
Dates, dry	5 dates	271
Figs, dry	2 figs	271
Kiwi fruit, raw	1 medium	252
Lima beans	1 cup	955
Melons, honeydew	1 cup	461
Milk, fat free or skim	1 cup	407
Nectarines	1 nectarine	288
Orange juice	1 cup	496
Oranges	1 orange	237
Pears (fresh)	1 pear	208
Peanuts dry roasted, unsalted	1 ounce	187
Potatoes, baked	1 potato	1081
Prune juice	1 cup	707
Prunes, dried	1 cup	828
Raisins	1 cup	1089
Spinach, cooked	1 cup	839
Tomato products, canned sauce	1 cup	909
Winter squash	1 cup	896
Yogurt, plain, skim milk	8 ounces	579

37. Jake read that the headaches he was enduring after running were caused by potassium depletion. Although he was consuming 3,200 milligrams of potassium daily, he was told he needed at least 10% more potassium than was recommended by nutritionists. To accrue this amount, Jake has decided to consume an extra potato and a cup of lima beans in his daily diet. If he consumes these extra items each day, how much more potassium will he consume than is recommended for his augmented need of this nutrient?

38. Joan consumes 22,400 milligrams of potassium each week. She has decided to add a serving of spinach and a glass of orange juice each day. If she maintains this addition to her daily diet, how many more milligrams of potassium will Joan need to reach the recommended milligrams per week?

ANSWER KEY
Practice Test 6

Section 1: Reading

1. **B**	14. **C**	27. **D**	40. **D**
2. **A**	15. **C**	28. **A**	41. **A**
3. **D**	16. **D**	29. **C**	42. **C**
4. **A**	17. **C**	30. **B**	43. **C**
5. **B**	18. **D**	31. **C**	44. **A**
6. **D**	19. **D**	32. **C**	45. **C**
7. **D**	20. **C**	33. **D**	46. **B**
8. **C**	21. **D**	34. **A**	47. **C**
9. **C**	22. **D**	35. **C**	48. **A**
10. **B**	23. **A**	36. **A**	49. **D**
11. **D**	24. **C**	37. **D**	50. **A**
12. **B**	25. **B**	38. **C**	51. **D**
13. **C**	26. **C**	39. **D**	52. **B**

Number Correct _____

Number Incorrect _____

Section 2: Writing and Language

1. **C**	12. **C**	23. **B**	34. **D**
2. **A**	13. **D**	24. **D**	35. **C**
3. **D**	14. **B**	25. **C**	36. **D**
4. **C**	15. **D**	26. **A**	37. **A**
5. **B**	16. **A**	27. **B**	38. **D**
6. **C**	17. **D**	28. **C**	39. **C**
7. **D**	18. **B**	29. **B**	40. **A**
8. **B**	19. **C**	30. **D**	41. **D**
9. **C**	20. **C**	31. **B**	42. **B**
10. **A**	21. **D**	32. **C**	43. **C**
11. **A**	22. **A**	33. **B**	44. **B**

Number Correct _____

Number Incorrect _____

ANSWER KEY
Practice Test 6

Section 3: Math (No Calculator)

1. **D**   5. **A**   9. **A**   13. **B**
2. **C**   6. **C**   10. **B**   14. **D**
3. **D**   7. **B**   11. **B**   15. **C**
4. **B**   8. **C**   12. **D**

16. **54**   17. **6**   18. **4**   19. **40**

20. **243**

Number Correct   _____

Number Incorrect   _____

ANSWER KEY
Practice Test 6

Section 4: Math (Calculator)

1. **D**	7. **D**	13. **B**	19. **B**	25. **B**
2. **C**	8. **C**	14. **C**	20. **D**	26. **D**
3. **B**	9. **C**	15. **B**	21. **D**	27. **B**
4. **A**	10. **B**	16. **C**	22. **B**	28. **A**
5. **C**	11. **A**	17. **B**	23. **B**	29. **D**
6. **B**	12. **A**	18. **C**	24. **B**	30. **A**

31. **438**

32. **67.6**

33. **18**

34. **36**

35. **0**

36. **50**

37. **66**

38. **1,155**

Number Correct _____

Number Incorrect _____

SCORE ANALYSIS

Reading and Writing Test

Section 1: Reading   _____ = _____ (A)
                         # correct   raw score

Section 2: Writing   _____ = _____ (B)
                         # correct   raw score

To find your Reading and Writing test scores, consult the chart below; find the ranges in which your raw scores lie and read across to find the ranges of your test scores.

_____ + _____ = _____ (C)
   range of Reading   range of Writing   range of Reading + Writing
      test scores   test scores   test scores

To find the range of your Reading and Writing Scaled Score, multiply (C) by 10.

Test Scores for the Reading and Writing Sections

Reading Raw Score	Writing Raw Score	Test Score
44–52	39–44	35–40
36–43	33–38	31–34
30–35	28–32	28–30
24–29	22–27	24–27
19–23	17–21	21–23
14–18	13–16	19–20
9–13	9–12	16–18
5–8	5–8	13–15
less than 5	less than 5	10–12

Math Test

Section 3:   _____ = _____ (D)
                 # correct   raw score

Section 4:   _____ = _____ (E)
                 # correct   raw score

Total Math raw score: (D) + (E) = _____

To find your Math Scaled Score, consult the chart below; find the range in which your raw score lies and read across to find the range for your scaled score.

Scaled Scores for the Math Test

Raw Score	Scaled Score	Raw Score	Scaled Score
50–58	700–800	20–25	450–490
44–49	650–690	15–19	400–440
38–43	600–640	11–14	350–390
32–37	550–590	7–10	300–340
26–31	500–540	less than 7	200–290

Answer Explanations

Section 1: Reading Test

1. **(B)** No information about the cause of hotspots is given in Passage 1. The author concentrates on explaining what J. Tuzo Wilson's "hotspot" theory says is caused by hotspots. Information is provided explaining all of the other choices.

2. **(A)** Wilson's theory predicts that a hotspot exists "beneath the present-day position of the Island of Hawaii" (also called the "Big Island") (lines 24–25). The fact that "new volcanic rock is continually being formed" (lines 54–55) suggests that the "Big Island" is located over a hotspot because it is consistent with the hotspot theory.

3. **(D)** The author says, "The vast majority of earthquakes and volcanic eruptions occur near tectonic plate boundaries, but there are some exceptions" (lines 1–3). The passage describes how the "hotspot" theory explains at least some of these exceptions. The "hotspot" theory explains how volcanoes form in the interior of tectonic plates.

4. **(A)** This is the best choice because the passage says that Wilson first "*noted that* in certain locations . . . volcanism has been active for very long periods of time" (lines 12–15). Wilson then "*reasoned* [that] if . . . hotspots existed below the plates that would provide . . . energy . . . to sustain volcanism" (lines 15–20). Finally, he "*hypothesized*" (line 20) about how volcanism occurred in a specific area, creating an island volcano, and about how plate movement affects this process. Note that the process of reasoning Wilson used was *deduction*—reasoning that infers something from a general principle.

5. **(B)** The author describes the "hotspot" theory: "[Wilson suggested that] continuing plate movement eventually carries the island beyond the hotspot, cutting it off from the magma source, and volcanism ceases. As one island volcano becomes extinct, another develops over the hotspot, and the cycle is repeated" (lines 34–39). The final paragraph describes how the structure and age of the Hawaiian Islands support the hotspot theory.

6. **(D)** As mentioned above, these lines provide the best evidence for the answer to question 5.

7. **(D)** The author says, "They [a team of scientists] deployed a large network of sea-floor seismometers . . . , opening up a window into the Earth" (lines 64–68). The word *window* as it is used here means "a means of observing."

8. **(C)** It can be inferred that the earthquakes mentioned in line 95 were largely or entirely unrelated to geological activity on or near the Hawaiian Islands because the purpose of recording the seismic waves from the earthquakes was to "determine whether seismic waves travel more slowly through hot rock as they pass beneath Hawaii" (lines 91–93).

9. **(C)** The focus of the passage is on efforts that have been made by scientists to discover the processes that created the Hawaiian Islands. The sentence in which the word *resolve* (lines 105–107) appears is about a difficulty in scientifically establishing the facts about the processes that created the islands' "deep structure."

10. **(B)** Both passages are concerned mainly with what causes volcanic islands to form in the middle of tectonic plates when both the theory of tectonic plates and observation of volcanic activity show that most volcanic activity occurs near places where two tectonic plates meet. Passage 1 describes a theory to explain this, called the "hotspot" theory, which examines the case of Hawaii as a good example of the phenomenon. Passage 2 describes efforts to confirm this theory, again focusing on the Hawaiian Islands as an example of the phenomenon.

11. **(D)** Much of Passage 1 describes the hotspot theory in considerable detail. The final paragraph describes the geology of the Hawaiian Islands, providing evidence for the theory. Most of Passage 2 is devoted to describing PLUME, an experiment that produced strong evidence for the hotspot theory described in Passage 1.

12. **(B)** In lines 4–19 ("It is in . . . a vast veil."), the author describes how as a child he came to realize that black people are treated differently than white people and are not accepted by them.

13. **(C)** The author says, "The exchange was merry, till one girl . . . refused my card . . . . Then it dawned upon me . . . that I was different from the others; or like, mayhap, in heart and life and longing, but shut out from their world by a vast veil" (lines 13–19).

14. **(C)** The author says, "With other black . . . mine own house?" (lines 34–40).

15. **(C)** These lines provide the best evidence for the answer to the previous question.

16. **(D)** In lines 40–47 ("The shades of . . . of blue above") the author describes how "the prison-house closed round us all." The prison house symbolizes the prevailing attitudes and limited opportunities available to both whites and blacks. The author says that the prison's walls were "stubborn"—that is, difficult, but not impossible to scale—to the white people but "unscalable" to blacks.

17. **(C)** The author says, "the Negro is . . . gifted with second-sight in this American world . . . a world which . . . only lets him see himself through the revelation of the other world" (lines 49–54).

18. **(D)** We can infer that "end" means *goal* in this context because the author is stating what he believes should be the goal of the African American

19. **(D)** The author does not appeal to authority. He makes use of all the others.

20. **(C)** This would be the most appropriate title for the passage because this is the author's main concern in the passage—how, as he says in lines 64–67, "The history of this strife,—this longing to attain self-conscious manhood, to merge his double self into a better and truer self."

21. **(D)** The phrase "latent genius" is not symbolic. It refers to intellectual abilities that are not being used. The other choices are used symbolically.

22. **(D)** In context, we can infer that *humoring* means "indulging" because it is stated that Jim is worth a lot to his employers. Thus, they would be likely to indulge him.

23. **(A)** *Fidelity* means "loyalty" and a *fiend* is a "devil."

24. **(C)** *Dryly humorous* is the best choice because the narrator is indirectly and somewhat humorously making the point that not many people are suited by character or temperament for an occupation that calls for qualities such as kindness and patience.

25. **(B)** This can be inferred from information provided in the passage: "Nevertheless . . . he would throw up the job suddenly and depart" (lines 50–51); "His incognito, which . . . go to another . . . ." (lines 60–65); "He retreated in . . . casually but inevitably"(lines 69–71). We can infer that the "fact" mentioned in line 62 refers to a secret about Jim.

26. **(C)** These lines provide the best evidence for the answer to the previous question. "The fact broke through the incognito" means a fact about him becomes known despite his attempt to conceal it and his true identity.

27. **(D)** The word *incognito* means "false identity." The phrase "as many holes as a sieve" means that the false identity did not do a good job of keeping Jim's real identity secret.

28. **(A)** This can be inferred from the reason that is given for Jim's leaving seaports: "When the fact . . . go to another" (lines 62–65).

29. **(C)** Jim is described as "powerfully built" (line 2) and "very popular" (line 14).

30. **(B)** These lines provide the best evidence for the answer to the previous question.

31. **(C)** The word "casually" is used to describe the manner in which "the fact" follows Jim. A secret about Jim eventually becomes known in the seaport in which he is working. The word "casually" describes how the secret becomes known after various intervals of time.

32. **(C)** The author is discussing American Indian worship in the past. He says "It [the worship] was silent" (lines 8–9). By "ascended to God" he means they did not literally ascend to God but rather that their souls drew close in worship. This is supported by the fact that he says "They believed that He is *nearer to us* in solitude" (lines 12–13).

33. **(D)** Because the author is concerned with the religious beliefs of Indians in the past, it is reasonable to conclude that he uses the word "original" in line 1 to suggest that these beliefs have changed from what they were in earlier times.

34. **(A)** In lines 24–40 ("There . . . cathedral!") the author describes how God can be perceived in many forms. It is reasonable to infer that the author uses a variety of capitalized names for God to reinforce the idea that God has many forms. Whether God is called "the Unseen" or "Him" does not matter because words can never convey His true nature.

35. **(C)** In the second paragraph (lines 7–23) the author contrasts traditional American Indian religious belief and practice with that of organized religions like Christianity. This comparison portrays Indian religion as superior because it does not have priests, creeds, preaching, proselytizing, or persecution.

36. **(A)** The author is describing the American Indians' experience of God. In lines 26–32 ("He . . . sky!") he describes where Indians believed God could "be met face to face." This "meeting" of man and God is, presumably, spiritual and emotional rather than literal, so the author most likely uses an exclamation mark to help convey to the reader a sense of the religious ecstasy experienced by Indians. The use of an exclamation mark in the next line ("He . . . cathedral!"—lines 32–40) conveys a similar emotion.

37. **(D)** *Rhapsodic* is the most accurate word to describe the language of the third paragraph because *rhapsodic* means "extravagantly enthusiastic; ecstatic." As mentioned in the explanation of the previous question, the author is trying to convey the sense of ecstasy experienced by the Indians. He uses extravagant poetic language to help convey this sense of ecstasy.

38. **(C)** In the fifth paragraph ("The . . . existence"—lines 48–69) the author describes the *bambeday*, which would be an important event in the life of a young man. The word *epoch* in context thus means "an important event."

39. **(D)** The author's description of American Indians is very positive, so he would be likely to agree with this statement. There is no evidence for choice (A) and choice (B); choice (C) is rebutted in lines 70–85 ("The . . . men").

40. **(D)** This provides the best evidence for the answer to the previous question.

41. **(A)** A *sage* is a "wise person," and *untutored* means "lacking formal education."

42. **(C)** A *hothouse* in this context is "an environment conducive to vigorous development." Thus, a "grammatical hothouse" is an environment in which a great effort is made to teach children about grammar.

43. **(C)** From the fact that the author's brother "was raised in the same grammatical hothouse" (lines 9–10) as the author, it is reasonable to conclude that he, like the author, would be unwilling to consider using substitute words for "his."

44. **(A)** A *neologism* is a "new word." The author is discussing new words that have been suggested to replace the word "his" used to refer to both males and females.

45. **(C)** The author quotes her father to illustrate the fact that in the past men "viewed the world . . . of artistic creation as a world of males" (lines 53–55). She says she doesn't believe her father was a misogynist (a man who hates women), but that he and other men in the past didn't "really see women" (lines 59–60). In context, therefore, *see women* means "take women seriously." Clues to the meaning are "blind spot" (line 61) and "invisibility" (lines 61–62).

46. **(B)** In context the word *reactionary* means "extremely conservative." The author's "reactionary self" would most likely write "his book" because as a conservative she would follow the traditional and accepted practice.

47. **(C)** The author uses the word "slowed" figuratively to mean the sentence would not have been as graceful and effective if E.B. White had used the word "woman" instead of the word "girl."

48. **(A)** In the last paragraph (lines 93–95) the author argues that although "Changing our language to make men and women equal has a cost. . . . That doesn't mean it shouldn't be done." In the phrase "heedless grace" the word *grace* refers to "elegant writing" and the word *heedless* means "unconcerned." The author is saying that we should be sad about losing the opportunity to write elegantly, but that we should accept its necessity.

49. **(D)** The author is suggesting that we should accept the necessity of changing our language so that it isn't sexist, but that doing so will undoubtedly be difficult for some people to do graciously. The word *muster* in context means "summon up" and has a connotation of "exerting great effort to summon up." The author is being somewhat jocular in the last sentence of the passage.

50. **(A)** As mentioned in the explanation of question 49, the author is being somewhat humorous in the last sentence of the passage. We can conclude that she mainly uses the expression "his'er" to remind us that every writer has to deal with the His'er Problem and must decide how to do so. The author's use of "his'er," although humorous, suggests that she might even consider using this expression she thinks is "hideous" (line 7) regularly.

51. **(D)** The author would almost certainly agree with this statement because she argues, "Changing our language has a cost. . . . That doesn't mean it shouldn't be done" (lines 93–95).

52. **(B)** The author would almost certainly change the sentence so that it doesn't suggest that all writers are all female or all male. Choice (A) does this but would not generally be considered graceful, a quality valued by the author. She probably wouldn't like choice (C) because it uses "his'er," which she believes is "hideous" (line 7). She would probably reject choice (D) as unnecessarily wordy. Choice (B) changes the sentence so that the His'er Problem is avoided.

Section 2: Writing and Language Test

1. **(C)** Choices (B) and (D) create run-on sentences. Choice (B) is grammatical but somewhat awkward. Choice (C) is a better choice because it creates two sentences, each of which clearly expresses an idea.

2. **(A)** Choices (C) and (D) do not create grammatical sentences. Choice (B) does not agree in number with the subject, "species." Choice (A) is correct because the verb "cause" (which is the singular form of the verb) agrees in number with the subject, "*P. falciparum* and *P. vivax*," which is plural.

3. **(D)** This is the best choice because the part of the sentence after the comma gives contrasting information to that given in the part of the sentence before the comma. The first part of the sentence tells about "the majority" of cases, whereas the second part tells about less common cases (signaled by the word "also"). The subordinating conjunction *although* creates a dependent clause, effectively linking it to the preceding independent clause. Choice (A) and choice (C) make little sense. Choice (B) creates a run-on sentence.

4. **(C)** This choice is correct because it creates a clear and grammatical sentence in which the participial phrase beginning with "concerning" and ending with "States" modifies the preceding noun, "reports." Choice (A) creates a run-on sentence. Choice (B) and choice (D) are awkward and wordy.

5. **(B)** This is correct. The context requires the simple past tense because the sentence is about cases that occurred "in 2010."

6. **(C)** This is the best choice because it is reasonable that it would have been difficult to understand two of the many cases. In context *cryptic* means "puzzling."

7. **(D)** This is the best choice. In context *acquisition* means "the act of acquiring," which makes good sense because the context is a description of information about where people contracted malaria. Choice (A), *procurement*, means "to obtain by effort," and so is not correct.

8. **(B)** This can be seen from the graph. Cases peaked first in January, declined, and rose to a higher peak in July.

9. **(C)** This can be seen from the graph. Cases peaked in August, declined, and then reached a much smaller peak in November.

10. **(A)** This is the best choice. The independent clause after the semicolon provides additional information directly relevant to that provided in the independent clause before the semicolon. Choices (C) and (D) create run-on sentences. Choice (B) is not as good as choice (A) because the colon is not normally used this way.

11. **(A)** This is the correct answer because paragraph 5 provides more information on the main topic discussed in paragraph 4, which is imported cases of malaria in the United States.

12. **(C)** All of the choices are grammatically correct, but choice (C), unlike the others, is both idiomatic and makes good sense in context.

13. **(D)** *Bolster*, meaning "increase" in context, is the best choice. It makes good sense because there are already teachers, but more are needed.

14. **(B)** This is the only choice that is grammatical and makes good sense.

15. **(D)** The correct answer can be determined from the information in the bar graph.

16. **(A)** Choice (A) is correct because the rest of the paragraph only discusses achieving UPE by 2020 or 2030.

17. **(D)** The correct answer can be determined from the information in the bar graph.

18. **(B)** The correct answer can be determined from the information in the bar graph.

19. **(C)** This is the best choice because sentence 2 explains the reason referred to in sentence 1. Also, sentence 2 provides an appropriate transition from the preceding paragraph and a good introduction for the paragraph that it is in.

20. **(C)** Choices (A) and (B) create run-on sentences. Choice (D) does not make good sense. Choice (C) creates a complete sentence that makes good sense. The previous sentence described the situation in sub-Saharan Africa. The phrase "across the region" refers back to the situation there, providing a transition to the next sentence.

21. **(D)** *Deteriorate*, which means "worsen" in context, is the best choice. The answer can be inferred from the context, which describes factors that are predicted to cause the situation to worsen in sub-Saharan Africa.

22. **(A)** This is the correct choice because the information given after the colon gives detailed information about the problem that will be caused by "growing school-age populations" mentioned in the independent clause before the colon.

23. **(B)** This is the correct choice because it creates a sentence that makes good sense and is grammatical. The modal verb may be used here to express a certain measure of likelihood that the "general standard of living" will be high in the future. Choices (A) and (D) are grammatically correct but do not make good sense in context. Choice (C) is not grammatical.

24. **(D)** This is the only choice that is grammatical and makes good sense. "Had," the simple past tense of the verb "have," is used to describe America's past.

25. **(C)** Choice (A) creates a run-on sentence. Choice (C) corrects this error by creating two complete sentences. Choice (D) is grammatical but awkward and wordy.

26. **(A)** This is the correct choice because the context requires a word meaning "in spite of that," which *however* means here. Note that although the punctuation is a bit unusual, it is nevertheless correct. The author uses dashes to highlight one area (industrial growth) of America's growth.

27. **(B)** This sentence should be added here because in the previous sentence the writer said that political rights, while vital, are not sufficient. This sentence states what else is essential— "economic security and independence"—and provides a transition to the rest of the passage.

28. **(C)** All of the other choices are not grammatical and do not make good sense. In Choice (C) the modal verb "can" is used with the linking verb "be" to indicate possibility.

29. **(B)** The writer is describing "a second Bill of Rights under which a new basis of security and prosperity can be established," so *remunerative* (well-paying) makes good sense. Choice (A) is incorrect because a job cannot be *solvent*. Choice (C) is acceptable, but is not as appropriate in context as choice (B).

30. **(D)** This is the best choice because the word in this blank and "competition" are the objects of a prepositional phrase beginning with "from," so these two words should be the same part of speech (in this case, nouns).

31. **(B)** This is the correct choice because it creates two clear and grammatical sentences. Choice (A) is incorrect because the sentence beginning with "Since" is not a complete sentence. Choices (C) and (D) do not make good sense.

32. **(C)** Choices (A) and (B) do not create grammatical sentences. The present perfect tense is appropriate in context because the sentence describes events in a fairly recent period of American history that are continuing at present.

33. **(B)** This is the correct choice because it creates a grammatical sentence that makes good sense in the context of the paragraph. Note that the preposition *for* is being used here to mean *because*.

34. **(D)** This is the correct choice because it creates a grammatical sentence that makes good sense. *Whose* is a relative pronoun beginning an adjective clause that modifies the noun "club."

35. **(C)** This is the correct choice. It creates a sentence in which the participial phrase "built for the purpose" modifies the noun "theater."

36. **(D)** *Could hear* is the correct choice. In context *could hear* means "were able to hear," which makes good sense.

37. **(A)** All of the words are related to speech. However, choice (A) is correct because *declamation* in context means "forthright projection of words set to music."

38. **(D)** Choices (A) and (B) are incorrect because they create a run-on sentence. Choice (D) is correct because *forgetting* is the present participle of "forget." This creates a participial phrase beginning with "forgetting" and ending with "wished," which is grammatical.

39. **(C)** This is the best choice because sentence 6 is about a contrast with what was said in sentence 3. This contrast is signaled by the word "however."

40. **(A)** This is the correct choice. It creates a clear and grammatical sentence in which the word "projecting" is a present participle and the first word of a participial phrase that modifies the noun "building."

41. **(D)** All of the other choices are not grammatical because they create run-on sentences. This choice creates a clear and grammatical sentence in which the conjunction "but" joins the dependent clause beginning with "which" to the preceding dependent clause. The word "but" is used here to signal a contrast with what was said earlier in the sentence about the actors.

42. **(B)** This is the best choice because it makes sense that the dresses were moved to "the cadence [beat] of the music."

43. **(C)** Choice (A) is a run-on sentence. Choice (D) makes little sense and is not grammatical. Choice (B) is grammatical and makes good sense. However, choice (C) is the better choice because it is more appropriate to use a semicolon than a colon after the word "audience" because the independent clause after the punctuation elaborates on the audience, not on *N* drama.

44. **(B)** Choices (A) and (B) can be used to describe sound, but choices (C) and (D) cannot be so used. A *crackle* is a sharper sound than a *rustle* and is not as appropriate as *rustle* in context because the sound of pages being turned is not sharp. A *rustle* is "a low crisp rubbing sound," which is an appropriate description of the pages being turned by the ladies.

Section 3: Math Test (No Calculator)

1. **(D)** Combine like terms and isolate the variable.

    $$2n + n + n + n - 6 = 4 + n - 2n$$
    $$5n - 6 = 4 - n$$
    $$6n = 10$$
    $$n = \frac{10}{6} = \frac{5}{3}$$

2. **(C)** Solve for $2k$.

    $$\frac{2k}{7} = 30$$
    $$2k = 210$$
    $$2k + 7 = 217$$

    You do not have to solve for k in this problem.

3. **(D)** Parallel lines have the same slope. Since the slope of $y = \frac{5}{9}x + 7$ is $\frac{5}{9}$, then a line parallel to it will also have a slope that measures $\frac{5}{9}$. Perpendicular lines have slopes that are the opposite reciprocals of one another. Thus, a line perpendicular to a line with slope $\frac{5}{9}$ will have a slope of $-\frac{9}{5}$.

4. **(B)** Tina starts each month with 360 sinks to repair. As each week passes, Tina will have 88 fewer sinks to repair within the month.

5. **(A)** $(-4x^3y - xy^3 + 4x) - (7x - 4xy^3 + 2x^2)$
    Combine like terms.

    $$-xy^3 - (-4xy^3) = 3xy^3$$
    $$4x - 7x = -3x$$

    There are no other like terms so arrange the expression as shown in choice (A).

    $$-4x^3y + 3xy^3 - 2x^2 - 3x$$

6. **(C)** Use the ratio $\dfrac{62.5 \text{ pounds}}{1 \text{ cubic foot}}$ to find the weight of a liquid that has a specific gravity of 3.

    $$\frac{62.5}{1} = \frac{x}{3}$$
    $$(3)(62.5) = x$$
    $$187.5 = x$$

7. **(B)** Raise each side of the equation to the $\frac{2}{3}$ power to isolate a.

    $$\left(a^{\frac{3}{2}}\right)^{\frac{2}{3}} = 64^{\frac{2}{3}}$$
    $$a = 16$$
    $$\sqrt{16} = 4$$

8. **(C)** Note that when $x = -3$, $y = 0$. When a function intersects the x-axis in the xy-plane then $y = 0$; that x value is a root of the function. We therefore conclude that $x = -3$ is a root of the function and adding 3 to both sides yields $x + 3 = 0$.

9. **(A)** $\dfrac{m^{x^1}}{m^{y^2}} = m^{36}$

    When dividing like terms, subtract the exponents.

    $$m^{x^2 - y^2} = m^{36}$$

Since the bases are the same, drop m to get $x^2 - y^2 = 36$. Factor by using the difference of squares.

$$(x + y)(x - y) = 36$$

It was given in the question that $x + y = 9$, so $x - y$ must equal 4 because $9 \times 4 = 36$.

10. **(B)** After the first month of paying off 20% of his student loan, Sean's remaining balance looks like this.

$$p - .2p = .8p$$

Sean's loan balance after one month was $.8p$. He now must pay off 20% of the $.8p$ that remains as the loan balance.

$$.8p - (.2)(.8p) = .64p$$

11. **(B)** Multiply both the numerator and the denominator by $7 + 4i$, which is the conjugate of $7 - 4i$. Remember that $i = \sqrt{-1}$.

$$\frac{5 + 2i}{7 - 4i} \times \frac{7 + 4i}{7 + 4i} =$$

$$\frac{35 + 34i - 8}{49 + 16}$$

$$\frac{27}{65} + \frac{34i}{65}$$

12. **(D)** This problem can be solved by factoring or using the quadratic equation.

$$\frac{-b \pm \sqrt{b^2 - 4ac}}{2a}$$

$$a = 4 \quad b = -2 \quad c = -6$$

$$\frac{-(-2) \pm \sqrt{(-2)^2 - 4(4)(-6)}}{2(4)}$$

$$\frac{2 \pm \sqrt{4 - (-96)}}{8}$$

$$\frac{2 \pm 10}{8}$$

$$\frac{3}{2}, -1$$

The sum of the roots, -1 and $\frac{3}{2}$, is $\frac{1}{2}$.

13. **(B)** The sum of the angles above and below the line are each 180°. Use that information to solve for both x and y.

$$3x = 180$$
$$x = 60$$
$$4y = 180$$
$$y = 45$$

Inputting 60 and 45 for x and y, respectively, yields $105 \div 30 = 3.5$.

14. **(D)** In order to rewrite $\dfrac{6-4i}{2+4i}$ in the form of $a + bi$, multiply the denominator and numerator by $2 - 4i$, the conjugate of $2 + 4i$.

$$\frac{6-4i}{2+4i} \times \frac{2-4i}{2-4i} = \frac{-4-32i}{20} = -\frac{1}{5} - \frac{8}{5}i$$

Using the general form of a complex number, $a + bi$, we find that $a = -\frac{1}{5}$ and $b = -\frac{8}{5}$.

Substituting those values for a and b, we get:

$$a - 2b = -\frac{1}{5} - (2)\left(-\frac{8}{5}\right) = 3$$

15. **(C)** Set the bottom equation equal to y.

$$y + 7x + 28 = 0$$
$$y = -7x - 28$$

Use the substitution principle to solve for x.

$$x^2 + 5x + 8 = -7x - 28$$

Set the equation equal to 0 and solve for x.

$$x^2 + 5x + 8 = -7x - 28$$
$$x^2 + 12x + 36 = 0$$
$$(x+6)^2 = 0$$
$$x + 6 = 0$$
$$x = -6$$

Substitute $x = -6$ into the equation $y = x^2 + 5x + 8$ to find the value of y.

$$y = (-6)^2 + 5(-6) + 8$$
$$y = 14$$

There is exactly one solution, $(-6, 14)$, to the system of equations.

16. **54** The molding, which surrounds the floor, is equal to the rectangle's perimeter. We are missing the length, but we know the area and width. The area of a rectangle can be found by using the formula Area $=$ length $\times$ width.

Input the known information to solve for "l."

$$180 = l \times 12$$
$$15 = l$$

We now know the rectangular floor has the following dimensions:

We can use the formula Perimeter $= (2 \times l) + (2 \times w)$ to find the number of feet of molding Oscar needs to surround the floor:

$$(2 \times 15) + (2 \times 12) = 54$$

Oscar needs 54 feet of molding to surround the floor of his study.

17. **6** Factor by grouping.

$$x^3 - 6x^2 + 2x - 12 = 0$$
$$(x^3 - 6x^2) + (2x - 12) = 0$$
$$x^2(x - 6) + 2(x - 6) = 0$$
$$(x^2 + 2)(x - 6) = 0$$
$$x^2 + 2 = 0 \text{ or } x - 6 = 0$$
$$x = \pm i\sqrt{2} \text{ or } x = 6$$

Of the three solutions, only 6 is a real solution to the equation.

18. **4** In order for a system of equations to have infinitely many solutions, the two equations must be some multiple of one another. Note that $64 = 8 \times 8$, so 2 must be eight times the value of m and 8 must be eight times the value of n. We conclude that m must equal $\frac{1}{4}$ and n must equal 1. Therefore, $\frac{n}{m} = \frac{1}{\frac{1}{4}} = 4$.

19. **40** If three parallel lines intersect two transversals, they divide the transversals proportionally. The lakefront length that is 27 feet corresponds to a dock length of 36. The lakefront length that is 30 feet should have a docking length that is proportional to the 27:36 ratio. Set up a proportion to find the docking length of the wider dock length.

You will find it useful to simplify $\frac{27}{36}$ to $\frac{3}{4}$.

$$\frac{3}{4} = \frac{30}{x}$$
$$3x = 120$$
$$x = 40$$

20. **243** Use $f(x) = 2x + 3$ and $f(2x + 3)$ together to find the value of x. Since $f(x) = 2x + 3$, then $f(2x + 3)$ must equal $2(2x + 3) + 3$. Set that expression equal to $5x$ and solve for x.

$$2(2x + 3) + 3 = 5x$$
$$4x + 6 + 3 = 5x$$
$$9 = x$$

Substitute 9 for x in $3x^2$.

$$3(9^2) = 243$$

Section 4: Math Test (Calculator)

1. **(D)** Multiply the cost per pound of flour by the number of pounds.

$$(1.50)(2x + 6) = 3x + 9$$

2. **(C)** Gina has $240 saved so that sum will be part of the answer. Each month, for m months, she will save $125. Therefore, she will save an additional $125m$ after m months. Adding the initial savings and the monthly accumulation of money, we arrive at $240 + 125m$ as the amount saved after m months.

3. **(B)** Find the total number of juice containers by multiplying 5 by 12.

$$5 \times 12 = 60$$

There were 3 main groups of juice containers, so divide 60 by 3 to find how many containers are in each group.

$$60 \div 3 = 20$$

Finally, divide 20 by 5 to find how many containers are in each of the smaller groups.

$$20 \div 5 = 4$$

4. **(A)** The survey size of 80 is sizeable enough to draw conclusions about the class in general. Since 15.6% of the surveyed students felt that additional crosswalks were necessary, that fraction of the entire class will probably feel the same way.

Find 15.6% of 320.

$$320 \, (.156) = 49.92$$

Round the answer to 50 students that can be expected to favor additional crosswalks.

5. **(C)** The formula for the density of an object is presented as density $= \dfrac{\text{mass}}{\text{volume}}$. Input 4 grams per milliliter for the density and 30 grams for mass to find the volume.

$$4 = \frac{30}{V}$$

Multiply both sides of the equation by V.

$$V\left(4 = \frac{30}{V}\right)V$$
$$4V = 30$$
$$V = 7.5$$

6. **(B)** Since Virginia worked fewer hours than Chad, let her hours be represented by x. Chad worked three more hours than did Virginia, so let his hours be represented by $x + 3$. Their total community service hours were 47, leading to the following equation:

$$x + (x + 3) = 47$$
$$2x + 3 = 47$$
$$2x = 44$$
$$x = 22$$
$$x + 3 = 25$$

Chad provided 25 hours of community service this week for his high school graduation requirement.

7. **(D)** The x-intercepts of the graph of $y = x^2 - 8x + 15$ are the values of x when y equals 0. Replace y with zero and factor $y = x^2 - 8x + 15$.

$$0 = x^2 - 8x + 15$$
$$0 = (x - 5)(x - 3)$$

Note that $y = 0$ when $x = 5$ or $x = 3$. Thus, $y = (x - 5)(x - 3)$ displays the x-intercepts of the parabola as the constants 5 and 3.

None of the other choices, (A), (B), or (C), show the x-intercepts as constants or coefficients.

8. **(C)** Multiply the two parentheses using the FOIL method.

$$(4 - 3i)(6 + 5i) =$$
$$24 + 20i - 18i - 15i^2 =$$
$$24 + 2i - 15i^2 =$$
$$24 + 2i + 15 = 39 + 2i$$

Using the form of a complex number, $a + bi$, 2 is b.

9. **(C)** A linear function can be expressed in the form of $y = mx + b$, where m is the slope of the line and b is the y-intercept. Given that $f(4) = -14$ and $f(-3) = 14$, we know that $(4, -14)$ and $(-3, 14)$ are points on this line. Find the equation of the line connecting $(4, -14)$ and $(-3, 14)$ by first finding the slope.

$$\frac{14 - (-14)}{-3 - 4} = -4$$

The formula for the line is $y = -4x + b$. Find b by substituting either point for x and y.

$$-14 = -4(4) + b$$
$$2 = b$$

The formula for the line connecting $(4, -14)$ and $(-3, 14)$ is $y = -4x + 2$. Substitute 7 for x to find $f(7)$.

$$y = -(4)(7) + 2 = -26$$
$$f(7) = -26$$

10. **(B)** Find the number of servings of roasted asparagus that provide the same nutritional value of vitamin C as one serving of a red bell pepper.

$$123\% \div 12\% = 10.25$$

It takes 10.25 servings of roasted asparagus to equal the amount of vitamin C in one serving of red bell pepper. Multiply the grams in one serving of roasted asparagus, 134, by 10.25.

$$134 \times 10.25 = 1,373.5$$

Choice (B), 1,400, is closest to this value.

11. **(A)** Satisfying the minimum daily requirement means 100% of that nutrient has been consumed in a day. Since one serving of roasted asparagus provides 16% of the daily iron requirement, divide 100% by 16% to determine the number of servings needed each day.

$$100 \div 16 = 6.25$$

A person needs 6.25 servings of roasted asparagus to satisfy the minimum daily requirement of iron. Multiply 6.25 by 134 to find the number of grams of roasted asparagus needed to reach this goal.

$$134 \times 6.25 = 837.5$$

Of the selections provided, choice (A), 800, is closest to this value.

12. **(A)** The line of best fit predicted 38 meteors viewed per minute, but the actual number viewed was 42. Therefore, the line of best fit predicted 4 fewer meteors than actually were viewed.

13. **(B)** Use the proportion $\dfrac{\text{length}}{\text{diagonal}} = \dfrac{\text{length}}{\text{diagonal}}$ to calculate the apparent length of the truck on the television with a 44" diagonal.

$$\frac{11}{32} = \frac{x}{44}$$
$$(11)(44) = 32x$$
$$484 = 32x$$
$$15.13 = x$$

Rounded to the nearest inch, the truck would appear to be 15" long on the television with the 44" diagonal.

14. **(C)** The sum of the measures of the angles in a quadrilateral is 360°. Solve for x by adding the angle measures and set that value equal to 360.

$$1.5x + 3x + 1.5x + 2x = 360$$
$$8x = 360$$
$$x = 45$$

m$\angle BCD$ + m$\angle ECD$ = 180 because they form a linear pair. m$\angle BCD$ equals 67.5 because $1.5 \times 45 = 67.5$. Therefore, $2y - 12$ is 112.5 because it is supplementary to $\angle BCD$. Set $2y - 12$ equal to 112.5 and solve for y.

$$112.5 = 2y - 12$$
$$124.5 = 2y$$
$$y = 62.25$$

15. **(B)** Solve for n.

$$\frac{n}{3} = 6$$
$$n = 18$$

Solve for m.

$$m - 18 = 18$$
$$m = 36$$

Divide m by n.

$$\frac{m}{n} = \frac{36}{18} = 2$$

16. **(C)** Systems of equations have no solution if they are the equations of parallel lines. Although these equations can be graphed, it is much simpler to note the scale factor between the two equations. If the coefficients of x and y are multiples of one another, but the constants are not, the system has no solution.

$$5x + 13y = 17$$
$$bx + 54.6y = 37$$

Divide the coefficients of y.

$$54.6 \div 13 = 4.2$$

The value of b is $4.2 \times 5 = 21$.

Double-check to ensure the constants are not of the same scale factor.

$$37 \div 17 \neq 4.2$$

17. **(B)** The minimum value of $g(x)$ occurs at $(1, 0)$ on the graph. The value of x, then, that yields the minimum value of $g(x)$ is 1.

18. **(C)** The banners are sold in the same sequence of repeating colors:

Red   Yellow   Blue   Green   Orange   Purple

There are 6 banners in each sequence, so divide 59 by 6 the same way you did in 4th grade.

$$59 \div 6 = 9 \text{ remainder } 5$$

The quotient is not important but the remainder is. The quotient suggests that we have completed 9 full sequences, and we are now 5 deep into the 10th sequence of colors. Count 5 banners into the series to arrive at orange as the 59th banner.

19. **(B)** Although a plug-and-check strategy is possible for this problem, using a system of equations is easier.

Let $x =$ tacos sold
Let $y =$ enchiladas sold

There were 54 items sold so the first equation is $x + y = 54$. Tacos cost \$2.00 and enchiladas cost \$4.50, and the revenue generated was \$198.00, giving us $2x + 4.5y = 198$.

Use either elimination or substitution to proceed.

$$x + y = 54 \text{ so } y = 54 - x$$

Substitute $54 - x$ for y in the equation $2x + 4.5y = 198$.

$$2x + 4.5(54 - x) = 198$$
$$2x + 243 - 4.5x = 198$$
$$-2.5x = -45$$
$$x = 18$$

Substitute 18 into $y = 54 - x$ to find the number of enchiladas sold.

$$y = 54 - 18 = 36$$

20. **(D)** The graphing form of a circle is $y = (x - h)^2 + (y - k)^2 = r^2$, where (h, k) is the center of the circle and r is the radius. Convert the equation to graphing form by completing the square.

$$x^2 + y^2 + 6x - 8y = 12$$
$$x^2 + 6x + 9 + y^2 - 8y + 16 = 12 + 9 + 16$$
$$(x + 3)^2 + (y - 4)^2 = 37$$

The radius squared is 37, so find its square root to calculate the length of the radius.

$$r^2 = 37$$
$$r = \sqrt{37}$$

21. **(D)** Arrange the percentages in the table in ascending order.

$$11.6 \quad 13.6 \quad 17.4 \quad 17.9 \quad 22.0 \quad 28.1 \quad 38.3$$

The median of the data shown is 17.9% because it is the middle term. Subtract 16.8%, the median of all homeowners in Fort Myers, from 17.9%:

$$17.9\% - 16.8\% = 1.1\%$$

22. **(B)** If $x + 2$ is a factor of $C(x) = x^3 + 5x^2 + 5x - 2$, the remainder, after dividing, is 0.

$$\begin{array}{r} x^3 + 3x - 1 \\ x + 2 \overline{)\, x^3 + 5x^2 + 5x - 2} \end{array}$$

Since there is no remainder, we know that $x + 2$ is factor of $C(x) = x^3 + 5x^2 + 5x - 2$.

An alternate method to answering this question is to substitute -2 for x and assess the results.

$$(-2)^3 + 5(-2)^2 + 5(-2) - 2 = 0$$

The result is 0, which indicates -2 is a root of the function and $x + 2$ is a factor.

23. **(B)** Find the difference between the volume of the can and the volume of the three tennis balls. Use the formula $V = \pi r^2 h$ to calculate the volume of the can.

$$V = \pi (1.25)^2 (3)(2 \times 1.25) \approx 36.8 \text{ cubic inches}$$

Next find the volume of the three tennis balls. Use the formula $V = \frac{4}{3}\pi r^3$ to find the volume of a single tennis ball, and multiply that value by 3.

$$V = 3\left(\frac{4}{3}\right)\pi (1.25)^3 \approx 24.5 \text{ cubic inches}$$

Subtract the volume of the three tennis balls from the volume of the can.

$$36.8 - 24.5 = 12.3 \text{ cubic inches}$$

24. **(B)** Let $x =$ the population of type B peaches at the 30-day mark.

Type A peaches had reached a total of 5,200, which is 30% greater than the total for peach type B. Therefore, the number of type A peaches with respect to type B is $1.3x$. Set $1.3x$ equal to 5,200 to find how many of type B peaches exist at the 30-day mark.

$$1.3x = 5,200$$
$$x = 4,000$$

25. **(B)** The initial city expenditure was \$1,500,000, yet this amount decreased by 6.8% per year. To calculate the continuous decay of the budgeted amount provided by the city, subtract .068 from 1.0 to see what portion of the last year's budget will be provided this year.

$$1.0 - .068 = .932$$

The exponent t in this case will refer to time in years.

Only choice (B) appears to show moderate decay in the budget. The other answers are too small or too large; choice (D) would offer alternating negative and positive values.

26. **(D)** Although funding for the theater group started out at $1.5 million, we only know the balance on 1/1/2000, which was $975,000. The question asks what the balance will be on 1/1/04 so we can assess the financial contribution of the neighboring city. Use the model you derived correctly from question 25, but remember to start with $975,000.

$$975,000(.932)^4 = 735,645$$

The city would have $735,644 in its budget so subtract that figure from $1.2 million to find the contribution needed from the nearby community.

$$1,200,000 - 735,645 = 464,355$$

The nearby community would need to contribute $464,355 during its first year of the merger.

27. **(B)** A regular hexagon can be divided into six equilateral triangles. Divide $324\sqrt{3}$ by 6 to find the area of one of the equilateral triangles.

$$324\sqrt{3} \div 6 = 54\sqrt{3}$$

An equilateral triangle can be divided into two 30-60-90 triangles.

Multiply the base, x, by the height, $x\sqrt{3}$, and $\frac{1}{2}$ and set that product equal to $27\sqrt{3}$, which is one-half of $54\sqrt{3}$.

$$\left(\frac{1}{2}\right)(x)(x\sqrt{3}) = 27\sqrt{3}$$
$$\frac{1}{2}x^2 = 27$$
$$x^2 = 54$$
$$x = 3\sqrt{6}$$

Multiply $3\sqrt{6}$ by 2 to find one side of the hexagon.

$$3\sqrt{6} \times 2 = 6\sqrt{6}$$

The side length of the hexagon is also the side length of the square. Square $6\sqrt{6}$ to calculate the area of the square.

$$(6\sqrt{6})^2 = 216$$

28. **(A)** Combine like terms and solve for m and n.

$$3x + m = 5x - 6 \text{ becomes } m = 2x - 6$$
$$3y + n = 5y - 6 \text{ becomes } n = 2y - 6$$

Substitute $\left(n + \frac{1}{2}\right)$ for m as provided in the problem.

$$n + \frac{1}{2} = 2x - 6, \text{ so } n = 2x - \frac{13}{2}$$
$$n = 2y - 6 \text{ and } n = 2x - \frac{13}{2}, \text{ so } 2y - 6 = 2x - \frac{13}{2}$$

Solve for x because all of the answer choices express x as a function of y.

$$2y - 6 = 2x - \frac{13}{2}$$
$$2y + \frac{1}{2} = 2x$$
$$y + \frac{1}{4} = x$$

29. **(D)** Use the distance formula to find the missing coordinates of x.

$$\sqrt{(x_1 - x_2)^2 + (y_1 - y_2)^2}$$
$$\sqrt{(x_1 - 7)^2 + (4 - 5)^2} = 8$$
$$(x_1 - 7)^2 + 1 = 64$$
$$(x_1 - 7)^2 = 63$$
$$x - 7 = \pm\sqrt{63}$$
$$x = 7 \pm 3\sqrt{7}$$

30. **(A)** The \$75 fee for the lesson is a fixed cost. Subtract that amount from the \$110.00, the total charged for the lesson and the time on the boat.

$$\$110 - \$75 = \$35$$

Create a proportion based solely on the time paid for the boat. The question indicates the fee varies directly with the square root of the time spent on the boat.

$$\frac{\sqrt{\text{time}}}{\text{fee}} = \frac{\sqrt{\text{time}}}{\text{fee}}$$
$$\frac{\sqrt{25}}{35} = \frac{\sqrt{36}}{x} = \frac{5}{35} = \frac{6}{x}$$

Cross-multiply and solve for x.

$$5x = 210$$
$$x = 42$$

Add \$42.00, the fee for the time spent on the boat, to \$75.00, the fixed cost of the lesson.

$$\$75 + \$42 = \$117$$

Choices (B), (C), and (D) are incorrect due to erroneous calculation.

31. **438** Let x represent the weight of the rock on Earth.

$$\frac{1}{6}x = 73$$
$$(6)\left(\frac{1}{6}x\right) = 73(6)$$
$$x = 438$$

32. **67.6** A woman age 35 has a Target HR Zone of 93 to 157 beats per minute. Find the mean of that range by adding $93 + 157$ and dividing by 2.

$$93 + 157 = 250$$
$$250 \div 2 = 125$$

Find the percent that 125 is of 185 by dividing 125 by 185.

$$125 \div 185 = .6757$$

Rounded to the nearest tenth of a percent, .6757 is 67.6%.

A heart rate of 125 is 67.6% of the maximum heart rate.

33. **18** The volume of a cylinder is found by using the formula Volume $= \pi r^2 h$, where r is the radius and h is the height. Use simple numbers to verify the ratio.

Let $r = 1$ and $h = 1$ for the measures of the smaller cylinder.

$$\text{Volume} = \pi(1)^2(1) = \pi$$

Doubling the measure of the height gives $h = 2$. Tripling the measure of the radius gives $r = 3$.

$$\text{Volume} = \pi(3)^2(2) = 18\pi$$

The larger cylinder has a volume 18 times greater than the smaller.

34. **36**

$$g(x) = 2b + x^3$$

The point $(-4, 8)$ lies on the graph of the function $g(x) = 2b + x^3$. Therefore, we can say $g(-4) = 8$. Solve for b by substituting -4 for x and 8 for $g(x)$.

$$8 = 2b + (-4)^3$$
$$8 = 2b - 64$$
$$72 = 2b$$
$$36 = b$$

35. **0**

$$f(x) = \frac{1}{(x-3)^2 + 6(x-3) + 9}$$

Division by 0 is undefined so set the denominator of the function f equal to 0.

$$(x-3)^2 + 6(x-3) + 9 = 0$$
$$x^2 - 6x + 9 + 6x - 18 + 9 = 0$$
$$x^2 = 0$$
$$x = 0$$

When $x = 0$, the function f is undefined.

36. **50** The supermarket chain manager wants to earn an 80% customer service rating from its first 20 customer service surveys. Multiply 20 by 80 to get 1,600, the total number of additional percentage points to be amassed. We found that the first 10 reviews yielded an average score of 65% or 10 × 65 = 650 percentage points. Subtracting 650 from 1,600 we get 950, the total number of percentage points to be amassed to earn the overall 80% rating. The question asks what could be the lowest the 17th survey could earn and still achieve the goal of 80% customer satisfaction from the first 20 surveys. Suppose all of the surveys from 11 through 16 and 18 through 20 gave the chain a score of 100%. That would mean those 9 customers added 900 points to the total. Given that we need 950 points from the final 10 customers, the 17th survey could score the chain as low as 50% and the chain would still receive an 80% average from the first 20 surveys.

37. **66** Although the suggested consumption of potassium for men is 4,700 milligrams, Jake's daily running indicates he needs an additional 10% above the norm. Multiply 4,700 by 1.1 to find the potassium requirement for Jake because of his running.

$$4,700 \times 1.1 = 5,170$$

Jake consumes 3,200 milligrams currently so he needs an additional 1,970 milligrams. By adding an extra potato and a cup of lima beans, he will add 1,081 + 955 = 2,036 milligrams of potassium. Since he needs 1,970 milligrams, the addition of these new foods will provide 66 milligrams more than is necessary.

38. **1,155** Find Joan's daily consumption of potassium by dividing 22,400 by 7.

$$22,400 \div 7 = 3,200$$

If Joan adds a cup of spinach (839 mg) and a glass of orange juice (496 mg), she will be consuming a total of 4,535 milligrams of potassium per day. Subtracting 4,535 from 4,700 (the recommended amount), we arrive at a daily deficiency of 165 milligrams per day. Multiplying 165 by 7, we find that Joan needs an additional 1,155 milligrams of potassium in her diet each week.

Acknowledgments

Page 23: from *Indian Country* by Peter Matthiessen, copyright © 1979, 1980, 1981, 1984 by Peter Matthiessen. Used by permission of Viking Penguin, a division of Penguin Group (USA) Inc.

Page 26: from *Flappers and Philosophers* by F. Scott Fitzgerald, 1920.

Page 28: from "Hiroshima: A Soldier's View" by Paul Fussell. Reprinted by permission of *The New Republic*, © 1981.

Page 32: from "The Professionalization of Poetry" in *Heavy Lifting* by David Alpaugh. Copyright © 2007 Alehouse Press. Reprinted by permission of the author.

Page 35: from "Coasts in Crisis, Coastal Change," Jeffress Williams, Kurt Dodd, and Kathleen Krafft Gohn, in U.S. Geological Survey Circular 1075, 1990.

Page 38: from "Highlights of Women's Earnings in 2011," U.S. Department of Labor, U.S. Bureau of Labor Statistics, October 2012, Report 1038.

Page 42: from "United States Arctic Science Policy," Alaska Council of Science and Technology, January 1983.

Page 44: from *Museum of Antiquity: A Description of Ancient Life* by L.W. Yaggy M.S. and T.L. Haines A.M., published by J.B. Furman & Co., Western Publishing House, Chicago, IL, 1884.

Page 47: from *History of Woman Suffrage, Volume 1*, by Susan B. Anthony, 1887.

Page 97: from *Balzac and the Little Chinese Seamstress* by Dai Sijie. Published by Alfred A. Knopf, 2001. English translation Copyright © by Ina Rilke 2001.

Page 100 from *Reflections of a Neoconservative* by Irving Kristol. Copyright © 1983 Irving Kristol. Reprinted by permission of Basic Books, a member of the Perseus Books Group.

Page 103: from "The Clash of Civilizations?" by Samuel P. Huntington. Reprinted by permission of *Foreign Affairs*, Summer 1993. Copyright © 1993 by the Council on Foreign Relations, Inc., *www.foreignaffairs.com*.

Page 103: from "Do Civilizations Hold?" by Albert L. Weeks in *The Clash of Civilizations: The Debate* published by the Council on Foreign Relations, 2010. Copyright © 1993 by Albert L. Weeks. Reprinted by permission of the author.

Page 107: from Friend, Milton, 2014, "Why bother about wildlife disease?": U.S. Geological Survey Circular 1401, 76.

Page 110: from Alexis de Tocqueville, *Democracy in America*, originally published in 1835; translated from French into English by Henry Reeve.

Page 252: from John L. O'Sullivan, "The Great Nation of Futurity." It was originally published in 1839.

Page 255: from "Toxoplasmosis" by Hill, D.E., and Dubey, J.P., 2014, U.S. Geological Survey Circular 1389, *http://dx.doi.org/10.3133/cir1389*.

Page 259: from "Beyond Supply and Demand: Assessing the Ph.D. Job Market," Bureau of Labor Statistics, Occupational Outlook Quarterly, Winter 2002–2003.

Page 262: from *Myths & Legends of Babylonia & Assyria* by Lewis Spence, published by George G. Harrap & Company, Ltd., London, 1916.

Page 264: from "On the Art of Fiction" by Willa Cather, Knopf, The Borzoi, 1920.

Page 309: from *The Americanism of Washington* by Henry Van Dyke, 1906.

Page 311: from Suparna Choudhury, "Culturing the adolescent brain: what can neuroscience learn from anthropology?" *Social Cognitive and Affective Neuroscience*, 2010, 5(2–3), 159–167, by permission of Oxford University Press.

Page 314: from *The Art of Teaching* by Gilbert Highet, copyright © 1950, copyright renewed 1977 by Gilbert Highet. Used by permission of Alfred A. Knopf, a division of Random House, Inc.

Page 317: from Friend, Milton, 2014, "Why bother about wildlife disease?": U.S. Geological Survey Circular 1401, 76 p., *http://dx.doi.org/10.3133/cir1401*.

Page 320: from *The Autobiography of Charles Darwin* by Charles Darwin, 1887.

Page 323: from "Healthcare: Millions of Jobs," Bureau of Labor Statistics, Occupational Outlook Quarterly, Spring 2014.

Page 326: from *The Indian Today: The Past and Future of the First American* by Charles A. Eastman (Ohiyesa), published by Doubleday, Page & Company, 1915.

Page 329: from *The History of Cuba*, Volume I, by Willis Fletcher Johnson, 1920.

Page 331: from Hiwasaki, L., Luna, E., Syamsidik, Shaw, R. "Local & indigenous knowledge for community resilience: Hydro-meteorological disaster risk reduction and climate change adaptation in coastal and small island communities." Jakarta, UNESCO, 2014.

Page 379: from "Hotspots: Mantle Thermal Plumes" in *This Dynamic Earth: The Story of Plate Tectonics* by Jacquelyne Kious and Robert I. Tilling, U.S. Geological Survey, 1996.

Page 379: from "Scientists Locate Deep Origins of Hawaiian Hotspot," press release 09–232, December 3, 2009, National Science Foundation.

Page 383: from *The Souls of Black Folk* by W.E.B. Du Bois, 1903.

Page 385: from *Lord Jim* by Joseph Conrad, 1917.

Page 388: from *The Indian Today: The Past and Future of the First American* by Charles A. Eastman (Ohiyesa), published by Doubleday, Page & Company, 1915.

Page 391: from *Ex Libris: Confessions of a Common Reader* by Anne Fadiman. Copyright © 1998 by Anne Fadiman. Reprinted by permission of Farrar, Straus and Giroux, LLC.

Page 386: from Centers for Disease Control and Prevention, "Malaria Surveillance—United States, 2010," MMWR 2012; 61, pp. 4–6.

Page 399: from "Wanted: Trained teachers to ensure every child's right to primary education 2014," UNESCO, 2014, Policy Paper 15, factsheet 30.

Page 402: from President Franklin Delano Roosevelt's Message to Congress on the State of the Union, January 11, 1944.

Page 405: from *An Artist's Letters from Japan* by John La Farge, published by The Century Company, New York, 1897.